Teaching Behaviorally Disordered Students

Preferred Practices

Daniel P. Morgan
Utah State University

William R. Jenson
University of Utah

Merrill Publishing Company
A Bell & Howell Information Company
Columbus Toronto London Melbourne

About the cover: The cover image on this book was created using paint and string by a group of children in Denise Trudeau's class at West Central School in Columbus, Ohio.

Published by Merrill Publishing Company
A Bell & Howell Information Company
Columbus, Ohio 43216

This book was set in Korinna.

Administrative Editor: Vicki Knight
Production Coordinator: Anne Daly
Art Coordinator: Mark Garrett
Cover Designer: Cathy Watterson

Photo credits: All photos copyrighted by individuals or companies listed. Celia Drake, p. 279; Barbara Lagomarsino, p. 106; Merrill Publishing Company/photographs by Andy Brunk (pp. 243, 435), Bruce Johnson (pp. 1, 8, 31, 47, 49, 101, 143, 153, 159, 183, 195, 230, 271, 305, 325, 328, 363, 365, 387, 440), Vicki Knight (p. 399); David Phillips, p. 403; Harvey R. Phillips/PPI, p. 235; David Ryder, pp. 67; Steve and Mary Skjold Photographs, p. 257; Gale Zucker, p. 357.

Library of Congress Catalog Card Number: 87–062850
International Standard Book Number: 0–675–20543–3
Printed in the United States of America
1 2 3 4 5 6 7 8 9—92 91 90 89 88

Preface

The basic purpose of this text is to help you become an effective teacher of behaviorally disordered students. It offers you important information about how to plan, organize, and manage instructional programs for behaviorally disordered students in a variety of settings as well as suggestions for assessing your students' progress. The book's subtitle, *Preferred Practices,* reflects our strong belief that instructional strategies and practices are available that ought to be preferred because they tend to produce desired outcomes more consistently and more often than others.

Throughout this text we discuss teaching practices shown by research to be effective when used with behaviorally disordered students. However, research cannot reasonably be expected to resolve all issues or erase all differences of opinion. What is certain to one person may be inconclusive to another. It is not our intent to oversimplify the complex phenomena associated with teaching behaviorally disordered students, nor do we wish to suggest resolutions to ongoing controversies prematurely or precipitately when data are incomplete or inconclusive. All questions in the field have not been fully addressed or completely answered. Pat answers are simply not available. Some findings, though promising, are still preliminary and tentative. However, we believe that findings concerning many essential aspects of teaching behaviorally disordered students have accumulated to a degree that some phenomena can be identified, explained, and put into practice.

Consequently, this text has a practical orientation. And although this practical emphasis does not negate the importance of theoretical or conceptual models as a means of acquiring insight into the complex problems presented by behaviorally disordered students, positive improvements, achieved through humane and supportive interventions, are preferable to an in-depth understanding of a variety of disparate theoretical models in those students' overall school adjustment. Our basic message is this: Teachers can have more time to teach and can be more effective if they plan and systematically implement strategies designed to teach students new ways of behaving. Simply telling students how to behave is insufficient; to be effective, teachers must teach students how to behave.

This text is meant primarily for individuals preparing to teach students with significant school behavior problems. Since the text is classroom- and student-centered, we think it also has much to offer inservice teachers working with behaviorally disordered students. It may also be useful to consulting teachers, resource teachers, and school psychologists who work with behaviorally disordered students.

We have assumed that the student reading this textbook is already knowledgeable about the characteristics of behaviorally disordered children. The information in Chapter 1 dealing with characteristics is intended to serve as a brief review of this area, not as a comprehensive discussion. Similarly, we assume that the reader has completed a basic assessment course and a basic behavior management course. While a great deal of the information in the textbook is applicable to a wide age range of students, most of the suggestions in Chapters 7, 8, and 9, which deal with specific classroom settings, are geared for elementary- and middle-school age students. It is our belief that the problems and challenges presented by secondary-aged behaviorally disordered students are of sufficient scope and magnitude that they deserve to be addressed in a separate volume altogether.

Teaching Behaviorally Disordered Students: Preferred Practices is organized in the following manner. Chapter 1 provides an overview of several important issues in the field of behavioral disorders. Issues related to the definition, prevalence, and characteristics of behaviorally disordered children are briefly reviewed. The research base underlying the preferred instructional practices to be discussed is also briefly identified and explained. How and where special education services are delivered to behaviorally disorderd students are covered, and the current status of service delivery is discussed in the context of problems and impediments to effective service delivery. Preferred service delivery strategies are also identified and emphasize students' successful adjustment in the regular classroom as the ultimate goal of special education programs for behaviorally disordered students.

Chapters 2 and 3 discuss the foundational instructional skills of assessment and behavior management required to effectively teach behaviorally disordered students. Chapter 4 deals with a topic of major importance in this field — generalizing academic, behavioral, and social improvements from special education settings to regular classroom settings. Chapters 5 and 6 address the major curriculum areas of academic instruction and social skills training. Teaching behaviorally disordered students in regular classrooms, resource programs, and self-contained settings is covered in Chapters 7, 8, and 9. In these chapters, we emphasize that the basic elements of effective instruction are essentially similar across all settings. The specific techniques and strategies particularly suited for specific classroom settings are highlighted. Chapter 10 is concerned with working with parents of behaviorally disordered students. The book concludes in Chapter 11 with a review of legal issues associated with teaching behaviorally disordered students.

In writing an instructional methods book, any author undertakes a gamble that the information contained in the book will, in fact, show the reader "how to" teach. This is, of course, impossible. No amount of information or special style of writing or textbook organization will automatically lead to successful teaching. What an author can do is discuss problems, research findings, concepts, and practical recommendations in a straightforward manner. Ultimately, it is up to the reader to use the information to plan and implement effective instructional programs. Each chapter opens with a list of learning objectives and concludes with questions for review designed to assist you in organizing your thinking about the issues and topics covered in each chapter and to stimulate your thinking about what you read. We want you to actively think about what you are reading!

ACKNOWLEDGMENTS

We are grateful to many people who helped us complete this project. First, a special thank you to those people who contributed chapters: Stan Paine and Lynne Anderson-Inman for their chapter on academic instruction (Chapter 5); Ginger Rhode for her co-authorship on the generalization and resource room chapters (Chapter 4 and 8); and John Myers for his authorship of the chapter on legal issues (Chapter 11).

We would also like to thank those individuals who reviewed the manuscript at various stages of development; Dr. Wesley Brown, East Tennessee State University; Dr. John Platt, University of South Florida; Dr. Carl Smith, Buena Vista College; Dr. Richard Shores, Peabody College, Vanderbilt University; Dr. Rick Neel, University of Washington; and Dr. Sharon Huntze, University of Missouri-Columbia all provided thoughtful critiques and useful suggestions that significantly improved the text. A special note of thanks is due Dr. George Sugai, University of Oregon, who reviewed the manuscript twice — at the beginning and near the end; his comments were a valuable resource to us. To Deann Bidstrup and Ann Kelly who served as our "right arms" and to Lynda Seele and Co Brunner who typed and retyped the manuscript patiently and expertly we owe a sincere thank you. Vicki Knight, our editor, demonstrated more patience than can be expected of mere mortals. For that and her support, encouragement, and advice, we are especially grateful.

Finally, our families require special recognition for enduring long periods of physical and mental absence and for allowing our priorities to remain inappropriately skewed while this book was being written. To Kathy, Grayson, Seth, Connie, Andy, Jennie, and Mary, we offer our deep appreciation and our sincere pledge not to start another writing project for at least a couple of months.

Contents

7 Teaching Behaviorally Disordered Students in the Regular Classroom · 279

8 Teaching Behaviorally Disordered Students in Resource Room Programs · 325

1 An Overview of Behavioral Disorders

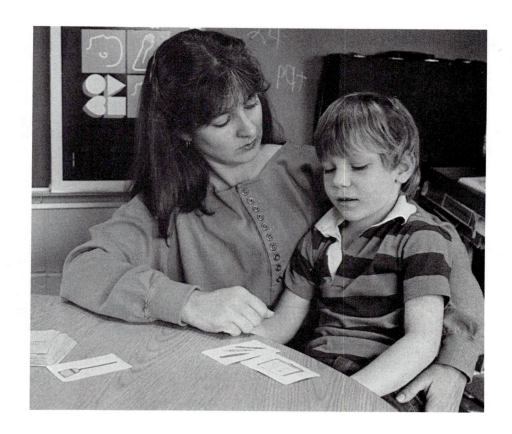

After completing this chapter, you should be able to

- *State the federal definition of* behavioral disorders.
- *Explain the importance of defining* behavioral disorders.
- *Explain why there is no single universally accepted definition of* behavioral disorders.
- *Discuss guidelines that can be used in developing definitions of* behavioral disorders.
- *Explain why the term* behavioral disorders *is preferred over* emotional disturbance.
- *Discuss prevalence of behavioral disorders.*
- *Describe primary types and characteristics of behavioral disorders.*
- *Identify the major findings from research on effective teaching for direct instruction, academic learning time, student success rates, and classroom management.*
- *Identify several emerging quality instructional practices in special education for the behaviorally disordered.*
- *Discuss the current status of service delivery in special education for the behaviorally disordered.*
- *Explain the Comprehensive Behavioral Services model.*
- *Define preferred practices.*

To provide high quality educational services to behaviorally disordered (BD) students, a teacher needs a thorough knowledge of the nature and dynamics of their problems. A firm understanding of these problems influences the teacher's approach to instruction and intervention. To provide quality educational services, the teacher must understand the essentials of effective instruction and service delivery. The purpose of this first chapter is to give you an overview of the field of behavioral disorders by describing these students and by introducing the types of effective instructional approaches and program arrangements that are the focus of the book.

The first section of the chapter introduces some of the more important concepts fundamental to understanding behaviorally disordered students. Who are they? How is the term *behavioral disorders* defined? How many behaviorally disordered students are there? What are their characteristics? The next section of the chapter introduces the concept of preferred practices by reviewing the findings from research on effective teaching and by identifying promising quality instructional practices in special education. The chapter concludes by examining some ways currently used to deliver services to behaviorally disordered students.

WHO ARE THEY?
BEHAVIORAL DISORDERS DEFINED

Teachers of behaviorally disordered students are often asked how they define *behavioral disorders.* However, even very experienced teachers may not have a ready response. They may give the official definition from their state's rules and regulations. Some may know the federal definition or other authoritative definitions well enough to recite. Some may even offer their own definition, one carefully honed over time. This should not be too surprising because there is no single, universally accepted definition of *behavioral disorders.* For a variety of theoretical, administrative, legal, and pedagogical reasons, many definitions have developed over the years, and each has its own proponents, admirers, and users.

Several distinct types of definitions of *behavioral disorders* have been identified (Cullinan & Epstein, 1979). For example, *research definitions* allow readers to better understand the results and potential practical implications of research by providing a precise description of the subject sample involved in a study. Unfortunately, samples in research studies involving these students are often inadequately described, primarily because a variety of terms are used to describe the sample (e.g. *conduct problems, behavior problems, acting out, emotionally disturbed, noncompliant, disruptive*), and the behavioral characteristics of the sample are vaguely or ambiguously defined (Kavale, Forness, & Alper, 1986). Knowledgeable individuals in the field have offered *authoritative definitions* of behavioral disorders. These definitions usually reflect the authority's experience and theoretical background and promote a particular point of view (see Exhibit 1.1).

Administrative definitions guide special education and related services at the local, state, and national levels. By defining *behavioral disorders,* the administrative unit—the federal government, a state government, or a local educational agency — sets the policies that determine who will receive services. There is much diversity among the administrative definitions that currently regulate behavioral disorders programs throughout the country (see Exhibit 1.2). There are also some things in common shared by most administrative definitions. According to Kauffman and Kneedler (1981), most administrative definitions of *behavioral disorders* include:

1. A statement that the child exhibits disorders of emotions and/or behaviors;
2. A statement that the child has interpersonal problems, such as being unable to relate satisfactorily to other children and adults;
3. A statement that the child's problems involve inability to learn or achieve at school;

EXHIBIT 1.1   Authoritative definitions of behavioral disorders

The emotionally disturbed child is one who, after receiving supportive educational services and counseling assistance available to all students, still exhibits persistent and consistent severe to very severe behavioral disabilities that consequently interfere with productive learning processes. This is the student whose inability to achieve adequate academic progress and satisfactory interpersonal relationships cannot be attributed primarily to physical, sensory, or intellectual deficits. (Algozzine, 1981, p. 4)

Children with behavior disorders (1) deviate from standards or expectations for behavior, and (2) impair the functioning of others or themselves. . . . Such deviations often involve behavior that is uncharacteristic of the pupil's age or sex. The frequency, intensity, and persistence of a behavior problem often, to an extreme degree, in multiple situations, and/or more or less continuously over a substantial period of time is more likely to be identified as behaviorally disordered. (Cullinan, Epstein, & Lloyd, 1983, p. 103)

Psychological disorder is said to be present when a child emits behavior that deviates from an arbitrary and relative social norm in that it occurs with a frequency or intensity that authoritative adults in the child's environment judge, under the circumstances, to be either too high or too low. (Ross, 1980, p. 9)

Emotional disturbance is a reciprocal condition which exists when intense coping responses are released within a human community by a community member's atypical behavior and responses. The triggering stimulus, the rejoinder of the microcommunity, and the ensuing transaction are all involved in emotional disturbance. (Rhodes, 1970, p. 311)

A behavior disorder is said to be present when a child or adolescent exhibits behavioral excesses and/or deficits that authoritative adults in the child's or adolescent's environment judge to be too high or too low. These behaviors are considered to be atypical because the frequency, intensity, and/or duration deviates from a relative social norm. The excesses and/or deficits which constitute a behavior disorder can be expressed through one or all behavioral systems or repertoires (cognitive/verbal, overt/motoric, or physiological/emotional) and occur across settings, situations, and time. (Gresham, 1985, p. 500)

EXHIBIT 1.2 State definitions

Utah: A behavior disordered student is defined as one whose behavior or emotional conduct over time adversely affects his/her educational performance and requires special education services.

Florida: The emotionally disturbed child is the student who, after receiving supportive educational assistance and counseling services available to all students, still exhibits persistent and consistent severe to very severe behavioral disabilities which interfere with productive learning processes. This is the student whose inability to achieve adequate academic progress and/or satisfactory interpersonal relationships cannot be attributed primarily to physical, sensory or intellectual deficits.

Iowa: "Behaviorally disordered" is the inclusive term for patterns of situationally inappropriate behavior which deviate substantially from behavior appropriate to one's age and significantly interfere with the learning process, interpersonal relationships, or personal adjustment of the pupil to such an extent as to constitute a behavioral disorder. . . . The determination of significantly deviant behavior is the conclusion that the pupil's characteristic behavior is sufficiently distinct from his or her peer group to qualify the pupil as requiring special education programs or services. . . . The behavior of concern shall be observed in the school setting for school-age pupils. It must be determined that the behavioral disorder is not maintained by primary intellectual, sensory, cultural, or health factors.

Michigan: "Emotionally impaired" means a person identified by an educational planning and placement committee, based upon a comprehensive evaluation by a school psychologist and social worker, a certified psychologist, a certified consulting psychologist, or a certified psychiatrist, and other pertinent information, as having 1 or more of the following behavioral characteristics:

(a) Disruptive to the learning process of other students or himself in the regular classroom over an extended period of time.
(b) Extreme withdrawal from social interaction in the school environment over an extended period of time.
(c) Manifestation of symptoms characterized by diagnostic labels such as psychosis, schizophrenia and autism.
(d) Disruptive behavior which has resulted in placement in a juvenile detention facility.

4. Comparison of the child's behavior to a norm or to age-appropriate expectations from which the child's behavior deviates;
5. A statement that the child's problem is of long standing, not a transient problem;
6. A statement that the problem is severe (i.e., serious, intense, or exhibited in a variety of settings); and
7. A statement that special education is needed if the child is to receive maximum benefit from schooling and that regular education is not suited to the child's needs. (p. 167)

A very important administrative definition is the one used by the federal government. The federal government uses the term *seriously emotionally disturbed* to refer to those students we refer to as *behaviorally disordered* (see Pointer 1.1). The current federal definition of *seriously emotionally disturbed* is as follows:

The term means a condition exhibiting one or more of the following characteristics over a long period of time and to a marked degree, which adversely affects educational performance:

(a) An inability to learn which cannot be explained by intellectual, sensory, or other health factors;
(b) An inability to build or maintain satisfactory interpersonal relationships with peers and teachers;
(c) Inappropriate types of behavior or feelings under normal circumstances;
(d) A general pervasive mood of unhappiness or depression;
(e) A tendency to develop physical symptions or fears associated with personal or school problems;
(f) The term includes children who are schizophrenic. The term does not include children who are socially maladjusted, unless it is determined that they are seriously emotionally disturbed.

This definition has not been universally embraced in the field. Kauffman (1982), a widely respected critic of the federal definition, has stated that it is too vague, making operational definition almost impossible. You need only to ponder such phrases as "to a marked extent," "over a long period of time," "satisfactory interpersonal relationships," "pervasive," and "adversely affects" to appreciate the difficulty of making this definition objective and reliable. Not mincing his words, Kauffman stated: "One is forced to conclude that the federal definition is, if not claptrap, at least dangerously close to nonsense" (p. 4).

The number and variety of definitions of *behavioral disorders* reflects the complexity of the problem and the diversity of the field. While there is no single, clear, and unambiguous definition that currently serves as a standard in special education, there are guidelines that can be help-

Pointer 1.1

EMOTIONALLY DISTURBED OR BEHAVIORALLY DISORDERED?

During the 98th Session, Congress requested a study which would help determine whether a change in both the federal definition and federal terminology (from *seriously emotionally disturbed* to *behaviorally disordered*) was needed (SRA Technologies, 1985). The results of the study suggested that there was no compelling reason to change either the definition or the terminology because (a) there would be no significant increase or decrease in the numbers of children served if changes were made, (b) services would neither be made more restrictive nor more available if changes were made, and (c) any reduction of the stigma caused by the seriously emotionally disturbed label would be small and temporary. On the other hand, the Council for Children with Behavioral Disorders (CCBD) recently issued the following statement in support of replacing the term *seriously emotionally disturbed* with the term *behaviorally disordered* (Huntze, 1985).

Statement to Support Replacing the Term Seriously Emotionally Disturbed with the Term Behaviorally Disordered as a Descriptor for Children and Youth Who Are Handicapped by Their Behavior

It is the official position of the Council for Exceptional Children with Behavior Disorders that the term *behaviorally disordered* is more descriptive and useful to educators in identifying and planning appropriate placements and services for students who are handicapped by their behavior than is the term seriously *emotionally disturbed.*

Rationale

The term *behaviorally disordered* has far greater utility for education than does the term *seriously emotionally disturbed.*

The term *behaviorally disordered* is not associated exclusively with any particular theory of causation and therefore with any particular set of intervention techniques. The term *seriously emotionally disturbed* is associated with a particular theory, usually called the *psychodynamic theory*, which stresses the hypothesis that problem behavior is a manifestation of disturbed thoughts and feeling (i.e., an "inner" emotional disturbance).

The term *behaviorally disordered* affords a more comprehensive assessment of the population.

The term *behaviorally disordered* is less stigmatizing than the term *seriously emotionally disturbed.* Parents, teachers, and students view the *seriously emotionally disturbed* label very negatively.

The term *behaviorally disordered* is more representative of the students who are handicapped by their behavior and currently served under Public Law 94–142.

It would appear that the judgment of the professional favors the term *behaviorally disordered* over *seriously emotionally disturbed.* Our choice of *behaviorally disordered* for this text was influenced by our judgment that a preferred practice is to focus on the behavior problems instead of covert emotional states. As Hewett and Taylor (1980) said, "Teachers can do something directly about disordered behavior that they cannot do about disturbed emotions" (p. 16).

Source: Statement from "A Position Paper of The Council for Children with Behavioral Disorders" by S.L. Huntze (1985), *Behavioral Disorders, 10,* p. 1.

ful in arriving at an educationally relevant and functional definition. For example, Wood (1979) proposed that a good definition should address the following questions:

1. The "disturber" element: What or who is perceived to be the focus of the problem?
2. The "problem behavior" element: How is the problem behavior described?
3. The "setting" element: In what setting does the problem behavior occur?
4. The "disturbed" element: Who regards the behavior as disturbed? (pp. 7–8)

In addition to answering these questions, a good definition must also be developed within the context of the concept of normalcy. The range of normal behavior is quite broad. In fact, many normal children behave problematically at some time during childhood or adolescence

Most of the problem behaviors displayed by behaviorally disordered students are also commonly displayed by normal children.

(Achenbach & Edelbrock, 1981). The existence of problem behaviors among children and adolescents is probably higher than most adults would like to admit. However, what is normal or common may not necessarily be appropriate or desirable. For example, smoking, drug abuse, and alcohol abuse are becoming more and more common among school-aged children in the United States. But does their popularity make these behaviors desirable or appropriate?

An unambiguous definition of *behavioral disorders* must also take into account the situational specificity of problem behavior. Apter (1982) described situational specificity as follows:

> Most of the behaviors attributed to children in conflict are normal behaviors; at least they are normal if one considers that normal children will sometimes cheat, or lie, or act out aggressive feelings by hitting other children. What often makes these behaviors deviant, and the children who exhibit them in conflict, is the fact that the behaviors are exhibited in the wrong places, at the wrong time, in the presence of the wrong people, and to an inappropriate degree. (p. 12)

Does disordered behavior, like beauty, lie in the eyes of the beholder? Hallahan and Kauffman (1977) thought so when they said, "The child is disturbed when an adult authority says he is, i.e., when the child's behavior is seriously discrepant from that desired by his adult caretakers" (p. 140). The classroom behavioral expectations, standards, and requirements of teachers vary widely and also play a big role in determining who is identified as behaviorally disordered (Walker & Rankin, 1983). Such situational variations make the task of identifying the behaviorally disordered student even more difficult.

Why is it important to define *behavioral disorders* in the first place? The answer is that special education does not have the human and fiscal resources or the legal mandates to serve every student having social, emotional, or behavioral difficulties in school. Thus, we need guidelines and criteria to ensure that those students who need service most receive it. These criteria should ensure that those children in need of service do in fact significantly deviate from what would be expected of most children of the same age in the same circumstances.

One criterion relates to the persistence of the behavior problem. Many childhood problems are transitory. While they may be quite serious for a short time, they tend to work themselves out without special education intervention. Of primary concern to the special educator are those problems that have been evident for some time. The problem here, however, is the lack of specificity of the term *persistent*. How long is long enough? Days? Weeks? Months? Years? While other factors (e.g., the magnitude of the problem) must be taken into account, sound practice suggests that 2 months be used as a minimum length of time a problem behavior is present before considering special education services, and 4 to 6 months would be more prudent.

Another guideline relates to the severity of the problem behavior. One way to establish it is to determine if the problem has been resistant to attempts at change. That is, those people who work with the child (e.g., a regular classroom teacher) should make a concerted attempt to deal with the problem, using appropriate intervention strategies. If the problem remains unchanged after several attempts to correct it, then the teacher may reasonably conclude that the problem is severe.

As can be seen, there are many opinions as to what constitutes a behaviorally disordered student. In view of the state of the art, the goal of arriving at one best definition of *behaviorally disordered* is very elusive. Nearly every text in the field includes a definition unique to its authors, and most of them have had little impact beyond the covers of the book in which they are used to structure the discussion (Kauffman & Kneedler, 1981). It is still important, however, to define *behavioral disorders* in order to narrow our focus here to those children whose behavior deviates from the norm enough that specially designed instruction (i.e., special education) is required to meet their unique learning needs.

The lack of a clear definition and continuing disagreements on terminology have consumed a great deal of time and energy over the last 2 decades in this field. Until the many assessment and measurement problems associated with defining and classifying behaviorally disordered students are resolved—that is, reliably and validly differentiating between normal and abnormal, adaptive and maladaptive, or appropriate and inappropriate behavior—we will continue to be better able to design and develop effective therapeutic interventions for these students than to define and describe who it is we serve.

PREVALENCE OF BEHAVIORAL DISORDERS

How many behaviorally disordered students are there? The question depends on the definition of *behavioral disorders* and the methods used to arrive at an estimate. Consequently, prevalence data vary widely. Depending on who you ask, from 1% to 40% of the school-aged population is behaviorally disordered. These estimates have been obtained through several methods — from actual headcounts to armchair guesstimating. For example, using teacher reports of the rate of problem behaviors in school, Wickman (1929) found that 42% of the students included in his sample displayed at least mild forms of behavior problems. Bower (1969) estimated that 10% of the school-aged population was behaviorally disordered. The Carnegie Council on Children reported that approximately 25 to 33% of all American children grow up in conditions that significantly damage their intellectual, emotional, and physical well-being

(Gliedman & Roth, 1980). Kauffman (1985) estimated that 6 to 10% of school-aged children need special education because they are behaviorally disordered.

Cullinan and Epstein (1986) proposed a "rule of one third." They estimated that one-third of all students in any given year display behavior problems. Of this number, about one-third need to have something done to deal with the problem above and beyond the regular program. About one-third of that group requires special education or related services to deal with their much more severe problems.

Kelly, Bullock, and Dykes (1977) asked 2,664 regular classroom teachers to classify each of their students in one of the following ways: (a) no perceived behavioral disorder, (b) a mild behavioral disorder, (c) a moderate behavioral disorder, or (d) a severe behavioral disorder. The teachers reported that 20.4% of their students displayed signs of behavioral disorders; 12.6% were identified as mild; 5.6%, as moderate; and 2.2%, as severe.

In a longitudinal study, Rubin and Balow (1978) surveyed 1,576 elementary teachers in Minnesota. Their findings indicated that, in any given year, 23 to 31% of the students were identified as displaying problem behavior. Over the 7-year period of this study, 59% of the students who were rated at least three different years by three different teachers were reported as manifesting behavior problems. Even more startling was the finding that 7.4% of the subjects were nominated by every teacher throughout the study. Rubin and Balow concluded by stating

> That the majority of children are perceived as presenting behavior problems by at least one teacher during the course of their elementary school careers may be more informative about the tolerance limits of teachers than about the inherent characteristics of children. Based on these findings, one might hypothesize that, given sufficient time and sufficient numbers of different classroom settings and different teachers, each with his or her own set of expectations and definitions of normal behavior, no child would be consistently exempt from classification as a problem. (p. 110)

In terms of special education, the most relevant prevalence figures are those determined by the federal government or a state educational agency. These figures typically represent the upper limit of the number of children who can be classified as behaviorally disordered for special education funding. The federal government has specified that 2% of the school-aged population may be considered seriously emotionally disturbed (i.e., behaviorally disordered) under the regulations of PL 94–142. How many of these children are we as a nation and as individual states actually serving? Are we serving an estimated 2% of the school-aged children and youth?

Actual national prevalence data are disconcerting. Using the 2% federal prevalence figure for behavioral disorders, there should be roughly 1,000,000 school-aged children who have been identified and are receiving special education services as behaviorally disordered. Available data indicate that only about 35% (i.e., 360,000 students) of those eligible to receive services are, in fact, getting those services. Stated differently, instead of 2%, the actual national prevalence figure is approximately 0.8%, based on the numbers of children actually identified and served. Very few states have identified and are serving 2% of their school children in special education programs for the behaviorally disordered. Some states have identified and served so few students as behaviorally disordered as to be virtually ludicrous. Prevalence rates as low as 0.2% to 0.5% of the school-aged population are not uncommon.

Commenting on the discrepancy between the number of served and unserved children, Huntze and Grosenick (1980) identified a number of problems associated with BD programs that help to explain this discrepancy. They concluded by saying, "There appears to be a general aversion to actively seeking out and progressively planning for behavior disordered students. The perception is that more behavior disordered children and programs equal more, not less, problems" (p. 33). While their analysis may be correct, it should not be taken as an excuse for what is a serious problem: a large number of unidentified and unserved behaviorally disordered students. Less than half of those behaviorally disordered students ostensibly eligible for special education actually receive it; as we shall see later, too many of those receiving services are receiving an inadequate educational program.

TYPES AND CHARACTERISTICS OF BEHAVIORAL DISORDERS

What are the major characteristics of behaviorally disordered students? No single set of characteristics can be used to describe all of them. Although it is clear that behaviorally disordered students are far from being a homogenous group (Hallahan & Kauffman, 1982), research from factor analytic studies as well as other classification efforts suggests that there are distinct dimensions to childhood behavior problems. For example, Quay (1979) has identified four major clusters of disordered behavior among school-aged children: conduct disorders, anxiety–withdrawal, immaturity, and socialized aggressive. Another classification scheme describes two broad groupings of behavior problems (Achenbach & Edelbrock, 1981). This system distinguishes between *externalizing* behaviors (aggressive, antisocial, undercontrolled behavior problems) and *internalizing* behaviors (fearful, withdrawn, immature, overcontrolled behavior problems). This section briefly examines some of the more common types of problem behaviors.

Conduct Disorders

Regardless of the term used— *acting out, antisocial, undersocialized, aggressive,* or *conduct disorders*—most teachers are very aware of the problems displayed by this child. These students are very aggressive—fighting, hitting, assaulting, making verbal threats, throwing temper tantrums, destroying property, stealing. Most of their problems are expressed overtly—aggression, tantrums, noncompliance. However, problems may also be expressed covertly — lying, stealing, vandalizing, abusing alcohol or other drugs (Walker & Fabre, in press).

In the classroom, conduct disordered students are defiant and noncompliant toward the teacher and school and classroom rules. They may be inattentive, hyperactive, disruptive, and distractible, may not complete assignments, may disturb their peers, and often lack academic skills. It is no wonder that teachers refer students with these types of behaviors more frequently than they refer students with other types of problem behavior (Kazdin, 1985). These students are perhaps the most potentially serious problem dealt with by the schools in terms of the risk for long-term failure in school and serious maladjustment in adulthood (Kazdin, 1987).

The behavioral characteristics associated with conduct disorders have been extensively described (see, for example, Achenbach & Edelbrock, 1981; Herbert, 1978; Kazdin, 1985; Patterson, 1975, 1982; Quay, 1975; Walker, 1979). Very common complaints about these children from parents and teachers would be: " 'He acts first and thinks (if he even thinks) afterwards,' 'He doesn't seem to know right from wrong,' 'He never listens,' 'He is *so* selfish, he never thinks of anyone but himself' " (Herbert, 1978). While most children commonly display some aggression (e.g., hitting, teasing, fighting) and noncompliance (i.e., not doing what they have been told or not adhering to established rules), conduct disordered children clearly display an *excess* of these highly noxious behaviors. The excess may be expressed in terms of *frequency* or *intensity* of the behavior. That is, these children are aggressive and noncompliant much more often than normal children and the intensity of their behavior often far exceeds routine petty fighting and arguing. They often injure others, either physically or psychologically. They may also destroy or damage property by vandalizing it, setting fires, or stealing. In addition, many conduct disordered children do not have the full repertoire of appropriate behaviors that their peers have.

There are several other characteristics that distinguish conduct disordered childen. As might be expected, most of them are boys; estimates range from four to eight times as many boys as girls (Herbert, 1982). Hyperactivity is a common characteristic; there is considerable overlap between conduct disorders and hyperactivity. Herbert maintains that hyperactive children and conduct disordered children have similar patterns of noncompliance, aggression, and learning problems. The amount of overactivity displayed by the hyperactive child is the principal difference. Others share the view that hyperactivity should not be considered independent from conduct disorders (Barclay, 1981; Quay, 1979), while still others argue that hyperactivity is a separate syndrome (Routh, 1980).

Conduct disordered children create considerable difficulty for those who work with, teach, or live with them. The extremely high rates of aggressive and noncompliant behaviors significantly cloud the prognosis for either short- or long-term satisfactory adjustment and challenge the school's ability to intervene effectively.

Personality Disorders

Children with personality disorders (fears, anxieties, social withdrawal, phobias, depression) display a behavior pattern almost directly opposite of the conduct disordered child. Quay (1979) has described the personality disordered child as "almost behaviorally paralyzed" (p. 19). Several common behavior problems associated with childhood personality disorders will be briefly discussed in this section.

Social Withdrawal

Increasingly, socially withdrawn children are coming to the attention of professionals who work with behaviorally disordered children (Guralnick, 1986; Hops & Greenwood, 1981; Strayhorn & Strain, 1986). Their characteristic behaviors include infrequent initiation to peers, lack of response to initiations from others, less verbal behavior in those social interactions that do occur, and a great deal of time spent in solitary activities (Greenwood, Walker, Todd, & Hops, 1979). Socially withdrawn children tend to have significant social skills deficits (Greenwood, Walker, & Hops, 1977), and often are rejected or neglected by their peers (Asher & Taylor, 1982).

Strain (1982) has attributed the stability of childhood social withdrawal to several powerful social influences:

1. By not engaging in behaviors that are reinforcing to peers (e.g., verbal compliments, following game rules, offering to share toys), withdrawn children become increasingly ignored and actively rejected by peers.
2. By not responding to peers' positive social initiations, withdrawn children may quickly extinguish any further attempts by classmates to play and make friends.
3. By misinterpreting the approach behaviors of peers (e.g., responding to rough and tumble play overtures as physical assaults) and not clearly communicating the intent of their own social behaviors (e.g., entering a play group without asking if they can participate), withdrawn children come to be viewed as bizarre, unpredictable individuals to avoid.

4. By not being in the close physical proximity of peers, withdrawn children have limited access to appropriate behavior models, spontaneous tutoring, and encouragement for outstanding performance. (pp. 94–95)

There are several potentially serious consequences of social withdrawal. First, because these children tend to be unpopular and because popularity with peers is positively associated with achievement, social withdrawal may interfere with academic achievement. Second, social withdrawal in childhood may predict later adjustment as an adult; i.e., children who do not interact with their peers are at risk for later psychopathology (Rolf & Hasazi, 1977). Because socially withdrawn children do not disrupt classrooms, lunchrooms, the school bus, or playground, they are often ignored when referrals are made for special education (Strain, Cooke, & Apolloni, 1976). However, an increased awareness of the potentially serious long-term effects of childhood social withdrawal has resulted in the development of social skill intervention programs and learning strategies. They will be discussed in detail in chapter 6.

Depression

Depression is one of the most prevalent forms of mental illness in adults. Despite controversy over definition, diagnostic criteria, and prevalence (Kazdin & Strober, 1982), childhood depression is increasingly being recognized as a significant mental health problem (Cantwell & Carlson, 1983; Petti, 1983; Schloss, 1983; Schulterbrandt & Raskin, 1977). However, scant attention has been devoted to the identification and treatment of childhood depression in special education programs for the behaviorally disordered (Cullinan, Schloss, & Epstein, 1987).

The general picture of a depressed child is one of an unhappy looking child who conveys an overall impression of pervasive sadness (Cantwell, 1982). Exhibit 1.3 presents a composite of the myriad symptoms of childhood depression. Similar characteristic patterns of behavior have been reported by Kovacs and Beck (1977) and Gittelman-Klein (1977), among others.

Estimates of the incidence of childhood depression vary so widely that it is extremely difficult to draw conclusions (Cantwell, 1982). A conservative estimate would place the incidence as relatively low in the general population of school-aged children (Schwartz & Johnson, 1985). Estimating the prevalence of childhood depression is again made more difficult by disagreements over definition. As with virtually all behavior problems, the behavioral characteristics associated with childhood depression are not unusual or abnormal by themselves. As Lefkowitz and Burton (1978) said,

> The list of feelings and behaviors observed in depressed children becomes so broad as to necessarily include, at one time or another dur-

EXHIBIT 1.3   Composite picture of a depressed child's behavioral characteristics

Withdrawal
Little interest in any activity
Listlessness
Physical pain (headaches, abdominal complaints, dizziness)
Insomnia, sleeping, and eating disturbances
Feels unloved or rejected
Negative self-concept
Low frustration tolerance
Irritability
Conveys a sense of needing comfort and reassurance
Self-deprecatory
Can become a scapegoat
A "born-loser" image
Obsessive-compulsive behavior

Source: Drawn from "Childhood Depression: A Clinical and Behavioral Perspective" by C. P. Malmquist, in J. G. Schulterbrant and A. Raskin (Eds.), *Depression in Childhood: Diagnosis, Treatment, and Conceptual Models* (pp. 33–59), 1977, New York: Raven Press.

ing development, almost all children. When the masked symptoms and depressive equivalents such as hyperactivity, aggressive behavior, psychosomatic disturbances, hypochondrias, delinquency, temper tantrums, disobedience, boredom, and restlessness . . . are added to the list, then virtually no child can escape the classification. (p. 718)

Clearly, more attention needs to be devoted to the reliable and valid identification of depressed children. This effort would include not only improved criteria, but the development of reliable and valid assessment instruments and procedures (Cantwell, 1982).

Additional research is also needed on the causes of and effective treatments for childhood depression. As with so many other childhood behaviors, a variety of causes and correlates of childhood depression have been suggested. Freudian psychoanalytic theories (Freud, 1977), cognitive theories (Beck, 1974), behaviorally oriented theories (Lewinsohn, 1974), and learned helplessness theories (Seligman, 1974) have all attempted to account for childhood depression. More recently, genetics, heredity, biochemical make-up, and family dynamics have been proposed as explanations (Strober, 1983; Strober & Carlson, 1982).

Given the problems of definition and assessment coupled with the fact that we know very little about the causes of childhood depression, it should come as no surprise that we also know very little about effective treatment for it. It is difficult to talk to depressed children as in traditional psychoanalytic therapy; therefore, play therapy is sometimes used as a substitute (Gelfand, Jenson, & Drew, 1982). Drug therapy is also used (Petti, 1983). Social skills training has also been proposed as a potentially useful alternative (Kazdin & Strober, 1982). However, the search continues for effective treatments for childhood depression because there are few available today.

Learning Problems

Although behaviorally disordered children are primarily characterized by their serious social, emotional, and behavioral problems, it has long been recognized that another major common identifying characteristic relates to school learning problems (Morse, Cutler, & Fink, 1964). Generally, these students exhibit intellectual and academic deficiencies; that is, slightly below-average IQ levels and academic achievement levels below that predicted by ability tests (Kauffman, 1985; Mastropieri, Jenkins, & Scruggs, 1985).

The intellectual and academic achievement characteristics of behaviorally disordered children have sparked a "Which came first? The chicken or the egg?" debate. Some have argued that a child's academic deficiencies lead to the development of social/emotional problems. The truth is that there is no conclusive evidence to support either position (Kauffman, 1985). Furthermore, continued attention to a question that probably can never be satisfactorily answered only obscures the fact that there are a significant number of children who have serious behavior problems *and* serious academic deficiencies and who need intensive, specialized instructional interventions.

Another characteristic associated with learning problems is poor academic survival skills. Academic survival skills—attending to tasks, following directions, working on or responding to an assignment, staying in seat, and following classroom rules—are prerequisites to school achievement (Cobb, 1972; Greenwood, Delquadri, Hops, & Walker, 1977). If a student has poor survival skills, it is likely that that child will have serious problems with academic achievement.

It is clear that behaviorally disordered students' learning problems should not take a back seat to their social/emotional problems. There appears to be a reciprocal relationship between learning problems and behavior problems; a child's behavior problems reduce the chances for academic success and the lack of academic success further exacerbates the behavior problem. Both problems must be addressed, with a coordinated and comprehensive program, if the child's long-term chances for adjustment are to be significantly improved. This issue is addressed in more depth in chapters 5 and 6 on academic instruction and social skills training.

Childhood Psychosis

A very small number of children display behavior patterns so bizarre and atypical that they can be classified as psychotic.[1] The most common form of childhood psychoses is childhood schizophrenia. The characteristic symptoms of childhood schizophrenia — thought disorders, delusions, hallucinations, altered mood — are very similar to those of adult schizophrenia. So close is the resemblance that the DSM-III (American Psychiatric Association, 1980) does not include a separate category for childhood schizophrenia and, instead, considers the essential features of schizophrenia to be the same in children and adults (Achenbach, 1982).

Schizophrenia in children is rare. Although precise estimates are difficult, about 3 children out of 10,000 is a conservative figure (Gelfand et al., 1982). Despite the low rate of occurrence, childhood schizophrenia has been extensively studied (Erickson, 1978). We still cannot state with certainty what causes schizophrenia or what treatments are required to produce positive, long-lasting changes. Neurological, biochemical, and genetic factors seem to be among the most promising areas of current investigations. Similarly, psychoanalytic, behavioral, and pharmacological approaches have all been tried as treatments for schizophrenic children. The results of these efforts are disappointing, and no other treatment approach has consistently resulted in major improvements (Achenbach, 1982).

Summary

Our purpose in this section was not to present a comprehensive description of every subgroup of behavioral disorders. Instead, our purpose was to define by example the nature of the students and the problems addressed in this text. We have only scratched the surface. Many excellent books have been written about the characteristics and etiology of behaviorally disordered children and youth (c.f. Clarizio & McCoy, 1983; Epanchin & Paul, 1987; Gelfand et al., 1982; Kauffman, 1985; Ollendick & Hersen, 1983; Schwartz & Johnson, 1985; Wicks-Nelson & Israel, 1984).

FOUNDATIONS OF EFFECTIVE TEACHING

Just as disagreement and occasional controversy surround the issues of definition and prevalence, the question of how you teach these children

---

[1]Our discussion of childhood psychosis will not include a discussion of infantile autism. While autistic children clearly display significantly deviant behavior patterns, we believe that the basic nature of the problems of autistic children is fundamentally different from those of behaviorally disordered students. Contemporary thinking in the field considers autism to be sufficiently distinct from behavioral disorders in terms of etiology, characteristics, and treatment that separate coverage, in much greater depth, is warranted.

has also been answered in ways that vary considerably in philosophy. You may read a book, attend a workshop, or enroll in a college course concerned with the education and treatment of behaviorally disordered students only to discover that definitive answers to questions of instructional methods and strategies are not always readily available.

We know considerably more about classroom teaching today than we did a decade ago. Research investigating the relationship between teaching and student achievement has made many important advances (see, for example, Brophy & Good, 1986; Medley, 1982; Rosenshine & Stevens, 1986; Stevens & Rosenshine, 1981). Even though this research has primarily been done in regular education settings, we think it has rich application value in special education as well. Several common themes cut across the research on effective teaching. These themes are direct instruction, academic learning time, student success rates, and classroom management.

Direct Instruction

When teachers explain exactly what students are expected to learn, demonstrate the steps needed to accomplish a particular task, and provide opportunities to practice and feedback, students learn more (U.S. Department of Education, 1986). Sometimes referred to as *active teaching* (Good, 1983) or *explicit instruction* (Rosenshine & Stevens, 1986), direct instruction has several essential components:

- Setting clear goals and making sure students understand those goals
- Presenting lessons that are well-organized and carefully sequenced
- Giving students clear, concise explanations and illustrations of the concepts to be learned
- Demonstrating how to perform new tasks
- Checking students' understanding of a lesson by asking frequent questions
- Providing students with frequent opportunities to practice newly learned skills
- Monitoring student progress, providing appropriate feedback, and reteaching if necessary

In short, in direct instruction, "the teacher carries the content to the students personally rather than depending on the curriculum materials to do so" (Brophy & Good, 1986, p. 361).

A more detailed examination of the instructional functions associated with direct instruction was provided by Rosenshine and Stevens (1986). They developed a general model of effective instruction that includes the following steps:

- Begin a lesson with a short review of previous, prerequisite learning.
- Begin a lesson with a short statement of goals.
- Present new material in small steps, with student practice after each step.
- Give clear and detailed instructions and explanations.
- Provide a lot of active practice for all students.
- Ask a lot of questions, check for student understanding, and obtain responses from all students.
- Guide students during initial practice.
- Provide systematic feedback and corrections.
- Provide explicit instruction and practice for seatwork exercises and, where necessary, monitor students during seatwork.

Rosenshine and Stevens have stressed that there is nothing extraordinary about these techniques; many teachers use them. What is worth noting, however, is that the most effective teachers use these techniques much more often than other teachers do.

Academic Learning Time

One of the most pervasive findings of recent years may also be one of the most self-evident. The amount of time students are actively engaged in learning is positively associated with achievement. Put another way, students learn more when they have more opportunity to learn and when they take maximum advantage of that opportunity. The strongest and most consistent findings have linked student achievement to the quantity of instruction delivered (Berliner, 1979). That is, when teachers make the best use of the time allocated for instruction by keeping students continuously and actively engaged and when they do not waste time on relatively unimportant activities, students achieve more (see Exhibit 1.4).

Studies of elementary classrooms have discovered that the amount of time actually allocated for instruction can vary from 50 to 90% of the total school time available for teaching (Rosenshine, 1980). Time is lost organizing instruction, managing transitions, dealing with student misbehavior, and responding to rather simple matters such as requests for assistance (Paine, Radicchi, Rosellini, Deutchman, & Darch, 1983). Thus, decisions about how time should be allocated among various content areas and how that allocated time is managed are very important in maximizing student achievement when teachers are successful.

Student Success Rate

The evidence of the importance of success on academic tasks is also very clear. Students should consistently be moderately to very successful on their academic assignments. A high success rate would be approximately 90 to 100% accurate; moderate success would be no less than 80% ac-

EXHIBIT 1.4 Managing classroom time

How much time students are actively engaged in learning contributes strongly to their achievement. The amount of time available for learning is determined by the instructional and management skills of the teacher and the priorities set by the school administration.

Teachers must not only know the subjects they teach, they must also be effective classroom managers. Studies of elementary school teachers have found that the amount of time teachers actually used for instruction varied between 50 and 90 percent of the total time available to them.

Effective managers in the classroom do not waste valuable minutes on unimportant activities; they keep the students continuously and actively engaged. Good managers perform the following time-conserving functions:

- *Planning class work:* Choosing the content to be studied, scheduling time for presentation and study, and choosing those instructional activities (such as grouping, seatwork, or recitation) best suited to learning the material at hand;
- *Communicating goals:* Setting and conveying expectations so students know what they are to do, what it will take to get a passing grade, and what the consequences of failure will be;
- *Regulating learning activities:* Sequencing course content so knowledge builds on itself, pacing instruction so students are prepared for the next step, monitoring success rates so all students stay productively engaged regardless of how quickly they learn, and running an orderly, academically focused classroom that keeps wasted time and misbehavior to a minimum.

When teachers carry out these functions successfully and supplement them with a well-designed and well-managed program of homework, they can achieve three important goals:

- They capture students' attention.
- They make the best use of available learning time.
- They encourage academic achievement.

Source: From *What Works: Research About Teaching and Learning,* 1986, Washington, DC: U.S. Department of Education.

curate (Brophy & Good, 1986). High success rates promote achievement by reducing confusion and frustration while still providing practice opportunities that challenge students to apply what they have just been taught.

High success rates are desirable in a variety of instructional contexts — independent seatwork, homework, group discussion and recitation, and small group work with the teacher. They are best achieved when the concept to be learned is carefully taught, the skill to be demonstrated by the student is clearly explained and demonstrated, the teacher checks the student's understanding of the concept and skill prior to the assignment, the task to be assigned is thoughtfully selected following an accurate assessment of the student's ability, and the student's performance is closely monitored. High success rates are especially desirable when students must work independently for long periods without teacher supervision or assistance.

Classroom Management

Student achievement is maximized in classrooms that run smoothly, where little time is spent in organizational or housekeeping chores and dealing with student misbehavior. The key to effective classroom management is a teacher who *acts* much more than he or she *reacts* (Brophy, 1986). How teachers prevent misbehavior is a more important determinant of classroom management skills than how they deal with behavior problems after they have occurred (Good & Brophy, 1987).

Much of what we currently know about effective classroom management was originally described by Kounin (1970) and has been subsequently elaborated by others. Kounin identified several variables that seem to differentiate effective from ineffective classroom managers:

1. *With-itness* — Being aware of student behavior and communicating that awareness to students
2. *Overlapping* — Dealing with two or more things simultaneously
3. *Smoothness* — Staying on-task by not interrupting the flow of a lesson with comments or behaviors that are disruptive to student learning
4. *Momentum* — maintaining a brisk pace by keeping the lesson moving ahead
5. *Alerting* — Attempting to keep students engaged by telling them their work will be checked
6. *Accountability* — following up on alerting behaviors and assessing students' understanding of the content being taught

Effective classroom managers also have clear expectations about student behavior and convey these expectations to students in the form of rules that are systematically and consistently enforced (Emmert, Evertson, & Anderson, 1980). Effective classroom managers also devote time, especially at the beginning of the school year, to actively teaching classroom rules, procedures, routines, and contingencies and then consistently follow through to enforce the standards and consequences (Evertson & Anderson, 1979).

Summary

The research on classroom teaching has focused on identifying classroom management and instructional strategies that promote student achievement. Students achieve more in classrooms and schools where:

1. There is an obvious instructional focus and ample time is committed to teaching.
2. Teachers actively teach content by demonstrating the concepts
   and skills to be learned, providing plenty of practice opportunities, monitoring student performance, and giving feedback.
3. Students display high levels of engagement with the instructional tasks and experience high rates of success.
4. There is a pervasive positive expectation that students will
   learn conveyed by all those involved with the instructional
   program.

The composite profile of an effective teacher drawn from this research is
that of someone who can manage instructional time and student behavior
and who is adept at instructional presentations, monitoring, and feedback. Teachers who provide an organized, structured, task-oriented,
emotionally warm and supportive learning environment usually provide
higher achievement from their students.

What do we know about effective teaching? We do know that teachers can and do make a difference (Good & Brophy, 1987). There is also
much that we do not yet know. Teaching is a complex act. No single factor or characteristic can entirely explain the qualities of effective teaching. In fact, what works in some situations may not work in other school
settings with different students, different subjects, or different instructional goals. There may be teachers who break all the rules and yet are
very successful.

The effective instructional practices that have emerged from the literature are generic practices that all teachers—both special and regular
— can implement with students of varying abilities (Goodman, 1985).
They certainly are not scripts that should be mechanically followed. Instead, they should be blended with a rich variety of personal, social, and
professional qualities and skills. They are a set of *starter skills* that should
be mastered to the point of automaticity (Brophy, 1986). While some of
these effective practices may not work with all students all of the time,
they provide a solid foundation to an effective instructional program for
all students, including behaviorally disordered ones.

EMERGING QUALITY INSTRUCTIONAL
PRACTICES IN SPECIAL EDUCATION

The knowledge obtained from research on effective instructional practices in regular education has potentially important applications in the
special education of behaviorally disordered students. The next section
will briefly highlight several of the more promising practices to emerge

from special education in recent years—data-based instruction, curriculum-based assessment, transfer of training procedures, peer tutoring, and parent involvement.

Data-Based Instructional Decision Making

Monitoring student performance was identified earlier as being positively associated with student achievement. In special education, monitoring student performance has been recognized for some time as essential to quality instruction. Effective special education teachers constantly monitor their students by collecting objective performance data and deciding whether to continue a specific intervention program, modify it, or implement a new program based on analysis of the data (Kerr & Nelson, 1983).

One of the more widely used instructional decision-making systems is known as *precision teaching*. Precision teaching is a set of procedures based on direct and daily measurement of academic or behavioral performance in terms of specific, observable behaviors. Precision teaching is a way of evaluating the effectiveness of instruction that enables the teacher to make decisions about how to improve the students' instructional program (White, 1986). According to White (1986), precision teaching is based on five guiding principles:

1. *The learner knows best.* The best indicator of the effectiveness of an instructional program is the student's performance. If the data indicate satisfactory progress, then the program must be appropriate for that child.
2. *Focus on direct observable behavior.* Precision teaching focuses on behaviors, or "pinpoints," which are countable, have a definite beginning and end, and are repeatable. Public events, such as oral reading, are the focus of precision teaching, while private events, such as silent reading, are not.
3. *Frequency is the basic measure of performance.* In precision teaching, all behaviors observed are described in terms of their frequency of occurrence in a given amount of time. Behavior is usually expressed in terms of the number of correct responses per minute or the number of errors per minute on any given task.
4. *The standard 'celeration chart is critical.* Special education teachers often use graphs or charts to visually display student performance data. Precision teaching uses the standard 'celeration chart to record, display, and analyze student performance data (see Exhibit 1.5). The standard 'celeration chart differs from other graphing or charting conventions because rate of change (or progress) is always depicted in a

EXHIBIT 1.5   The standard 'celeration chart and charting conventions

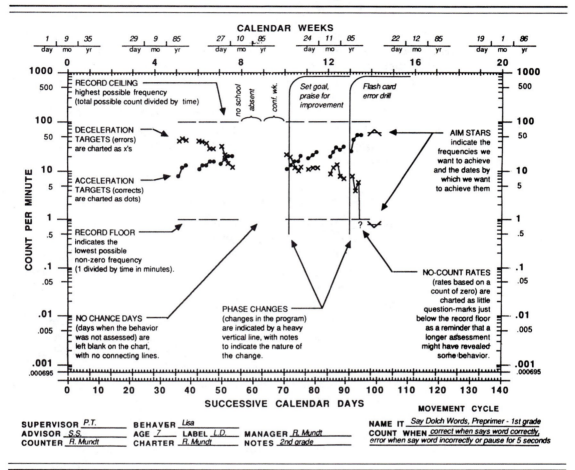

standard manner; a ratio, or semi-logarithmic, scale is used rather than the standard add–subtract scale used on most graphs. The use of a ratio scale enables equal dimensions of changed performance to appear equivalent regardless of their absolute frequencies.

5. *Analyze environmental conditions.* It is a well-established principle of learning that environmental events, both antecedents and consequences, can influence a behavior by increasing, decreasing, or maintaining its rate. Precision teaching emphasizes the analysis of those environmental conditions

(e.g., settings, materials, tasks, reinforcers, punishers) that seem to influence the performance of students.

Whether a teacher uses precision teaching per se is not as important as the fact that some method of systematic and continuous monitoring of student performance be employed.[2] Perhaps the best way to guarantee that students receive effective instruction is to systematically and continuously evaluate their performance and make instructional decisions based on an analysis of those data (Fuchs & Fuchs, 1986). The primary task for teachers is to find and use a procedure that allows them to collect and graphically display student performance data as efficiently and effectively as possible.

Curriculum-Based Assessment

Effective teaching requires that teachers understand the instructional needs of each student. To engage their students and achieve high student success rates, teachers must be able to accurately assess their students' current levels of educational performance and provide appropriate instruction that has been carefully matched to the students' identified instructional needs (Zigmond & Miller, 1986).

While many teachers agree with the need to assess students' instructional needs, they may not practice what they believe. A wide range of assessment procedures is observed in practice. The techniques teachers use to assess their students' current level of performance vary greatly in reliability, validity, and functional utility. For example, standardized tests of achievement typically provide grade-level scores, a measure too imprecise to serve as a guide for instructional planning. Teacher judgments and observations of student achievement and instructional levels may also be flawed in terms of accuracy and reliability.

What emerges is a picture of students, both nonhandicapped and handicapped, who are being taught without the benefit of having their instructional needs accurately and precisely assessed. The implications of this situation are serious. As Gickling and Thompson (1985) have indicated, the mismatch between students' instructional needs and the demands of the curriculum provides a fertile basis for the sprouting of many school learning and behavior problems.

In recent years, increasing attention has been given to an approach that provides optimal levels of success for all students. The approach, along with its associated procedures, is called *curriculum-based assessment*. Curriculum-based assessment (CBA) has been defined as "the prac-

---

[2]See Kerr and Nelson (1983), especially chapter 3, and Deno and Mirkin (1977) for additional examples of systems and procedures for the continuous monitoring of student performance.

tice of obtaining direct and frequent measures of a student's performance on a series of sequentially arranged objectives derived from the curriculum used in the classroom" (Blankenship & Lilly, 1981, p. 81). Characteristics of CBA include:

- Objective measurement of student performance in virtually all areas of the curriculum
- Careful sampling of behaviors to allow the student to be appropriately placed in the curriculum
- Performance data on skills collected over several days to increase reliability of data
- Frequent probing, or measurement, of skill acquisition throughout the school year to measure student progress

Curriculum-based assessment is not new in special education. For years special educators have been urged to focus their assessment efforts on pinpointing specific learner needs and providing instruction specifically geared to those identified needs. This approach contrasts with a more traditional view of assessment, which emphasizes assessment for diagnosis and placement. That view, while necessary, too often leaves the teacher with little useful or meaningful information about what students need to learn *today*.

The collective results of a significant number of research and development efforts with curriculum-based assessment underline several clearly evident advantages of CBA: (a) it improves the quality of information teachers have that can be used to make better-informed decisions about a student's progress and instructional program; (b) it is much more sensitive to changes in student skill levels than traditional, standardized tests of student performance; (c) the data gathered provide a base of information that allows teachers to generate more sophisticated empirical decisions about student progress; (d) CBA provides the opportunity to gather data on nonhandicapped students that can be used for meaningful normative comparisons; and (e) it is cost-effective when compared to the actual and hidden costs of administering commercially available standardized tests and using the results provided by those tests (Deno, 1985).

Strategies That Promote Generalization

The success of special education programs for the behaviorally disordered is often measured by the extent to which academic and behavioral improvements generalize, or transfer, from a special education setting to other places and people (e.g., mainstream classrooms, regular classroom teachers). Achieving generalization and maintenance is a key ingredient in the overall success of a BD student's education.

However, it is often very difficult to achieve generalization. Gains made in special education settings do not consistently transfer to regular classrooms. When a behaviorally disordered student is removed from a regular classroom and placed in special education, the student does not automatically generalize or maintain academic and behavioral improvements achieved in the special setting after returning to the regular classroom.

Our knowledge of the nature of this problem has increased dramatically in the last 10 years with the emergence of a number of promising practices that facilitate generalization. For example, a new set of procedures known as *transenvironmental programming* is especially appropriate for use with behaviorally disordered students (Anderson-Inman, 1986; Anderson-Inman, Walker, & Purcell, 1984). Self-management procedures, peer reprogramming techniques and academic strategy training are other promising approaches to generalization. Given the complexity of the problem and its central relationship to the overall success of special education for behaviorally disordered students, teachers must give priority to systematic planning for generalization. So important is this practice to the task of teaching these students that we have devoted an entire chapter to a detailed explanation of the problem and potential solutions.

Involving Peers

Students have been used as tutors and peer helpers in education for a very long time. Recently considerable attention and effort have been devoted to programmatic research in several areas where peers have been involved in the classroom:

- The use of peer confederates in social skills interventions with socially withdrawn children (Strain, 1981; Strain & Odom, 1986);
- The use of peer tutors for basic academic skills, exemplified by the work done at the Juniper Gardens Children's project (Delquadri, Greenwood, Whorton, Carta, & Hall, 1986);
- The use of peer monitors to decrease the disruptive behaviors and increase appropriate classroom behaviors of elementary-aged students (Carden-Smith & Fowler, 1984; Fowler, 1986);
- The use of cooperative learning strategies to promote positive relationships between handicapped and nonhandicapped students in mainstreamed settings (Johnson & Johnson, 1986)

Evaluations of the effectiveness of peer tutoring indicate several benefits to both the tutor and the tutee. The academic achievement of tutees increases, as does their behavioral and social functioning (Delquadri et al., 1986). Both nonhandicapped and handicapped tutors may benefit in similar ways (Cooke, Heron, & Heward, 1983). Peer involvement strategies are more effective when they are used as a complement to the classroom teacher (as opposed to being a substitute for the teacher) (Young, 1981). Peer-mediated interventions have been widely used with behaviorally disordered students with positive results (Scruggs, Mastropieri, & Richter, 1985). Effectiveness increases when both tutors and tutees are carefully taught the procedures and routines and when the teacher carefully monitors the program.

Parent Involvement

Many children who have significant behavioral problems at school also behave maladaptively in their homes. Thus, the importance of involving parents in the overall educational program provided behaviorally disordered students is clear. Common sense would seem to indicate that teachers should make a concerted effort to involve parents of these students in their child's program.

Despite the relatively long history of actively involving parents in intervention programs for BD students, teachers may not always enthusiastically embrace this concept. While some teachers acknowledge the role of the family home environment in shaping and maintaining maladaptive behavior, they believe that teachers should be primarily concerned with a student's behavior during school hours only. Furthermore, they believe that because teachers are only responsible for what occurs in the classroom and because there is only so much time available in the day to fulfill the teaching role, somebody else should be responsible for working with parents.

It is true that teachers of behaviorally disordered students already have an arduous role without the added responsibility of actively involving parents. However, we also believe that teachers ought to be involved with their students' parents on a consistent and planned basis in several key areas at least: (a) jointly planning the student's individualized educational program (IEP), (b) regularly monitoring and discussing the student's progress, (c) participating in home–school behavior management programs, and (d) intervening, as needed, with specific home or school academic or behavioral problems.

There is a growing body of knowledge related to involving parents of BD students in comprehensive treatment programs. A number of effective programs have been developed that teach parents specific behavior management skills to use with their children (cf. Becker, 1971; Blechman, 1985; Fleischman, Horne, & Arthur, 1983; Forehand & McMahon, 1981; Patterson, 1975; Pinkston, 1984; Sloaner, 1979). Data from programs training parents to use specific behavior management skills with their children indicate that parents can be taught to effectively manage and improve their child's behavior (McMahon & Forehand, 1980).

While we recognize the practical constraints associated with actively involving parents in the overall program for behaviorally disordered students, we also see the potential for positive outcomes. While schools can have a positive impact *without* parental involvement, it is clear they can have a potentially more positive and more durable impact on these students *with* active parental involvement. The benefits to students, parents, and schools are of such magnitude that the effort is worthwhile and cost-effective.

Summary

All the instructional practices presented here have certain features in common (Algozzine & Maheady, 1986). Active teacher and student involvement in teaching and learning, precise and functional assessment of instructional needs, continuous progress monitoring, reprogramming the social environment, and mobilizing resources beyond the classroom seem to fall out as basic ingredients of effective instructional programming. Perhaps the most salient characteristic permeating all the quality practices is the notion of *positive expectancy* (Bickel & Bickel, 1986): the almost passionate, "can do" belief that the primary mission of the school —student learning and growth— will be accomplished regardless of how difficult it may appear.

The practices described here are in no way intended to represent a finite list of quality indicators in special education for behaviorally disordered students. There are many more practices (e.g., social skills training, teacher consultation) we could add to these, and we will present a number of them in later chapters.

PREFERRED STRATEGIES IN SERVICE DELIVERY

The problems presented by behaviorally disordered students are complex, dictating the need for a coordinated array of services. A number of human service systems may play a role in the delivery of services to these students—the educational system, the mental health system, the social welfare system, the legal/correctional system. This section will review service delivery strategies. While primarily focusing on the role of the educational system, the overall intent is to describe how providing quality, comprehensive services requires collaboration, coordination, and communication among all those involved.

Current Status of Service Delivery

One of the most comprehensive pictures drawn of service delivery for behaviorally disordered students was developed by the National Needs Analysis in Behavior Disorders project (Huntze & Grosenick, 1980a), a federally funded project whose purpose it was to conduct a full-scale analysis of the field of behavior disorders. One of the key elements investigated was service delivery. The project found that most behaviorally disordered students are served in one of three service configurations — public schools, mental health agencies, and facilities for neglected and delinquent children and youth.

Public Schools

The public school system is the largest provider of services in terms of the numbers of students served. Typically, the continuum of services offered includes itinerant services, resource rooms, self-contained classes,

The amount and quality of services provided to behaviorally disordered students are on the rise.

special schools, out-of-district residential placement, consulting teachers, and homebound instruction. The most commonly employed service delivery option is the self-contained classroom. Resource rooms are the next most frequently used, followed by special schools, itinerant services, out-of-district placements, and homebound instruction.

The degree to which out-of-district placements (i.e., private day care and residential facilities) are used varies considerably from state to state. For example, in one state nearly 30% of all behaviorally disordered students are served in out-of-district day or residential placements, while in other states out-of-district placements are infrequent. Alternative schools are not typically used to serve these students.

One particularly perplexing finding related to the use of *school demissions* as a means of dealing with behaviorally disordered students. Grosenick (1981) has asserted that being severely behavior disordered is more likely to result in removal from school than any other disability. Exhibit 1.6 describes common school demission techniques. These procedures probably became more prevalent when courts determined that it was improper to expel behaviorally disordered students from school for rule breaking or disruptive behavior. Nevertheless, demission mechanisms can be viewed as a means to remove behaviorally disordered students from school through the back door.

Mental Health Agencies

Facilities such as state hospitals, regional mental health facilities, and community mental health facilities constitute another placement option for approximately 2,000 to 4,000 behaviorally disordered students across the nation. Other service options may include foster care programs, group homes, partial hospitalization for students requiring less than full-time residential placement but more than outpatient care, and outpatient evaluations including screening, diagnosis, evaluation, counseling, crisis intervention, and education. Students are placed in these facilities primarily through voluntary commitment by their parents, though some placements may be made by the courts.

The treatment program usually consists of an educational program, individual and group therapy, and other services such as occupational therapy, recreational therapy, and speech therapy. The length of stay in a residential facility averages 8 to 9 months; in larger state institutions, the stay is somewhat longer. Two major problems are evident in the programs delivered by mental health agencies: (a) there are very few data to document the effectiveness of this service delivery system, and (b) there is a lack of communication and coordination between mental health agencies and the public schools who take students back after their placement in a mental health facility (Huntze & Grosenick, 1980b).

EXHIBIT 1.6   School demission procedures

In-school suspension—Assigning a student to a class other than his or her own class or classes; BD students may be continuously or permanently assigned to the "temporary" class.

Continuous suspensions—Student may be suspended for 3 days, return to school for a half day, and be suspended for 3 more days, and so on; many schools do not have a limit on the number of times a student may be suspended in one school year.

Shortened school day—May be a legitimate tool for educating BD students; however, it is also used as a means of reducing the amount of contact school personnel must have with a student, which is not a legitimate use of this procedure.

Homebound instruction—Conceivably, another legitimate intervention/service option; contact with a teacher limited to 1 to 5 hours per week; relies on "independent study"; not likely to be an effective intervention for BD students on a long-term basis (i.e., more than 2 weeks).

Alternative school placement—An option that may be chosen by school officials or students; again, effectively removes the BD student from the regular school environment; not used frequently with BD students.

Ignored truancy—Some districts may be reluctant to follow-up on chronic truancy when the student is behaviorally disordered.

Source: Adapted from *National Needs Analysis in Behavior Disorders: Severe Behavior Disorders* by S. L. Huntze and J. K. Grosenick, 1980, Columbia: University of Missouri–Columbia, Department of Special Education.

Facilities for Delinquent Youth

There are approximately 72,000 children incarcerated in juvenile correction facilities in the United States (Rutherford, Nelson, & Wolford, 1985). Of these, approximately 40% may meet PL 94–142 criteria for being handicapped. Correctional education programs (formal instructional programs offered in correctional facilities) are covered by the PL 94–142 regulations stating that a free appropriate public education is to be provided handicapped persons up to 21 years old in correctional facilities. However, according to Rutherford and his colleagues, very few states comply with this provision of the law. Hampered by the sometimes short period of confinement and by typically long histories of antisocial behavior and school failure, the states find providing appropriate and effective educational programs for adjudicated youth to be extremely difficult.

After reviewing the current status of program development and service delivery for behaviorally disordered students, Kauffman (1986) concluded that it can be best characterized as one of "confusion, disorder, diversity, inadequacy" (p. 263). Grosenick (1986) provided some data to substantiate this description with the results of a survey of 145 programs for behaviorally disordered students intended to provide information about program plan and design. The components deemed essential to well-designed programs were program philosophy, student needs and identification, goals, instructional methods and curriculum, community involvement, program design and operation, exit procedures, and evaluation. Among the findings of this study were the following:

1. Only about half of the programs had established a written philosophy describing not only where services were to be provided but also why and how.
2. Similarly, about half of the programs had a written set of guidelines that described the aims and purposes of the program.
3. Curriculum and instructional methods are determined by the particular teacher in a specific program. Teachers had the primary responsibility for developing the curriculum and designing the interventions. Administrators indicated that their policies on curriculum and instructional methods were flexible enough to accommodate a range of instructional orientations.
4. The least well-developed program component was community involvement and interagency cooperation.
5. Regular education personnel (teachers and administrators) were not routinely involved in developing program goals or providing inservice training on matters pertaining to the program.
6. Only half of the programs had formalized criteria and procedures governing student exit from programs.
7. Only one-third of the programs used formal program evaluation procedures.

It was findings similar to these that led Noel (1982) to conclude that there was too much haphazard program development for students with behavioral disorders and insufficient coherence. What is needed instead are system-wide service plans based on practices that have been empirically demonstrated to be effective with these students.

A Model Continuum of Services

Expressing deep concern over the quality of programming and service delivery for behaviorally disordered students, Walker, Reavis, Rhode, and Jenson (1985) proposed an alternate service delivery system. The Comprehensive Behavioral Services model (CBSM) presented in Exhibit 1.7 meets the requirements of an effective service delivery system because it contains the following three elements: "(a) a range of placement options

EXHIBIT 1.7 Comprehensive behavioral services model (CBSM) for a continuum of education settings

Settings	Remediation Procedures
Regular classroom	Programs and procedures applied on a classwide basis by the teacher. No consultant teacher assistance required. For mild behavioral disorders.
Regular classroom	Consultant-based remediation programs/ procedures applied on a classwide or individual basis. Teacher eventually assumes program control under consultant supervision. For mild–moderate behavior disorders.
Resource or self-contained classrooms	Direct instruction and direct intervention based model programs containing the following elements: rules, praise, point systems, backup rewards, time-out, cost contingency, parent involvement. For moderate behavioral disorders.
Special day schools, residential settings, mental health facilities	Intensive, complex, and restrictive intervention procedures. Compliance training level systems, small teacher/pupil ratios, mental health support services, parent involvement, social skills training, careful monitoring and supervision. For severe behavioral disorders.

Source: Adapted from "A Conceptual Model for Delivery of Behavioral Services to Behavior Disordered Children in Educational Settings" by H. M. Walker, H. K. Reavis, G. Rhode,, and W. R. Jenson, in P. H. Bornstein and A. E. Kazdin (Eds.), *Handbook of Clinical Behavior Therapy with Children* (p. 717), 1985, Homewood, IL: Dorsey Press.

to accommodate different levels of severity, (b) rational and empirically based entry and exit criteria governing placement in such settings, and (c) transition strategies to facilitate transfer and integration across settings" (p. 716). The CBSM is a scheme for the delivery of services to the full range of behaviorally disordered students along a continuum of settings from regular classrooms to residential settings. More complex and very intensive interventions are required for more severely disordered students (Level IV); less intensive procedures are required as you move up the continuum. The CBSM's remediation procedures are predicated on the fact that validated effective intervention programs have been developed, and school personnel can be taught to use these procedures correctly with positive results.

After a student is initially placed along the continuum of services, the major focus of all programming efforts would be on preparing to meet the requirements for the next least restrictive setting. The final goal is full-time retention within the regular classroom. That is why pinpoint-ing the requirements and standards of each setting along the continuum (the entrance and exit criteria governing movement in and out of each setting) is so important. The student's fluid movement along the con-tinuum is also the reason the CBSM places a premium on strategies to facilitate transition from one setting to another (i.e., generalization of treatment effects).

The CBSM assumes that the regular classroom is the service deliv-ery option of choice for the majority of students. However, for a variety of reasons, it is not easy to keep all BD students there. Hersh and Walker (1983) have described the logistical barriers that must be overcome in mainstreaming behaviorally disordered students:

   (a) the technical competence required of regular educators to accom-
       modate the special needs of handicapped children. . . .
   (b) the provision of sufficient diversity, specialization, and individualiza-
       tion of instructional programming to accommodate the needs of
       handicapped children in less restrictive settings;
   (c) the task of persuading regular educators that a mainstreamed handi-
       capped child is *their* responsibility and that such children are entitled
       to large amounts of time, energy, and instructional attention to
       achieve a satisfactory rate of progress; and
   (d) the task of expanding the teacher's tolerance limits for bizarre forms
       of child social behavior they are not used to seeing and/or are
       unwilling to accept. (p. 162)

The CBSM also highlights the itinerant consulting teacher and the re-source teacher/consultant as crucial resources who must be available to assist regular teachers working with behaviorally disordered students placed in their classrooms.

The CBSM, its creators point out, is a conceptual model, a collec-tion of ideas about effective service delivery. Many obstacles currently stand in the way of its full implementation. For example, the shortage of competent consulting teachers who can work within regular classrooms is a significant problem. By and large, however, most of the potential ob-stacles can be overcome through the innovative use of current personnel and creative programming aimed at the goal of providing behaviorally disordered students a high quality and cost-effective program.

Summary

Because so many service providers are involved—special education, reg-ular education, mental health, juvenile justice, health, child welfare, and vocational rehabilitation—improved service delivery for behaviorally dis-ordered students is a complex challenge (Office of Special Education and Rehabilitative Services, 1986). While the problem of quality service delivery is especially acute for adolescents, there are also many problems facing younger students with mild and moderate behavior disorders. Specifically, there is a pressing need for special education and regular education to cooperate to develop strategies to accommodate the students in regular classrooms (National Association of State Directors of Special Education, 1985). The purposes of a meaningful alliance between regular education and special education would be (a) to enhance the ability of regular education, with support from special education, to provide quality educational experiences to behaviorally disordered students, (b) to prevent mild behavior problems from developing into more severe behavior disorders, and (c) to develop more cost-effective treatment approaches through prevention-oriented services.

CHAPTER SUMMARY

This chapter has provided a broad overview of several important issues in the field of behavioral disorders. Definitions and prevalence, characteristics of behaviorally disordered children, effective instructional practices in both regular and special education, and the current status of service delivery and programs were addressed.

Defining *behavioral disorders* has proven to be very difficult, and there is still no single, widely accepted definition. One of the major impediments is that most of the problem behaviors displayed by behaviorally disordered children are also commonly displayed by normal children. The difference between normal children and behaviorally disordered children, then, lies in the frequency of occurrence, degree of severity, and persistence of problem behaviors. Thus, for special education purposes, a student's behavior must differ significantly from the norm over an extended period to be classified as a behavioral disorder.

There are similar disagreements concerning the prevalence of behavioral disorders. Estimates of the number of BD students range from a low of 1% to as high as 30 to 40%. The federal government and most state governments estimate the prevalence to be approximately 2% of the school-aged population. Even with this rather conservative estimate, relatively few behaviorally disordered students have been identified and are currently receiving special education services. Only a little more than a third of the estimated 2% eligible to receive special education services are currently placed in programs across the country.

The major characteristics of behaviorally disordered students fall into one of two categories. Externalizing behavior problems (e.g., aggression, noncompliance, acting out) are characterized by behavioral excesses directed out toward the social environment. Internalizing behavior problems (e.g., social withdrawal, depression) are directed inward and usually involve deficits associated with a personal disturbance. Cutting across both externalizing and internalizing problems are the significant learning problems experienced by most of these students in school. Generally speaking, then, behaviorally disordered students are "unhappy youngsters who are behavioral misfits at school, likely to cause the consternation of teachers, and almost certain to be avoided or rejected by their peers" (Cullinan, Epstein, & Kauffman, 1984, p. 18).

There are no quick and easy cures available for use with all behaviorally disordered students. However, a growing body of knowledge is available that suggests that there are instructional procedures that tend to produce positive changes predictably and consistently. We have termed these instructional procedures *preferred practices*. Preferred practices can be identified when the contributions of educational and psychological research to practice are recognized and understood. We believe that the field of special education for behaviorally disordered students is at the point where we can now state with reasonable confidence that certain educational practices ought to be preferred over others because they facilitate desired changes in the student behavior.

When viewed from an historical perspective, the amount and quality of services provided to behaviorally disordered students is on the rise. However, there is still a long way to go in terms of the availability of enough trained teachers, better techniques for identification and assessment, enhanced coordination among various agencies, increased sensitivity to the needs of students, significantly improved program evaluation techniques, and more widespread adoption and application of validated, effective instructional practices. Service delivery can never be better than the persons who teach in the various programs. However, weak programs have a profoundly limiting effect and substantially restrict the beneficial influence of an effective teacher.

THE REST OF THIS BOOK

Chapters 2 and 3 of *Teaching Behaviorally Disordered Students: Preferred Practices* discuss the foundation instructional skills of assessment and behavior management required in teaching behaviorally disordered students. Chapter 4 deals with a topic of major importance in this field — generalizing academic, behavioral, and social improvements from special education to the regular classroom. Chapters 5 and 6 address the major curriculum areas of academic instruction and social skills training. How to teach behaviorally disordered students in regular classrooms, resource programs, and self-contained classrooms is covered in chapters 7, 8 and 9. Chapter 10 is concerned with working with parents. The book concludes in chapter 11, with a review of legal issues associated with teaching these students.

REVIEW QUESTIONS

1. Define the term *behavioral disorders* in your own words.
2. Explain what is meant by the statement, "Behaviorally disordered students do not have a monopoly on problem behaviors."
3. Why is the term *behaviorally disordered* preferred over the term *emotional disturbance?*
4. Why are there large differences in the estimates of the prevalence of behaviorally disordered students?
5. Give some reasons why there is such a large gap between the number of students estimated to be behaviorally disordered and the number of students actually receiving special education services.
6. Differentiate between externalizing and internalizing behavior problems. Provide examples of each.
7. Summarize the characteristics of effective teaching identified in this chapter. Relate these characteristics to the instructional needs of behaviorally disordered students.
8. It appears as if the current status of service delivery for behaviorally disordered students is, at best, inadequate. What do you think accounts for this? What are some things that can be done about it?

REFERENCES

Achenbach, T. M. (1982). *Developmental psychopathology* (2nd ed.). New York: John Wiley.

Achenbach, T. M., & Edelbrock, C. S. (1981). Behavioral problems and competencies reported by parents of normal and disturbed children aged 4 through 16. *Monographs of the Society for Research in Child Development, 46* (Serial No. 188).

Algozzine, R. (1981). Introduction and perspective. In R. Algozzine, R. Schmid, & C. D. Mercer (Eds.), *Childhood behavior disorders: Applied research and educational practice.* Rockville, MD: Aspen Systems Corp.

Algozzine, R., & Maheady, L. (1986). Assessment for instructional planning. *Exceptional Children, 52,* 501–509.

American Psychiatric Association. (1980). *Diagnostic and statistical manual of mental disorders* (3rd ed.). Washington, DC: Author.

Anderson-Inman, L. (1986). Bridging the gap: Student-centered strategies for promoting the transfer of learning. *Exceptional Children, 52,* 562–572.

Anderson-Inman, L., Walker, H. M., & Purcell, J. (1984). Promoting the transfer of skills across settings: Transenvironmental programming for handicapped students in the mainstream. In W. L. Heward, T. E. Heron, D. S. Hill, & J. Trap-Porter (Eds.), *Focus on behavior analysis in education.* Columbus, OH: Merrill.

Apter, S. J. (1982). *Troubled children/Troubled systems.* New York: Pergamon Press.

Asher, S. R., & Taylor, A. R. (1982). Social outcomes of mainstreaming: Socio-metric assessment and beyond. In P. Strain (Ed.), *Social development of exceptional children.* Rockville, MD: Aspen Systems Corp.

Barclay, R. A. (1981). *Hyperactive children: A handbook for diagnosis and treatment.* New York: Guilford Press.

Beck, A. T. (1974). The development of depression: A cognitive model. In R. Friedman & M. Katz (Eds.), *The psychology of depression: Contemporary theory and research.* Washington, DC: V. H. Winston.

Becker, W. C. (1971). *Parents are teachers.* Champaign, IL: Research Press.

Berliner, D. C. (1979). Tempus educare. In P. L. Peterson & H. J. Walberg (Eds.), *Research on teaching: Concepts, findings, and implications.* Berkeley, CA: McCutchan.

Bickel, W. E., & Bickel, D. D. (1986). Effective schools, classrooms, and instruction: Implications for special education. *Exceptional Children, 52,* 489-500.

Blankenship, C., & Lilly, M. S. (1981). *Mainstreaming students with learning and behavior problems: Techniques for the classroom teacher.* New York: Holt, Rinehart and Winston.

Blechman, E. A. (1985). *Solving child behavior problems at home and at school.* Champaign, IL: Research Press.

Bower, E. M. (1969). *Early identification of emotionally handicapped children in school.* Springfield, IL: Charles C Thomas.

Brophy, J. (1986, April). *Synthesizing the results of research linking teacher behavior to student achievement.* Paper presented at annual meeting of American Educational Research Association, San Francisco.

Brophy, J., & Good, T. L. (1986). Teacher behavior and student achievement. In M. C. Wittrock (Ed.), *Handbook of research on teaching* (3rd ed.). New York: Macmillan.

Cantwell, D. P. (1982). Childhood depression: Current research. In B. B. Lahey & A. E. Kazdin (Eds.), *Advances in clinical child psychology* (Vol. 5). New York: Plenum Press.

Cantwell, D. P., & Carlson, G. A. (Eds.). (1983). *Affective disorders in childhood and adolescence: An update.* New York: Spectrum.

Carden-Smith, L., & Fowler, S. A. (1984). Positive peer pressure: The effects of peer monitoring on children's disruptive behavior. *Journal of Applied Behavior Analysis, 17,* 213-227.

Clarizio, H. F., & McCoy, G. F. (1983). *Behavior disorders in children* (3rd ed.). New York: Thomas Y. Crowell.

Cobb, J. A. (1972). Relationship of discrete classroom behaviors to fourth-grade academic achievement. *Journal of Educational Psychology, 63,* 74-80.

Cooke, N. L., Heron, T. E., & Heward, W. L. (1983). *Peer tutoring: Implementing classwide programs in the primary grades.* Columbus, OH: Special Press.

Cullinan, D., & Epstein, M. H. (1979). Administrative definitions of behavior disorders: Status and directions. In F. Wood & K. C. Lakin (Eds.), *Disturbing, disordered or disturbed? Perspectives on the definition of problem behavior in educa-*

tional settings. Minneapolis: University of Minnesota, Department of Psychoeducational Studies.

Cullinan, D., & Epstein, M. H. (1986). Behavior disorders. In N. Haring (Ed.), *Exceptional children and youth* (4th ed.), Columbus, OH: Merrill.

Cullinan, D., Epstein, M. H., & Kauffman, J. M. (1984). Teacher's ratings of students' behaviors: What constitutes behavior disorder in school? *Behavioral Disorders, 10,* 9–19.

Cullinan, D., Epstein, M. H., & Lloyd, J. (1983). *Behavioral disorders.* Englewood Cliffs, NJ: Prentice-Hall.

Cullinan, D., Schloss, P. J., & Epstein, M. H. (1987). Relative prevalence and correlates of depressive characteristics among seriously emotionally disturbed and non-handicapped students. *Behavioral Disorders, 12,* 90–98.

Delquadri, J., Greenwood, C. R., Whorton, D., Carta, J. J., & Hall, R. V. (1986). Classwide peer tutoring. *Exceptional Children, 52,* 535–542.

Deno, S. L. (1985). Curriculum-based measurement: The emerging alternative. *Exceptional Children, 52,* 219–232.

Deno, S. L., & Mirkin, P. K. (1977). *Data-based program modification: A manual.* Reston, VA: Council for Exceptional Children.

Emmert, E. T., Evertson, C. M., & Anderson, L. M. (1980). Effective management at the beginning of the school year. *Elementary School Journal, 80,* 219–231.

Epanchin, B. C., & Paul, J. L. (1987). *Emotional problems of childhood and adolescence. A multidisciplinary perspective.* Columbus, OH: Merrill.

Erickson, M. T. (1978). *Childhood psychopathology: Assessment, etiology, and treatment.* Englewood Cliffs, NJ: Prentice-Hall.

Evertson, C., & Anderson, L. (1979). Beginning school. *Educational Horizons, 57,* 164–168.

Fleischman, M. J., Horne, A. M., & Arthur, J. L. (1983). *Troubled families: A treatment program.* Champaign, IL: Research Press.

Forehand, R. L., & McMahon, R. J. (1981). *Helping the noncompliant child: A clinician's guide to parent training.* New York: Guilford Press.

Fowler, S. A. (1986). Peer-monitoring and self-monitoring: Alternatives to traditional teacher management. *Exceptional Children, 52,* 573–581.

Freud, A. (1977). Fears, anxieties, and phobic phenomena. *The Psychoanalytic Study of the Child, 32,* 85–90.

Fuchs, L. S., & Fuchs, D. (1986). Effects of systematic formative evaluation: A meta-analysis. *Exceptional Children, 53,* 199–208.

Gelfand, D. M., Jenson, W. R., & Drew, C. J. (1982). *Understanding child behavior disorders.* New York: Holt, Rinehart and Winston.

Gickling, E. E., & Thompson, V. P. (1985). A personal view of curriculum-based assessment. *Exceptional Children, 52,* 205–218.

Gittelman-Klein, R. (1977). Definitional and methodological issues concerning depressive illness in children. In J. G. Schulterbrandt & A. Raskin (Eds.), *Depression in childhood: Diagnosis, treatment, and conceptual models.* New York: Raven Press.

Gliedman, J., & Roth, W. (1980). *The unexpected minority: Handicapped children in America.* New York: Harcourt Brace Jovanovich.

Good, T. L. (1983). Recent classroom research: Implications for teacher education. In D. C. Smith (Ed.), *Essential knowledge for beginning educators.* Washington, DC: American Association of Colleges for Teacher Education.

Good, T. L., & Brophy, J. (1987). *Looking in classrooms* (4th ed.). New York: Harper & Row.

Goodman, L. (1985). The effective school movement and special education. *Teaching Exceptional Children, 17,* 102–105.

Greenwood, C. R., Delquadri, J., Hops, H., & Walker, H. M. (1977). *Program for academic survival skills: Consultant manual.* Eugene, OR: Center at Oregon for Research in the Behavioral Education of the Handicapped.

Greenwood, C. R., Walker, H. M., & Hops, H. (1977). Some issues in social interaction/withdrawal assessment. *Exceptional Children, 43,* 490–499.

Greenwood, C. R., Walker, H. M., Todd, N. M., & Hops, H. (1979). Selecting a cost-effective screening device for the assessment of preschool social withdrawal. *Journal of Applied Behavior Analysis, 12,* 639–652.

Gresham, F. M. (1985). Behavior disorder assessment: Conceptual, definitional, and practical considerations. *School Psychology Review, 14,* 495–509.

Grosenick, J. K. (1981). Public school and mental health services to severely behavior disordered students. *Behavioral Disorders, 6,* 183–190.

Grosenick, J. E. (1986, November). *Preliminary findings on the plan and design of SED programs.* Paper presented at Tenth Annual TECBD National Conference on Severe Behavior Disorders of Children and Youth, Tempe, AZ.

Guralnick, M. J. (1986). The peer relations of young handicapped and nonhandicapped children. In P. S. Strain, M. J. Guralnick, & H. M. Walker (Eds.), *Children's social behavior: Development, assessment, and modification.* Orlando, FL: Academic Press.

Hallahan, D. P., & Kauffman, J. M. (1977). Categories, labels, behavioral characteristics: ED, LD, and EMR considered. *Journal of Special Education, 11,* 139–149.

Hallahan, D. P., & Kauffman, J. M. (1982). *Exceptional children: Introduction to special education* (2nd ed.). Englewood Cliffs, NJ: Prentice-Hall.

Herbert, M. (1978). *Conduct disorders of childhood and adolescence: A behavioral approach to assessment and treatment.* New York: John Wiley.

Herbert, M. (1982). Conduct disorders. In B. B. Lahey & A. E. Kazdin (Eds.), *Advances in clinical child psychology* (Vol. 5). New York: Plenum Press.

Hersh, R., & Walker, H. M. (Eds.). (1983). Great expectations: Making schools effective for all children. *Policy Studies Review* [Special issue], *2,* 147–188.

Hewett, F. M., & Taylor, F. D. (1980). *The emotionally disturbed child in the classroom: The orchestration of success* (2nd ed.). Boston: Allyn & Bacon.

Hops, H., & Greenwood, C. R. (1981). Social skills deficits. In E. J. Mash & L. G. Terdal (Eds.), *Behavioral assessment of childhood disorders.* New York: Guilford Press.

Huntze, S. L. (1985). A position paper of The Council for Children with Behavioral Disorders. *Behavioral Disorders, 10,* 167–174.

Huntze, S. L., & Grosenick, J. K. (1980a). *National needs analysis in behavior disorders: Human resource issues in behavior disorders.* Columbia: University of Missouri–Columbia, Department of Special Education.

Huntze, S. L., & Grosenick, J. K. (1980b). *National needs analysis in behavior disorders: Severe behavior disorders.* Columbia: University of Missouri–Columbia, Department of Special Education.

Johnson, D. S., & Johnson, R. T. (1986). Mainstreaming and cooperative learning strategies. *Exceptional Children, 52,* 553–561.

Kauffman, J. M. (1982). Social policy issues in special education and related services for emotionally disturbed children and youth. In M. M. Noel & N. G. Haring (Eds.), *Progress or change: Issues in educating the emotionally disturbed: Vol. 1. Identification and program planning.* Seattle: University of Washington.

Kauffman, J. M. (1985). *Characteristics of children's behavior disorders* (3rd ed.). Columbus, OH: Merrill.

Kauffman, J. M. (1986). Educating children with behavior disorders. In R. J. Morris & B. Blatt (Eds.), *Special education: Research and trends.* New York: Pergamon Press.

Kauffman, J. M., & Kneedler, R. D. (1981). Behavior disorders. In J. M. Kauffman & D. P. Hallahan (Eds.), *Handbook of special education.* Englewood Cliffs, NJ: Prentice-Hall.

Kavale, K. A., Forness, S. R., & Alper, A. E. (1986). Research in behavioral disorders/emotional disturbance: A survey of subject identification criteria. *Behavioral Disorders, 11,* 159–167.

Kazdin, A. E. (1985). *Treatment of antisocial behavior in children and adolescents.* Homewood, IL: Dorsey Press.

Kazdin, A. E. (1987). *Conduct disorders in childhood and adolescence.* Newbury Park, CA: Sage Publications.

Kazdin, A. E., & Strober, M. (1982, November.). *Assessment and diagnosis of childhood and adolescent depression.* Paper presented at 9th Annual Convention of the Association for the Advancement of Behavior Therapy, Los Angeles.

Kelly, T. J., Bullock, C. M., & Dykes, M. K. (1977). Behavioral disorders: Teachers' perceptions. *Exceptional Children, 43,* 316–318.

Kerr, M. M., & Nelson, M. (1983). *Strategies for managing behavior problems in the classroom.* Columbus, OH: Merrill.

Kounin, J. (1970). *Discipline and group management in classrooms.* New York: Holt, Rinehart and Winston.

Kovacs, M., & Beck, A. T. (1977). An empirical-clinical approach toward a definition of childhood depression. In J. G. Schulterbrandt & A. Raskin (Eds.), *Depression in childhood: Diagnosis, treatment, and conceptual models.* New York: Raven Press.

Lefkowitz, M. M., & Burton, N. (1978). Childhood depression: A critique of the concept. *Psychological Bulletin, 85,* 716–726.

Lewinsohn, P. M. (1974). A behavioral approach to depression. In R. Friedman & M. Katz (Eds.), *The psychology of depression: Contemporary theory and research.* Washington, DC: V. H. Winston.

McMahon, R. J., & Forehand, R. (1980). Self-help behavior therapies in parent training. In B. B. Lahey & A. E. Kazdin (Eds.), *Advances in clinical child psychology* (Vol. 3). New York: Plenum Press.

Malmquist, C. P. (1977). Childhood depression: A clinical and behavioral perspective. In J. G. Schulterbrandt & A. Raskin (Eds.), *Depression in childhood: Diagnosis, treatment, and conceptual models.* New York: Raven Press.

Mastropieri, M. A., Jenkins, V., & Scruggs, T. E. (1985). Academic and intellectual characteristics of behaviorally disordered children and youth. In R. B. Rutherford (Ed.), *Monograph in behavioral disorders: Severe behavior disorders of children and youth.* Reston, VA: Council for Children with Behavior Disorders.

Medley, D. M. (1982). Teacher effectiveness. In H. M. Mitzel (Ed.), *Encyclopedia of educational research* (Vol. 4) (5th ed.) New York: Free Press.

Morse, W. C., Cutler, R. L., & Fink, A. H. (1964). *Public school classes for the emotional handicapped: A research analysis.* Washington, DC: Council for Exceptional Children.

National Association of State Directors of Special Education. (1985). *Progress report: Special study on terminology.* Washington, DC: Author.

Noel, M. M. (1982). Public school programs for the emotionally disturbed: An overview. In M. M. Noel & N. G. Haring (Eds.), *Progress or change: Issues in educating the emotionally disturbed: Vol. 2. Service delivery.* Seattle: University of Washington, Program Development Assistance Team.

Office of Special Education and Rehabilitative Services (1986). *Eighth Annual Report to Congress on the Implementation of The Education of the Handicapped Act* (Vol. 1). Washington, DC: U.S. Department of Education.

Ollendick, T. H., & Hersen, M. (Eds.). (1983). *Handbook of child psychopathology.* New York: Plenum Press.

Paine, S. C., Radicchi, J., Rosellini, L. C., Deutchman, L., & Darch, C. B. (1983). *Structuring your classroom for academic success.* Champaign, IL: Research Press.

Patterson, G. R. (1975). *Families: Applications of social learning to family life* (Rev. ed.). Champaign, IL: Research Press.

Patterson, G. R. (1982). *Coercive family process* (Vol. 3). Eugene, OR: Castalia.

Petti, T. A. (1983). Depression and withdrawal in children. In T. H. Ollendick & M. Hersen (Eds.), *Handbook of child psychopathology.* New York: Plenum Press.

Pinkston, E. M. (1984). Individualized behavioral intervention for home and school. In R. F. Dangel & R. A. Polster (Eds.), *Parent training.* New York: Guilford Press.

Quay, H. C. (1975). Classification as an aid to treatment in delinquency and antisocial behavior. In N. Hobbs (Ed.), *Issues in the classification of children* (Vol. 1). San Francisco: Jossey-Bass.

Quay, H. C. (1979). Classification. In H. C. Quay & J . S. Werry (Eds.), *Psychopathological disorders of childhood* (2nd ed.). New York: John Wiley.

Rhodes, W. C. (1970). A community participation analysis of emotional distur-bance. *Exceptional Children, 37,* 309–314.

Rolf, J. E., & Hasazi, J. E. (1977). Identification of preschool children at risk and some guidelines for primary interaction. In G. W. Albec & J. M. Joffe (Eds.), *Pri-mary prevention of psychopathology: The issues* (Vol. 1). Hanover, NH: University Press of New England.

Rosenshine, B. (1980). How time is spent in elementary classrooms. In C. M. Den-ham & A. Lieberman (Eds.), *Time to learn.* Washington, DC: National Institute of Education.

Rosenshine, B., & Stevens, R. (1986). Teaching functions. In M. D. Wittrock (Ed.), *Handbook of research on teaching* (3rd ed.). New York: Macmillan.

Ross, A. O. (1980). *Psychological disorders of children: A behavioral approach to theory, research, and therapy* (2nd ed.). New York: McGraw-Hill.

Routh, D. K. (1980). Developmental and social aspects of hyperactivity. In C. K. Whalen & B. Henker (Eds.), *Hyperactive children: The social ecology of identifica-tion and treatment.* New York: Academic Press.

Rubin, R. A., & Balow, B. (1978). Prevalence of teacher identified behavior prob-lems: A longitudinal study. *Exceptional Children, 45,* 102–111.

Rutherford, R. B., Nelson, C. M., & Wolford, B. I. (1985). Special education in the most restrictive environment: Correctional/special education. *Journal of Special Education, 19,* 59–71.

Schloss, P. J. (1983). Classroom-based intervention for students exhibiting de-pressive reactions. *Behavioral Disorders,* 231–236.

Schulterbrandt, J. G., & Raskin, A. (Eds.). (1977). *Depression in childhood: Diagnosis, treatment, and conceptual models.* New York: Raven Press.

Schwartz, S., & Johnson, J. H. (1985). *Psychopathology of childhood: A clinical-experimental approach* (2nd ed.). New York: Pergamon Press.

Scruggs, T. E., Mastropieri, M. A., & Richter, L. (1985). Peer tutoring with behav-iorally disordered students: Social and academic benefits. *Behavioral Disorders, 10,* 283–294.

Seligman, M. E. P. (1974). Depression and learned helplessness. In R. J. Fried-man & M. M. Katz (Eds.), *The psychology of depression: Contemporary theory and research.* Washington, DC: V. H. Winston.

Sloane, H. (1979). *The good kid book: A manual for parents.* New York: New American Library.

SRA Technologies (1985). *Special study on terminology: Comprehensive review and evaluation report.* Contract No. 300-84-0144, Report No. MV-85-01. Mountain View, CA: Author.

Stevens, R., & Rosenshine, B. (1981). Advances in research on teaching. *Excep-tional Education Quarterly, 2,* 1–9.

Strain, P. S. (1981). Peer-mediated treatment of exceptional children's social withdrawal. *Exceptional Educational Quarterly, 1,* 83–95.

Strain, P. S. (1982). Peer-mediated treatment of exceptional children's social withdrawal. In P. S. Strain (Ed.), *Social development of exceptional children.* Rock-ville, MD: Aspen Systems Corp.

Strain, P. S., Cooke, T. P., & Apolloni, T. (1976) . *Teaching exceptional children: Assessing and modifying social behavior.* New York: Academic Press.

Strain, P. S., & Odom, S. L. (1986). Peer social initiations: Effective intervention for social skills development of exceptional children. *Exceptional Children, 52,* 543–551.

Strayhorn, J. M., & Strain, P. S. (1986). Social and language skills for preventive mental health: What, how, who, and when. In P. S. Strain, M. J. Guralnick, & H. M. Walker (Eds.), *Children's social behavior: Development, assessment, and modification.* Orlando, FL: Academic Press.

Strober, M. (1983). Clinical and biological perspectives on depressive disorders in adolescence. In D. Cantwell & G. Carlson (Eds.), *Affective disorders in childhood and adolescence.* New York: Spectrum.

Strober, M., & Carlson, G. (1982). Bipolar illness in adolescents with major depression: Clinical, genetic, and psychopharmacologic predictors in a three-to-four year follow-up. *Archives of General Psychiatry, 39,* 549–555.

U.S. Department of Education. (1986). *What works: Research about teaching and learning.* Washington, DC: Author.

Walker, H. M. (1979). *The acting-out child: Coping with classroom disruption.* Boston: Allyn & Bacon.

Walker, H. M., & Fabre, T. R. (in press). Assessment of behavior disorders in the school settings: Issues, problems, and strategies revisited. In N. Haring (Ed.), *Measuring and managing behavior disorders.* Seattle: University of Washington Press.

Walker, H. M., & Rankin, R. (1983). Assessing the behavioral expectations and demands of less restrictive settings. *School Psychology Digest, 12,* 274-284.

Walker, H . M., Reavis, H. K., Rhode, G., & Jenson, W. R. (1985). A conceptual model for delivery of services to the behavior disordered children in educational settings. In P. H. Bornstein & A. E. Kazdin (Eds.), *Handbook of clinical behavior therapy with children.* Homewood, IL: Dorsey Press.

White, O. R. (1986). Precision teaching — Precision learning. *Exceptional Children, 52,* 522–534.

Wickman, E. K. (1929). *Children's behavior and teachers' attitudes.* New York: Commonwealth Fund.

Wicks-Nelson, R., & Israel, A. C. (1984). *Behavior disorders of childhood.* Englewood Cliffs, NJ: Prentice-Hall.

Wood, F. H. (1979). Defining disturbing, disordered and disturbed behavior. In F. H. Wood & K. C. Lakin (Eds.), *Disturbing, disordered or disturbed: Perspectives on the definition of problem behavior in educational settings.* Minneapolis: Advanced Institute for Training of Teachers for Seriously Emotionally Disturbed Children and Youth.

Young, C. C. (1981). Children as instructional agents for handicapped peers: A review and analysis. In P. S. Strain (Ed.), *The utilization of classroom peers as behavior change agents.* New York: Plenum Press.

Zigmond, N., & Miller, S. E. (1986). Assessment for instructional planning. *Exceptional Children, 52,* 501–509.

2 Assessment of Behaviorally Disordered Students

After completing this chapter, you should be able to

- *Identify the primary purposes for assessing behaviorally disordered students.*
- *Differentiate between traditional and behavioral models of assessment.*
- *Describe assessment procedures used for assessing behavior problems, social skills, and academic achievement.*
- *List advantages and disadvantages of behavior problem checklists, behavioral observation, interviews, sociograms, role-play tests, standardized achievement tests, criterion-referenced tests, curriculum-based assessment.*
- *Explain the current status of procedures and determine eligibility for special education in the area of behavioral disorders.*
- *Describe a recommended procedure for determining if a student is eligible for special education due to a behavioral disorder.*

T he accurate assessment and classification of children with behavioral disorders is generally accepted as a professional standard. However, the processes involved in accurately assessing these students are not well understood, and there is very little professional agreement about the specific assessment procedures to be used (Walker & Fabre, in press).

This chapter will review preferred practices in the assessment of behaviorally disordered students. Initially, the purposes of assessment and two different models are discussed. Specific procedures used in the assessment of behavior problems, social skills, and academic skills are described. Problems related to classifying students as behaviorally disordered are also reviewed, and solutions are suggested. Also included is a description of emerging assessment practices.

PURPOSES OF ASSESSMENT

Assessment is defined as an information-gathering process that leads to decisions about a student's classification, appropriate instructional programs, evaluation of progress, and predictions about future adjustment (P. Cole, personal communication, 1978; Cronbach, 1970; Lidz, 1981; Swanson & Watson, 1982). What is critical to this two-part definition is that assessment first involves information gathering. How this information is gathered greatly affects the decisions made about a child. The gathered information can be collected in rigorously structured approaches such as academic achievement testing, formal behavioral observations, and structured interviews. It can also be collected in less structured approaches such as anecdotal reports, social histories, and projective testing.

There are no perfect assessment procedures. All have some error associated with their use that affects reliability (the consistency of measurement) or validity (the ability to actually measure what a test purports to measure). Because they all are imperfect, using *multiple assessment measures* is the best way to control individual assessment error and obtain more accurate results. For example, if one procedure is prone to

Behavioral observation is a critical component in the assessment of behaviorally disordered students.

one type of error, then another procedure can be used to evaluate the same behavior. In a sense, one measure helps cancel out the other measure's error.

Because assessment leads to decisions, it must be *continuous*. Assessments are sometimes made before an intervention and again after an intervention to determine if the intervention has been effective. However, educating behaviorally disordered children is not a static process. Decisions are needed each day to change a program or fine-tune an instructional intervention. Teachers cannot wait until the end of the year to determine if a program has been effective. Preferred assessment practices are continuous and directly affect decisions every day.

The main reason to assess a behaviorally disordered child is to make well-informed decisions that will benefit the child. These decisions include (a) determining whether a child is eligible to be classified as behaviorally disordered and (b) planning an appropriate instructional program. If information is gathered only to label the child without developing a treatment plan or instructional program, time and money are wasted. Worse, harm can be done to the child.

Data-based decisions are critical to assessment (Lidz, 1981). For behaviorally disordered children, these decisions should include the following elements (Gelfand, Jenson, & Drew, in press; Lidz, 1981; Salvia & Ysseldyke, 1985):

1. *Screening*—Assessment methods such as tests and checklists can be used with relatively large numbers of children to identify those who might need special services. Screening acts as a first step in identifying children for more in-depth assessment and classification. Classification and labeling are needed to qualify students for special services and placements; they are not ends in themselves.

2. *Placement*—Different special education placements remediate different types of problems, provide different services, and differ in restrictiveness (how different they are from regular classrooms). Objective information should be used in identifying appropriate educational placements for referred students. For example, accurate information from behavioral observations, structured interviewing, and testing can be used in deciding whether a child can stay in a regular classroom with help or needs more intensive services in a resource room or self-contained classroom. Good assessment practices should also help prevent educators from placing children on the basis of subjective impressions and biases.

3. *Behavioral interventions*—Behaviorally disordered children exhibit a range of behavior problems from severe social withdrawal to aggression and noncompliance. Objective assess-

ment of a student should lead to specific recommendations about appropriate instructional interventions. Many intervention strategies that are effective with specific behavioral problems have been identified. Detailed recommendations that realistically can be implemented in the classroom depend greatly on the quality of the assessment information.

4. *Academic interventions*—The behavior problems of these children are frequently the central focus, obscuring significant academic deficits. There is a clear connection between behavior problems and poor academic performance, particularly in reading ability (Rutter & Yule, 1973). Any assessment of a behaviorally disordered student should include a precise description of the child's current academic skills, enabling educators to make specific recommendations for academic intervention.

5. *Research and program evaluation*—Although research and program evaluation have less direct impact on individual children, they have a wide impact on programs that affect large numbers of children. Assessment information compiled on a number of students can help to change and improve programs to make them more effective. Even assessment information on individual students can be disseminated as individual case reports and have a meaningful impact (Kazdin, 1981).

In summary, the assessment of behaviorally disordered children is a two-step process. First, structured information is gathered constantly, using multiple sources. Second, practical decisions concerning the child are based on the information gathered. The quality or fidelity of the information limits the appropriateness of the decisions that professionals and parents make. Assessment information that is unreliable or invalid can lead to poor placements, inappropriate interventions, and ineffective educational procedures.

MODELS OF ASSESSMENT

We have defined assessment as an information-gathering process that leads to instructional decisions about students. The assumptions we make about possible causes of behavior underlying assessment can affect how the information is gathered and what type of information is gathered. Professionals engaged in assessment, however, are frequently not aware that a model of behavior forms the foundation of their approach to assessment and that they use a model each time they conduct an assessment (Lidz, 1981; McReynolds, 1968). Lidz (1981) has pointed out that "the model the assessor uses determines the variables that become the focus of the assessment, the measures that are selected for use, the interpretations of these measures, and the recommendations that result from these interpretations" (p. 5). Assessment models can be divided into two broad categories, traditional and behavioral.

Traditional Models of Assessment

There have been several different approaches or models considered traditional in special education and psychology. These models have been given various names including the *medical model,* the *state-developmental model,* and the *trait-attribute model* (Mischel, 1968). Although the terms may vary, these models share similar assumptions about behavior and personality.

A basic assumption of traditional models is that abnormal behavior is a function of an underlying cause, which can be biological or emotional (Fagley, 1984; Hartmannn, Roper, & Bradford, 1979). The problematic abnormal behavior is only a superficial symptom or correlate of the underlying cause (state or trait). If the surface abnormal behavior is treated without treating the underlying cause, then another abnormal behavior will be substituted (symptom substitution). It follows that the major focus of traditional assessment should not be on abnormal surface behavior, but instead on the assumed underlying cause. "In the traditional approach to assessment, emphasis is placed on uncovering the historical roots of current intrapsychic problems" (Hartmann et al., 1979, p. 5).

There are several other assumptions that follow from these models. For example, the child's history is emphasized and indirect information-gathering techniques are employed (unstructured interviews, projective tests) to help uncover important painful or emotional past events. In addition, most traditional approaches assume that behavior is stable across time and different situations. This assumption is a function of the belief that behavior is consistent because it is the product of a stable underlying cause. It puts little emphasis on the use of multiple assessment measures in different settings or assessment of generalization.

The overall purpose of the traditional assessment approach has been to diagnose, classify, and predict future outcomes. Less emphasis is placed on making everyday decisions for interventions. Most traditional assessments are conducted pre-intervention and post-intervention, instead of continuously during intervention.

Behavioral Models of Assessment

The behavioral model directly contrasts with many of the assumptions of traditional assessment models. While traditional models emphasize what an individual *has* (underlying cause), the nontraditional, behavioral model places far more emphasis on what the individual *does* (Hartmann et al., 1979; Mischel, 1968). Far less importance is placed on the historical causes of behavior, and more importance is placed on an accurate sample and descriptions of behavior and the current situational factors that may be controlling a behavior (Mash, 1979; O'Leary, 1979). The behavioral assessment model stresses directly assessing current antecedent variables (that come before a behavior) and consequence variables (that follow a behavior) that may control problem behaviors. For example, behavioral observation techniques, behavior problem checklists, and structured interviewing are used to pinpoint antecedent events such as teacher or peer behavior that may set the occasion for the inappropriate behavior. Similarly, these techniques can assess the consequences that follow a behavior and reinforce it.

This approach has gained popularity in education in the past 10 years primarily because it does not make many inferences about underlying causes of behavior and it does emphasize effective intervention. Practical assessment that leads directly to intervention appeals to educators and to parents who put a premium on utilitarian, cost effective procedures. This appeal extends to the idea of continuous assessment, which allows midcourse corrections with interventions instead of taking the "wait-and-see" approach of a pre-post traditional assessment.

In the behavioral approach, behavior is assumed to be a function of current environmental conditions and to be stable only as long as the environment is stable. If conditions change, then the behavior will probably also change (Mischel, 1979). This assumption is different from the traditional approach, which assumes that behavior will be stable across environments. This difference has important implications. For example, the behavioral approach would assume that behaviors trained and measured in one environment may not occur in a different environment. Again, the behavioral approach focuses on multiple and continuous measurement, particularly across environments. Because it does not assume generalization of behaviors, generalization must be planned to ensure success. The assumption of planned generalization with multiple and continuous assessment feedback across environments is at the heart of preferred practices in assessment.

There are several advantages of behavioral assessment over traditional assessment in special education. These advantages are based on the fundamental differences between the two approaches (see Exhibit 2.1). However, not all behavioral assessment procedures are preferred practices. Some behaviorally based assessment procedures have not been adequately field-tested and do not meet minimum standards for technical adequacy. They should not be used if alternative measures are available. In addition, there is also a place for some selected traditional assessment procedures with behaviorally disordered children (e.g., stan-

EXHIBIT 2.1 Differences between behavioral and traditional approaches to assessment

	Behavioral	Traditional
I. Assumptions		
1. Conception of personality	Personality constructs mainly employed to summarize specific behavior patterns, if at all	Personality as a reflection of enduring underlying states or traits
2. Causes of behavior	Maintaining conditions sought in current environment	Intrapsychic or within the individual
II. Implications		
1. Role of behavior	Important as a sample of person's repertoire in specific situation	Behavior assumes importance only insofar as it indexes underlying causes
2. Role of history	Relatively unimportant, except, for example, to provide a retrospective baseline	Crucial in that present conditions seen as a product of the past
3. Consistency of behavior	Behavior thought to be specific to the situation	Behavior expected to be consistent across time and settings
III. Uses of data	To describe target behaviors and maintaining conditions	To describe personality functioning and etiology
	To select the appropriate treatment	To diagnose or classify
	To evaluate and revise treatment	To make prognosis; to predict
IV. Other characteristics		
1. Level of inferences	Low	Medium to high
2. Comparisons	More emphasis on intraindividual or idiographic	More emphasis on interindividual or nomothetic
3. Methods of assessment	More emphasis on direct methods (e.g., observations of behavior in natural environment)	More emphasis on indirect methods (e.g., interviews and self-report)
4. Timing of assessment	More ongoing; prior, during, and after treatment	Pre- and perhaps posttreatment, or strictly to diagnose
5. Scope of assessment	Specific measures and of more variables (e.g., of target behaviors in various situations, of side effects, context, strengths as well as deficiencies)	More global measures (e.g., of cure, or improvement) but only of the individual

Source: From "Some Relationships Between Behavioral and Traditional Assessment" by D. P. Hartmann, B. L. Roper, and D. C. Bradford, 1979, *Journal of Behavioral Assessment, 1,* p. 4. Published by Plenum Publishing Corporation. Used by permission.

dardized educational and psychological tests such as academic achievement tests and intelligence tests).

ASSESSING BEHAVIOR PROBLEMS

Special educators should be able to recognize, define, and assess the problem behaviors of individual students referred to their programs. Assessment procedures that they can use include behavior problem checklists, structured interviewing, and behavioral observation.

Behavior Problem Checklists

The use of behavior problem checklists has increased substantially in special education because they are easy to administer and useful in identifying behavioral disorders. Behavior problem checklists have been used to reliably identify behaviorally disordered children and to identify specific problems such as hyperactivity, conduct disorder, childhood depression, and personality disorder. These checklists are based on the behavioral model of assessment. Someone who is familiar with the child —often a teacher or parent—completes the checklist. The person filling out the checklist decides if the behavior described by each of the checklist's items applies to the child being assessed. Generally, this person is deciding either from observation or memory whether the behavior has occurred (a yes or a no) or to what degree or frequency the behavior is evident (not a problem, sometimes a problem, or often a problem). Exhibit 2.2 shows a sample of items from a checklist.

Most checklists take from 10 to 20 minutes to fill out. They are norm-referenced in that they compare the child's score to the mean score of a population of nonhandicapped children. This indication of deviation aids in determining both the identification and severity of behavioral disorder. For example, the *Conners Parent and Teacher Checklist* (Conners, 1969) is commonly used to help identify children with attention deficit disorder (hyperactivity). Children with scores in the upper 2% of the range (whose scores are at least two standard deviations from the mean) have a high probability of having attention deficit disorder. Some checklists are sensitive enough that they clearly show when interventions are effective (Achenbach, 1979; Conners, 1969; Quay & Petersen, 1975).

One of the best checklists available is the *Child Behavior Checklist and Profile* (CBCL) (Achenbach, 1979; Achenbach & Edelbrock, 1978).[1] This checklist, which is completed by the child's parents or teacher, uses

---

[1]Several other behavior problem checklists are also well suited for use with behaviorally disordered students. They are identified in the last section of this chapter, "Preferred Assessment Practices."

EXHIBIT 2.2 A sampling of questions from the *Child Behavior Checklist—Teacher's Report Form*

Below is a list of items that describe pupils. For each item that describes the pupil now or within the past 2 months, please circle the 2 if the item is very true or often true of the pupil. Circle the 1 if the item is somewhat or sometimes true of the pupil. If the item is not true of the pupil, circle the 0.

0	1	2	1.	Acts too young for his/her age
0	1	2	2.	Hums or makes other odd noises in class
0	1	2	3.	Argues a lot
0	1	2	4.	Fails to finish things he/she starts
0	1	2	5.	Behaves like opposite sex
0	1	2	6.	Defiant, talks back to staff
0	1	2	7.	Bragging, boasting
0	1	2	8.	Can't concentrate, can't pay attention for long
0	1	2	9.	Can't get his/her mind off certain thoughts; obsessions (describe): _____
0	1	2	10.	Can't sit still, restless, or hyperactive
0	1	2	11.	Clings to adults or too dependent
0	1	2	12.	Complains of loneliness
0	1	2	13.	Confused or seems to be in a fog
0	1	2	14.	Cries a lot
0	1	2	15.	Fidgets
0	1	2	16.	Cruelty, bullying, or meanness to others
0	1	2	17.	Day-dreams or gets lost in his/her thoughts
0	1	2	18.	Deliberately harms self or attempts suicide

0	1	2	31.	Fears he/she might think or do something bad
0	1	2	32.	Feels he/she has to be perfect
0	1	2	33.	Feels or complains that no one loves him/her
0	1	2	34.	Feels others are out to get him/her
0	1	2	35.	Feels worthless or inferior
0	1	2	36.	Gets hurt a lot, accident-prone
0	1	2	37.	Gets in many fights
0	1	2	38.	Gets teased a lot
0	1	2	39.	Hangs around with others who get in trouble
0	1	2	40.	Hears things that aren't there (describe): _____
0	1	2	41.	Impulsive or acts without thinking
0	1	2	42.	Likes to be alone
0	1	2	43.	Lying or cheating
0	1	2	44.	Bites fingernails
0	1	2	45.	Nervous, highstrung, or tense
0	1	2	46.	Nervous movements or twitching (describe): _____
0	1	2	47.	Overconforms to rules
0	1	2	48.	Not liked by other pupils
0	1	2	49.	Has difficulty learning
0	1	2	50.	Too fearful or anxious

Source: From *Child Behavior Checklist—Teacher's Report Form* (p. 3) by T. M. Achenbach and C. Edelbrock, 1980, Burlington: University of Vermont. Copyright by T. M. Achenbach. Reproduced by permission.

a 3-point scale (0 = not true, 1 = sometimes true, 2 = often true). There are 118 items in the CBCL covering behavior problems that are split into two broad-spectrum factors, an externalizing factor and an internalizing factor. These two broad factors are further divided into more specific or narrow-band factors. For example, contained within the broad externalizing factor (problems directed out toward the environment) are the narrow-band factors of aggression and hyperactivity (see Exhibit 2.3). The narrow-band factors are different for males and females and for children of different ages because problems differ.

When completed, the checklist is then scored and the scores are plotted on the Behavior Problem Profile (Exhibit 2.3). Again, the publisher provides different Behavior Problem Profiles for males and females and for different age groups (ages 4 to 5, 6 to 11, and 12 to 16). The Behavior Problem Profile lists the individual checklist items under each behavioral factor. For example, in Exhibit 2.3, under the behavioral factor Aggressive (VIII), the specific items from the checklist include item 3, argues; item 6, defiant; item 19, demands attention; item 37, fights; and item 95, temper tantrums. A teacher can look at the profile and see any factor that appears to be a problem. The teacher can then look for items given a score of 2 by a parent. These items may be important behaviors that should be targeted for intervention if they are confirmed by other assessment measures.

In addition to identifying individual problem behaviors, the Behavior Problem Profile is norm-referenced and indicates the severity of the behavior problems as compared to nonhandicapped children. On the profile, the average factor score for nonhandicapped children is T–50 (see Exhibit 2.3, on the right side); a score of T–70 indicates a problem that is clinically significant. Scores above T–70 are in the upper 2% of the population (98% of the standardization group have scores lower than this score). These scores are two or more standard deviations from the mean. That is, for example, 98% of the standardization group would have scores lower than a child with a raw score of 22 (score of T–70) on Aggressive (Factor VIII). This type of comparison helps answer one question frequently asked by parents, "How different is my child from other children?"

The Child Behavior Checklist and Behavior Problem Profile have other important information that is also helpful to a teacher. For instance, Exhibit 2.3 is a parent profile for a checklist filled out by both the mother and father. When the two lines are close together, the parents agreed about the problem; when the two lines are far apart, the parents disagreed. This information can be useful to the teacher.

In addition, the checklist has 20 items covering social activities and adjustment in school, the home, and the community. These items are plotted on a separate profile that again allows norm-referenced compari-

EXHIBIT 2.3 (a) Profile from parent responses; (b) Teacher's report

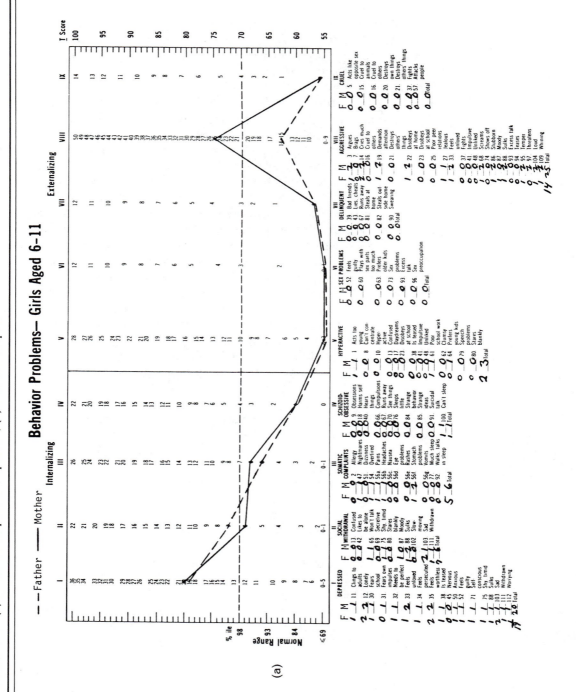

(a)

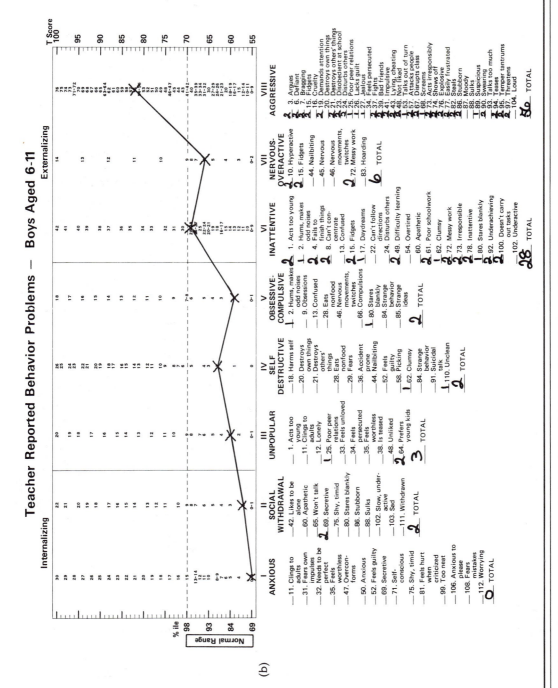

Teacher Reported Behavior Problems — Boys Aged 6-11

Source: From *Child Behavior Checklist and Profile* by T. M. Achenbach and C. S. Edelbrock, 1982, Burlington: University of Vermont. Copyright by Craig S. Edelbrock and Thomas M. Achenbach. Reproduced by permission.

sons to nonhandicapped children. This social information can be especially useful in determining if a child needs social skills training. The CBCL also yields a Total Social Competency Score and a Total Behavior Problem Score.

The primary function of behavior problem checklists and rating scales is the identification of behavioral disorders in children. The advantages of checklists include their low cost, comprehensive assessment information and utility as pre- and post-measures to determine treatment effectiveness. In addition, norm-referenced checklists provide some indication of the severity of problem behaviors. Checklists serve these purposes well if they are used in conjunction with other assessment measures. However, they should not be the sole source of information used in identifying and classifying a child.

There are also several disadvantages of behavior checklists. First, an informant can intentionally over- or underreport the severity of a problem behavior. The only validity check for false reporting is to use another assessment procedure, such as behavioral observations, to confirm a suspicious finding. Second, the individual items of a checklist may not be reliable, even though the overall reliability of the checklist may be acceptable. This weak point can be a problem if intervention target behaviors are selected from individual items. Again, the way to counter this problem is to use several measures to confirm the problem behaviors. Third, most checklists only describe problem behaviors; they do not prescribe. That is, they do not recommend interventions for these problem behaviors. However, a new generation of behavior problem checklists under development will be prescriptive. Jenson, Reavis, Rhode, Clare, and Evans (1986) have developed a checklist that recommends five interventions (based on the research) for each individual problem behavior identified by the checklist.

Interviewing

Interviewing is a frequently used assessment technique that has been called the universal tool for collecting information about a child's behavior and its possible causes (O'Leary & Johnson, 1979). It is not too difficult to see why interviewing is so universal and popular. It is used early in the assessment process; that is, an interview is usually conducted before psychological testing, behavioral observation, and filling out a checklist. It would be difficult to select the proper assessment technique or know how to interpret it without the information gathered from an interview with a teacher or parent familiar with the child.

In educational settings, there are a number of reasons for interviewing former teachers, the child's parents, and the child. The interview provides a limited sample of behavior from the person who is being interviewed; thus it is a form of limited behavioral observation (Anastasi, 1982). Characteristics such as the child's use of language, compliance with an unfamiliar adult, social skills, and general appearance can be evaluated. However, the child's behavior in an interviewer's office is only a limited sample of behavior and may not generalize across settings. For example, a hyperactive child with Attention Deficit Disorder may seem perfectly normal in an interview, but may act differently in the classroom (Barkley, 1981).

Interviewing also allows the assessor to gather basic information such as past history, developmental data, and the subject's perception of the problem. A history of what has happened in the past is possibly one of the best predictors of what may happen in the future (Anastasi, 1982). Interviewing a child or parent offers unique perceptions and information that cannot be gathered well by other assessment techniques such as psychological testing. For example, the child may identify preferred rewards or reinforcers (Mash & Terdal, 1981; Nay, 1974) that could be used in a behavior management program, or the child may describe a problem and the contributing circumstances (Evans & Nelson, 1977). The interview also allows a personal interaction that other standardized assessment approaches do not. A relationship can be established with the child, parent, or teacher that can be an effective aid in developing an instructional intervention.

For our purposes, a structured approach to behavioral interviewing is most productive because it is reliable and yields specific information. Structured interviewing contrasts with unstructured interviewing, in which the interviewer does not use a specific set of questions. Several different models for structured interviewing of parents, children, and teachers have been developed (Evans & Nelson, 1977; Gelfand & Hartmann, 1984; Holland, 1970; Wahler & Cromier, 1970). Using these models, interviewers try to obtain a specific description of the problem behavior, its rate and duration, and events or consequences that precede or follow it. Other important information to be gathered in an interview includes the child's strengths, past attempts to change the problem behavior, and the role of peers in escalating or rewarding the misbehavior. Exhibit 2.4 contains questions that interviewers typically ask of teachers who have had a behaviorally disordered child in their classroom. Pointer 2.1 offers a series of simulated answers to these questions.

A number of factors can influence the reliability and validity of the information gathered in an interview. Reliability appears to be partially a function of the degree of structure of the interview. The more structured and standardized the interview questions are, the more consistent the interview will be over time (test–retest reliability) and across interviewers (interrater reliability). Reliability will be lower when the interview questions are stressful or have great emotional significance (Haynes & Jensen,

EXHIBIT 2.4   Interview with the teacher

---

1. Is there a problem with any of the following situations: working alone, working in groups, structured activities, unstructured activities, recess, lunch, free time, or a particular academic period (or subject)?
2. If there is a problem, what specifically does the child do?
3. What is the frequency of the child's problem behavior?
4. What is the duration of the child's problem behavior?
5. What is the teacher's response to this problem behavior?
6. How do classmates respond to this problem behavior?
7. What interventions has the teacher tried?
8. What were the child's responses to the teacher's intervention?
9. What are the common classroom rules that the child violates?
10. Does the child leave his or her desk inappropriately?
11. Does the child bother his or her classmates while they are working?
12. Does the child talk out of turn?
13. Does the child demand excessive attention from the teacher?
14. What does the teacher consider appropriate behavior in each of the identified problem areas?
15. What are the child's strengths? Does he engage in any of the appropriate classroom behaviors?
16. What are the possible rewards and punishers available in the classroom that could be used in a management program for this child?
17. Is the teacher willing to use these rewards and punishers?

Source: Adapted from "Conduct Disorders" by B. M. Atkeson and R. Forehand (1981) in *Behavioral Assessment of Childhood Disorders* edited by E. J. March and L. G. Terdal, New York: Guilford Press.

1979; Wenar & Coulter, 1962). When parents or families are interviewed, several variables affect the validity of the information. Parents tend to distort information in the direction of precocity (McCord & McCord, 1961). They also tend to report information that fits cultural stereotypes (McCord & McCord, 1961) or idealized expectations (Chess, Thomas, Birch, & Hertzig, 1960). Essentially, families may try to present the best "idealized" picture of themselves and minimize the seriousness of a stressful problem with a child. The opposite may be true when a child's teacher is interviewed. A regular classroom teacher who is interested in having a child removed from the classroom may overreport the severity of the problems. A second measure, such as behavioral observation in the regular classroom, may be needed to validate the interview information.

The reliability and validity of information gathered from a behaviorally disordered child in an interview is questionable. Although some earlier research (Herjanic, Herjanic, Brown, & Wheatt, 1977) reported good reliability between parent and child responses to interview questions, other, more recent research has shown poorer agreement (Herjanic & Reich, 1982; Reich, Herjanic, Welner, & Gandy, 1982). Information from younger children is less reliable than information from older children (Edelbrock, Costello, Duncan, Kalas, & Conover, 1985). The overall value of interviewing a child may be confined to establishing rapport, assessing possible reinforcers for use in an intervention, and eliciting the child's view of the problem. However, most behaviorally disordered children will have limited insight into their problems.

> In my experience, interviews with the child may not prove particularly productive for treatment planning, except in establishing a necessary rapport and in elaborating on some of his or her physical, cognitive, and behavioral characteristics. Interviews usually reveal the children to have little perception of their difficulties, because their self-reflection is generally poor, and to have little insight into the reactions toward them. Lying or distorting information in a more socially acceptable or pleasing direction is more frequent, as are impulsive responses to questions. (Barkley, 1981, p. 154)

All teachers use interviews either informally or formally. Because few structured models of interviewing report reliability or validity findings, general guidelines must suffice. First, use a structured format with predetermined questions and try to elicit specific answers. Second, discourage gossip or second-hand information. Third, realize parents may underreport a problem and referring teachers may overreport a problem. Fourth, use interviewing with other assessment measures, particularly behavior problem checklists and behavioral observation. Fifth, realize that most behaviorally disordered children have limited insight into their difficulties and will underreport their problem behaviors.

Behavioral Observation

Observation has been used to assess behaviorally disordered children in the home (Patterson, 1982; Reid, 1978), in the school classroom (Deno, 1980; O'Leary, Romanczyk, Kass, Dietz, & Santagrossi, 1971), and on the playground (Walker et al., 1978). The techniques to be described here are very different from simply looking at a child for a while and writing a description of what you see. Behavioral observation uses structured recording techniques to collect data and a set of codes to define the target behaviors. The observation codes for target behaviors are defined following the general rule that the behaviors must be observable and measurable to be included in the code. Other dimensions of behavior

Pointer 2.1

REGULAR CLASSROOM TEACHER INTERVIEW:
FOR JOHNNY, A DIFFICULT BOY

1. Is there a problem in any of the following situations: working alone, working in groups, structured activities, recess, lunch, free time, or a particular academic teaching time?

   Johnny has his most difficult times in structured settings that require independent study skills. He constantly is off-task and bothering other students. He has particular difficulty during reading workbook assignments, and doesn't seem to have the self-control to read silently and answer written questions.

2. If there is a problem, what does he specifically do?

   He just can't seem to work without bothering someone. This bothering can involve poking a child, talking out for attention, making strange noises, or trying to talk with a neighbor to get him or her off-task.

3. What is the frequency of the child's problem behavior?

   Taking a rough count, it appears that Johnny makes from 5 to 10 noises each 45-minute classroom period. He also disturbs other children approximately 10 times in the same class period.

4. What is the duration of the child's problem behavior?

   Johnny is generally off-task for about 30 minutes out of the 45-minute class period.

5. What is the teacher's response to this behavior?

   The teacher is tired of Johnny and feels that there is nothing she can do in her class to stop him. She feels that things are getting worse, and she might lose control of other children if Johnny's behavior is not stopped.

6. How does class respond to this behavior?

   The class loves it. They think that Johnny is the class clown, and they continuously give him attention for the behavior. However, socially Johnny is not well accepted by the other children.

7. What interventions have been tried by the teacher?

   At first the teacher tried to reason with Johnny, but that had no effect. Then she started to ask him to get back on task and finally yelled at him and sent him to the principal's office. All of this just seemed to make things worse.

8. What is the child's response to the teacher's intervention?

   It makes him worse.

9. What are the common classroom rules that are violated?

   The teacher has not specified many rules for the class, although for Johnny, she implemented two rules: (1) Keep your hands in your own personal space, and (2) Do not bother your neighbor. He frequently violates both of these rules.

10. Does the child leave his or her desk inappropriately?

    Yes, Johnny will frequently leave his desk and wander around the room looking for attention.

11. Does the child bother his or her classmates while they are working?

    Constantly.

12. Does the child talk out of turn?

    Constantly.

13. Does the child demand excessive teacher attention?

    Yes, because she is having to constantly correct his inappropriate behavior.

14. What is considered appropriate student behavior in each of the identified problem areas?

    Appropriate behavior includes: (1) independent seatwork for 45-minute blocks of time, (2) to not bother other children, (3) to ask permission to talk during

structured academic session, and (4) to not wander around the classroom.

15. What are the child's strengths? Does he engage in any appropriate classroom behaviors?

    Johnny is a really loving boy, which is really a strength. He does work consistently for 45 minutes or more when the topic is reading adventure stories. Getting to pick the next adventure story for the class or extra reading time might be used as a reinforcer.

16. What are the possible rewards and punishers available in the classroom that could be used in a management program for this child?

    Johnny loves attention. Appropriate peer attention, extra free time, getting to be a classroom monitor, and getting to choose a friend to play a game would all be rewards. Possible punishers in the classroom might involve having to stay after school to work on academics that have been missed, having to sit in the corner as a form of time-out, and loss of recess time.

17. Is the teacher willing to use these rewards and punishers?

    The teacher is desperate and willing to do anything. However, close consultation is needed because the teacher feels powerless.

EXHIBIT 2.5   Classroom observation codes for noise and aggression

---

Noise—Symbol = N

Purpose:	Noise is intended to monitor the frequency of distracting sounds produced by the child, other than vocalization.
Description:	Child is creating any audible noise, without permission, other than vocalization. For the sake of consistency, *any audible* sound is to be recorded even though in the observer's opinion, it did not "seem" disruptive.
Critical Points:	The observer must *actually hear* the sound to rate it. Inferences are not acceptable.
Includes:	Turning pages in an exaggerated manner, producing noise. Moving desk around. Pencil tapping. Banging of any object. Fishing in desk without coming out with anything or coming out with an inappropriate object (if noise is actually made in the process). Shuffling feet more than once each way. Any noises made while getting out of chair without permission. In general, any noise made in conjunction with any disruptive behavior, e.g., any noise made when child throws a book or another object at another (A).
Excludes:	Shuffling feet if only once each way. Accidental dropping of a task-related object (book or pencil). Pushing chair back and forth once during a permitted act (e.g., to get a task-related object).

Aggression—Symbol = A

Purpose:	To measure the highly disruptive behavior of physical assaults.
Description:	Child makes an intense movement directed at another person so as to come into contact with him/her, either directly or by using a material object as an extension of the hand.
Critical Points:	Intention is to be recorded rather than just accuracy of assault, e.g., aggression is recorded if child throws pencil or swings at another, *regardless* of whether or not the pencil or motion hits the other child.
Includes:	Blocking others with arms or body to keep from attaining goal (e.g., while walking up aisle). Tripping, kicking, throwing.
Excludes:	Brushing against another (*include* if action is continually repeated so as to tease or annoy).

Source: From *Procedures for Classroom Observation of Teachers and Children,* by K. D. O'Leary, R. G. Romanczyk, R. E. Kass, A. Dietz, and D. Santagrossi, 1971, Unpublished manuscript. Used by permission.

such as the intensity of the response, its shape or topography, or whether it is discrete (has a clear beginning and ending) are also important to a good definition of a behavior (see Exhibit 2.5). For example, *in-seat behavior* in a classroom may be defined as "at least one buttock on the seat of the chair, neither foot above the level of the desk or in the desk, head above the level of the desk top, and the chair not more than one foot away from the desk" (Kesler & Jensen, 1986). This particular definition does not permit much interpretation or guesswork by the observer. The

Assessment should be an ongoing process.

less interpretation and judgment required of the observer, the more reliable the observational system will be between observers (interrater reliability).

There are five basic observation recording techniques; each is suited for a specific purpose and type of behavior (Alessi, 1980; Gelfand & Hartmann, 1984; Sulzer-Azaroff & Mayer, 1986). The easiest method to understand is the *event* or *tally* recording system. With this method, the observer records the number of times a behavior occurs within a defined time. The number of times a child talks out in class within 30 minutes would be an example of event recording. Although event recording is easy to conceptualize, it is often difficult to implement in the classroom. To use event recording, an observer has to focus on well-defined behavior with a clear beginning and end, in order to know when one instance of the behavior stops and the next one starts. For example, it is difficult to use event recording with the behavior "attends to a teacher in the classroom." Because attending is a continuous behavior with no clear beginning or end, it is virtually impossible to record as a frequency. Event recording is also limited with very frequent behaviors because the observer becomes overwhelmed and loses count. For example, it would be extremely difficult to keep an accurate count of wiggles of all the students in a classroom. There are just too many.

The *time-sampling interval* method of recording observational data is possibly the most useful in classes with behaviorally disordered children. All time-sampling methods use a period separated into a number of smaller intervals for observation. For example, a 10-minute sample of an academic period might be divided into sixty 10-second intervals for recording a child's attending behavior. The behavioral code for attending might be "child is in seat, with the head and eyes oriented to work or teacher who is instructing, with hands on desk, and responding when called upon by the teacher."

There are three basic types of time sampling: whole-interval time sampling, partial-interval time sampling, and momentary time sampling (Sulzer-Azaroff & Mayer, 1986).

1. *Whole-interval time sampling*—With the whole-interval method, a child would need to be attending throughout the whole 10-second interval to be scored and recorded as attending. If the child momentarily stopped attending, then the entire interval would be scored as "not attending." This is a strict and conservative estimate of an observed behavior because it does not count any appropriate behavior (such as attending) in an interval if any instance of the inappropriate behavior (nonattending) occurs.

2. *Partial-interval time sampling*—This approach is more liberal in estimating the occurrence of an observed behavior. With the partial-interval time-sampling method, a single occurrence of a behavior results in the entire interval being scored. For the example with attending, if a child attends for half of the 10-second interval and is off-task for the other half, then the entire interval is scored for attending.

3. *Momentary time sampling*—This is the most liberal time-sampling procedure for estimating a behavior. It is a good system when a teacher does not have a lot of time to observe. With the momentary time-sampling system, an external system such as a prerecorded "beep" on a tape would signal the end of each 1-minute interval. The teacher would then quickly observe the target student and, if the student was attending, the teacher would record the behavior. In a 10-minute

academic period, a teacher would have 10 momentary samples of behavior using this method.

For busy teachers, partial-interval and momentary-time sampling are probably the best methods to use in observing most discrete and non-discrete behaviors. However, it is important to realize that these two methods are the more liberal approaches and may overestimate the actual occurrence of an observed behavior.

Two additional types of time observation procedures can be useful with discrete responses. *Duration recording* simply involves recording the length of time a response lasts. It generally requires timing the behavior with a stopwatch. This method could be used to measure the time a student spends working on academics, appropriately interacting on the playground, or having tantrums. *Latency recording* is very similar; it measures the time from a specified event to the start of the target behavior. For example, it could be used to measure the time between a request from a teacher to stop an inappropriate behavior to the cessation of the behavior by the child. Another example might involve the amount of time between the distribution of assignments and the initiation of work. An observer must know when a behavior starts or stops to accurately record the time of a response.

If a child attends in class only half of the time, as found by a partial-interval time-sampling procedure, is this average, below average, or exceptional performance in a classroom? Most observation systems do not include group standardization data for norm-referenced comparisons. It may be easy to collect the observation data but difficult to interpret because there is no comparison group. For example, a *response-discrepancy* system of observation allows meaningful normative comparisons (Alessi, 1980; Deno, 1980). The term *response discrepancy* suggests a difference or discrepancy between the observed behavior of a target child (referred child) and an index child (nonreferred child). Data are collected simultaneously on the target and index child across each interval and then compared. One approach (Alessi, 1980) even collects data on the teacher's reactions across each interval to determine if there is a difference in the reactions to the target and index child.

The response-discrepancy system generally uses a partial-interval time-sampling procedure to collect data. The major advantage of such a system is that it helps answer the question "Just how different is the target child's performance from that of other children in the classroom?" An example of the data collected from a response-discrepancy system is displayed in Exhibit 2.6. With this system four behaviors are observed: physical contact, noise, off-task, and out-of-place. In Exhibit 2.6, significant differences for the observed behaviors for the three identified target children (Pe, Pa, and Ma) and their classroom peers can be identified. Both Pe and Pa have difficulty being out-of-place, compared to their

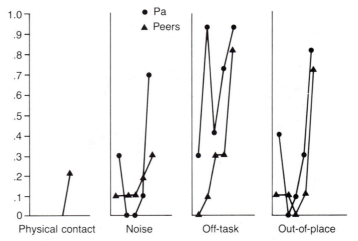

Number of behaviors emitted per minute by Pa and his peers over 5 days.

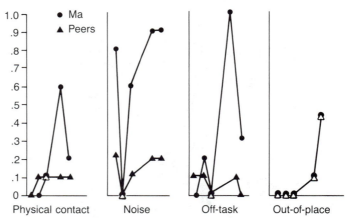

Number of behaviors emitted per minute by Ma and his peers over 5 days.

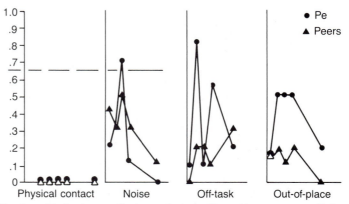

Number of behaviors emitted per minute by Pe and her peers over 5 days.

peers. This is not a significant problem, however, for Ma. Being off-task is a problem for both Pa and Ma, but not for Pe, as compared to their peers. Being noisy is a serious problem for Ma, with no difference for Pa, and Pe is actually less noisy than her peers. Response-discrepancy observation can be a valuable tool in selecting target behaviors for intervention. In this example, Pe does not need a program for being disruptive; however, she might need a program for being out-of-place. In fact, this problem is the only one in which Pe differs from her peers. Response-discrepancy observation is also valuable as a validity check for other measures such as structured interviewing and behavior checklists. An observer can take the most serious behavior problems reported in an interview or behavior checklist and use them to observe the target child, the index child, and the teacher's behavior.

Although behavioral observation has a number of advantages, like most assessment techniques it also has trade-offs and disadvantages. It can be expensive in terms of the time required to train observers and actually collect data. Many school districts cannot afford to train observers to be highly skilled and then allow them hours of observation time in the classroom and playground. Teachers generally have to collect observation data themselves, though aides, volunteers, school psychologists, and others can be recruited to help.

The last type of observation procedure to be discussed is *permanent product* observation. With this system, a teacher observes the product of a child's behavior. The actual behavior itself is not observed. For example, a teacher might check an academic assignment or a test (the product) after an academic period. Another example might involve checking the litter on a playground after a child has been assigned to pick it up. In both of these situations, only the products and not the actual behaviors are observed. The advantages of a permanent product system are that little time is required to observe, the product is just waiting to be checked, and the observer's reactions do not affect the child. The basic disadvantage of the system is that the behavior is assumed to have been done by the child. Cheating can occur with academic assignments; a child might coerce a smaller child into picking up the playground litter. The best approach to reducing this problem is to randomly observe the child actually performing the task.

◀ **EXHIBIT 2–6**   A comparison of three behaviorally disordered children (Pa, Ma, and Pe) and their peers using a response-discrepancy model of observation

Source: From "Direct Observation Approach to Measuring Classroom Behavior" by S.L. Deno, 1980, *Exceptional Children, 46,* pp. 396-399. Reproduced by permission.

ASSESSING SOCIAL SKILLS

There are three primary purposes for assessing social skills: (a) to initially identify children and youth who need training, (b) to pinpoint skill areas to be taught, and (c) to evaluate student progress and the effectiveness of social skills instruction. Achieving these purposes while satisfying the requirements of accuracy, reliability, and validity is easier said than done, however. Numerous reviews have underlined the generally weak state of social skills assessment (Bellack, 1979; Foster & Ritchey, 1979; Gresham, 1981, 1983; Hops, 1982).

Generally, preferred practice in social skills assessment is to use several methods (Hops & Greenwood, 1981). Naturalistic observation, teacher ratings, sociometric measures, and role-play tests are the procedures most commonly used to assess social skills in children.

Naturalistic Observation

Systematically collected observational data provide very specific information regarding both the quality and quantity of social behavior in real-life situations. A number of behavioral observation systems have been developed for observing children's social interactions. While most have been developed for research purposes, one observation system developed for use by practitioners is the *Accepts Observation Form* (Walker et al., 1983). This system employs a duration method of behavioral observation. The observer starts a stopwatch whenever the student being observed is engaging in appropriate social participation, which is defined as follows: "An active exchange of social signals between two or more children that may involve verbal interaction, physical contact, active gesturing, playing catch, participating in a structured game or activity, or playing on playground equipment" (p. 133). When the child stops participating appropriately, the observer stops the stopwatch. The watch is turned on and off with the child's behavior. At the conclusion of a 20-minute observation period, if the stopwatch totals 11 minutes, you know that the child has been engaged in appropriate social participation 55% of the time (11/20 = 55%).

Another method that has been suggested for assessing social skills through observation is frequency recording (Gresham, 1983). An observer would tally how many times a child says "please," initiates to another, shares, and so on in a given period. A basic problem with frequency recording is that appropriate social interaction is a continuous behavior, much like attending to task. While certain discrete bits of social behavior can be counted (e.g., saying "please," inviting others to play), it would be erroneous to conclude anything about an individual's overall social skills on the basis of frequency data alone. For example, a child might say "please" three times, "nice going" twice, and invite someone to play four times during a 20-minute observation period, but those events probably would take up only 15 seconds of the period. Conceivably, the child could have spent the rest of the time engaged in inappropriate social interactions or could have been isolated and not engaged at all. Clearly, any observation system used to assess a child's social skills should take into account the nature of the behavior. Duration and interval recording systems do, while frequency recording does not.

The relative advantages and disadvantages of behavioral observation as a method for assessing social skills are summarized in Exhibit 2.7. In general, behavioral observation procedures provide the most specific and representative data on social skills. However, cost factors, somewhat limited practicality in applied settings, and less than satisfactory validity data suggest that observational procedures alone are insufficient to assess social skills adequately.

Teacher Ratings

The use of behavior problem checklists to pinpoint child behavioral excesses and deficits was discussed earlier. While some conclusions may be drawn about a child's social skill deficits from the results of a behavior problem checklist, more specific information may be obtained by using checklists that are part of a social skills training program. A curriculum-imbedded social skills rating scale is shown in Exhibit 2.8.

The advantages and disadvantages of using teacher ratings to assess social skills are also summarized in Exhibit 2.7. Perhaps the most apparent weakness of these checklists is that most lack data attesting to their reliability, validity, and norms. This can be a real disadvantage if the assessment information will be used to classify or place a child. However, if the goals are to identify treatment goals and establish a baseline against which future progress can be assessed, social skills checklists such as the one presented in Exhibit 2.8 are appropriate.

Sociometric Measures

Sociometric procedures estimate the level of social acceptance or rejection among an individual student and the peer group. There are two types of sociometric measures.

1. *Peer nomination*—Students are asked, in an interview or with paper-and-pencil, to answer the following types of questions: "Who are your three best friends in class?" "Who do you like to play with?" "Who do you like to work with?" Negatively oriented questions may also be used: "Who would you *not* like to play with?" Results indicate the most popular and unpopular children in a group.

EXHIBIT 2.7   Advantages and disadvantages of four procedures for assessing social skills

Procedure	Advantages	Disadvantages
Behavioral observation	Sensitive to changes in social behavior due to training	Involve a great deal of time to collect data
	Can be used frequently to monitor progress	Cannot always detect low frequency behaviors
	Identifies quantity and quality of social behavior	All observed behavior may not be importantly related to overall social competence or acceptance
	Can be used to assess generalization	Poorly trained observers may gather unreliable data
	Can focus on specific behaviors (e.g., hitting) instead of global behaviors (e.g., aggression)	
	Can provide information regarding social interaction; i.e., what happens before and after the observed behaviors	
Teacher ratings	Good initial screening device	Frequent use of a rating scale may have a reactive effect
	Good source of information	Not likely to be sensitive to subtle changes in behavior
	Low cost	Psychometric characteristics are generally weak
	Can be used to pinpoint treatment goals, if checklist items are specific rather than global behaviors	
	Can be used to evaluate treatment effects	

2. *Peer rating*—Each student in a class rates every other student on a number of items related to peer acceptance and social competence. Results indicate overall level of acceptance by peers.

There is a large body of literature on the use of sociometric assessment of the social status of handicapped children (cf. Asher & Hymel, 1981; Asher & Taylor, 1981; Gottlieb, Semmel, & Veldman, 1978; MacMillan & Morrison, 1980; McConnell & Odom, 1986). An important distinction is whether social acceptance is best judged by the number of best friends a student has or by the overall level of acceptance by the peer group. The peer nomination method assesses best friendship status, and the rating scale method assesses overall acceptance. It might be a more desirable and realistic goal for handicapped students in mainstream peer

Exhibit 2-7 *continued*

Procedure	Advantages	Disadvantages
Sociometric measures	Very useful as a screening device Good predictive validity Can be used to identify rejected and neglected students	Provide limited diagnostic information regarding specific social skill deficiencies Cannot be used to monitor progress because students may become bored with completing sociogram Not always sensitive to changes in social behavior (as a general treatment evaluation procedure) May possibly be negative repercussions if sociogram becomes a prime topic of conversation among students May not identify students who are simply "tolerated"
Role-play tests	Flexible in providing a wide range of situations otherwise inaccessible Close monitoring of discrete, hard-to-observe behaviors	Lack of correspondence between competence demonstrated on role-play tests and competence demonstrated in naturalistic settings Lack of reliability data Lack of normative data

groups to become generally accepted rather than becoming everyone's best friend (Asher & Taylor, 1981; Gresham, 1983).

One disadvantage of sociometric measures (see Exhibit 2.7) is that they do not pinpoint specific social skills deficits. Other assessment techniques (observation, teacher ratings) must also be used for this kind of specific information. However, sociometric measures are an integral part of the overall assessment process because they identify the extent to which a child is accepted by peers, a major goal of social skills training.

Role-Play Tests

The nature of most social skills makes it difficult to obtain direct measures of an individual child's skills in natural settings (e.g., conversation skills, greetings, assertiveness, negotiation skills, eye contact). That is,

EXHIBIT 2.8   Representative items from a social skills checklist

---

Area II: Basic Interaction Skills

---

1. The student maintains eye contact
   while speaking or when spoken to.   1 .... 2 .... 3 .... 4 5

2. The student speaks in a moderate
   tone of voice (neither too loud/too
   soft)   1 .... 2 .... 3 .... 4 5

3. The student seeks out others to
   interact with and initiates a
   conversation.   1 .... 2 .... 3 .... 4 5

4. The student pays attention when
   spoken to.   1 .... 2 .... 3 .... 4 5

5. The student responds/answers when
   spoken to.   1 .... 2 .... 3 .... 4 5

6. The student converses by saying
   things which are relevant to the
   topic.   1 .... 2 .... 3 .... 4 5

7. The student shares a conversation
   by speaking for about the same
   amount of time as they listen.   1 .... 2 .... 3 .... 4 5

8. The student asks questions that
   request information about
   someone/something.   1 .... 2 .... 3 .... 4 5

9. The student keeps a conversation
   going.

Source: From *The Walker Social Skills Curriculum: The Accepts Program* (p. 137) by H. M. Walker, S. McConnell, D. Holmes, B. Todis, J. Walker, and N. Golden, 1983, Austin, TX: Pro-Ed. Used with permission.

these behaviors may not occur during any given observation period. Many researchers, therefore, have developed role-play tests to assess otherwise inaccessible behaviors.

In a role-play test, students are asked to demonstrate how they would behave in a particular situation. The teacher would carefully observe, record, and evaluate each student's responses to a simulated scene. For example:

> *Teacher says:*   You are sitting alone at lunch and a new kid in school sits next to you.
>
> *Question:*   Show me what you would do or say.

The student's response to this question would be evaluated for the presence or absence of specific behaviors or qualities (e.g., eye contact, length of response, tone, assertiveness).

The rationale underlying role-play tests is that direct observation may not be possible in every situation and that an artificial setting can be carefully controlled to elicit responses to specific situations (Hops, 1982). In addition, a role-play test may help determine whether a child has acquired the skill or whether the basic problem is performing the skill consistently. However, research indicates a significant lack of correspondence between the social competence demonstrated in role-play situations and competence demonstrated in natural settings (VanHasselt, Hersen, & Bellack, 1981). Consequently, if role-play tests are used to assess a child's social skills, the results should be interpreted very cautiously.

Issues in Assessing Social Skills

The assessment of children's social skills is a relatively new field. The problems of the reliability and validity of the assessment instruments and procedures and the lack of normative data should be a source of concern to practitioners.

There is no single best procedure to assess social skills. Therefore, more than one source of assessment data should be used. At a minimum, a social skills assessment should include behavioral observation, sociometric data, and teacher ratings. Role-play data can also be collected. The purpose here is to develop a treatment program to remediate any deficits found. It would be unwise to develop or implement a treatment program without an adequate assessment of the child's social skills. Admittedly, the assessment of social skills is less well developed than, for example, the assessment of academic skills. If implemented properly, however, these assessment strategies will provide the teacher with sufficient information to plan and monitor the effectiveness of a training program.

ASSESSING ACADEMIC SKILLS

Much of the time spent on the assessment of behaviorally disordered students is given to instruments and procedures such as behavioral observation and behavior problem checklists that assess social skills. However, the assessment of academic skills is also critical, even if, unfortunately, it sometimes is minimized or omitted. Clearly, academic skill deficiencies and behavioral disorders are associated. Lambert and Sandoval (1980) found 42% of the hyperactive children they studied had learning problems that could also qualify the child as learning disabled. Cullinan, Epstein, and McLinden (1986) found in their study of state definitions of behavior disorders that "more definitions explicitly recognize *learning/ achievement* problems as important accompaniments of a behavior disorder" (p. 389). Reading deficiencies are particularly clearly correlated with conditions called *antisocial* or *conduct disorders* (Rutter & Yule, 1973). If academic problems are ignored in behaviorally disordered students, then the children will continue to fail in spite of gains made in other areas such as social skills training and the management of behavior problems.

Standardized Achievement Tests

These traditional tests are frequently used to screen and assess students with learning problems. Achievement tests assess skills in several academic areas, often including reading recognition and comprehension, spelling, mathematics, science, and social studies. Some tests measure specific curricular areas such as reading and divide the area into multiple skills such as letter recognition, word attack skills, and reading comprehension. Achievement tests "sample the products of past formal and informal educational experiences. They measure the extent to which a student has profited from schooling and/or life experiences compared to others of the same age or grade" (Salvia & Ysseldyke, 1978, p. 125). As this definition suggests, most are norm-referenced, allowing normative comparisons. To make these comparisons valid, academic curricula must be sampled and the content area adequately represented in the test.

Achievement tests are administered individually or in a group, depending on the particular test used. With behaviorally disordered students, individually administered tests are preferable because the student's motivation to take the test is maximized and the assessor can get information about the student's test-taking behavior (i.e, attention to a task, impulsivity in answering). Achievement tests are used with behaviorally disordered students to determine if there is a deficit in any of a number of general academic areas. If screening reveals a deficit, a diagnostic achievement test can assess specific skills within that specific area. For example, a general achievement test like the *Peabody Individual Achievement Test* (PIAT) (Dunn & Markwardt, 1970) could be given to a child. If a child's score in reading is low, then a diagnostic achievement test such as the *Woodcock Reading Mastery Test* (Woodcock, 1973) can be given. Achievement tests can also be used as a gross measure of improvement (pre- and post-measurement) in academic skills.

Some of the most frequently used achievement tests are the *Metropolitan Achievement Test* (MAT) (Balow, Farr, Hogan, & Prescott, 1978), the *Stanford Achievement Test* (SAT) (Gardner, Rudman, Karlsen, & Merwin, 1982), the *California Achievement Test* (CAT) (Tiegs & Clarke, 1970), the PIAT (Dunn & Markwardt, 1970), and the *Wide Range Achievement Test* (WRAT) (Jastak & Jastak, 1965). The WRAT has been one of the most popular achievement tests in special education because it is short and easy to administer, and it has been recently revised (WRAT-R). However, it is based on a limited standardization group, and it has limited item sampling from standard school curricula.

Standardized achievement tests have been criticized for several reasons. Jenkins and Pany (1978) have criticized the use of norm-referenced achievement tests because of the poor overlap between what an achievement test actually measures and what is taught in the classroom (content validity). Some tests overestimate a child's achievement, while others underestimate achievement, depending on which test is used with which particular curriculum materials. "It appears that measured progress may be more reflective of test and curriculum combinations than of teaching and learning" (Jenkins & Pany, 1978, p. 451). Such test bias can have real effects on students and the educational interventions used with them. For example, if a student is using a test that does not correspond to the curriculum materials he is using, his achievement may be overestimated and he may be denied extra services such as resource room help.

Daily measurement of rate and accuracy of a student's academic performance is needed along with achievement test data to make meaningful and specific educational recommendations. Merely using an achievement test score as a pre- and post-measure to evaluate academic success is too biased and the information is generally too delayed to be a preferred assessment strategy. In addition, Shapiro and Lentz (1985, 1986) have criticized standardized tests because they yield a composite or average score but do not give information about specific subskills. For example, a third grader may receive a 3.0 grade level score in arithmetic; however, some subskills may be above average and some, below average. The utility of standardized achievement tests for academic intervention has also been criticized (Shapiro & Lentz, 1985). It is difficult, if not impossible, to design specific academic interventions for deficits described by average or composite scores.

Criterion-Referenced Testing

An alternative to norm-referenced testing has been criterion-referenced testing to assess absolute mastery of a skill. Criterion-referenced testing was first proposed by Glaser (1963) in response to the limitations of many norm-referenced tests. Norm-referenced tests are designed to give information about an individual's standing in relation to a standardization population. The information provided by norm-referenced achievement tests, however, is only of a composite or global nature. It indicates how different a child is from the average of the standardization group with global numbers such as percentiles or grade level scores. These tests do not give specific information about a child's deficits so that interventions can be designed from the scores (Shapiro & Lentz, 1986).

Criterion-referenced tests compare an individual student's performance against objectives to assess the mastery of those objectives (Lidz, 1981). A simple definition is that a criterion-referenced test is "constructed to assess the performance level of examinees in relation to well-defined objectives" (Popham, 1978). The success of criterion-referenced tests depends on how well the objectives are defined and analyzed into small steps, and how the criterion is determined. The word *criterion* suggests the mastery level or how correct a student must be on each objective. Frequently the criterion level is set between 85% and 100% correct.

Criterion-referenced tests are based on a behavior sampling model that emphasizes very structured and specific information. Few assumptions are made about why a skill has not developed, but it is assumed that within broad limits of intelligence, most skills can be acquired. Criterion-referenced tests are available for most academic areas, such as math (Connolly, Nachtman, & Pritchett, 1971), reading (Woodcock, 1973), and general academic skills (Brigance, 1978). These tests are not associated with any particular set of academic materials. However, some criterion-referenced tests are actually part of a published academic curriculum such as *Corrective Reading* (Engelmann, 1978).

The basic advantage of criterion measures is that the information is so specific that direct educational interventions can be developed (Shapiro & Lentz, 1986). In addition, criterion-referenced measures are excellent for evaluating a child's progress in a program because learning is demonstrated with the mastery of each new objective (Lidz, 1979). Most norm-referenced tests can only give global pre- and post-scores as evaluation points, and thus offer a far less detailed analysis of progress than do criterion-referenced tests.

Although there are distinct advantages to using criterion-referenced tests with behaviorally disordered children, there are also a number of limitations. Sometimes reliability measures for the subtests vary greatly across grades (Shapiro & Lentz, 1986). It is also difficult to use these tests continuously because the student can become "test wise" if one form of the test is repeatedly given. The adequacy of criterion-referenced tests is directly related to how well the test samples the content area. The test must contain enough items to measure each content area reliably and still be of manageable length (Anastasi, 1982).

The content areas that lend themselves to complete sampling by criterion-referenced objectives are generally elementary-level academic areas (Ebel, 1971, 1972). However, there is no complete agreement among educators concerning which objectives are essential or necessary for demonstrating mastery (Ebel, 1971, 1973; Lidz, 1979). Even if there were complete agreement among educators about the necessary content areas and their adequate sampling, there is still the difficult question of setting acceptable performance levels for mastery (Anastasi, 1982). Few academic skills must be completely mastered before other skills are learned; however, many criterion-referenced tests require absolute mastery. This requirement can delay learning by slowing the pace of instruction, particularly with some complex skills that do not require absolute mastery. For example, a socially deficient child may successfully make friends at school without mastering all the friendship-making skills in a social skills training program. (This argument may be more true for non-handicapped children than for behaviorally disordered children who have severe skill deficiencies and who may require overlearning of a skill before they can advance in the curriculum.)

Direct Academic Assessment

Direct assessment of academic skills involves using several related approaches that have been reported in the educational literature, such as curriculum-based assessment (Deno, 1985; Tucker, 1985), direct assessment (Howell, 1986; Lentz & Shapiro, 1986), functional assessment of learning environments (Lentz & Shapiro, 1986), and formative evaluation of individual student programs (Deno, 1986). All of these approaches are related and emphasize (a) using the child's classroom academic materials to assess progress and (b) assessing the child's learning environment for signs of motivation and learning problems. These approaches view academic difficulties as either a skill or a performance deficiency. With a skill deficiency, the child does not have the minimum skills to perform the required academic task. With a performance deficiency, the child may have the minimum skills but the environment may not provide the opportunity or the motivation to respond.

As indicated in chapter 1, curriculum-based assessment uses a child's classroom academic materials as the actual assessment instruments (Idol, Nevin, & Paolucci-Whitcomb, 1986). Several steps are followed in a curriculum-based assessment.

1. Most publishers of curricular materials and many school districts define where a child should be in an academic curriculum by the age of the child and the time of the academic year. The difference between where a child's skills actually place her in the curriculum and where she is expected to be at the time of assessment is a *progress discrepancy* (Deno & Mirkin, 1977; Lentz & Shapiro, 1986). This difference defines a skill area that a child must master.

2. Most teachers using curriculum-based assessment develop a series of items that serve as assessment probes directly from the curriculum. These items reflect the important skills and

are sequenced logically from the start to the finish of the
curriculum (Blankenship, 1985). Some types of curriculum
materials (such as arithmetic, spelling, and writing) will take
structured written forms that define the tasks exactly. Other
task items, such as reading, will require performance probes,
such as selecting three or more passages from a basal reader
and having the child read aloud for one minute (Lentz &
Shapiro, 1986). With this procedure, the number of words read
and the errors per minute can be calculated. In addition, the
child can be quizzed about the passage's meaning. Other
examples in reading may have students supply words deleted
from the text (cloze procedures), read aloud from the text, say
the meanings of underlined words, and discuss the meaning of
the passage (Deno, 1985). Teachers can easily cover and
underline words in a basal reader that is used as the testing
book. All of these procedures have excellent reliability and
validity when compared to more traditional forms of academic
testing (Deno, 1985).

3. Some end-of-the-book tests from academic series can be used
   or modified for use as curriculum-based tests. For example,
   the end-of-the-book tests in the Scott-Foresman *Mathematics
   Around Us* were used by Lentz and Shapiro (1986) as assessment probes for arithmetic progress. It is important that end-
   of-the-book tests have items that reflect the instructional
   objectives across all the curriculum and that there is an indication where each of the items should be administered.

4. Samples of a child's academic progress can be made with
   these techniques. However, the child's mastery of the academic material in a classroom needs to be assessed. For
   example, if a sample is collected with a child reading aloud in
   a basal reader, then the teacher can calculate the number of
   errors, the fluency, and the reading comprehension in three
   one-minute timings (Gickling & Thompson, 1985). A ratio of
   mastered material to errors can then be calculated. For
   example, a child might have an accuracy ratio of 90% to 95%
   correctly read words with 5% to 10% errors and a 75%
   comprehension level. For a particular classroom, this might be
   a reasonable instructional level. Drill and practice with pin-
   pointed difficult words could be used to improve the 5% to
   10% error level. If the ratio is larger, with a higher error ratio
   (75% correct words and 25% incorrect words with a 50%
   comprehension level), then a child would be at the frustration
   level with more guessing, more off-task behavior, and more
   behavior problems. For a child at the frustration level, the

curriculum, teaching techniques, and previous skills would have to be reviewed.

Curriculum-based assessment does not, however, directly assess academic performance deficiencies that are caused by the instructional environment. The quality of the classroom learning environment must be directly assessed to assess performance problems (Lentz & Shapiro, 1986). This functional assessment involves behavioral observation, a structured interview of the teacher, and a review of the child's work.

The quality of classroom instruction can be sampled by observing in the classroom. Important variables to assess include academic engaged time, pacing of instruction, the teacher as a model, prompts provided, feedback on performance, and patient, positive, and instructive error correction. In addition, observations can be made of the organization of the classroom and the number of distracting simuli that compete with academic instruction (i.e., classroom noises, people coming into the classroom, bells ringing, hall noise).

The classroom contingencies can be assessed through observation, interviews, and reviewing children's work samples. What types of incentives does a teacher use for academic work? Is there a high ratio of positive reinforcers to punishers? Does the teacher use attention effectively? Does the teacher move around the class during independent seatwork and provide quiet praise for on-task behavior? Are there formal motivational systems (publicly posted performance feedback systems; direct reinforcement for on-task behavior and accurate academic performance such as tokens, material reinforcers, or contingent positive activities)?

The Instructional Environment Scale (TIES) (Ysseldyke & Christenson, 1987) is designed to systematically analyze instructional environments by identifying areas of strengths and weaknesses and the relationship between a student's academic and behavioral difficulties and the instructional environment. Using interviews of teacher and students and structured classroom observations, TIES examines the extent to which the environment can be characterized along several indicators of effective instruction (e.g., teacher expectations, academic engaged time, relevant practice, motivational strategies, informed feedback, progress evaluation). As such, TIES is inextricably linked to intervention.

Both curriculum-based assessment and the functional assessment of the instructional environment have advantages as preferred assessment practices. They are relatively inexpensive, plus they relate directly to educational interventions. Curriculum-based assessment and functional assessment are important for new referrals and for assessing the progress of a behaviorally disordered student in a special education program. These techniques are also particularly important in the students' transition back to regular education settings. Curriculum-based assess-

Pointer 2.2

DIAGNOSTIC AND STATISTICAL MANUAL (DSM-III) CLASSIFICATION SYSTEM

DSM-III is a psychiatric classification system developed by the American Psychiatric Association (1980) to classify mental disorders in adults and children. The number of categories for use with children has been greatly expanded from previous editions. DSM-III includes such categories as mental retardation, attention deficit disorder (with or without hyperactivity), conduct disorder (undersocialized or socialized, aggressive or nonaggressive), anxiety disorder, pervasive development disorder (childhood onset, infantile autism), and eating disorders (anorexia nervosa, bulimia, pica).

Instead of classifying a child with only one category, the DSM-III has *multiple axes.* One of the axes gives the main category of the disorder (i.e., attention deficit disorder with hyperactivity), while the added axes give additional information such as developmental information, intellectual capability, learning problems, and psychosocial factors. All of the axes add more than just a label for a disorder and provide a better picture of the child. The DSM-III axes are: axis 1 — the clinical psychiatric syndrome;

axis 2 — developmental or personality disorders; axis 3 — physical disorders; axis 4 — psychosocial stressors; and axis 5 — intellectual and social functioning.

An example of a DSM-III diagnosis for a behaviorally disordered child found in a psychiatric evaluation might look like this:

- Axis 1:   312.00* Conduct Disorder — Undersocialized, Aggressive
- Axis 2:   315.00 Developmental Reading Disorder
            315.10 Developmental Arithmetic Disorder
- Axis 3:   Physical condition: Asthma
- Axis 4:   Psychosocial stressor: Divorce of parents in the past year Severity: 5—Severe
- Axis 5:   Highest level of adaptive functioning: 5—Poor

*The number code refers to specific condition and allows the coding of additional information (i.e., 314.01 refers to attention deficit disorder with hyperactivity [.01]; 314.00 refers to the condition without hyperactivity [.00]).

---

ment can be used to determine a child's ability to adjust to the new curriculum of a regular classroom. Functional assessment can also help a child prepare for the teaching style, organization, and expectations of a regular classroom teacher.

DETERMINING ELIGIBILITY FOR SPECIAL EDUCATION

Before a student is placed in a special education program for behaviorally disordered students, the school must determine whether the student is

In this example, the behaviorally disordered child who is classified has poor social relations with peers and adults, is aggressive, has significant learning problems in reading and mathematics, has asthma, has parents who are recently divorced, and currently is not functioning well.

Overall, DSM-III is superior to most classification systems because it provides more detailed information. However, it is not perfect. Like other assessment procedures, DSM-III has significant associated error. The categories were developed by a committee, not by research and statistical procedures such as factor analysis. This weakness has led to criticism of the validity of some of the classification categories (Achenbach, 1980; Rutter & Shaffer, 1980). The reliability of the system has also been questioned. For the broad categories of childhood conditions, the interrater reliability is acceptable. However, for the finer discriminations demanded by a multiaxial system and complex conditions, reliability falls to poor levels.

DSM-III also reflects a traditional medical model that stresses underlying causes (Schacht & Nathan, 1977). DSM-III includes classifications for several educational conditions (i.e., reading disorder, arithmetic disorder, language disorder, and articulation disorder) that physicians are not as well trained as educators to assess (Harris, 1979). DSM-III is currently being revised to improve some of these difficulties, and DMS-III-R is expected in the near future.

Teachers of behaviorally disordered students should be familiar with DSM-III because all or parts of it will be used with their students at some point. Many teachers will receive psychiatric reports on children with DSM-III diagnoses, and they will hear other professionals use terms from DSM-III in meetings. Teachers should remember that DSM-III is an imperfect model or approximation of a child who has a disorder. As a model, it is always prone to some error when applied with an individual child. The child's DSM-III classification is not the child.

eligible to be classified as behaviorally disordered. Historically, this decision has been heavily influenced by clinical diagnostic systems such as the American Psychiatric Association's *Diagnostic and Statistical Manual* (DSM-III) (1980) (see Pointer 2.2).

Most states outline procedures and classification guidelines to assist in the determination of eligibility. Some states provide extensive and detailed information in an effort to provide support and assistance to those responsible for the classification of behaviorally disordered students (cf., Wood, Smith, & Grimes, 1985). Yet the specific criteria and their interpretation differ among states, among districts in a state, and

EXHIBIT 2.9   Procedures for classifying students as behaviorally disordered—Suggested evaluation checklist

1. At least two of the following five apply.
   a. The student is rated above the 98th percentile on two different acceptable problem behavior rating scales (or similar-named subscales) by *two* or more current teachers.
   b. The student is rated at or above the 98th percentile on two different acceptable problem behavior rating scales (or similar-named subscales) by his/her current teacher and at least one previous year's teacher.
   c. The student is rated at or above the 98th percentile on two different acceptable problem behavior rating scales (or similar-named subscales) by one or more parents/guardians.
   d. The student is currently displaying behavior which is endangering his/her life or seriously endangering the safety of others.
   e. The student's observable school and/or classroom problem behavior is documented to be more severe than approximately 98% of his/her peers.

All these apply:

2. Behavior management consultation to the classroom teacher(s) has been provided over a period of at least 4 weeks by a behavioral specialist and *documentation* indicates that specifically prescribed and consistently employed classroom management interventions have not reduced the inappropriate behavior within acceptable limits suggested by these eligibility criteria.

even among different schools in the same district (Waksman & Jones, 1985).

However, there is reason to believe that there is a serious lack of data — both qualitative and quantitative — to determine eligibility of behaviorally disordered students for special education (McGinnis, Kiraly, & Smith, 1984; Smith, Frank, & Snider, 1984). The primary problem appears to be that the assessment information collected is insufficient to justify classifying a student as handicapped. That is, very little documentation related to the behavioral/social/emotional status of behaviorally disordered students is available. When there is documentation, it tends to be unstructured (e.g., general verbal or written statements about a student's behavior, self-concept inventory, family history, school history). Structured assessment data (e.g., behavior problem rating scales, checklists, systematically collected observational data, environmental analyses) are not consistently used.

Exhibit 2-9
continued

3. The problem behaviors have been exhibited for over 6 months. This may be waived if the child is endangering his/her life or seriously endangering the safety of others.
   Waived: __ Yes __ No

4. No recent acute stressor or isolated traumatic event in the child's environment (e.g., divorce or death in the family, loss of property) can *adequately* explain the problem behavior.

5. No medical problem or health impairment can *adequately* explain the problem behavior pattern.

6. An inappropriate education program cannot *adequately* explain the problem behavior pattern.

7. Culturally different norms or expectations cannot *adequately* explain the problem behavior pattern.

8. The child is *either:*

   a. Performing markedly below his/her academic potential on acceptable academic tests or school report cards (__ Yes __ No) or,

   b. Severely deficient in social skills or social competence (__ Yes __ No)

9. Direct observation by a school psychologist and/or behavioral specialist has documented that *either:*

   a. The student is displaying problem behaviors at a high frequency (__ Yes __ No) or,

   b. The student is displaying low frequency behaviors which grossly deviate from acceptable social norms (__ Yes __ No)

Source: Adapted from *A Suggested Procedure for the Identification and Provision of Services to Seriously Emotionally Disturbed Students* (Technical Assistance Paper #5) by S. Waksman and V. Jones, 1985, Salem: Oregon Department of Education. Used with permission.

An excellent set of procedures for determining eligibility and classifying students as behaviorally disordered was developed by Waksman and Jones (1985). This system requires gathering information about a student from more than one person, across a variety of settings, using multiple sources of verifiable information. (See Exhibit 2.9 for an outline of these procedures.) Assessment information gathered using these kinds of procedures is much more likely to lead to correct eligibility decisions as well as to yield useful information for planning interventions.

Clearly, preferred assessment practices such as behavior problem checklists, systematic behavioral observations, and structured interviewing should always be used to help determine whether a student should be classified as behaviorally disordered. Standardized achievement tests, criterion-referenced tests, curriculum-based assessment, and the functional assessment of the learning environment are also important. Deviation from the norm and severity can be assessed with norm-referenced behavior problem checklists and response-discrepancy observations. Chronicity, the need for special education, and possible etiology can be assessed through structured interviewing of parents and teachers.

There are still serious problems in the practices used to assess, classify, and declare eligible students for special education services. Problems with the nature and quality of the assessment data, as well as how the data are used to make decisions, have been identified in all areas of special education, including the behaviorally disordered (Ysseldyke, Algozzine, & Epps, 1982; Ysseldyke, Algozzine, Richey, & Graden, 1982; Ysseldyke, Christenson, Pianta, & Algozzine, 1983). Using the procedures proposed in this section and explained in greater detail throughout this chapter will help to reduce these problems and provide the basis for making better informed decisions.

EMERGING PROCEDURES IN ASSESSING BEHAVIORALLY DISORDERED STUDENTS

New assessment procedures are currently being developed that promise to improve the educational programs received by behaviorally disordered students. Some of these systems depend on advances made with microcomputers; others are the products of long years of development.

A *multiple-gating* approach for the systematic screening of behaviorally disordered children is currently being developed at the University of Oregon and the University of Washington (Walker, Severson, & Haring, 1985). The system consists of three separate stages. It is called a *multiple-gating* approach because each step involves more rigorous assessment through which a student must pass. The first gate involves a teacher's systematic evaluation of all children in the classroom who may be at risk for behavior problems. At the first gate, the teacher ranks students according to a profile that describes externalizing and internalizing behaviors.

The second gate also relies on the teacher's judgment. At this stage, the teacher rates the top 10 ranked students on the externalizing list and the top 10 ranked students on the internalizing list in terms of the frequency and nature of their problem behaviors when compared to a list of critical problem behaviors. The frequencies and types of problem behaviors are then compared to normative data. If they exceed the norms, then the child advances to gate three. With gate three, the child is assessed through behavioral observation on two important dimensions: academic engagement time during classroom seat work and the quality and amount of social interaction behavior at recess and on the playground.

Children who significantly deviate from the norm for academic engaged time and social interaction are then considered for special education services.

The advantage of the multiple-gating system is that it involves teacher judgment at the first two gates. A teacher is generally the person most familiar with a student's behavior in educational settings. This system also screens entire classrooms for behavior problems so that fewer children are missed, and more difficult children are detected before a crisis develops. Overall assessment costs are lowered because the least expensive assessment procedures are used for screening while the more expensive and more precise procedures are used only with high probability cases.

The Child Behavior Checklist and Profile (Achenbach, 1979) has already been reviewed. This checklist completed by parents has been greatly expanded, particularly for applications in educational settings. A Teacher Behavior Checklist with the teacher as informant parallels the parent checklist (Achenbach & Edelbrock, 1980). In addition, a Direct Observation Form allows direct observation in the classroom of items from the parent and teacher checklist (Achenbach & Edelbrock, 1983). The Direct Observation Form also includes a section for observation across ten 5-second intervals of classroom on-task behavior. The last part of this system is a Youth Self-Report Form on which a child rates his or her own behaviors on a checklist similar to the parent and teacher checklists.

The advantages of this system are that it allows multiple measures across several data sources (parent, teacher, observer, and child). The individual assessment devices are very similar so that items checked on one measure can be compared with items checked on another measure. Personal computer scoring and plotting of the profiles are available for some of the measures. The basic drawback of the system is that not all of the measures have been standardized to date.

Another system for the assessment of behaviorally disordered children uses the judgment capabilities of a microcomputer. This system, developed at Utah State University, involves artificial intelligence (Hofmeister & Ferraro, personal communication, 1986). The formal assessment process, done by an *expert system,* uses an IBM personal computer and an MI inference engine developed at Stanford University for applications with medical diagnoses. Essentially, the computer is programmed to hold hundreds of research findings and regulations concerning the assessment of behaviorally disordered children. Assessment information is fed into the computer, which evaluates the quality of the information and calculates a probability that the child is actually behaviorally disordered. This system is used for a second opinion for difficult cases in which human judgment may be in error.

SUMMARY: PREFERRED ASSESSMENT PRACTICES

In this chapter the major approaches to the assessment of behaviorally disordered children in educational settings have been reviewed. No single assessment method or procedure can suffice as an adequate assessment for behaviorally disordered students. *Multiple* methods or measures are required (Achenbach, 1982; Ciminero & Drabman, 1977; Nay, 1979). Because all assessment methods are prone to error, balance is achieved by using assessment methods that are not subject to the same error.

Diagnosing mental retardation from a single IQ test, learning disabilities from a single achievement test, or behavioral disorders from a single behavior problem checklist can lead to serious assessment errors. Failure to use several assessment methods has led to legal action in some cases, particularly with minority children. A carefully planned assessment strategy includes a number of different types of appropriate assessment methods that are culturally fair and are administered and interpreted by adequately trained personnel. To cut corners by using only one or two measures or to use staff members who are not adequately trained can result in inappropriately classified and placed children and probable legal problems.

A comprehensive assessment strategy for the classification and placement of behaviorally disordered children should include a structured interview, a diagnostic screening measure, behavioral observation, and academic achievement assessment. The child, teachers, and parents should be interviewed to objectively identify and describe problem behaviors, problem environments, the child's strengths, and possible management strategies for both the classroom and home. Measures such as behavior problem checklists can indicate the severity of the behavioral disorder. Behavior problem checklists have an added advantage in that the individual items can be used as tentative target behaviors for intervention.

Behavioral observation is a critical component in the assessment of these children. Interviews, checklists, and rating forms generally involve the teacher or parent as the main informant, and this information can be biased. Systematic observation of the child in structured settings such as the classroom or unstructured settings such as the playground or lunchroom offers a check on the validity of other information. Response-discrepancy observations should also include the behavior of the teacher, the identified child, and a nonhandicapped index peer. This practice gives some additional normative information that many observation systems do not give.

Academic assessment is necessary because a majority of behaviorally disordered children experience significant academic problems. This type of assessment should include normative- or criterion-referenced aca-

EXHIBIT 2.10 Selected preferred assessment measures

Structured Interview Methods
The Caretaker Interview (Gelfand & Hartmann, 1984)
Child Behavior Schedule (Hodges et al., 1982)

Behavior Checklists
Child Behavior Checklist (Achenbach & Edelbrock, 1983)
Walker Problem Identification Checklist–Revised (Walker, 1983)
Revised Behavior Problem Checklist (Quay & Petersen, 1983)
Conners Parent and Teacher Checklist (Conners, 1969)
Behavior Rating Profile (Brown & Hammill, 1983)

Behavioral Observation Systems
Response-Discrepancy Observation (Alessi, 1980)
Classroom Observation System (O'Leary, Romanczyk, Kass, Dietz, & Santagrossi, 1979)
CORBEH Observation Systems—RECESS, PASS, CLASS, & PEERS (Greenwood, Guild, & Hops, 1977; Hops, Beickel, & Walker, 1976; Hops & Stevens, 1978; Walker et al., 1978)

Social Skills Checklists
Schools Social Skills Rating Scale (Brown, Black, & Downs, 1984)
The Walker-McConnell Test of Children's Social Skills (Walker & McConnell, 1985)

Nonstandardized Academic Assessment
Curriculum-based probes (teacher-made)
Corrective Reading Placement Test (Engelmann, Carnine, & Johnson, 1978)

Standardized Academic Assessment
Peabody Individual Achievement Test (PIAT) (Dunn & Markwardt, 1970)
California Achievement Test (CAT) (Tiegs & Clarke, 1970)
Metropolitan Achievement Test (MAT) (Balow et al., 1978)
Stanford Achievement Test (SAT) (Gardner et al., 1982)
Stanford Diagnostic Reading Test (Karlsen, Madden, & Gardner, 1977)
Woodcock Reading Mastery Test (Woodcock, 1973)
KeyMath Diagnostic Arithmetic Test (Connolly et al., 1971)
Woodcock–Johnson Psychoeducational Battery (Woodcock & Johnson, 1977)

Adaptive Behavior Scales
Adaptive Behavior Scale (American Association of Mental Deficiency) (Lambert, Windmiller, Cole, & Figueroa, 1974)
Scales for Independent Behavior (Bruininks, Woodcock, Weatherman, & Hill, 1984)
Adaptive Behavior Inventory for Children (Mercer & Lewis, 1978)

Intelligence Tests
Wechsler Intelligence Scales (WISC–R, WIPPSI, WAIS–R) (Wechsler, 1967, 1974, 1981)
Stanford-Binet Intelligence Scale (Terman & Merrill, 1973)
Stanford-Binet Intelligence Scale–Revised (Thorndike, Hagen, & Sattler, 1986)

demic testing, curriculum-based assessment procedures, and a functional assessment of the learning environment. It is important to assess the child's academic skill deficits and performance deficits. The most direct approach is curriculum-based methods that use the child's current academic curriculum. The best approach for performance deficits is a functional assessment of the learning environment, which may include classroom observations, structured interviewing, and a review of permanent products such as the child's academic work. Preferred assessment practices for behavioral, academic, and social skills are summarized in Exhibit 2.10.

Preferred practice suggests that the assessment should be an ongoing process during the course of a special education intervention. All too often a child is assessed, a report is written, and the child is placed—with nothing further except infrequent subjective reports to determine the effectiveness of the placement. Such a limited assessment can leave a child in special education with little data to help determine when the child is ready to leave the program or if the program needs to be changed because it is not effective.

EXHIBIT 2.11   Outline for a preferred assessment strategy

1. Make a referral.
2. Obtain permission to assess from parents.
3. Conduct structured interviews with the teacher, parent, and child.
4. Conduct response-discrepancy behavioral observation in an unstructured and a structured setting.
5. Give behavior problem checklists to teachers and parents.
6. Perform academic assessment, which can include a standardized achievement test, a criterion-referenced academic test, a curriculum-based assessment, and a functional assessment of the learning environment.
7. Perform intellectual assessment, including IQ testing and adaptive behavior scales if retardation or a learning disability is suspected.
8. Perform social skills assessment that includes part of the behavioral observation and a social skills checklist from the teacher or parent.
9. Get a youth report to assess the referral problem from the child's perspective.
10. Hold interdisciplinary team meeting with parents to discuss special services and possible placements.
11. Negotiate individual education plan with the parents for special services or placement.
12. Select on-going assessment measures and include them in the IEP to evaluate the effectiveness of the services or placement.

Preferred assessment practices also involve a multidisciplinary team. A multidisciplinary assessment should be a cooperative process with a common goal of high quality assessment that is complementary instead of fragmentary. The special education teacher should not be the primary person responsible for the entire assessment process. For example, school psychologists can help with formal testing and observations. Social workers can help with interviewing and rating a child's behavior. Classroom aides can help with academic assessment and observation. However, they should all understand that preferred assessment practices require measures with good reliability and validity, use multiple measures to reduce bias errors, and are employed continuously to determine the utility and effectiveness of special interventions (see Exhibit 2.11).

REVIEW QUESTIONS

1. Why is it important to use multiple methods when assessing behaviorally disordered students?
2. Define *continuous assessment* as it relates to teachers of behaviorally disordered students. Why is it important?
3. Design a system for conducting a behavioral observation for noncompliance with teacher's requests, disruptive talk-outs, accuracy on math assignments, tardiness, physical aggression, and academic engaged time.
4. Which assessment model — traditional or behavioral — yields data that are more useful for planning instructional programs? Why?
5. Why is it important to assess the instructional environment? How is this done?
6. Using your own state's definition and classification procedures for behavioral disorders as a guide, state the types of assessment procedures you would use to collect the data necessary for determining eligibility for special education.
7. In the final analysis, in determining eligibility for special education, is clinical judgment our best guide or can we objectively determine whether a student is behaviorally disordered? Explain and support your answer.

REFERENCES

Achenbach, T. M. (1979). The Child Behavior Profile: An empirically based system for assessing children's behavioral problems and competencies. *International Journal of Mental Health, 7,* 24–42.

Achenbach, T. M. (1980). The DSM III classification of psychiatric disorders of infancy, childhood, and adolescence. *Journal of the American Academy of Child Psychiatry, 19,* 395–412.

Achenbach, T. M. (1982). *Developmental psychopathology.* New York: Wiley.

Achenbach, T. M., & Edelbrock, C. (1980). *Child Behavior Checklist — Teacher's report form.* Burlington: University of Vermont, Department of Psychiatry.

Achenbach, T. M., & Edelbrock, C. (1983). *Manual for the Child Behavior Checklist and Revised Child Behavior Profile.* Burlington: University of Vermont, Department of Psychiatry.

Alessi, G. F. (1980). Behavioral observation for the school psychologist: Response-discrepancy model. *School Psychololgy Review, 9,* 31–45.

American Psychiatric Association (1980). *Diagnostic and statistical manual of mental disorders* (DSM III). Washington, DC: Author.

Anastasi, A. (1982). *Psychological testing* (5th ed.). New York: Macmillan.

Asher, S. R., & Hymel, S. (1981). Children's social competence in peer relations: Sociometric and behavioral assessment. In J. Wine & M. Smye (Eds.), *Social competence.* New York: Guilford.

Asher, S. R., & Taylor, A. R. (1981). Social outcomes of mainstreaming: Sociometric assessment and beyond. *Exceptional Education Quarterly, 1,* 13–30.

Atkeson, B. M., & Forehand, R. (1981). Conduct disorders. In E. J. March & L. G. Terdal (Eds.), *Behavioral assessment of childhood disorders.* New York: Guilford.

Balow, H. I., Farr, R., Hogan, T. P., & Prescott, G. A. (1978). *Metropolitan Achievement Test* (5th ed.). San Antonio, TX: Psychological Corp.

Barkley, R. A. (1981). *Hyperactive children: A handbook for diagnosis and treatment.* New York: Guilford.

Bellack, A. S. (1979). A critical appraisal of strategies for assessing social skills. *Behavioral Assessment, 1,* 157–176.

Blankenship, C. S. (1985). Using curriculum-based assessment data to make instructional decisions. *Exceptional Children, 52,* 233–238.

Brigance, A. H. (1978). *Brigance Diagnostic Inventory of Early Development.* Woburn, MA: Curriculum Associates.

Brown, L., & Hammill, D. (1983). *Behavior Rating Profile.* Austin, TX: Pro-Ed.

Brown, L. J., Black, D. D., & Downs, J. C. (1984). *School social skills.* East Aurora, NY: Slosson Educational Publications.

Bruininks, R. H., Woodcock, R. W., Weatherman, R. F., & Hill, B. K. (1984). *Scales for Independent Behavior.* Allen, TX: DLM Teaching Resources.

Chess, S., Thomas, A., Birch, N. G., & Hertzig, M. (1960). Implications of a longitudinal study of child development for child psychiatry. *American Journal of Psychiatry, 117,* 434–441.

Ciminero, A. R., & Drabman, R. S. (1977). Current developments in the behavioral assessment of children. In B. B. Lahey & A. E. Kazdin (Eds.), *Advances in clinical child psychology* (Vol. 1). New York: Plenum Press.

Conners, C. K. (1969). A teacher rating scale for use in drug studies with children. *American Journal of Psychiatry, 126,* 884–888.

Connolly, A., Nachtman, W., & Pritchett, E. (1971). *Manual for the KeyMath Diagnostic Arithmetic Test.* Circle Pines, MN: American Guidance Service.

Cronbach, L. J. (1970). *Essentials of psychological testing* (3rd ed.). New York: Harper & Row.

Cullinan, D., Epstein, M. H., & McLinden, D. (1986). Status and change in state administrative definitions of behavior disorders. *School Psychology, 15,* 383–392.

Deno, S. L. (1980). Direct observation approach to measuring classroom behavior. *Exceptional Children, 46,* 396–399.

Deno, S. L. (1985). Curriculum-based measurement: The emerging alternative. *Exceptional Children, 52,* 219–232.

Deno, S. L. (1986). Formative evaluation of individual school programs: A new role for school psychologists. *School Psychology Review, 15,* 358–374.

Deno, S., & Mirkin, P. (1977). *Data-based program modification: A manual.* Minneapolis: University of Minnesota, Leadership Training Institute/Special Education.

Dunn, L. M., & Markwardt, F. C. (1970). *Peabody Individual Achievement Test.* Circle Pines, MN: American Guidance Service.

Ebel, R. L. (1971). Criterion-referenced measurements: Limitations. *School Review, 79,* 282–288.

Ebel, R. L. (1972). Some limitations of criterion referenced measurement. In G. H. Bracht, K. D. Hopkins, & J. C. Stanley (Eds.), *Perspectives in educational and psychological measurement.* Englewood Cliffs, NJ: Prentice Hall.

Ebel, R. L. (1973). Evaluation and educational objectives. *Journal of Educational Measurement, 10,* 273–279.

Edelbrock, C., Costello, A. J., Dulcan, M. K., Kalas, R., & Conover, N. C. (1985). Age differences in the reliability of the psychiatric interview of the child. *Child Development, 56,* 265–275.

Engelmann, S. (1978). *SRA Corrective Reading Program.* Chicago: Science Research Associates.

Engelmann, S., Carnine, D., & Johnson, G. (1978). *Word attack basics—corrective reading and decoding.* Chicago: Science Research Associates.

Evans, I. M., & Nelson, R. O. (1977). Assessment of child behavior problems. In A. R. Ciminero, K. S. Calhoun, & H. E. Adams (Eds.), *Handbook of behavior assessment.* New York: John Wiley.

Fagley, N. (1984). Behavioral assessment in the schools: Obtaining and evaluating information for individualized programming. *Special Services in the Schools, 1,* 45–57.

Foster, S. L., & Ritchey, W. L. (1979). Issues in the assessment of social competence in children. *Journal of Applied Behavior Analysis, 12,* 625–638.

Gardner, E. R., Rudman, H. C., Karlsen, B., & Merwin, J. C. (1982). *Stanford Achievement Test.* San Antonio, TX: Psychological Corp.

Gelfand, D. M., & Hartmann, D. P. (1984). *Child behavior analysis and therapy* (2nd ed.). New York: Pergamon Press.

Gelfand, D. M., Jenson, W. R., & Drew, C. (in press). *Understanding child behavior disorders* (2nd ed.). New York: Holt, Rinehart and Winston.

Gickling, E. E., & Thompson, V. P. (1985). A personal view of curriculum-based assessment. *Exceptional Children, 52,* 205–218.

Glaser, R. (1963). Instructional technology and the measurement of learning outcome: Some questions. *American Psychologist, 18,* 519–522.

Gottlieb, J., Semmel, M. I., & Veldman, D. J. (1978). Correlates of social status among mainstreamed mentally retarded children. *Journal of Educational Psychology, 70,* 396–405.

Greenwood, C. R., Guild, J. J., & Hops, H. (1977). *Program for Academic Survival Skills (PASS).* Eugene: University of Oregon, Center at Oregon for Research in the Behavioral Education of the Handicapped.

Gresham, F. M. (1981). A model for the behavioral assessment of behavior disorders in children: Measurement consideration and practical application. *Journal of School Psychology, 20,* 131–145.

Gresham, F. M. (1983). Social skills assessment as a component of mainstreaming placement decisions. *Exceptional Children, 49,* 331–336.

Harris, S. L. (1979). DSM III — Its implications for children. *Child Behavior Therapy, 1,* 37–48.

Hartmann, D. P., Roper, B. L., & Bradford, D. C. (1979). Some relationships between behavioral and traditional assessment. *Journal of Behavioral Assessment, 1,* 3–21.

Haynes, S. N., & Jensen, B. J. (1979). The interview as a behavioral assessment instrument. *Behavioral Assessment, 1,* 97–106.

Herjanic, B., Herjanic, M., Brown, G., & Wheatt, T. (1977). Are children reliable reporters? *Journal of Abnormal Child Psychology, 3,* 41–48.

Herjanic, B., & Reich, W. (1982). Development of a structured psychiatric interview for children: Agreement between child and parent on individual symptoms. *Journal of Abnormal Child Psychology, 10,* 307–324.

Hodges, K., Kline, J., Kashani, D., Cytyrn, L., Stern, L., & McKnew, D. (1982). *Child assessment survey.* Unpublished manuscript, University of Missouri.

Holland, C. J. (1970). An interview guide for behavioral counseling with parents. *Behavior Therapy, 1,* 70–79.

Hops, H. (1982). Behavioral assessment of exceptional children's social development. In P. S. Strain (Ed.), *Social development of exceptional children.* Rockville, MD: Aspen Systems Corp.

Hops, H., Beickel, S. L., & Walker, H. (1976). *Contingencies for learning academic and social skills (CLASS).* Eugene: University of Oregon, Center at Oregon for Research in the Behavioral Education of the Handicapped.

Hops, H., & Greenwood, C. R. (1981). Social skills deficits. In E. J. Mash & L. G. Terdal (Eds.), *Behavioral assessment of childhood disorders.* New York: Guilford.

Hops, H., & Stevens, T. (1978). *PEERS observation training manual.* Eugene: University of Oregon, Center at Oregon for Research in the Behavioral Education of the Handicapped.

Howell, K. W. (1986). Direct assessment of academic performance. *School Psychology Review, 15,* 324–335.

Idol, L., Nevin, A., & Paolucci-Whitcomb, P. (1986). *Practices in curriculum-based assessment.* Rockville, MD: Aspen Systems Corp.

Jastak, J. F., & Jastak, S. R. (1965). *Wide Range Achievement Test.* Wilmington, DE: Guidance Associates.

Jenkins, R. J., & Pany, D. (1978). Standardized achievement tests: How useful for special education. *Exceptional Children, 44,* 448–453.

Jenson, W. R., Reavis, K., Rhode, G., Clare, S., & Evans, C. (1986). *Prescriptive checklist for behaviorally disordered students.* Unpublished manuscript.

Karlsen, B., Madden, R., & Gardner, E. F. (1977). *Stanford Diagnostic Reading Test.* New York: Harcourt Brace Jovanovich.

Kazdin, A. E. (1981). Drawing valid inferences from case studies. *Journal of Consulting and Clinical Psychology, 49,* 183–192.

Kesler, J., & Jenson, W. R. (1986). *Children's behavior therapy observation codes.* Salt Lake City: Salt Lake Mental Health.

Lambert, N. M., & Sandoval, J. (1980). The prevalence of learning disabilities in a sample of children considered hyperactive. *Journal of Abnormal Child Psychology, 8,* 33–50.

Lambert, N. M., Windmiller, M., Cole, L., & Figueroa, R. (1974). *AAMD Adaptive Behavior Scale—Public school version.* Washington, DC: American Association of Mental Deficiency.

Lentz, F. E., & Shapiro, E. (1986). Functional assessment of the academic environment. *School Psychology Review, 15,* 346–357.

Lidz, C. S. (1979). Criterion referenced assessment: The new bandwagon? *Exceptional Children, 46,* 131–132.

Lidz, C. S. (1981). *Improving assessment of schoolchildren.* San Francisco: Jossey Bass.

MacMillan, D. L., & Morrison, G. M. (1980). Correlates of social status among mildly handicapped learners in self-contained special classes. *Journal of Educational Psychology, 72,* 437–444.

Mash, E. J. (1979). What is behavioral assessment? *Behavioral Assessment, 1,* 23–29.

Mash, E. J., & Terdal, L. G. (1981). Behavioral assessment of childhood disturbance. In E. J. Mash & L. G. Terdal (Eds.), *Behavior assessment of childhood disorders.* New York: Guilford.

McConnell, S. R., & Odom, S. L. (1986). Sociometrics: Peer-referenced measures and the assessment of social competence. In P. S. Strain, M. J. Guralnick, & H. M. Walker (Eds.), *Children's social behavior: Development, assessment, and modification.* New York: Academic Press.

McCord, J., & McCord, W. (1961). Cultural stereotypes and the validity of interviews for research in child development. *Child Development, 32,* 171–185.

McGinnis, E., Kiraly, J., & Smith, C. R. (1984). The types of data used in identifying public school students as behaviorally disordered. *Behavioral Disorders, 9,* 239–246.

McReynolds, P. (1968). An introduction to psychological assessment. In P. Mc-Reynolds (Ed.), *Advances in psychological assessment* (Vol. 1). Palo Alto, CA: Science and Behavioral Books.

Mercer, J. R., & Lewis, J. F. (1978). *System of Multicultural Pluralistic Assessment (SOMPA).* New York: Psychological Corp.

Mischel, W. (1968). *Personality assessment.* New York: John Wiley.

Mischel, W. (1979). On the interface of cognition and personality: Beyond the person-situation debate. *American Psychologist, 34,* 740–754.

Nay, R. W. (1979). *Multimethod clinical assessment.* New York: Gardner Press.

O'Leary, K. D. (1979). Behavioral assessment. *Behavioral Assessment, 1,* 31–36.

O'Leary, K. D., & Johnson, S. B. (1979). Psychological assessment. In H. C. Quay & J. S. Werry (Eds.), *Psychopathological disorders of children* (2nd ed.). New York: John Wiley.

O'Leary, K. D., Romanczyk, R. G., Kass, R. E., Dietz, A., & Santagrossi, D. (1971). *Procedures for classroom observation of teachers and children.* Unpublished manuscript.

Patterson, G. R. (1982). *Coercive family process.* Eugene, OR: Castalia.

Popham, W. J. (1978). The case for criterion referenced measurements. *Educational Researcher, 7,* 6–10.

Quay, H. C., & Petersen, D. R. (1975). *Manual for the Problem Behavior Checklist.* Unpublished paper.

Quay, H. C., & Petersen, D. R. (1983). *Manual for the Revised Problem Behavior Checklist.* Unpublished paper.

Reich, W., Herjanic, B., Welner, Z., & Gandy, P. R. (1982). Development of a structured psychiatric interview for children: Agreement on diagnosis comparing child and parent interviews. *Journal of Abnormal Child Psychology, 10,* 325–336.

Reid, J. B. (1978). *A social learning approach to family intervention: Observation in the home setting* (Vol. 2). Eugene, OR: Castalia.

Rutter, M., & Shaffer, D. (1980). DSM III: A step forward or backward in terms of the classification of child psychiatric disorders. *Journal of the American Academy of Child Psychiatry, 19,* 371–394.

Rutter, M., & Yule, W. (1973). Specific reading retardation. In L. Mann & D. Sabatino (Eds.), *The first review of special education.* Philadelphia: Buttonwood Farms.

Salvia, J., & Ysseldyke, J. E. (1978). *Assessment in special education and remedial education.* Boston: Houghton Mifflin.

Salvia, J., & Ysseldyke, J. E. (1985). *Assessment in special education and remedial education* (3rd ed.). Boston: Houghton Mifflin.

Schacht, T., & Nathan, P. E. (1977). But is it good for psychologists? Appraisal and status of the DSM III. *American Psychologist, 32,* 1017–1025.

Shapiro, E. S., & Lentz, F. E. (1985). Assessing academic behavior: A behavioral approach. *School Psychology Review, 14,* 325–338.

Shapiro, E. S., & Lentz, F. E. (1986). Behavioral assessment of academic skills. In T. R. Kratochwill (Ed.), *Advances in school psychology* (Vol. 5). Hillsdale, NJ: Lawrence Erlbaum.

Smith, C., Frank, A., & Snider, B. (1984). School psychologists' and teachers' perceptions of data used in the identification of behaviorally disordered students. *Behavioral Disorders, 10,* 27–32.

Sulzer-Azaroff, B., & Mayer, R. G. (1986). *Achieving educational excellence.* New York: Holt, Rinehart and Winston.

Swanson, H. L., & Watson, B. L. (1982). *Educational and psychological assessment of exceptional children: Theories, strategies, and applications.* Columbus, OH: Merrill.

Terman, L., & Merrill, M. (1973). *Stanford-Binet Intelligence Scale, 1972 Norms Edition.* Boston: Houghton Mifflin.

Thorndike, R. L., Hagen, E. P., & Sattler, J. M. (1986). *The Stanford-Binet Intelligence Scale — Revised.* Chicago: Riverside.

Tiegs, E. W., & Clarke, W. W. (1970). *California Achievement Test.* Monterey, CA: CTB/McGraw-Hill.

Tucker, J. A. (1985). Curriculum-based assessment: An introduction. *Exceptional Children, 52,* 199–204.

VanHasselt, V. B., Hersen, M., & Bellack, A. S. (1981). The validity of role play tests for assessing social skills in children. *Behavior Therapy, 12,* 202–216.

Wahler, R. G., & Cromier, W. H. (1970). The ecological interview: A first step to out-patient child behavior therapy. *Journal of Behavior Therapy and Experimental Psychiatry, 1,* 279–289.

Waksman, S., & Jones, V. (1985). *A suggested procedure for the identification and provision of services to seriously emotionally disturbed students* (Technical Assistance Paper #5). Salem: Oregon Department of Education.

Walker, H. M. (1983). *Walker Problem Behavior Identification Checklist–Revised.* Los Angeles: Western Psychological Services.

Walker, H. M., & Fabre, T. R. (in press). Assessment of behavior disorders in the school settings: Issues, problems, and strategies revisited. In N. Haring (Ed.), *Measuring and managing behavior disorders.* Seattle: University of Washington Press.

Walker, H. M., McConnell, S., Holmes, D., Todis, B., Walker, J., & Golden, N. (1983). *The Walker Social Skills Curriculum.* Austin, TX: Pro-Ed.

Walker, H. M., Severson, H., & Haring, N. (1985). *Standardized screening and identification of behavior disordered pupils in the elementary age range: Rationale, procedures, and guidelines.* Eugene: University of Oregon.

Walker, H. M., Street, A., Garrett, B., Crossen, J., Hops, H., & Greenwood, C. R. (1978). *Reprogramming environmental contingencies for effective social skills (RECESS): Consultant manual.* Eugene: University of Oregon, Center at Oregon for Research in the Behavioral Education of the Handicapped.

Wechsler, D. (1967). *Manual for the Wechsler Preschool and Primary Scale of Intelligence.* New York: Psychological Corp.

Wechsler, D. (1974). *Manual for the Wechsler Intelligence Scale for Children — Revised.* New York: Psychological Corp.

Wechsler, D. (1981). *Manual for the Wechsler Adult Intelligence Scale.* San Antonio, TX: Psychological Corp.

Wenar, C., & Coulter, J. B. (1962). A reliability study of developmental histories. *Child Development, 33,* 453–462.

Wood, F. H., Smith, C. R., & Grimes, J. (Eds.). (1985). *The Iowa assessment model in behavioral disorders: A training manual.* Des Moines: Iowa State Department of Public Instruction.

Woodcock, R. W. (1973). *Woodcock Reading Mastery Tests.* Circle Pines, MN: American Guidance Service.

Woodcock, R. W., & Johnson, M. B. (1977). *Woodcock-Johnson Psychoeducational Battery.* Hingham, MA: Teaching Resources.

Ysseldyke, J., Algozzine, B., & Epps, S. (1982). A logical and empirical analysis of current practices in classifying students as handicapped. *Exceptional Children, 49,* 160–166.

Ysseldyke, J., Algozzine, B., Richey, L., & Graden, J. (1982). Declaring students eligible for learning disability services: Why bother with the data? *Learning Disability Quarterly, 5,* 37–44.

Ysseldyke, J. E., & Christenson, S. L. (1987). *The Instructional Environment Scale: A comprehensive methodology for assessing an individual student's instruction.* Austin, TX: Pro-Ed.

Ysseldyke, J., Christenson, S., Pianta, B., & Algozzine, B. (1983). An analysis of teachers' reasons and desired outcomes for students referred for psychoeducational assessment. *Journal of Psychoeducational Assessment, 1,* 73–83.

3 Basic Principles of Behavior Management

After completing this chapter, you should be able to

- *Discuss the assumptions underlying this chapter's approach to behavior management.*
- *Define functional analysis of behavior and three-term contingency.*
- *Describe basic procedures that can be used to increase or decrease behavior.*
- *Explain why reinforcement and punishment are defined in terms of their effects on behavior.*
- *Identify factors that influence the effectiveness of reinforcement and punishment procedures.*
- *Define positive educational programming.*

A reasonable level of order and control is needed in a classroom before teachers can effectively teach their students. Problems such as poor attending skills, disobedience, and poor motivation to learn can significantly reduce student learning. More serious problems, such as aggression, tantrums, noncompliance, and school vandalism, can produce chaos and disorganization. It doesn't take too many children fighting, talking out and disturbing the class, or defying the teacher before order and control are lost.

Teachers need effective and practical strategies to help manage problem behavior. The focus of this chapter will be on those preferred practices that teachers can use in regular, resource, and self-contained classrooms to produce orderly and productive learning environments. The term used to describe these practices is *behavior management.* The chapter begins with a discussion of the assumptions underlying our approach to behavior management, followed by a review of the importance of functional analysis of the behavior in behavior management strategies. Two major types of behavior management interventions are presented: procedures to increase behavior (reinforcement, shaping, modeling) and procedures to decrease behavior (time-out, overcorrection, response cost).

ASSUMPTIONS OF BEHAVIOR MANAGEMENT

Many of the assumptions underlying a behavior management approach overlap the assumptions of the behavioral assessment model outlined in chapter 2. The behavioral model holds that a child's past learning experiences and biological make-up are important to understanding that child's current performance. However, the significance of assumed underlying emotional causes, which are impossible to measure directly, is deemphasized. Measurable and observable behaviors are the main building blocks of behavior management approaches.

Another central assumption is that both normal and abnormal behavior are lawfully governed by the same principles. The science of behavior becomes unnecessarily complex if we assume that different principles and variables control abnormal behavior. The variables that affect both abnormal and normal behaviors fall into four basic categories: genetic-constitutional factors, past learning, current physiological state, and current environmental conditions (Ross & Nelson, 1979). Genetics and past learning are very difficult to change with current scientific techniques. However, current physiological and environmental conditions and their effects on behavior can be changed. For example, a vitamin deficiency or an allergy that makes the problem behaviors of a child worse can be remediated with a vitamin supplement or diet change. Similarly, tantrumming behavior that is consistently rewarded by a teacher's attention can be changed by changing the environment. Behaviors that at one time were assumed to be primarily biologically caused, such as epileptic seizures (Mostofsky & Balaschak, 1977), chronic bed-wetting (Doleys, 1977), asthma (Sirota & Mahoney, 1974), colitis (Yonnell & McCullough, 1975), and juvenile diabetes (Melamed & Johnson, 1981), have been helped by environmental interventions.

There are very few instances where the cause of a behavior problem can be solely attributed to biology or environment. Instead, they interact. The biological make-up of each individual sets certain limits on behavior, and much of the behavior that occurs within those limits is controlled by the contingencies of the environment and the principles of learning.

The behavior management approach assumes that the best way to discover the contingencies that govern behavior is through the scientific method (Ross & Nelson, 1979). The scientific method requires (a) hypotheses to be generated, (b) experiments to be designed to test the hypotheses, (c) empirical data to be gathered objectively, and (d) the results to be openly and fairly evaluated. This method involves a series of experiments in which behavior (the dependent variable) is carefully measured and observed while under the effects of a series of interventions (the independent variable). Not all of the interventions will produce significant changes in behavior. They must be tested and the ineffective ones abandoned. A process of hypothesized interventions, data collection, trial and error, and chance comes into play in testing interventions. Only after the scientific homework has been done will a set of procedures and principles emerge that form a technology of behavior change. At this point we do not have a complete set of behavior management principles for every behavior problem in every situation. However, there is enough of a technology that we can make major positive changes in the management of childhood behavior problems in educational settings.

Like the field in general, working with an individual student involves using the scientific method to evaluate and change a behavior management program. Work with individual cases requires a fine-tuning approach in which a series of interventions may be tried before the most effective procedure is identified. There are no single "silver bullets" that work for the same problem each and every time in an educational setting. Children differ in their learning history, biological make-up, and the particular environmental conditions that contribute to behavior. The best way to identify an effective and preferred technique is to apply the scientific method for each case individually. For example, a teacher could choose a promising technique from the research literature and apply it in a specific situation. Empirical data are collected to assess if the technique is practical and if it significantly changes the child's behavior. If the technique is too expensive in time or resources for the corresponding behavior change, then the technique is replaced by a more efficient and cost-effective one. If the technique is cost effective but does not significantly change the child's behavior, it is discontinued for a more effective technique.

The last assumption of behavior management is that each case must be treated individually to determine the variables that actually change behavior. Behavior management programs must be constantly monitored to ensure success. An objective evaluation of an intervention requires that a teacher have a working knowledge of continuous assessment procedures and understand the principles associated with a functional analysis of behavior. The evaluation of behavior management techniques is not simply another procedure added to an intervention. Instead, evaluation is an integral part. Starting an intervention without a plan for evaluation is like shooting in the dark at a moving target. The intervention will be incomplete and will very likely fail if on-going data are not collected to verify its effectiveness. Exhibit 3.1 summarizes the assumptions of behavior management discussed here.

THE FUNCTIONAL ANALYSIS OF BEHAVIOR

The rules that govern behavior are called *behavioral principles* or *functions*. Webster (*Webster's New World Dictionary,* 1960) defines a *function* as "a variable quantity whose value depends on and varies with another quantity or quantities." In a *functional analysis of behavior* (Ferster, 1965), a behavior varies in value depending upon changes in the environment. The function is explained by a *three-term contingency* consisting of *antecedents* (what comes before the behavior), the *behavior,* and the *consequence* (what follows the behavior) (Bijou, Petersen, Harris, Allen, & Johnston, 1969; Paine, Radicchi, Rosellini, Deutchman, & Darch, 1983). This has been called the A, B, C (A = antecedent; B = behavior; C = conse-

EXHIBIT 3.1   Assumptions of behavior management

1. Behaviors that are observable and measurable are the targets for change rather than underlying causes, which are difficult or impossible to measure.
2. Both normal and abnormal behavior follow the laws of nature and are controlled by essentially the same variables.
3. Past learning histories, genetics, and physiological variables set limits on behavior; however, many behaviors that occur within these limits are controlled by the principles of learning and environmental contingencies.
4. The scientific method with empirical data is the only reliable way to establish which interventions effectively change behavior.
5. The interventions that are validated as being effective by the scientific method form a group of procedures or a technology of behavior change.
6. Not all the procedures that form a technology of behavior change are effective in every situation with every child. Rather, each technique must be tested individually until an effective technique is identified.
7. Applications of behavior management techniques require constant monitoring and assessment to insure their effectiveness.

quence) function of behavior (see Exhibit 3.2). The environmental antecedents that precede the behavior actually set the occasion for the behavior. Behavior is the important variable of observable and measurable change. The consequence increases or decreases the frequency of the behavior (Gelfand, Jenson, & Drew, in press).

For example, a teacher might turn his or her back to the class to write on the blackboard, leave the class for an emergency, or require a substitute teacher because of illness. In a functional analysis, we say that all of these instances might serve as an antecendent for some students to become disruptive by leaving their seats, talking out, or disobeying. These behaviors were preceded by the teacher diverting attention or being absent from the classroom. Understanding the antecedents of a problem behavior in terms of which people are present or absent, the

EXHIBIT 3.2   The ABCs of a functional analysis of behavior

A	**B**	**C**
Antecedents	**Target Behaviors**	**Consequences**
1. People	1. To increase	1. Positive reinforcers
2. Times of the day	2. To decrease	2. Negative reinforcers
3. Events	3. Observable	3. Punishers
4. Special environments	4. Measurable	

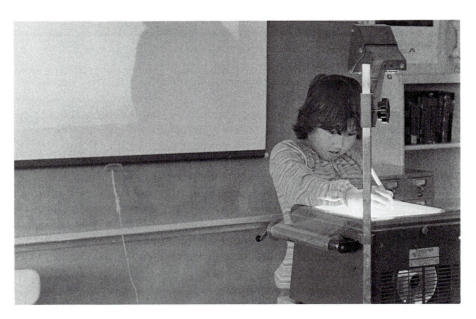

There is a functional relationship between student behavior and the instructional environment.

time of day, and the physical environment (structured classroom, transition time, or unstructured play time) can greatly enhance the effectiveness of a behavior management program. If antecedents can be changed or manipulated, then in some instances a problem behavior can be changed (see Pointer 3.1).

The behavior component of a functional analysis of behavior is critically important to the successful implementation and evaluation of a behavior management procedure. The B in the ABC equation is often referred to as a *target behavior* because it is the target or reason for the program. Specifically defining the target behaviors requires that the behavior be observable, measurable, and repeatable (Alberto & Troutman, 1986; Jenson, Sloane, & Young, in press). If a behavior cannot be seen or measured by two or more people, then it is impossible to know when to apply an intervention or how effective the intervention has been. The behavior must also be repeatable (happen more than once).

Common behavior problems are sometimes expressed in ways that do not meet these criteria. For example, "poor attitude," "lack of responsibility," "poor self-esteem," and "immaturity" are all ambiguous descriptions for specific behaviors that could be defined in more observable and measurable terms. Poor responsibility might refer to a child who is chronically late for class, one who does not respond when called on in class, or one who seldom hands in assigned academic work unless prompted.

Pointer 3.1

SILKY AND THE THUMBSUCKING KID

Jason was a real 5-year-old well-adjusted boy with only one bad habit: He liked to suck his thumb and hold his blanket. As a matter of fact, Jason's blanket, Silky, was about the most important object he owned. He could not sleep without Silky, and whenever anxious, Jason would search frantically until he found Silky. Jason's dentist, however, was concerned about his new permanent teeth and the constant thumbsucking that Jason did while he held Silky. Some of the other children in the neighborhood had also started to make fun of Jason's blanket and thumbsucking so Jason's father decided to try to stop those behaviors.

His father noticed that Jason always picked up Silky first and started to stroke the blanket (the antecedent) before he popped his thumb in his mouth (the behavior). While Jason was watching television or having stories read to him, or if he was anxious because of some event, he would pick up Silky and then start to suck his thumb. The father decided to see if he could get Jason to give up Silky voluntarily and see if that would decrease his thumbsucking. If Jason always picked up and stroked Silky before sucking his thumb, Jason's father reasoned that having the blanket out of the picture might stop the thumbsucking. If this strategy worked, the father would have reduced both socially stigmatizing behaviors and would not have to intervene directly with the thumbsucking.

Jason's father decided to make a contract with him about the blanket and took Jason to his favorite toy store to look at new toys. The deal offered was that Jason could have the toy of his choice (up to $35.00) if he would give up Silky permanently. When Jason heard the deal he immediately began searching for Silky and started to suck his thumb! However, over the next 2 weeks, Jason asked to go back to the toy store several times and "look." Jason was thinking, and one day he announced that he was big now and was willing to give Silky up. He selected a toy spaceship that cost $34.95 and handed the blanket to his father. The father stored the blanket in a safe place in case Jason had a blanket fit; however, that never happened. A couple of times Jason asked where Silky was and the father told him that the blanket was gone for a very long time. To Jason's parents' relief, he never again sucked his thumb. He had such a conditioned habit that having the blanket gone disrupted the thumbsucking chain permanently. By taking the antecedent away, the target behavior was stopped without a direct intervention. Jason's parents also socially reinforced him for not sucking his thumb after Silky was gone, a strategy that had never worked while Silky was around.

Target behaviors are generally measured by direct behavioral observation or by an analysis of permanent products (see chapter 2). Data on target behaviors are generally collected as a frequency (event), by duration or latency (time), or as an event within an interval. The teacher, an aide, or the child may collect the data. *Permanent products* are not directly observed but, instead, are enduring changes in the environment that leave physical evidence (Sulzer-Azaroff & Mayer, 1986).

Target behaviors for behavior management programs fall into three general problem areas (Bijou & Petersen, 1971; Kanfer & Saslow, 1965). *Response excesses* occur too often and are, therefore, a problem for a classroom. Behaviors such as tantrums, noncompliance, talking back to adults, and high motor activity are all problems of excess. Teachers frequently associate these problem behaviors with behavioral disorders in children (Walker, 1982). The second class of problem behaviors is *response deficits.* These behaviors do not occur frequently enough to ensure a child's adjustment. Examples of response deficits include infrequent social interaction with other children, infrequent and inaccurate academic work, and delayed language skills. Third, *stimulus control* problems occur when an appropriate behavior is emitted in an inappropriate environment. For example, laughing at a friend's jokes at lunch is generally considered appropriate. However, to start to laugh during a serious classroom lecture and to continue to laugh day after day would be inappropriate.

As we saw in chapter 1, most of the problems that mental health specialists and educators consider abnormal or deviant in behaviorally disordered children are exhibited by most normal children at some point in their lives. For example, all children are sexually curious, tell lies, become aggressive, throw tantrums, or occasionally do not interact well socially with their peers. These behaviors are tolerated as long as the quantity, intensity, and appropriateness remain within acceptable limits. Generally, it is not the bizarreness or strangeness of a behavior, but rather its frequency or inappropriate setting, that leads to labeling a child as behaviorally disordered.

The last element of the ABC function is the consequence that follows the behavior. Consequences that act as rewards or *positive reinforcers* for the behavior will increase the strength of the behavior (Skinner, 1953). Positive reinforcers can take the form of material things such as food, money, or toys; activities such as games, recess, or sports; and social reinforcement such as attention from a teacher or recognition from peers. In essence, positive reinforcement is anything that a child will increase a behavior to obtain. In contrast, *negative reinforcement* is anything (material, activity, or social) that a child will increase a behavior to avoid or escape. For example, if a child increased his rate of homework completion to avoid going to bed early, going to bed early would be a negative reinforcer. Both positive and negative reinforcers *increase* the frequency of a behavior.

This effect is contrasted with *punishment,* which decreases the frequency of a behavior by applying some type of noxious stimulus (Azrin & Holz, 1966). For example, if a teacher's praise and attention for a child's appropriate behavior reduce its frequency, then praise and attention are punishing stimuli. A very common mistake is to believe that we know exactly which stimuli reinforce or punish a child without observing the child's behavior. The same stimulus can be a reinforcer at one time and a punisher at another time. The category into which we put a particular stimulus depends on whether the child's behavior increases or decreases. The rest of this chapter will deal primarily with the use of consequences to increase or decrease behaviors in educational settings.

BEHAVIOR MANAGEMENT INTERVENTIONS

Again, the basic procedures that constitute the technology of behavior management can be divided into procedures that increase behaviors and procedures that decrease behaviors. With behaviorally disordered students there is frequently a tendency to focus on behaviors that disturb a classroom and, therefore, should be reduced. It is, however, a mistake to decrease problem behaviors without simultaneously increasing appropriate behaviors as replacements for them. An annoying behavior may serve a practical purpose for the child and need to be replaced with appropriate behaviors that serve a similar purpose. Few things could be more unethical in the treatment of children than to teach them only how to be still, quiet, and docile (Winett & Winkler, 1972).

Many of the behavior problems seen in a classroom are a function of children's not knowing how to behave appropriately and effectively. Others are a reaction to inadequate or frustrating instruction. For each behavior that is to be decreased, an appropriate replacement behavior should be increased. The antecedents and consequences of inappropriate behaviors should be assessed and understood so that replacement behaviors serve primarily the same function as the inappropriate behaviors but in a socially appropriate way.

INCREASING APPROPRIATE BEHAVIORS

We have already stressed that behaviorally disordered students demonstrate many behaviors that interfere with school learning and that it is easy to focus on reducing these disruptive behaviors. However, these students do not make meaningful educational progress unless they are taught skills that increase their overall adaptation to school.

We must also distinguish between increasing new behaviors that a student has not mastered (acquisition) and increasing the frequency of behaviors that a student has mastered but may be reluctant or unmotivated to perform (maintenance). Acquisition and maintenance are closely linked because new skills are developed by modifying and practicing skills that have already been mastered. For example, many academic skills, such as reading and arithmetic, build on simple skills that are modified and expanded. In addition, a skill acquired and maintained in one setting will need to be applied to new settings, people, and times (generalization). A reading skill learned and mastered with one teacher in a morning reading group will be expanded to different classrooms (settings), different periods of the day (times), and different teachers (people). A program to increase prosocial behaviors and academic skills in behaviorally disordered children should take into account acquisition, maintenance, and generalization of those behaviors to be a preferred practice.

Reinforcement

Certain events, foods, activities, and material objects are pleasurable to children, and children are willing to work to obtain them. A problem occurs, however, in that all children are not interested in the same things. One child may love sports activities while another child may dislike sports and prefer something else. Even with the same child, the value of a reward may change over time. It is a mistake to try one type of reward with a child and, when the child is not interested in it, proclaim that all rewards and reinforcers have failed. Every child is interested in earning *some* type of reward or reinforcer. The trick is to find out what.

Because children are so different in their likes and dislikes, it is impossible to specify which stimuli will be positive reinforcers. They can only be defined in terms of their *effects on behavior*. According to Skinner (1953), a positive reinforcer is any event that follows a response that increases the probability that the response will be repeated. This definition allows a reinforcer to be anything that increases the strength, number, frequency, percentage, duration, or amount of a behavior (Favell, 1977). In positive reinforcement, a behavior is followed by receiving something—perhaps food, water, or sleep. Some stimuli are neutral in that they have no direct effect on behavior. However, if they are paired with a primary reinforcer, they may acquire reinforcing properties over time. These *secondary* or *conditioned reinforcers* can include social rewards, money, grades, and stickers.

The only way we can tell if a stimulus is truly positive and rewarding is if the behavior that it follows increases in strength and is repeated. If the behavior stays the same or decreases in frequency or strength, then the event is not a reinforcer. One of the most common mistakes is to assume an event or stimulus is or is not a reinforcer. Some of the events that many educators assume are not reinforcers are "a good talking to," "being sent home or to the principal's office," or "yelling at a child for being out of the seat." However, if after yelling at child he is out of his seat more often than before, then this assumed negative event is actually a positive reinforcer. That is, the quality of reinforcement is defined by an event's functional relationship to the event it follows.

Assessing Reinforcers

To assess possible positive reinforcers, a teacher can have a child identify what he or she would like to earn. However, the teacher should explain that expense and the time involved must be kept to a minimum. There are a number of low-cost, low-time-investment reinforcers for behaviorally disordered children. Tourigny-Dewhurst and Cautela (1980) surveyed a number of children who had been labeled *behaviorally disturbed, learning disabled, autistic, mentally retarded,* or *developmentally disabled.* The children ranged from 5 to 12 years of age. They divided 100 possible reinforcers into 50 food and 50 nonfood reinforcers. Exhibit 3.3 identifies the 10 most valued food and nonfood reinforcers for each of three age categories. Food items that were rated in the top 10 for all three age categories included cookies, french fries, ice cream, and pudding. For the nonfood items, only stickers were rated by all three age groups as preferred. The results suggest strong age differences for nonfood reinforcers. It should be noted that these items are only *possible* reinforcers that have some likelihood of being valued by children of different ages. Again, the only way to be sure if an item is a reinforcer for an individual child is to see if it works—if the child will work to gain access to it.

A second method for determining which items are reinforcing for a child is simply to observe the child in an unrestricted, natural setting. The things the child does frequently are reinforcing, and the things that the child does less frequently are less reinforcing. Grandmothers have known this principle for ages. More importantly, they have realized that if access to a high frequency behavior depends upon engaging in a low frequency behavior, then the low frequency behavior will increase. For example, using "Grandma's principle," many children have been made to eat their peas (low frequency) before they are given ice cream (high frequency). This principle, formally known as the "Premack principle" (Premack, 1959), states that

> If two behaviors are observed to occur at different rates in the natural, unrestricted environment, the opportunity to engage in the more frequent behavior can be used as a positive reinforcer to increase the rate of the less frequent behavior. (Favell, 1977, p. 91)

EXHIBIT 3.3   Food and nonfood reinforcers most frequently preferred by a group of special needs children

		Food Reinforcers						
		Ages					Ages	
Item	5–6	7–9	10–12	Item	5–6	7–9	10–12
1. Apples	70	98*	72	26. Ice cube	65	83	78
2. Bananas	93*	92	78	27. Jello	72	95	80
3. Cake	80	97	87	28. Koolaid	79	97	67
4. Cereal—milk	59	63	72	29. Lollipop	94*	96	74
5. Cereal—dry	55	49	38	30. Milk	59	78	74
6. Cheese	72	103*	88	31. Milkshake	111*	97	101*
7. Cheeseburger	62	92	82	32. Orange	54	90	69
8. Cheesecracker	70	71	73	33. Peach	89	94	71
9. Cherry	83	98*	75	34. Pears	88	100*	76
10. Chewing gum	59	86	70	35. Pickle	60	72	69
11. Chocolate bar	85	93	74	36. Pie	88	95	73
12. Chocolate milk	88	92	73	37. Plums	46	73	68
13. Cookie	102*	105*	92*	38. Popcorn	66	94	87
14. Corn chip	57	82	68	39. Popsicle	94*	102*	71
15. Cracker jacks	90	65	89*	40. Potato chips	97*	90	78
16. Donuts	67	100*	87	41. Pretzel	88	70	86
17. French fries	109*	111*	103*	42. Pudding	93*	101*	100*
18. Fruit juice	80	102*	70	43. Raisin	68	81	96*
19. Fudgsicle	73	91	68	44. Saltines	67	58	61
20. Graham cracker	86	86	72	45. Soda	96*	90	98*
21. Gumdrops	88	79	72	46. Strawberry	70	94	89*
22. Hamburger	82	96	100*	47. Sugar cone	88	84	63
23. Hot chocolate	84	83	66	48. Water	76	89	77
24. Hot dog	92	95	84	49. Watermelon	70	94	80
25. Ice cream	107*	113*	105*	50. Yogurt	83	76	81
Mean	79.08	88.70	76.72				
Median	80.00	92.16	75.50				
Range	67	64	65				

*Ranks as one of top ten preferred items

Source: From "A Proposed Reinforcement Survey for Special Needs Children" by D. L. Tourigny-Dewhurst and J. R. Cautela, 1980, *Journal of Behavior Therapy and Experimental Psychiatry, 11,* 109–112. Copyright 1980, Pergamon Press, Ltd. Reprinted with permission.

EXHIBIT 3.3

continued

	Nonfood Reinforcers							
		Ages					Ages	
Item	5–6	7–9	10–12		Item	5–6	7–9	10–12
1. Aquarium	105*	94	98*		26. Play ball	82	84	68
2. Bells	65	73	35		27. Play drum	74	88	61
3. Bicycle	106*	100*	78		28. Play horn	69	63	55
4. Blocks	74	68	38		29. Pull toys	42	56	12
5. Blow bubbles	101*	99*	63		30. Puppets	69	85	71
6. Books	64	88	78		31. Puzzles	102*	79	78
7. Camera	94	98*	88		32. Radio (listen)	46	81	79
8. Chalkboard	63	107*	51		33. Records (listen)	76	94	110*
9. Cars—trucks	75	88	49		34. Rhythm sticks	74	72	40
10. Clay	67	89	68		35. Sandbox	110*	70	43
11. Climbing	99*	96	57		36. Singing	73	90	87
12. Coloring	77	101*	93*		37. Shaving cream	79	49	28
13. Dolls	74	66	59		38. Stay up late	88	85	98*
14. Eat out	91	97	84		39. Stickers	101*	100*	98*
15. Fingerpaint	78	93	61		40. Swimming	99*	111*	64
16. Go to park	91	89	85		41. Swinging	94	97*	77
17. Go to store	91	98*	77		42. Tape recorder	97	71	107*
18. Gym	99*	110*	92		43. Television	99*	97	96*
19. Legos	88	88	72		44. Time with adult	91	77	101*
20. Magnifying glass	66	79	83		45. Tinker toys	65	81	20
21. Music box	72	77	57		46. Toy telephone	83	71	37
22. Paint—brush	78	97	82		47. Typewriter	85	92	96*
23. Pegboard	63	70	46		48. Waterplay	91	65	56
24. Play—kids	86	66	93*		49. Workbench	65	65	29
25. Play-doh	93	91	69		50. Zoo	95	89	95*
Mean	80.20	84.68	70.44					
Median	82.50	88.00	72.50					
Range	68	62	98					

Educational applications of the Premack principle are used almost naturally by good teachers and include such contingencies as "Do your math assignment before you go to recess" and "Increase your positive interactions with other children before you play alone."

Some important points need to be highlighted concerning the use of the Premack principle in the classroom. First, the behaviors that are used as positive reinforcers need only meet the requirement that they are more frequent than the target behavior that you want to increase. It is not the behavior or activity in itself that is important, but instead the natural frequency of the behavior relative to a second, target behavior. If working on spelling words occurs at a low frequency, but working on math problems occurs even less frequently, then the rate or frequency of doing math problems will increase if the child must do them before being allowed to do the spelling words (Konarski, 1982). Second, the Premack principle depends on the assessment of the frequencies of behaviors occurring in natural and unrestricted settings. If the setting is artificial and the child's behaviors are guided or restricted, then it may be difficult to assess the natural frequencies of the behaviors.

Reinforcement Effectiveness

Several factors affect the ability of positive reinforcers to strengthen a target behavior. *Immediacy* is critical in maximizing the effectiveness of positive reinforcement (Skinner, 1938; Sulzer-Azaroff & Mayer, 1986). When a reinforcer is delayed, other behaviors occur between the end of the target behavior and the reinforcement. These intervening behaviors may also be inadvertently reinforced and increase in strength (Reynolds, 1968). In this situation, the target behavior is only partially reinforced and the unwanted intervening behaviors are increased.

The *amount* of reinforcement and *deprivation* (how long it has been since being reinforced) are also important factors in determining the potency of reinforcers. The larger the number or amount of reinforcers, within limits, the stronger the response will be (Favell, 1977). As a rule, reinforcement should be large enough to be truly reinforcing, but not so large as to quickly cause *satiation* (temporary reduction in response resulting from too much reinforcement).

Deprivation is the opposite of satiation; it increases the effectiveness of a reinforcer because the individual has not recently been reinforced. *Novelty* is related to deprivation in that unusual or varied reinforcers are preferred. In effect, novelty can be a reinforcer by itself and can be used to motivate behaviorally disordered children. For example, Exhibit 3.4 shows a spinner (Jenson, Neville, Sloane, & Morgan, 1982) that maximizes novelty, amount of reinforcement, variety, and variability. A child simply spins the arrow after a target behavior (e.g., an aca-

EXHIBIT 3.4 A spinner and a reinforcement list for either school or home use

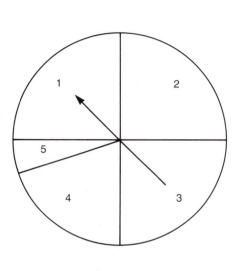

Examples of School Reinforcers

1. Five minutes of free time
2. Recess game leader
3. Candy treat
4. Get to sit in the back of the class
5. Teacher's lunch helper

Example of Home Reinforcers

1. Five minute back scratch
2. Get to choose TV program for 1 hour
3. Game with mom for 15 minutes
4. Horse back ride from dad
5 Gets to stay up 30 minutes later

Source: From "Spinners and Chartmoves: A Contingency Management System for School and Home" by W. R. Jenson, M. Neville, H. Sloane, and D. Morgan, 1982, *Child & Family Behavior Therapy*, 4(1), 83. Published by The Haworth Press, Inc., New York. Used with permission.

demic assignment) has been completed. The circle of the spinner is divided into a number of possible reinforcers, with larger, more desirable reinforcers on the smaller wedges and smaller, less costly reinforcers on the larger wedges. Whatever reinforcer the arrow randomly points to is what the child earns. The size of the wedge regulates the probability that a particular reinforcer will be delivered, the smaller wedges (bigger reinforcer) being less likely than the larger wedges (smaller reinforcer). With a spinner, a child earns selected reinforcers listed on the spinner. Moreover, the novelty and unpredictability of the spinner itself are reinforcing for many children. The convenience of obtaining and dispensing the reinforcer affects the likelihood that a teacher or parent will consistently deliver reinforcers when they are earned.

Consistency in giving a reinforcer each time a new behavior occurs (acquisition) is also important if a new behavior is to be strengthened. If reinforcement is haphazard, the child will learn the new target behavior slowly or not at all. However, behaviors that have been already learned are better maintained by irregularly scheduled reinforcement. The schedules of reinforcement that maintain performance will be discussed in greater detail later in the chapter.

Shaping

A teacher who waits for the perfect target behavior so that it can be reinforced may have an extremely long wait. Target behaviors may never occur in exact, perfect form. Therefore, we need a process to prompt the target behavior. This process, *shaping,* is defined as reinforcing successive approximations to a final behavior (Gelfand & Hartmann, 1984). In a shaping procedure, any behavior that remotely resembles the target behavior is reinforced. Then, gradually, the standards required before reinforcement increase until the child's behavior closely approximates the final target. Sometimes *prompts* are necessary to get the child to make the first response. For example, a physical prompt (manually guiding the child) may be needed to get a child to start cleaning up a mess or start getting dressed. Exhibit 3.5 lists a number of shaping steps used to teach a child to dress himself fully (Gelfand & Hartmann, 1984). Prompts are slowly *faded* out (withdrawn). The child completes the behavior alone and earns the reinforcer. Prompts can take several forms, including verbal, modeled, and written forms, but eventually they all must be faded.

Shaping is often used in educational settings to increase new behaviors. Many complex skills taught at school are gradually shaped; examples include athletic skills, self-help skills, and academic skills. Behavioral level systems (see chapter 9) found in many special education classrooms serving behaviorally disordered children are basically shaping procedures. With these systems, a student at first must control only the most rudimentary disruptive behaviors, such as being out of seat or aggressive, to receive reinforcement. The child who masters these skills, however, moves up to another level that requires more complex skills, such as reinforcing peers and working independently, and earns better, unique reinforcers.

Although shaping is indispensable for teaching new behaviors to children, it is also a complex procedure that requires practice. For example, the final target behavior must be defined in objective terms so that it can be used as a standard to judge behavior approximations. If the definition is ambiguous, reinforcing successive approximations to the target behavior will be difficult. Consistency of reinforcement is critical in the beginning stages of shaping. The reinforcement must also be contingent and potent. Clearly, shaping is long and sometimes very laborious. A particularly useful short cut to teaching new behaviors to children is called *modeling.*

Modeling

Most complex behaviors that children learn are acquired through modeling rather than shaping. Modeling involves learning new behaviors by

EXHIBIT 3.5   Sample program including a shaping procedure: Training a child to dress himself

Step   1. Child's legs are inserted into his underpants. Underpants are drawn up to his knees. Contingency: Child must draw underpants up into wearing position in order to receive hug and praise (probably conditioned reinforcers). He is verbally requested to do so (prompt).

Step   2. Child performs Step 1 consistently (near 100%) upon request. Now only one of child's legs is inserted into underpants. Contingency: Child must insert other leg, then draw pants up to receive a hug and praise.

Step   3. Child performs Step 2 consistently upon request. Now he is required to pick up underpants, insert both legs, and draw pants up to receive positive consequences (hug and praise).

Step   4. Child consistently puts on underpants upon request. Now he is required to put on slacks. (Note: In this and in each succeeding step, positive consequences follow successful performance.)

Step   5. Putting on a pullover shirt. The shirt is put over child's head; he must locate the sleeves, insert his arms, and pull down his shirt.

Step   6. Child picks up pullover shirt, pulls it over his head, locates sleeves, inserts his arms, and pulls shirt into place.

Step   7. Putting on socks. Socks are placed over child's toes. He must pull them up over his ankles. Shoes are put on him.

Step   8. Child must pick up socks, gather each one together, put it over his toes, and pull it up over his ankle. Shoes are put on him.

Step   9. Putting on shoes. Child puts on socks. Shoes are placed before him in correct arrangement, right shoe in front of right foot. He must slip his foot into the shoe. Shoes are buckled or tied for him.

Step 10. Shoes are not placed before child. He finds shoes and puts them on the correct foot.*

*If this sounds difficult and tedious, you are right. Winter weather in a cold climate further complicates matters by requiring boots, hats, mittens, and snowsuits. Even adults may have difficulty in outfitting themselves for excursions in subfreezing weather.

Source: From *Child Behavior Analysis and Therapy* (p. 114) by D. M. Gelfand and D. P. Hartmann, 1984, New York: Pergamon Press. Copyright 1984 Pergamon Press. Reprinted with permission.

first observing a model and then imitating the model's behavior (Bandura, 1973). The successful imitation of a peer or prestigious model may be reinforcing in itself. The economy of modeling in comparison to shaping is readily apparent. Many of the time-consuming steps required in shaping are replaced by observation.

A number of factors affect the use of modeling with behaviorally disordered students in educational settings. First, the child needs to have the basic skills for modeling, including the willingness to attend to the model and to imitate a behavior when instructed to do so. If the child

Pointer 3.2

SELF-AS-A-MODEL WITH BEHAVIORALLY DISORDERED STUDENTS

This study was unique because it did not use models of other children to influence the behavior of a self-contained class of behaviorally disordered students. Instead, the model was the child himself. In this study, four male behaviorally disordered students, ages 10 to 13 years, served as subjects. During the first phase of the study, varying length baseline measures were taken on the percentage of inappropriate behaviors in the classroom for each child (see Exhibit 3.6). The approximate average percentages of inappropriate behavior for each child were 50% of the time.

The intervention involved videotaping each child in the classroom and then editing out all inappropriate behavior (i.e., aggression, off-task, talk-outs, playing, and touching). The children then watched 11-minute edited videotapes (self-as-a-model tapes) of only their appropriate and on-task behavior each day. The control child, Child 4, saw his unedited (both appropriate and inappropriate behavior)

during the unedited-tape phase of the study (see Exhibit 3.6).

The results were dramatic. After seeing tapes of themselves engaging in appropriate behaviors only, all of the children improved their classroom behavior significantly. The control child, Child 4, did not improve his behavior when he watched the unedited tape and improved his behavior only when exposed to the edited tapes of only appropriate behaviors. Interestingly, for every child, when the self-as-a-model tape was withdrawn, behavior continued to improve. This improvement lasted into a 6-week follow-up period.

The authors stated in their article that these results were probably a function of a child viewing himself as an appropriate model. Behaviorally disordered children receive constant feedback about their inappropriate behaviors. Possibly the uniqueness of having only positive feedback and serving as the positive model themselves helped make this result so robust and lasting.

Source: Drawn from "Effectiveness of the Self-Modeling Procedure with Behaviorally Disturbed Elementary Age Children" by T. Kehle, E. Clark, W. R. Jenson, and B. Wampold, 1986, *School Psychology Review, 15,* 289–295. Exhibit 3.6 from pg. 294. Used with permission.

does not have the skills or is too anxious, then the skill must be taught and the child prompted through it. Pointer 3.2 gives a unique example of children serving as their own model, or self-as-a-model, for appropriate behavior. This technique has been used successfully to reduce inappropriate behaviors in a self-contained classroom for behaviorally disordered children (Kehle, Clark, Jenson, & Wampold, 1986). Similarly, modeling has been used to treat children with fears (dental, medical, animal, and school), social withdrawal, severe social deficits (autism and mental retardation), and social aggression (Kirkland & Thelen, 1977).

EXHIBIT 3.6 Percentages of disruptive classroom behaviors from four children before and after viewing themselves in self-as-a-model videotapes

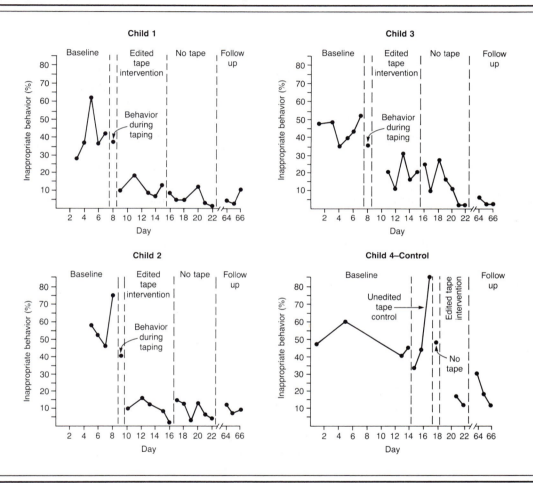

Factors that affect modeling include the age and sex of the child. Younger children imitate more frequently than do older children. Children are more likely to imitate the behavior of a model of the same sex with similar characteristics (Bandura, 1968; Fryrear & Thelen, 1969). Children are also more likely to imitate a prestigious model, such as a successful and socially valued peer, than one who is less prestigious (Bandura, Ross, & Ross, 1963). The consequences the model receives for the behavior will affect whether the child imitates the behavior. If the model is reinforced for the behavior, then another child will be more likely to imitate (Thelen & Rennie, 1972). If the model is punished for the behavior, then another child is likely to avoid the behavior and is less likely to imitate it (Bandura, 1965).

Sometimes the effects of modeling and shaping can backfire with behaviorally disordered children. For example, if a child is phobic in a specific situation and the model also displays fear, then the child's avoidance and fearful behaviors may actually increase. With aggressive or tantrumming children, a common practice is to have the child "get it out of the system" by expressing anger in a socially appropriate manner such as pounding a pillow, throwing the tantrum under an adult's supervision, punching a plastic doll, or fighting with rubber foam bats. This process is called a *cathartic therapeutic release of pent-up aggressive drives,* and a teacher may initially model this cathartic behavior to help a child. Practitioners of cathartic therapy assume that a child has a reservoir of hostility that can be drained by socially appropriate aggression. However, the research on cathartic treatment indicates that it actually maintains or increases the aggressive behavior instead of decreasing it (see Bandura, 1973). If the child is aggressive in a permissive setting, then the child may imitate, practice, and develop these skills for possible later use in a less permissive setting.

Negative Reinforcement

Up to this point in the discussion of reinforcement, we have focused on positive reinforcement, where the frequency or strength of a behavior increases following a favored stimulus or event. A second type of reinforcement, negative reinforcement, also increases the frequency or strength of a behavior; however, in this case, the individual avoids or escapes an aversive stimulus. For example, a child may increase academic work to avoid (postpone) a poor grade. In another example, a child may escape (turn off) the negative stimulus of being called names by peers by increasing aggressive behavior. (Negative reinforcement is often confused with punishment. Punishment decreases a behavior by the delivery of an aversive stimulus. Punishment will be covered in greater detail later in this chapter.)

Many of the same factors that affect positive reinforcement also influence negative reinforcement, including immediacy, intensity, and consistency. Moreover, conditioned negative reinforcers can gain their effects by being paired with an unconditioned negative reinforcer. For example, verbal reprimands and frowning are probably neutral stimuli that gain their negatively reinforcing characteristics by being paired with an aversive stimulus such as spanking (Favell, 1977).

Negative reinforcement can be successfully applied with behaviorally disordered students. Hendersen, Jenson, and Erken (1986) used both negative and positive reinforcement to increase the attending behavior (working consistently and on-task) of behaviorally disordered and developmentally delayed students. In this study, the classroom contained a tape recorder that played soft beeps at random. The students never knew when it might beep. If the students were working when it beeped, they earned points they could exchange later for rewards (positive reinforcement). However, if the students were not attending to their work when the beep sounded, then they did not get the points. In this example, avoiding the negative reinforcement contingencies (i.e., not getting points) required the children to increase their attending behavior. The handicapped children in this study increased their attending and working behavior from baselines of 10% to 20% up to 80%. The random beep sustained the attending behavior in this study at the 80% level. This arrangement of reinforcement is called a *variable schedule* of reinforcement, and such schedules are critical in maintaining performance.

Schedules of Reinforcement

The schedule of a reinforcer (either positive or negative) specifies the amount of work required or the time between reinforcers. The most basic reinforcement schedule is to deliver a reinforcer each time the child makes the target response. This is called *continuous reinforcement,* and it is the reinforcement schedule that should be used when a child is learning a new behavior (acquisition). It is a very poor schedule, however, for maintaining performance simply because the child will become easily satiated. Maintenance requires a different schedule for reinforcement to keep the child responding without satiation.

The other reinforcement schedules are classified as two basic types: (a) time schedules, known as *interval schedules,* and (b) work schedules, known as *ratio schedules* (Ferster & Skinner, 1957). Both interval and ratio schedules can be broken down further into *fixed* or *variable* schedules. For example, a *fixed ratio* schedule requires that the child make some specified number of responses before being reinforced. A child might have to finish five arithmetic problems (abbreviated as FR5) before reinforcement. With a *fixed interval* schedule of reinforcement, a fixed amount of time must pass before reinforcement. A child might work on arithmetic problems for five minutes (FI5) before a reinforcer is given. Fixed interval schedules of reinforcement are commonly found in the everyday environment—a paycheck every 2 weeks, a test each Friday.

Although both fixed ratio and fixed interval schedules of reinforcement produce higher rates of performance of acquired skills than continuous schedules, they have a serious drawback. When reinforcement is fixed, the child knows that no additional reinforcers will be available. As a result, the child's work may decrease or stop immediately after a reinforcement (postreinforcement pause). For example, with FI scheduling, a student may stop studying after an examination or find it hard to start work on a Monday morning after a weekend of fun. Although the postreinforcement pause is more characteristic of FI schedules than FR schedules for humans, pauses can occur with FR schedules if the work requirement of the schedule is large. Postreinforcement pauses reduce the steady, independent work required of many teachers. Furthermore, with FR schedules there may be a tendency for errors to increase after reinforcement (Davidson & Osborne, 1974).

Each type of reinforcement schedule has a characteristic work pattern that can be graphed. In Exhibit 3.7, the lines represent the cumulative work produced for each type of schedule of reinforcement. The hatchmarks indicate the delivery of a reinforcer. The slopes of the lines for the various schedules indicate how much work was performed, with the steeper slopes showing more work accomplished. As shown in Exhibit 3.7, the fixed interval schedule has scallops (increases and then decreases) around the reinforcement marks. A child will work harder when getting closer to a reinforcement and then pause or slow down after reinforcement is given.

A classic example of scalloping on a fixed interval schedule of reinforcement is the Congress of the United States. Exhibit 3.8 graphs the

EXHIBIT 3.7   Behavior performance curves of four schedules of reinforcement

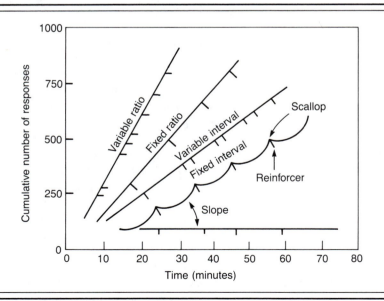

EXHIBIT 3.8 Scalloping of the U.S. Congress of cumulative bills passed from 1961 to 1968 — Work habits on a fixed interval schedule

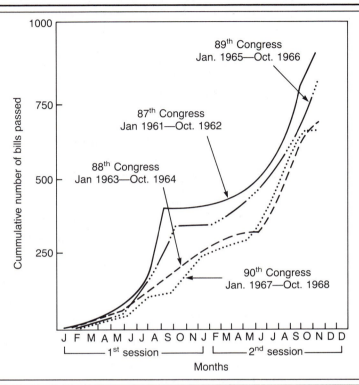

Source: From "Fixed-Interval Work Habits of Congress" by P. Weisberg and P. B. Waldrop, 1972, *Journal of Applied Behavior Analysis, 5,* 95. Copyright 1972 by the Society for the Experimental Analysis of Behavior, Inc. Used with permission.

number of bills passed from 1961 through 1968. In the early part of each Congressional session, the legislature passed few bills; however, as the time for adjournment approached, the number increased rapidly. Adjournment may serve as a reinforcer for members of Congress in several ways, such as going home, receiving public acclaim for working, or attracting voters' attention. Legislators, writers, college students, workers on a job, and behaviorally disordered students respond with the same characteristic patterns to fixed schedules of reinforcement.

Intermittent or variable schedules of reinforcement maintain responding at consistent rates over long periods. A *variable* ratio schedule programs a reinforcer after a variable or random amount of work has been accomplished. For example, a variable ratio 5 (VR5) means that a reinforcer will be given after the child has made an average of five responses. The child may be reinforced after seven responses, then three responses, then nine responses, and then only one response. The child never knows the exact response requirement for the next reinforcement. Gambling is an excellent example of a variable ratio schedule of reinforcement, with slot machines the prime example. Variable interval reinforcement schedules are similar to variable ratio schedules in that the time between reinforcements is variable or random. The variable beep tapes used to increase students' attending is an example of a variable interval schedule of reinforcement (Hendersen et al., 1986). Variable schedules of reinforcement do not have postreinforcement pauses because there is a chance that the very next response after a reinforcement could also be reinforced.

All the schedules of reinforcement that we have discussed have utility in educational settings, and each type has limitations worth noting. Continuous reinforcement schedules are excellent for shaping new behaviors; however, these schedules are very poor for maintaining behaviors because of satiation. Both fixed ratio and interval schedules are commonly found in classrooms because they convey explicit requirements to the students. These schedules seem fair because they spell out exact requirements, but they may induce postreinforcement pauses and more errors after reinforcement. Variable schedules of reinforcement are not effective in shaping new behaviors; however, they are excellent in maintaining performance once a behavior has been learned. Unfortunately, it may be difficult to use variable schedules of reinforcement in the classroom because these students need to have exact performance requirements specified. Applications of variable reinforcement schedules will be discussed in later chapters, particularly in reference to the maintenance and generalization of target behaviors.

DECREASING INAPPROPRIATE BEHAVIORS

If increasing social and academic behaviors is at the heart of education, then decreasing behaviors that interfere with learning is a necessary reality of teaching. All children display some behaviors that are incompatible with learning — they wander around, fail to pay attention, make noise, and daydream. Behaviorally disordered students engage in those behaviors more frequently and intensely. Behaviors such as aggression, noncompliance, tantrumming, and property destruction not only interfere with learning but may also interfere with classmates' performance.

Effective behavior management procedures for decreasing inappropriate behaviors quickly, effectively, permanently, and with few side effects are critical ingredients of a well-managed classroom. These techniques, however, present difficult ethical and legal issues. Teachers must be aware of the limitations of behavior reduction techniques, using them sparingly while constantly evaluating their effectiveness.

Punishment

Punishment is "a reduction of the future probability of a specific response as a result of the immediate delivery of a stimulus for that response" (Azrin & Holz, 1966, p. 381). Like positive and negative reinforcement, punishment is relatively stimulus-independent. That is, some stimuli are assumed to be always noxious and punishing (e.g., electric shock or physical restraint). Yet even shock (Lovaas & Bucher, 1974) and physical restraints (Favell, McGimsey, & Jones, 1978) have been found to be positively reinforcing to some people. The only way to determine if a stimulus is noxious and punishing is to carefully assess its effects on a specific behavior. If the behavior decreases, the stimulus is a punisher. If the target behavior increases, then the stimulus is a reinforcer.

Punishment is pervasive in everyday social interactions. For example, children rapidly learn that they should not touch a hot stove. By learning rapidly, children experience minimal injury and are not likely to repeat the behavior in the future. If the natural process involved a slow shaping procedure to teach a decrease in a dangerous behavior, a great deal of harm could be done. The efficiency of punishment is also one of its greatest drawbacks in educational and clinical settings. The rapid behavior change can be very reinforcing to a teacher, parent, or clinician. As a result, punishment may be overused and more positive approaches may be ignored (Neisworth & Smith, 1973). This tendency must be constantly monitored.

Types of Punishment

The first type of punishment involves the delivery of an aversive stimulus each time an undesirable behavior occurs. *Aversive stimuli* include such stimuli as a verbal reprimand (Van Houten & Doleys, 1983) and shame (Serber, 1970). Other aversive stimuli that have been used successfully include slaps (Foxx & Azrin, 1972), contingent electric shock (Birnbrauer, 1968; Risley, 1968), and aversive substances such as a fine water mist (Jenson, Rovner, Cameron, & Petersen, 1985) or lemon juice in the mouth (Sajwaj, Libet, & Agras, 1974). These latter procedures (e.g., slaps, electric shock, and substances) have *no* ethical use with behaviorally disordered children in schools. Only for the most severe behaviors (e.g., serious self-injury) and only under stringent legal and clinical supervision should these procedures ever be used with a child. Other commonly employed forms of punishment with behaviorally disordered children include response cost, time-out, and overcorrection.

Response Cost

Response cost is essentially a penalty or fine used to reduce maladaptive behaviors. It is used in situations in which children have already earned

Pointer 3.3

THE RESPONSE COST LOTTERY

This study was conducted in a regular fourth grade classroom of 28 students. The subjects were three male students with a history of severe behavior problems; each had been suspended from school at least once, and each had recently been referred for placement in a self-contained special education program because of their disruptive classroom behavior. The Response Cost Lottery procedures were implemented during a 30-minute period in the afternoon when the class was either engaged in seatwork or listening to teacher-led instruction and discussion.

The basic intervention procedures were as follows:

- The classroom rules in effect during that period were explained. The boys were told that slips of paper would be placed on their desks at the beginning of the study time. The slips had the student's name on them. The boys were told that one slip of paper would be taken away if they broke any of the classroom rules.
- All slips of paper remaining at the end of a work period were collected and placed in a box for the lottery drawing at the end of the week. The person whose slip of paper was drawn in the lottery could select a reward from the reinforcement menu (low-cost activities and prizes).
- The idea that the better they behaved, the better chance they had to win the lottery was emphasized.
- When the teacher observed the students breaking a rule, she removed a slip of paper and briefly explained why it was removed.

The Response Cost Lottery procedures were effective in increasing the students' appropriate behavior. In addition, the students' accuracy on assignments also increased during the study. Interestingly, the procedure was effective even though

points or tokens for appropriate behaviors or where a privilege, such as a field trip, is earned and then lost. Response cost has been used successfully to reduce off-task behavior and violation of classroom rules (Iwata & Bailey, 1974; Witt & Elliot, 1982), aggressive verbalizations and tardiness (Phillips, 1968; Phillips, Phillips, Fixsen, & Wolf, 1971), and school vandalism (Kalish, 1981). (See Pointer 3.3.) Before response cost can be used, there must be a program of positive reinforcement involving items such as privileges, money, points, or tokens that can be taken away.

While response cost can be effective in modifying inappropriate classroom behavior, teachers are urged to use caution. A behavior management system that relies on response cost may focus too heavily on decreasing inappropriate student behaviors instead of increasing appropriate behaviors. It is counterproductive to totally remove opportunities the teacher did not notice every incident of student misbehavior during the work period in which procedures were in effect. The teacher took slips of paper away for only the most flagrant rule violations. Perhaps more stringent decisions by the teacher might have produced more dramatic results.

For the teacher interested in adopting or adapting the basic Response Cost Lottery procedures, several modifications could be considered:

1. Extend the time in which the procedures are in effect (e.g., all morning, reading and math, or all day).
2. Involve only one student or involve up to six students.
3. Conduct a lottery at the end of every day (at least in the initial stages of the program).
4. In addition to a daily lottery, consider having a "grand prize drawing" every

Friday. This is for the student who may have kept all of the slips of paper each day of the week but did not win a daily lottery due to the luck of the draw. Tickets not drawn in the daily lottery could be carried over to the weekly lottery drawing.

5. After the procedures have been in effect for a while, teach the student to self-monitor and self-consequate for rule violations. In other words, teach the student to surrender a slip of paper for each rule violation.
6. This system also greatly simplifies recording frequency data on student behavior. Each slip of paper taken away from a student represents one occurrence of a specific class of inappropriate behaviors. In a sense, the slips of paper are permanent products of student performance.

Source: Drawn from "The Response Cost Lottery: A Time Efficient and Effective Classroom Intervention," by J. C. Witt and S. N. Elliot, 1982, *Journal of School Psychology, 20,* 155–161.

to earn positive reinforcers or for a child to go in the hole (i.e., have a negative point balance) (Walker, 1983). Effective response cost procedures require that more reinforcement should be earned than lost. The behaviors that result in response cost and the amounts of each fine should be decided before a program is started to ensure objectivity and fairness. It is very easy to take away a large number of points or overuse the technique when you are upset about a misbehavior (Pazulinec, Meyerrose, & Sajwaj, 1983). Response cost should never be punitive or personalized. ("Now look what you've done! This is going to cost you!")

Taking away reinforcers from a student for misbehavior can be difficult for several reasons. If the child physically has the reinforcers (points or tokens), he or she might refuse to surrender them freely. Physical struggles should be avoided at all costs. Instead, the teacher can increase the response cost for failures to relinquish the reinforcers or make sure that some points and tokens are always saved in a bank the teacher controls.

As with all behavior management procedures, response cost will not work with all students. It will be a punisher for some but, for others, it may actually increase the problem behavior and function as a reinforcer (Burchard & Barrera, 1972). In that case, the only recourse is to try a different technique and evaluate its effectiveness.

Time-out

Time-out is a procedure that temporarily excludes a pupil from the opportunity to receive reinforcement (Sloane, Buckholt, Jenson, & Crandal, 1979). Of all the punishment procedures used with behaviorally disordered students, time-out is possibly the best known. It also has great potential for misuse by people who are not well trained in applying it appropriately.

It is useful to look at time-out on a continuum of restrictiveness. Among the least restrictive forms of time-out would be the situation where reinforcers (work materials, food, or toys) were removed for a short time (usually seconds) when a child is misbehaving. The advantage of removing materials is that the child remains in the classroom. This procedure can work as long as the child's behavior does not disrupt other children.

The next, more restrictive step in the time-out continuum is contingent observation, in which a child is seated a few feet from the work setting and observes but cannot earn reinforcement for a short period (Porterfield, Herbert-Jackson, & Risley, 1976). Contingent observation is also possible only if the child does not disturb other children. A similar procedure that is particularly effective with younger children is the time-out ribbon described in Pointer 3.4 (Foxx & Shapiro, 1978).

The last step in the continuum of time-out procedures involves isolating the child in a restricted environment. An example of time-out with isolation is seating a child in a chair facing the corner of the classroom so the child is unable to see the classroom. It can also involve removing a child from one class to another class in a different grade (for example, removing a disruptive third grader to a sixth grade classroom to work for a while). This approach works because the third grade child is not likely to have friends in the sixth grade class.

For severe misbehavior such as aggression, time-out with isolation might require that the child be placed in a well-lighted and ventilated booth or empty room. A child placed in such a restricted environment is being taken away from a reinforcing environment and going to a "boring" environment for a very short period. The booth or empty room should not be an unhealthy environment that is poorly ventilated, dark, or dangerous. The procedural do's and don't's of time-out are outlined in more detail in Exhibit 3.9.

Pointer 3.4

THE TIME-OUT RIBBON

One of the most innovative uses of time out with younger children is the time-out ribbon. The time-out ribbon is a nonexclusionary time-out procedure involving a ribbon or necklace that the child wears. Initially, the child learns to wear the ribbon in class. Each time the teacher reinforces the child, the teacher mentions the appropriate target behavior and wearing the ribbon. The pairing of the ribbon with reinforcement helps to establish the ribbon as a secondary or conditioned reinforcer and a signal that the child is behaving well and can earn reinforcement. After pairing the reinforcer and ribbon for a week to 10 days, the teacher then removes the ribbon for a short period (from 3 to 5 minutes) when the child misbehaves. The teacher informs the child that he has misbehaved, describes the behavior, and takes the ribbon. While the ribbon is off, the teacher and other students ignore the misbehaving child, and the child can not participate in reinforcing activities. The teacher removes objects and materials near the child. After the short time-out period, the child receives the ribbon again and rejoins classroom activities. A few seconds after the child receives the ribbon, the teacher looks for an appropriate behavior to reinforce.

The time-out ribbon has a number of advantages with behaviorally disordered students. First, the child remains in the classroom and can see other students enjoying the reinforcing activities. This advantage possibly helps students refrain from behaving inappropriately. Second, the procedure can be implemented immediately when the misbehavior occurs and does not involve the delay of escorting a child to a corner or booth. Third, removing the ribbon is less disruptive to the classroom's activity than removing the child from the classroom. Fourth, the removal of the ribbon is a clear signal to other teachers, aides, and students that time-out is in effect and that they should ignore the misbehaving child. The disadvantages of the ribbon could include any struggle or resistance when the teacher removes the ribbon. If this problem happens repeatedly, the technique might be inappropriate. Another disadvantage is the time involved in establishing the ribbon as a conditioned reinforcer.

In one study using the time-out ribbon with older boys who were labeled *retarded* and *emotionally disturbed,* the procedure effectively reduced disruptive classroom behavior. For one boy, failure to follow instructions dropped from a baseline of 3 per hour to 0 per hour. Another boy's inappropriate speech declined from 10 words per hour to approximately 1 per hour. In a third boy, inappropriate disturbing noises dropped from an average of 3 per hour to 0 per hour. We have also found the time-out ribbon to be particularly effective when negative attention from the teacher and attention from peers for misbehavior reinforce a behaviorally disordered child. Simply taking the ribbon off is a signal to other children that all reinforcing peer attention should stop for the misbehaving child.

Source: Drawn from "The Time-Out Ribbon: A Nonexclusionary Time-Out Procedure," by R. M. Foxx and S. T. Shapiro, 1978, *Journal of Applied Behavior Analysis, 11,* 125–136.

EXHIBIT 3.9   The *dos* and *don'ts* of time-out

1. Do explain the total procedure to the child before starting time-out.

   Don't start the procedure without explaining time-out to the child first in a calm setting that is not emotionally charged.

2. Do prepare a time-out setting for the child that is clean, well lighted, and ventilated.

   Don't just pick any place. Make sure that it isn't dark, too confining, dangerous, or not ventilated.

3. Do pick a place or situation for time-out that is boring or less reinforcing than the classroom activity.

   Don't pick a place that is scary or that could be more reinforcing than the classroom (for example, sitting in the hall).

4. Do use a set of structured verbal requests with a child, such as the recommended precision request format.

   Don't threaten a child repeatedly with time-out.

5. Do remain calm, and don't talk with a child when he or she is being taken to time-out.

   Don't get into a verbal exchange with a child on the way to time-out or while in time-out.

6. Do place a child in time-out for a set period of time that you control.

   Don't tell a child to come out of time-out when "you are ready to behave."

7. Do require the child to be quiet for 30 seconds at the end of the time-out period, before being let out.

   Don't let a child out of time-out while crying, screaming, yelling, or tantrumming.

8. Do use a short period for time-out, such as 5 or 10 minutes.

   Don't use exceedingly long periods.

9. Do require the child to complete the request that led to time-out or missed academic work.

   Don't allow a child to avoid compliance to a request or miss academic work by going to time-out.

Time-out has been used effectively with a number of very difficult behavior problems including physical aggression (LeBlanc, Busby, & Thomson, 1974), tantrums (Nordquist, 1971), and severe noncompliance (Bean & Roberts, 1981; Roberts, 1982). Its major advantage is that it is usually very effective in decelerating misbehavior. However, to make time-out as effective as possible, the teacher should plan several steps and contingencies before beginning. The teacher must define the types of misbehaviors that will result in time-out and explain the exact procedures to the child *before* time-out is used. Time-out should be long enough to

EXHIBIT 3.9 *continued*

10. Do have someone responsible for the child in time-out, preferably equipped with an audible signaling device (egg timer) to signify when a child should come out.

    Don't put a child in time-out without a responsible person checking on the child or knowing what to do in an emergency.

11. Do ignore a child who says he or she likes time-out or will not leave time-out.

    Don't beg a child to leave time-out.

12. Do make a child clean up any mess made in time-out.

    Don't let a child mess up the time-out room and avoid cleaning it.

13. Do add minutes to the length of time-out for each request you make to a child who refuses to go to time-out.

    Don't threaten, yell, beg, or physically fight a child to get him to go to time-out.

14. Do keep data on the use of time-out such as who is respnsible for the child, time in and time out, reason for being placed in time-out, and date.

    Don't assume you can remember or don't need the data.

15. Do write the basic steps and procedures of time-out in your classroom, have the staff read them, and post them along with the data sheets on the door of the time-out room.

    Don't leave the data sheets back in the room, or assume that all staff will read and remember the time-out procedure.

16. Do get the parents' permission before you use the procedures, show them the time-out room if one is used, have them sign a permission sheet, have them read the time-out procedures, and include the procedures in the child's IEP.

    Don't assume it is all right with the parents if you use the procedures and that it doesn't need to be included on the IEP.

17. Do change the time-out procedure or parameters (length of time, place, or type of time-out) if the data indicate that it is not working over a reasonable period (2 weeks).

    Don't assume that time-out will work for every child or all inappropriate behaviors, in all settings.

have an effect but not so long as to be abusive. Deciding on a time period is difficult. A few minutes for a younger child and up to 15 minutes or more for older children who exhibit severely disruptive behavior are very general guidelines (Clark, Rowbury, Baer, & Baer, 1973; Tyler, 1965). An hour or more is too long. Long periods of confinement constitute seclusion, not time-out, and can have serious legal ramifications.

The teacher should also think about the type of learning environment the child is leaving when going to time-out and what the child does in time-out. If the classroom environment is boring or aversive (i.e., not reinforcing), the child may prefer time-out. A teacher should make sure that the child completes any academic assignments that he or she missed because of being in time-out. A child who is allowed to miss work may selectively misbehave to avoid certain academic subjects. Time-out is effective only if it is a boring, nonreinforcing situation, making the child want to return to the reinforcing classroom.

If the time spent in time-out is more reinforcing than the classroom, then misbehavior will increase. Activities that might be reinforcing for a child in time-out include daydreaming, rocking and singing, playing with a smuggled toy, and masturbating. It is not effective to try to stop these behaviors directly while the child is in time-out; the attention will probably be reinforcing. If the child exhibits these behaviors in time-out and the misbehavior remains frequent, another behavior management technique will be necessary.

Teachers who use time-out should also be prepared for some ploys and problems. If the child reports liking time-out, the teacher should ignore the report and continue to use it for a trial period and then review the data. Similarly, if the child refuses to leave time-out when the period is over, the teacher should leave the door open and inform the child that missed work will have to be made up. Urinating or defecating in a time-out room is another problem behavior that some children use to coerce their teachers into not using the technique. If this happens, the child should clean up the mess. These examples are attempts used by behaviorally disordered children to persuade teachers and parents to stop using time-out.

Another difficult problem to control with behaviorally disordered students is peer reinforcement for misbehavior. A child may be rewarded by friends for getting into trouble and going to time-out. Peer reinforcement for misbehavior will produce dramatic increases in problem behaviors and undermine the teacher's control. A group contingency where the whole classroom has something to gain or lose depending on the number of time-outs in a classroom can effectively address this type of problem. Group contingencies will be covered in more detail in chapter 9.

To reiterate, the *only* way to determine if a child likes time-out is to review the data after the technique has been in effect for a week or two. If the misbehavior does not change or if it increases, then the child may indeed enjoy time-out.

Overcorrection

This is a technique that teachers have used for centuries, though clinical research on it is recent. Essentially, overcorrection is a procedure for reducing behaviors in which a child who misbehaves repeats a behavior many times. A classic example of overcorrection is the girl who, after constantly teasing a little boy at recess (the misbehavior), is required by her teacher to write "I will not tease at recess" 100 times (the repeated behavior) on the blackboard. With this example, the girl is not only punished for her misbehavior, but she also improves her writing skill through the overcorrection.

Overcorrection is actually a much more complex punishment procedure than our simple example implies. It has been used with children and adults to reduce out-of-seat and talking-out behavior (Azrin & Powers, 1975), aggression (Klinge, Thrasher, & Myers, 1975), self-stimulation (Foxx & Azrin, 1973), fire setting (Koles & Jenson, 1985), noncompliance (Doleys, Wells, Hobbs, Roberts, & Cartelli, 1976), and fecal soiling (Doleys & Arnold, 1975). It has been used to increase sharing and reduce nonsharing in kindergartners (Barton & Osborne, 1978), to increase spelling accuracy while reducing mistakes in elementary students (Foxx & James, 1978), and to improve toileting skills in preschoolers while reducing accidents (Foxx & Azrin, 1973). Because overcorrection has an instructional component, it is the only punishment procedure that decreases an unwanted behavior while improving a desirable behavior (see Pointer 3.5).

There are two basic types of overcorrection procedures used with children. The first type is *restitutional* overcorrection, which requires a child to restore a disrupted environment to a state that is better than before the misbehavior. For example, if a child urinates on a time-out room floor, the child might be required to wash the walls as well as the floor. Similarly, if a child throws a tantrum in a classroom and overturns a desk, the requirement might be to straighten all the other classroom desks and dust them.

The second type of overcorrection is *positive practice,* in which a child who makes a mistake or is disruptive practices the correct behavior. If the misbehavior has not physically disturbed the environment, then positive practice rather than restitutional overcorrection is generally appropriate. The case of the girl who teased at recess is an example of positive practice overcorrection. Messy behavior such as dropping coats in the middle of a room or leaving boots scattered around could be changed by having the messy student hang up the coat or put the boots away five times.

To make overcorrection maximally effective, Foxx and Azrin (1972) make the following recommendations:

1. Repeated or practiced behavior should be related if possible to the misbehavior (i.e, picking up clothes for throwing clothes around).
2. Overcorrection procedures should follow misbehavior immediately.
3. Duration or number of repetitions should require work and not merely be a game. "An increased work or effort requirement is

Pointer 3.5

POSITIVE PRACTICE OVERCORRECTION FOR CLASSROOM DISTURBANCES

This study was designed to assess the effectiveness of positive practice overcorrection on disruptive behavior in the classroom. The procedures were implemented in a summer school for boys who ranged in age from 7 to 11 years old and who had been referred for severe academic delays and extremely disruptive behavior. During the baseline phase of the study, the classroom was generally chaotic: "Students were continuously walking around and running about, hitting, talking, and shouting and interfering with the learning activities of students that did try and learn" (Azrin & Powers, 1975, p. 530). The main disruptive behaviors targeted for intervention in this study were talking-out and being out of seat without permission.

The positive practice principle "states that when an error or disruptive action occurs, the individual be required to practice the correct manner of behaving" (Azrin & Powers, 1975, p. 530). For being out-of-seat and talking-out, the principle does not require the child to practice the misbehavior but rather to ask permission first before talking or leaving a seat.

The basic design of the study included four phases: (1) warning, reminders, and reinforcement, (2) loss of recess, (3) positive practice (delayed), and (4) positive practice (immediate). Data on the disruptive behaviors were recorded by observers on a special form.

1. *Warning, reminders, and reinforcement* — This phase served basically as a baseline in which the teacher warned the students before each class that no one was allowed to talk out or be out of seat without permission. If a student did talk out or get out of seat without permission, the teacher identified the child and restated the rule.

2. *Loss of recess* — During this phase, a child lost 10 minutes of recess for getting out of seat or talking out in class. The child simply stayed in the classroom during recess, did not talk, and did not enage in any type of constructive activity.

3. *Positive practice procedure (delayed)* — As with the other two procedures, the teacher warned the students of the rule before class and the students lost recess if they broke the rules. In addition, the student had to practice asking permission by raising their hands and asking for permission to talk or get out of their seats. If one or two students had to stay in and practice during recess, the time spent practicing was 5 minutes. Then they could join the other students at recess. If more than one student had to stay in during recess, the practice time was equally divided among the students. If a student delayed or was incorrect in practicing, the teacher had the student start practicing all over again.

4. *Positive practice (immediate)* — This phase was the same as the other phases except that a student was required to practice by asking permission immediately after breaking a rule for one trial (immediate). Then, during recess, the student practiced for the 5-minute period. Exhibit 3.10 shows the results of the study across all phases of the intervention.

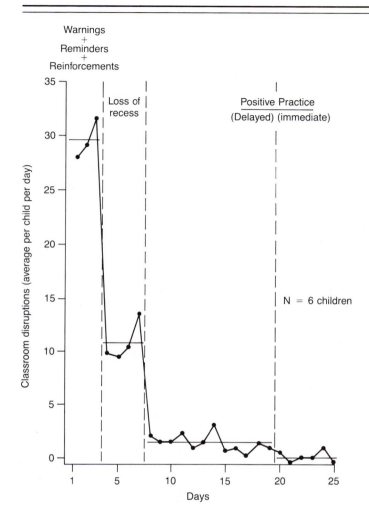

EXHIBIT 3.10
Eliminating classroom
disturbances; disruptive
episodes by six children in
a special class for children
with behavior problems

During the baseline of warnings, reminders, and reinforcement, the average number of disruptions per day was 29. This average decreased by 60% to an average of 11 disruptions per day with the loss of recess intervention; however, this was still relatively high. During the positive practice (delayed) phase, disruptions declined by 95% to an average of 2 per day. With positive practice (immediate), disruptions decreased to 98% of the baseline level, with only 0.4 per day. After the positive practice (immediate) procedure, the overall practicing time was slowly faded out. Clearly, the positive practice procedure was effective in reducing classroom disruptions. As described by Azrin and Powers, the general appearance of the class was relaxed but with direct attention to learning and consideration of other students. None of the children were shouting and walking about.

Source: From "Eliminating Classroom Disturbances of Emotionally Disturbed Children by Positive Practice Procedures" by N. H. Azrin and M. A. Powers, 1975, *Behavior Therapy, 6,* 529. Used with permission. Exhibit 3.10 from pg. 529. Used with permission.

known to be annoying and serves as an inhibitory event" (Foxx & Azrin, 1972, p. 16).

4. Required repetitions should involve active participation without pausing, excessive help, or prompts from an adult, though some physical guidance may be necessary to get a child started.

5. Access to reinforcement (peer attention, praise, or approval) should be removed while the child is busy with the overcorrection. In this sense, overcorrection is like time-out because the child loses access to a reinforcing environment.

Some researchers (Axelrod, Brantner, & Meddock, 1978; Hobbs, 1976; Matson, Ollendick, & Martin, 1979) have questioned the long-term effectiveness of overcorrection. Although it has been documented (Osborne, 1976), its effectiveness depends upon many of the same factors as do other punishment techniques. The main drawback of overcorrection is that it requires one-to-one supervision from an adult. If a child is not monitored, he or she may simply stop doing the overcorrection activity because it is too much work. A child must also be fairly compliant and willing to follow instructions from an adult even in times of stress. Some children require physical guidance to start the activity. If the child is abusive or assaultive, however, physically prompting the child may be impossible.

The length of time that a child should engage in an overcorrection activity may be difficult to gauge. Studies have reported times ranging from a few minutes up to 45 minutes or longer (Osborne, 1976). With children, 45 minutes is excessive. Educators should also be aware that long periods of overcorrection may have legal implications: "This point (length of time) is particularly important in light of *Morales v. Turman* (1973) which declares that repetitive nonfunctional tasks lasting many hours constitute cruel and unusual punishment in violation of the Eighth Amendment to the Constitution" (Sulzer-Azaroff & Mayer, 1977, p. 301).

Even with these limitations, overcorrection is a very useful technique that combines a behavior reduction component with an educational component. It has been used informally for many years, and it will continue to be used, we hope, as a preferred behavior management strategy with an enlarged data base to evaluate its effectiveness.

Factors That Influence the Effectiveness of Punishment

As with reinforcement, the timing of punishment is critical. A punishing stimulus should be delivered *immediately* with as little delay as possible between the inappropriate behavior and the punishment. For optimal effectiveness, a punishing stimulus should be presented in the early stages of a misbehavior instead of at its conclusion (MacMillan, Forness, & Trumbell, 1973; Parke, 1970). Many misbehaviors are linked together like a chain, with less severe responses leading to more intense responses until, at the end of the chain, the child is totally out of control. For example, time-out would be more effective at the beginning of a tantrum than it would be after the child has been screaming and crying for 10 minutes.

The *intensity* of the punishing stimulus is an important and difficult choice (Walters & Grusec, 1977). If the punishing stimulus is too mild, it will not be effective; if it is too intense, it may be unethical or abusive. The size of a fine in response cost, the duration of time-out, or the number of repeated behaviors in overcorrection can be estimated on the basis of what has been published in the literature for a handicapped child of similar age. Erring on the conservative side by using a weak intensity or short duration may be a disservice to the child. Although all educational and clinical procedures should use the least restrictive approach to punishment, we may do children great harm by slowly adapting them to greater intensities or durations of a punishing stimulus. For example, to begin by using one minute of time-out and increasing the requirement gradually up to an hour teaches the child to withstand intense punishment, not to change misbehavior. The least restrictive punishing stimulus is one that will not be constantly increased and is effective in reducing an inappropriate behavior. The best strategy is to be familiar with the educational and clinical literature and know what intensities have been successfully used in studies with different populations. Age of children, mental ability, and type of target behavior are other important factors.

The type of person who delivers a punishing stimulus for a misbehavior and the nature of the delivery greatly influence the effectiveness of punishment. The teacher who has been fair and caring with the child and has formed a *positive attachment* with the child will be far more effective in using punishment than a cold disciplinarian (MacMillan et al., 1973; Parke, 1970; Parke & Walters, 1967).

The *consistency* of the person who is implementing the punishment procedure is important from two perspectives. First, it is important that the procedure is done correctly and consistently each time the child misbehaves. If the behavior is sometimes punished correctly and at other times ineffectively punished or even rewarded, then the behavior will be much more resistant to change (Banks, 1966). There may be a great temptation to comfort a child immediately after a punishment. However, Parke (1977) has noted that

> by reacting positively shortly after administering a reprimand, an adult may undermine the effectiveness of discipline. Not only is such inconsistency ineffective in achieving suppression of an unacceptable behavior in the immediate situation . . ., but it may also make it more difficult to control the child with this kind of discipline on future occasions. (p. 89)

The second aspect of consistency and the use of punishment deals with the most effective *schedules of punishment*. Initially, when a behavior is occurring frequently, it is important to punish the behavior each time it occurs. A consistent and continuous schedule is the most effective in reducing high frequency behaviors (Walters & Grusec, 1977). Once a behavior has decreased, however, a variable ratio of punishment can be used to maintain low rates (Clark et al., 1973; Harris & Ersner-Hershfield, 1978). Variable ratio schedules of punishment are important for teachers who cannot take the time to use time-out or overcorrection each time an infrequent misbehavior occurs.

Misbehavior occurs because of some consequence in the environment. A child might react aggressively because he is highly frustrated at not succeeding and not being rewarded. Another child might whine or cry to obtain attention from the teacher or peers. Similarly, a third child might throw a tantrum to escape or avoid following a teacher's request and work.

All of these examples demonstrate how children misbehave to gain positive and negative reinforcement from their environments. Of all the factors that make punishment permanently effective, the most important is identifying and rewarding an *alternative* behavior that leads to the same type of reinforcement. The child who seeks a peer's attention by disrupting the class can learn more appropriate social skills and gain attention without misbehaving. Teaching appropriate replacement behaviors is important so that a child can interact and claim the attention of others without misbehaving. No punishment for an inappropriate behavior can be permanently effective without building in an appropriate behavior that leads to rewards.

Drawbacks of and Myths Associated with Punishment

Some of the drawbacks associated with the use of punishment have already been mentioned; for example, the tendency to overuse it because of the rapid behavior change it produces. When punishment is overused, socially appropriate alternative behaviors are not being reinforced. If punishment is overused or inappropriately used, it can result in a child's withdrawing from the person or the environment in which the punishment occurs or becoming aggressive (Oliver, West, & Sloane, 1974). Withdrawal or aggression in children may be a function of overuse, unfair application, use of too intense a punishing stimulus, or use by a person who does not have a positive relationship with the child.

Imitation of a punishment procedure by other children can be a problem. Studies have documented the imitation of punishment such as response-cost procedures (Gelfand et al., 1974), reprimands and criticism (Mischel & Grusec, 1966), and aggressive acts (Steuer, Applefield, & Smith, 1971) by other children.

Possibly the greatest drawback with the use of punishment is its *misuse* and *abuse* by poorly trained staff. Physical punishments such as slapping or hitting a child; verbal punishments such as calling names, yelling, or screaming; or the use of aversive substances such as bad-tasting substances have no place in the classroom (Guess, Helmsetter, Turnbull, & Knowlton, 1987). Exhibit 3.11 identifies a number of questions that teachers and administrators should answer before and during the implementation of punishment procedures (Harris & Ersner-Hershfield, 1978).

There are several common myths about punishment as an intervention with humans. Some authors (Estes, 1944; Skinner, 1938, 1953) have suggested that the behavior-suppressing effects of punishment are temporary and not worth the emotional side effects it causes. Clearly, the ability of punishment to reduce an unwanted behavior can be permanent, and the permanence is a function of the intensity of the punishing stimulus and the establishment of an appropriate alternative response that leads to reinforcement (Solomon, 1964).

The second myth implies that punishment will result in numerous negative emotional side effects and possibly lead to neurosis. The negative side effects include anxiety, withdrawal, disorganization of behavior,

EXHIBIT 3.11   Procedural questions for the use of punishment procedures with humans

---

1. Does the procedure achieve complete suppression of the target behavior?
2. Does suppression generalize to other settings and other caretakers?
3. Is suppression sustained over time?
4. Are there side effects, positive or negative?
5. Is there physical risk to the subject?
6. Can the suppression procedures be consistently implemented by caretakers?
7. What level of training is required to use the procedure?
8. Are less drastic alternatives available?
9. Is provision made to teach the patient alternative responses?
10. What kinds of people benefit from the procedure?
11. Is an intermittent or continuous schedule of delivery more effective?
12. Where in the chain of responses can this procedure be most effectively imposed?
13. How intense must the punishment be to obtain suppression?

Source: From "Behavioral Suppression of Seriously Disruptive Behavior in Psychotic and Retarded Patients: A Review of Punishment and its Alternative" by S. L. Harris and R. Ersner-Hershfield, 1978, *Psychological Bulletin, 85,* 1368. Copyright 1978 by the American Psychological Association. Reprinted by permission of the author.

and avoidance of the situation in which punishment occurs. However, research has not found an overwhelming number of negative side effects when punishment has been *appropriately used.* Even with the most severe types of punishment used for the most difficult types of behavior (self-injury), more positive side effects have been reported than negative side effects (Lichstein & Schreibman, 1976). The positive side effects associated with the appropriate use of punishment include more appropriate social behavior, calmness, affection, social play, and an improved awareness of the environment (Newsom, Favell, & Rincover, 1983).

Using punishment procedures appropriately and providing an alternative response that leads to reinforcement are critical in permanently reducing inappropriate behaviors and avoiding negative side effects while maximizing positive side effects.

> It is apparent that, although punishment does have undesirable side effects, they are not as detrimental as some people have suggested. Used judiciously, punishment can be quite effective in suppressing unwanted behavior, without adversely affecting desirable behavior. This excludes extremely severe punishment, that is administered randomly so that the contingencies are unclear to the recipient, and that which is administered by a hostile and rejecting caretaker. What we are referring to is punishment used by a responsible and concerned person in teaching acceptable behavior. (Walters & Grusec, 1977, p. 177)

> Indeed, the case can be made for according them [positive side effects] *greater* weight than negative side effects since they tend to last longer and to make further desirable changes possible. This argument may be especially appropriate in situations where positive reinforcement approaches either have no impact alone or work too slowly to be of significant therapeutic value. (Newsom et al., 1983, p. 306)

Issues related to the negative side effects and the myths surrounding the use of punishment can be unsettling for teachers and school administrators. Some programs have tried to ban the use of punishment and replace it with only positive procedures. However, if punishment is banned, it is still possible that staff members would surreptitiously use it, without supervision. It is our view that punishment cannot be banned by administrative fiat. It will be clandestinely used. The best approach to punishment is to thoroughly train personnel, carefully regulate its practice, employ good data systems to evaluate its effectiveness, design appropriate alternatives to punishment, and learn to use it effectively and ethically. Wood (1978) also suggests that we remember:

> Using punishment should be a painful experience for the punisher as well as the punished. When our rationalizations come too easily and we cease to be sensitive about the infliction of pain on others, or even worse, begin to find satisfaction in punishing, we have lost some of our humanity. (p. 122)

ALTERNATIVE AND COMPLEMENTARY PROCEDURES TO PUNISHMENT

Several behavior management procedures decrease unwanted behavior but do not involve punishment. These procedures can sometimes be used as alternatives to punishment, or they can be used to complement punishment to make it more effective. The first of these procedures, called *extinction,* involves discontinuing reinforcement for a previously reinforced behavior. Extinction should not be confused with time-out, in which the child is removed from a reinforcing environment. With extinction, the child remains in the environment and reinforcement ceases. Extinction can involve eliminating any type of positive reinforcement. With children, however, extinction generally means the withdrawal of adult attention. If a misbehavior is reinforced by adult attention, then ignoring the child or reacting with stoney silence is an extinction procedure and should decrease the behavior. Many behaviors that are assumed to be attention-dependent (e.g., trantrumming, whining, or constantly clinging to an adult) decrease when the adult ignores the child.

With extinction, in the beginning, a child will temporarily increase the misbehavior (*extinction burst*). This increase will be temporary if the adult consistently uses the extinction. If the adult reinforces the child during an extinction burst, then the child learns that responding harder will eventually draw attention. Similarly, after a behavior has decreased following extinction, a child may abruptly behave inappropriately (*spontaneous recovery*). Spontaneous recovery of the misbehavior is also temporary and will become less frequent if the adult is consistent with the extinction.

Satiation can sometimes be used as a behavior management technique, but creative applications are required. Satiation is "the reduction in performance or reinforcer effectiveness that occurs after a large amount of that type of reinforcer has been delivered" (Sulzer-Azaroff & Mayer, 1986, p. 401). Generally, satiation works when the child's behavior is reinforcing in itself. For example, the mother of an autistic child was distressed by her son's constant perseverative question asking. No sooner had the mother answered one question than the boy would ask another question and want an answer. Finally, the mother decided to use a satiation technique because the perseverative questions were reinforcing and the answers meant little to the boy. Each time her son would ask a repetitious question, the mother would insist that the boy ask it again and again until he was tired of asking the question (usually more than 50 times). Only then would she answer him. Finally, the boy stated one day that he wanted to ask only once because it was too much work. Actually, satiation involves transforming a stimulus or behavior from being reinforcing to being aversive. Its greatest limitations are the time involved and the few practical instances where it can be used.

The most positive procedures for reducing misbehavior in behaviorally disordered children are *differential reinforcement procedures,* which selectively reinforce children for low rates of the inappropriate target behavior. There are essentially three types of differential reinforcement procedures. The first is differential reinforcement of *low rates* of behavior (abbreviated DRL). The child is positively reinforced for a rate of an inappropriate behavior that is lower than that observed before the intervention (Deitz & Repp, 1973). For example, Bolstad and Johnson (1972) reduced disruptive classroom behaviors by awarding eight points to each child for keeping the number of disruptive behaviors to five or less, four points for fewer than 10 disruptive behaviors, and zero points for more than 10 disruptive classroom behaviors. DRL is excellent for inappropriate behaviors that can be reduced gradually.

The second type is the differential reinforcement of an *incompatible behavior* (DRI). A behavior that physically interferes with the inappropriate target behavior is identified and reinforced (LaVigna & Donnellan-Walsh, 1976). Examples of the use of DRI would be reinforcement for standing quietly in line (incompatible with pushing) and reinforcement for being in seat (incompatible with being out of seat). DRI has been combined with extinction to reduce disruptive and aggressive behaviors (Madsen, Becker, & Thomas, 1968) and to increase in-seat behavior and attending in a hyperactive boy (Twardosz & Sajwaj, 1972).

The last type of differential procedure is the differential reinforcement of *zero rates of behavior* (DRO), which has also been called *omission training.* The child is reinforced after a specified interval if the inappropriate behavior has not occurred. Essentially, a DRO is like a DRL procedure in which no occurrences of the misbehavior are allowed. With DRO, an aggressive child would be reinforced only if there were a complete absence of aggression for a specified interval, such as 10 minutes. If any aggressive behavior occurred, the child would not be reinforced and the interval would start over. However, if the child was not aggressive during the 10-minute interval, he would receive a reinforcer; in effect, any *other* behavior that occurred in that interval would be reinforced. One of the basic disadvantages of DRO is that behaviors other than the target behavior are reinforced with this procedure, and these other behaviors can be less desirable than the original target behavior (Sulzer-Azaroff & Mayer, 1986).

The last alternative to punishment is perhaps the easiest to overlook. It is *positive educational programming* (LaVigna & Donnellan, 1976). Most teachers want their classrooms to operate with positive programming that maximizes learning and makes it enjoyable. Yet not all teachers are totally aware of the factors that create a positive educational program with behaviorally disordered students. A number of classroom behavior problems can be traced to a boring environment and a frustrat-

Rules:
1. Stay in chair
2. Pay attention
3. Don't talk or bother other people
...inish your work first.
...se your hand.
... HAPPY.

Positive educational programming maximizes learning and makes it enjoyable.

ing curriculum. These problems decrease significantly when academic skills are strengthened (Ayllon, Layman, & Burke, 1972; Ayllon & Roberts, 1974; Hay, Hay, & Nelson, 1977). Positive educational programming emphasizes a well-structured curriculum that rewards effort and maximizes success. In addition to a well-organized curriculum, positive programming includes a variety of tasks to keep a student interested in learning. Classroom rate or pace is another component of positive educational programming. The classroom rate does not refer to the speed at which a teacher presents material, but rather the pacing and transitions that the students demonstrate in academic work (West & Sloane, 1986). Brisk (but not frenetic) pacing from behaviorally disordered students with smooth and short transitions between academic activities improves performance and reduces disruptions and the need for punishment (West & Sloane, 1986). Teacher organization involves the schedule of classroom activities, predictable timing of events, and physical structure of the classroom. These characteristics are important variables in positive programming and reducing classroom problems (Paine et al., 1983). Disorganization and lack of structure invariably increase classroom behavior problems.

CHAPTER SUMMARY

This chapter has reviewed the underlying theory and applications of behavior management techniques with children. Behavior management was presented as a scientific technology of behavior change. The techniques covered are learning-based techniques because they focus on general principles of learning that have been scientifically investigated in experimental laboratories and applied settings over the past 50 years. The principles of behavior management are essentially "rules describing the relationship between what a person does and specific conditions" (Sulzer-Azaroff & Mayer, 1977, p. 3). "What a person does" is basically the behavior that we are interested in changing. The "specific conditions" generally represent environmental manipulations or interventions that change behavior. The rule represents a relationship between the intervention and the expected behavior change. Rules like this have also been referred to as *behavioral principles, contingencies,* or *functions.* When systematically followed, the rules represent a technology of behavior management.

The functional relationship between a child's environment and behavior was also stressed, with an emphasis on behavioral antecedents and consequences. Two major types of behavior management strategies were reviewed — procedures that increase appropriate behaviors and procedures that decrease inappropriate behaviors. The advantages and disadvantages of specific techniques such as positive and negative reinforcement, shaping, time-out, overcorrection, and response cost were reviewed. In addition, several alternatives to punishment techniques were also covered.

All the behavior management procedures presented in this book can contribute to the common goal of positive and efficient education of behaviorally disordered students. Yet the same behavior management techniques will not be effective with every child in all settings. Each technique has to be tried and evaluated on its own merits.

REVIEW QUESTIONS

1. If awarding stickers contingent upon appropriate behavior does not increase the rate of appropriate behavior, are the stickers reinforcers? Why? What is the best way to determine if a given consequence is reinforcing?

2. A student in your classroom is having a temper tantrum during which he throws his and others' books, papers, and chairs around the room. What would be an appropriate consequence for this behavior, overcorrection or time-out? If overcorrection, what type? If time-out, what type?
3. Explain how punishing a student might be negatively reinforcing to a teacher.
4. You are accused of bribing your students because you systematically reinforce their appropriate behavior. How would you respond?

REFERENCES

Alberto, P. A., & Troutman, A. C. (1986). *Applied behavior analysis for teachers: Influencing student performance* (2nd ed.). Columbus, OH: Merrill.

Axelrod, S., Branter, J. P., & Meddock, T. D. (1978). Overcorrection: A review and critical analysis. *Journal of Special Education, 12,* 367–391.

Ayllon, T., Layman, D., & Burke, S. (1972). Disruptive behavior and reinforcement of academic performance. *The Psychological Record, 22,* 315–323.

Ayllon, T., & Roberts, M. D. (1974). Eliminating discipline problems by strengthening academic performance. *Journal of Applied Behavior Analysis, 7,* 71–76.

Azrin, N. H., & Holz, W. C. (1966). Punishment. In W. K. Honig (Ed.), *Operant behavior: Areas of research and application.* New York: Appleton-Century-Crofts.

Azrin, N. H., & Powers, M. A. (1975). Eliminating classroom disturbances of emotionally disturbed children by positive practice procedures. *Behavior Therapy, 6,* 525–534.

Bandura, A. (1965). Influence of model's reinforcement contingencies on the acquisition of imitative responses. *Journal of Personality and Social Psychology, 1,* 589–595.

Bandura, A. (1973). *Aggression: A social learning analysis.* Englewood Cliffs, NJ: Prentice-Hall.

Bandura, A., Ross, D., & Ross, S. (1963). Imitation of film-mediated aggressive models. *Journal of Abnormal and Social Psychology, 66,* 3–11.

Banks, R. K. (1966). Persistence to continuous punishment following intermittent punishment training. *Journal of Experimental Psychology, 71,* 373–377.

Barton, E. J., & Osborne, J. G. (1978). The development of classroom sharing by a teacher using positive practice. *Behavior Modification, 2,* 231–250.

Bean, A. W., & Roberts, M. W. (1981). The effect of time-out release contingencies on changes in child noncompliance. *Journal of Abnormal Child Psychology, 9,* 95–105.

Bijou, S. W., & Peterson, R. F. (1971). Functional analysis in the assessment of children. In P. McReynolds (Ed.), *Advances in psychological assessment.* Palo Alto, CA: Science and Behavior Books.

Bijou, S. W., Peterson, R. F., Harris, F. R., Allen, K. E., & Johnston, M. S. (1969). Methodology for experimental studies of young children in natural settings. *Psychological Record, 19,* 77–210.

Birnbrauer, J. S. (1968). Generalization of punishment effects — A case study. *Journal of Applied Behavior Analysis, 1,* 201–211.

Bolstad, O. D., & Johnson, S. M. (1972). Self-regulation in the modification of disruptive classroom behavior. *Journal of Applied Behavior Analysis, 5,* 443–454.

Burchard, J. D., & Barrera, F. (1972). An analysis of time-out and response cost in a programmed environment. *Journal of Applied Behavior Analysis, 5,* 271–282.

Clark, H. B., Rowbury, T., Baer, A. M., & Baer, D. M. (1973). Time-out as a punishing stimulus in continuous and intermittent schedules. *Journal of Applied Behavior Analysis, 6,* 443–455.

Davidson, N. A., & Osborne, J. G. (1974). Fixed ratio and fixed interval schedule control of matching-to-sample errors by children. *Journal of the Experimental Analysis of Behavior, 1,* 27–36.

Deitz, S. M., & Repp, R. C. (1973). Decreasing classroom misbehavior through DRL schedules of reinforcement. *Journal of Applied Behavior Analysis, 6,* 457–463.

Doleys, D. M. (1977). Behaviour treatments for nocturnal enuresis in children: A review of the literature. *Psychological Bulletin, 84,* 30–54.

Doleys, D. M., & Arnold, S. (1975). Treatment of childhood encopresis: Full cleanliness training. *Mental Retardation, 13,* 14–16.

Doleys, S. M., Wells, K. C., Hobbs, S. A., Roberts, M. W., & Cartelli, L. M. (1976). The effects of social punishment on noncompliance: A comparison with time-out and positive practice. *Journal of Applied Behavior Analysis, 9,* 471–482.

Estes, W. K. (1944). An experimental study of punishment. *Psychological Monographs, 57* (3, Whole no. 263).

Favell, J. E. (1977). *The power of positive reinforcement: A handbook of behavior modification.* Springfield, IL: Charles C Thomas.

Favell, J. E., McGimsey, J. S., & Jones, M. L. (1978). The use of physical restraint in the treatment of self-injury and positive reinforcement. *Journal of Applied Behavior Analysis, 11,* 225–241.

Ferster, C. B. (1965). Classification of behavioral pathology. In L. Krasner & L.P. Ullmann (Eds.), *Research in behavior modification.* New York: Holt, Rinehart and Winston.

Ferster, C. B., & Skinner, B. F. (1957). *Schedules of reinforcement.* New York: Appleton-Century-Crofts.

Foxx, R. M., & Azrin, N. H. (1972). Restitution: A method of eliminating aggressive disruptive behaviors of retarded and brain damaged patients. *Behavior Research & Therapy, 10,* 15–27.

Foxx, R. M., & Azrin, N. H. (1973). Dry pants: A rapid method of toilet training children. *Behavior Research and Therapy, 11,* 435–442.

Foxx, R. M., & Jones, J. R. (1978). A remediation program for increasing the spelling achievement of elementary and junior high school students. *Behavior Modification, 2,* 211–230.

Foxx, R. M., & Shapiro, S. T. (1978). The time-out ribbon: A nonexclusionary time-out procedure. *Journal of Applied Behavior Analysis, 11,* 125–136.

Fryrear, J. L., & Thelen, M. H. (1969). The effect of sex of model and sex of observer on the imitation of affectionate behavior. *Developmental Psychology, 1,* 298.

Gelfand, D. M., & Hartmann, D. P. (1984). *Child behavior analysis and therapy* (2nd ed.). New York: Pergamon Press.

Gelfand, D. M., Hartmann, D. P., Lamb, A. K., Smith, C. L., Mahan, M. A., & Paul, S. C. (1974). The effects of adult models and descriptive alternatives on children's choice of behavior management techniques. *Child Development, 45,* 585–593.

Gelfand, D. M., Jenson, W. R., & Drew, C. (in press). *Understanding child behavior disorders* (2nd ed.). New York: Holt, Rinehart & Winston.

Guess, D., Helmsetter, E., Turnbull, R. H., & Knowlton S. (1987). *Use of aversive procedures with persons who are disabled: An historical review and critical analysis.* Seattle: The Association for Persons with Severe Handicaps.

Harris, L. L., & Ersner-Hershfield, R. (1978). Behavioral suppression of seriously disruptive behavior in psychotic and retarded patients: A review of punishment and its alternative. *Psychological Bulletin, 85,* 1352–1375.

Hay, W. H., Hay, L. R., & Nelson, R. O. (1977). Direct and collateral changes in on-task and academic behavior resulting from on-task versus academic contingencies. *Behavior Therapy, 8,* 431–441.

Hendersen, H., Jenson, W. R., & Erken, N. (1986). Focus article: Variable interval reinforcement for increasing on task behavior in classrooms. *Education and Treatment of Children, 9,* 250–263.

Hobbs, S. A. (1976). Modifying stereotyped behaviors by overcorrection: A critical review. *Rehabilitation Psychology, 23,* 1–11.

Iwata, B. A., & Bailey, J. S. (1974). Reward versus cost token systems: An analysis of the effects on students and teachers. *Journal of Applied Behavior Analysis, 7,* 567–576.

Jenson, W. R., Neville, M., Sloane, H., & Morgan, D. (1982). Spinners and chart-moves: A contingency management system for school and home. *Child & Family Behavior Therapy, 4,* 81–85.

Jenson, W. R., Rovner, L., Cameron, S., & Petersen, B. P. (1985). The use of a spray bottle plus startle response to reduce chronic self-injury in an autistic girl: A fading technique. *Journal of Behavior Therapy and Experimental Psychiatry, 16,* 77–80.

Jenson, W. R., Sloane, H. N., & Young, R. (In press). *Applied behavior analysis: A structured teaching approach.* Englewood-Cliffs, NJ: Prentice-Hall.

Kalish, H. I. (1981). *From behavioral science to behavior modification.* New York: McGraw-Hill.

Kanfer, F., & Saslow, G. (1965). Behavior analysis: An alternative to diagnostic classification. *Archives of General Psychiatry, 12,* 848–853.

Kehle, T., Clark, E., Jenson, W. R., & Wampold, B. (1986). Effectiveness of the self-modeling procedure with behaviorally disturbed elementary age children. *School Psychology Review, 15,* 289–295.

Kirkland, K. D., & Thelen, M. H. (1977). *Uses of modeling in child treatment.* In B. B. Lahey & A. E. Kazdin (Eds.), *Advances in child clinical psychology* (Vol. 1). New York: Plenum Press.

Klinge, V., Thrasher, P., & Myers, S. (1975). Use of bed-rest overcorrection in a chronic schizophrenic. *Journal of Behavior Therapy and Experimental Psychiatry, 6,* 69–73.

Koles, M., & Jenson, W. R. (1985). A comprehensive treatment approach for chronic firesetting in a boy. *Journal of Behavior Therapy and Experimental Psychiatry, 16,* 81–86.

Konarksi, E. A. (1982, May). *Recent and proposed response deprivation in applied settings.* Invited address presented at the Association of Behavior Analysis, Milwaukee.

LaVigna, G. W., & Donnellan-Walsh, A. (1976, October). *Alternatives to punishment in the control of undesirable behavior.* Paper presented at the Eighth Annual Southern California Conference on Behavior Modification, California State University, Los Angeles.

LeBlanc, J. M., Busby, K. H., & Thomson, C. L. (1974). The functions of time-out for changing the aggressive behaviors of a preschool child: A multiple-baseline analysis. In R. Ulrich, T. Stachnik, & J. Mabry (Eds.), *Control of human behavior* (Vol. 3). Glenview, IL: Scott, Foresman.

Lichstein, K. L., & Schreibman, L. (1976). Employing electric shock with autistic children: A review of the side effects. *Journal of Autism and Childhood Schizophrenia, 6,* 163–173.

Lovaas, I. O., & Bucher, B. D. (1974). *Perspectives in behavior modification with deviant children.* Englewood Cliffs, NJ: Prentice-Hall.

MacMillan, D. L., Forness, S. R., & Trumbull, B. M. (1973). The role of punishment in the classroom. *Exceptional Children, 40,* 85–96.

Madsen, C. H., Becker, W. C., & Thomas, D. R. (1968). Rules, praise, and ignoring: Elements of elementary classroom control. *Journal of Applied Behavior Analysis, 1,* 139–150.

Matson, J. L., Ollendick, T. H., & Martin, J. E. (1979). Overcorrection: A long-term follow-up. *Journal of Behavior Therapy and Experimental Psychiatry, 10,* 11–13.

Melamed, G. G., & Johnson, S. B. (1981). Chronic illness: Asthma and juvenile diabetes. In E. J. Mash & L. G. Terdal (Eds.), *Behavioral assessment of childhood disorders.* New York: Guilford.

Mischel, W., & Grusec, J. E. (1966). Determinants of the rehearsal and transmission of neutral and aversive behaviors. *Journal of Personality and Social Psychology, 3,* 197–205.

Morales v. Turman, 364 F. Supp. 166 (E.D. Texas 1973).

Mostofsky, D. I., & Balaschak, B. A. (1977). Psychobiological control of seizures. *Psychological Bulletin, 84,* 723–750.

Neisworth, J.T., & Smith, R.M. (1983). *Modifying retarded behavior.* Boston: Houghton Mifflin.

Newsom, C., Favell, J. E., & Rincover, A. (1983). Side effects of punishment. In S. Axelrod & J. Apsche (Eds.), *The effects of punishment on human behavior.* New York: Academic Press.

Nordquist, V. M. (1971). The modification of a child's enuresis: Some response-response relationships. *Journal of Applied Behavior Analysis, 4,* 241–247.

Oliver, S. D., West, R. C., & Sloane, H. N. (1974). Some effects on human behavior of aversive events. *Behavior Therapy, 5,* 481–493.

Osborne, J. G. (1976). Overcorrection and behavior therapy: A reply to Hobbs. *Rehabilitation Psychology, 23,* 13–31.

Paine, R., Radicchi, J., Rosellini, L. C., Deutchman, L., & Darch, C. B. (1983). *Structuring your classroom for academic success.* Champaign, IL: Research Press.

Parke, R. D. (1970). The role of punishment in the socialization process. In R. A. Hoppe, G. A. Milton, & E. Simmel (Eds.), *Early experiences in the process of socialization.* New York: Academic Press.

Parke, R. D. (1977). Punishment in children: Effects, side effects, and alternative strategies. In H. L. Ham & P. A. Robinson (Eds.), *Psychological process in early education.* New York: Academic Press.

Parke, R. D., & Walters, R. H. (1967). Some factors determining the efficacy of punishment for inducing response inhibition. *Monograph of the Society for Research in Child Development (32,* No. 109).

Pazulinec, R., Meyerrose, M., & Sajwaj, T. (1983). Punishment via response cost. In S. Axelrod & J. Apsche (Eds.), *The effects of punishment on human behavior.* New York: Academic Press.

Phillips, E. (1968). Achievement place: Token reinforcement procedures in a home styled rehabilitation setting for predelinquent boys. *Journal of Applied Behavior Analysis, 1,* 213–223.

Phillips, E. L., Phillips, E. A., Fixsen, D. L., & Wolf, M. M. (1971). Achievement place: Modification of the behavior of predelinquent boys within a token economy. *Journal of Applied Behavior Analysis, 4,* 45–59.

Porterfield, J. K., Herbert-Jackson, E., & Risley, T. R. (1976). Contingent observation: An effective and acceptable procedure for reducing disruptive behavior of young children in a group setting. *Journal of Applied Behavior Analysis, 9,* 55–64.

Premack, D. (1959). Toward empirical behavior laws: Positive reinforcement. *Psychological Review, 66,* 219–233.

Reynolds, G. S. (1968). *A primer of operant conditioning.* Glenview, IL: Scott, Foresman.

Risley, T. R. (1968). The effects and side effects of punishing the autistic behaviors of a deviant child. *Journal of Applied Behavior Analysis, 1,* 21–34.

Roberts, M. W. (1982). The effects of warned versus unwarned time-out procedures on child noncompliance. *Child and Family Behavior Therapy, 4,* 37–53.

Ross, A. O., & Nelson, R. O. (1979). Behavior therapy. In H. C. Quay & J. S. Werry (Eds.), *Psychopathological disorders of childhood* (3rd ed.). New York: John Wiley.

Sajwaj, T., Libet, J., & Agras, S. (1974). Lemon-juice therapy: The control of life threatening rumination in a six month-old infant. *Journal of Applied Behavior Analysis, 7,* 557–563.

Serber, M. (1970). Shame aversion therapy. *Journal of Behavior Therapy and Experimental Psychiatry, 1,* 213–215.

Sirota, A. D., & Mahoney, M. J. (1974). Relaxing on cue: The self-regulation of asthma. *Journal of Behavior Therapy and Experimental Psychiatry, 5,* 65–66.

Skinner, B. F. (1938). *The behavior of organisms.* New York: Appleton.

Skinner, B. F. (1953). *Science and human behavior.* New York: Macmillan.

Skinner, B. F. (1961). Teaching machines. *Scientific American, 205,* 90–102.

Sloane, H. N., Buckholdt, D. R., Jenson, W. R., & Crandal, J. A. (1979). *Structured teaching: A design for classroom management and instruction.* Champaign, IL: Research Press.

Solomon, R. L. (1964). *American Psychologist, 19,* 239-253.

Steuer, F. B., Applefield, J. M., & Smith, R. (1971). Televised aggression and the interpersonal aggression of preschool children. *Journal of Experimental Child Psychology, 11,* 442–447.

Sulzer-Azaroff, B. S., & Mayer, G. R. (1977). *Applying behavior analysis procedures with children and youth.* New York: Holt, Rinehart and Winston.

Sulzer-Azaroff, B., & Mayer, G. R. (1986). *Achieving educational excellence.* New York: Holt, Rinehart and Winston.

Thelen, M. H., & Rennie, D. L. (1972). The effect of vicarious reinforcement on limitation: A review of the literature. In B. A. Maher (Ed.), *Progress in experimental personality research: A review of the literature* (Vol. 6). New York: Academic Press.

Tourigny-Dewhurst, D. L., & Cautela, J. R. (1980). A proposed reinforcement survey for special needs children. *Journal of Behavior Therapy and Experimental Psychiatry, 11,* 109–112.

Twardosz, S., & Sajwaj, T. (1972). Multiple effects of a procedure to increase sitting in a hyperactive, retarded boy. *Journal of Applied Behavior Analysis, 5,* 73–78.

Tyler, V. O. (1965, September). *Exploring the use of operant techniques in the rehabilitation of delinquent boys.* Paper presented at the meeting of the American Psychological Association, Chicago.

Van Houten, R., & Doleys, D. M. (1983). Are social reprimands effective? In S. Axelrod & J. Apsche (Eds.), *The effects of punishment on human behavior.* New York: Academic Press.

Walker, H. M. (1982). Assessment of behavior disorders in the school setting: Issues, problems, and strategies. In N. Haring & M. Noel (Eds.), *Progress or change: Issues in educating the emotionally disturbed* (Vol. 1). Seattle: University of Washington.

Walker, H. M. (1983). Applications of response cost in school settings: Outcomes, issues, and recommendations. *Exceptional Education Quarterly, 3,* 47–55.

Walters, G. C., & Grusec, J. E. (1977). *Punishment.* San Francisco: W. H. Freeman.

Webster's New World Dictionary of the American Language. (1960). New York: Work Publishing Company.

Weisberg, P., & Waldrop, P. B. (1972). Fixed-interval work habits of Congress. *Journal of Applied Behavior Analysis, 5,* 93–97.

West, R., & Sloane, H. N. (1986). Teacher presentation rate and point delivery rate: Effects on classroom disruption, performance accuracy, and response rate. *Behavior Modification, 10,* 267–286.

Winett, R. A., & Winkler, R. C. (1972). Current behavior modification in the classroom: Be still, be docile. *Journal of Applied Behavior Analysis, 5,* 499–504.

Witt, J. C., & Elliot, S. N. (1982). The response cost lottery: A time efficient and effective classroom intervention. *Journal of School Psychology, 20,* 155–161.

Wood, F. H., (1978). Punishment and special education: Some concluding remarks. In F. H. Wood & K. C. Lakin (Eds.), *Punishment and aversive stimulation in special education: Legal, theoretical, and practical issues in their use with emotionally disturbed children and youth.* Minneapolis: Advanced Training Institute for Trainers of Teachers for Seriously Emotionally Disturbed Children and Youth.

Yonnell, K. J., & McCullough, J. P. (1975). Behavioral treatment of mucous colitis. *Journal of Consulting and Clinical Psychology, 43,* 740–745.

4 Teaching for Mainstreaming: Generalizing Improved Performance

This chapter was written with Ginger Rhode, Special Education Coordinator, Granite School District, Salt Lake City, Utah.

After reading this chapter, you should be able to

- *Define* generalization.
- *Identify four different types of generalization.*
- *Describe how the following strategies can be used to promote generalization: sequential modification, natural contingencies of reinforcement, sufficient teaching examples, loose training, indiscriminable contingencies, programming common stimuli.*
- *Explain how teaching skills required in mainstream settings facilitates generalization.*
- *Identify different types of self-management procedures.*
- *Describe the advantages and disadvantages of self-management as a means of facilitating generalization.*
- *Describe procedures for monitoring generalization.*

Chapter 3 reviewed and illustrated the principles and practices of effective behavior management. When used correctly, behavior management strategies are a powerful and effective means of improving the school behavior of behaviorally disordered students. Their effectiveness in producing short-term changes has been repeatedly documented. However, questions about the durability and generalizability of the improvements produced by behavior management programs continue to be raised. For example, do the improvements last for a long time or only a short period? Do they occur in other places and with other people? Isn't it meaningless to change behavior unless the improvements last and the changed behavior will occur in different settings, in the absence of the original teacher?

These questions have important implications for special education programs. Behaviorally disordered students are often placed in residential treatment facilities, full-time self-contained classrooms, or part-time resource programs. The primary purpose of these programs is to remediate social, behavioral, and academic deficiencies, thus enabling the students to return to a regular classroom full-time. Typically, when behaviorally disordered students are removed from their regular classrooms and placed in resource programs or self-contained classrooms, they make academic and behavioral gains in the special education setting, but those changes do not transfer or maintain after they return to the regular classroom (Walker & Buckley, 1972; Walker, Hops, & Johnson, 1975). While regrettable, this is not unusual (see Pointer 4.1). Changes in student behavior that occur outside the regular classroom (i.e., in special education programs) do not automatically generalize to the regular classroom (Vaughn, Bos, & Lund, 1986). In fact, generalization rarely occurs unless it has been carefully and purposefully programmed.

Pointer 4.1

A FAILURE TO GENERALIZE: THE CASE OF ANDREW

Before being placed in a private residential school for severely behaviorally disordered students, Andrew had a long history of school learning and behavior problems. His behavior in his fifth-grade classroom had earned him a place in the annals of his school as one of the most difficult-to-manage students his teachers and principal had ever encountered. He bullied his peers, extorted money from younger children, argued with bus drivers and cafeteria workers, taunted his teachers, and defied even the principal. He also had set several fires in the boys' restroom and was caught stealing money from his teacher's purse on two different occasions.

A residential school was selected because of the program's excellent reputation and because it specialized in the kinds of problems presented by children such as Andrew. The residential treatment program featured a very structured, behaviorally oriented milieu; its staff were competent and experienced. In addition to the educational program, a full range of ancillary support services (counseling, parent training, recreational therapy, group therapy for social skills training) was available.

After 5 months in the program, Andrew's behavior had improved so much that it was deemed appropriate to return him to his own school. A report was prepared summarizing the treatment program that had been used, and the effects of the program on Andrew's behavior were documented. In addition, the report contained numerous recommendations to the school concerning how best to manage Andrew in the future.

The first 2 weeks back in his fifth-grade classroom were, according to his teacher, a "honeymoon," though she added, "I'm just waiting and holding my breath for something to go wrong." It did— at the beginning of the third week, Andrew began getting into fights on the playground with his classmates. Once again, he refused to do his work in class; when his teacher would attempt to cajole him into working, he would tell her to "jump in a large lake." When sent to the principal's office, he shouted, "I ain't gonna take this s _____ anymore; I'm leavin' and you ain't gonna do a g _____ thing about it!"

That afternoon the principal called the district special education director and requested an emergency meeting to consider sending Andrew back to the residential program. "It just didn't work — they didn't have him long enough." The special education director assured the principal that he would try to arrange a meeting as soon as he could and added, "When I read their report, I couldn't help but think that most of their recommendations were unrealistic." After hanging up the phone, the principal realized he had never seen a copy of the report the residential program had sent to the district.

The success of programs for handicapped students should be measured by the extent to which students' improved classroom and social behavior and academic performance generalizes from special education settings to the regular classroom. There are many things that can be done within the special education setting to facilitate generalization. There are also many things that can be done within the regular setting after the student returns from the special education setting. This chapter will focus on a variety of empirically validated procedures that can be used to facilitate generalization of treatment effects. The chapter begins with an overview of the importance of generalization and identifies several different types of generalization. The next section covers specific procedures for promoting generalization. Teaching relevant academic and social behaviors, reprogramming the social environment in the generalization setting, and programming common stimuli from the regular classroom to the special education setting are three techniques discussed. Procedures for teaching self-management skills are given special attention because of their great promise as a preferred practice. Finally, recommendations for monitoring and following up on the generalization program are also provided.

GENERALIZATION DEFINED

Generalization has been defined as the extension of newly acquired behavior to settings in which treatment procedures have not been implemented (Wahler, Berland, & Coe, 1979). Stokes and Baer (1977) expanded this definition to include "the occurrence of relevant behavior under different, nontraining conditions . . . without the scheduling of the same events in those conditions as had been scheduled in the training conditions" (p. 350). According to this definition, generalization has occurred when the learner exhibits the target behavior outside the training setting, with no specific intervention. Generalization may also be claimed when an intervention is used, but its extent or cost in terms of teacher time and effort are considerably less than that of the original training program.

Another way of describing generalization is to view behavior change as a two-stage process: "In stage one, procedures must be implemented to produce changes in behavior. In stage two, a second set of procedures must be implemented to insure such changes endure over the long-term and generalize to other settings" (Walker 1979, pp. 286–287). Stage one procedures are part of an already highly developed and effective technology. However, the procedures used in stage two are part of a technology that is only in its infancy.

Generalization comprises several behavioral processes. Drabman, Hammer, and Rosenbaum (1979) have identified four specific categories, or types, of generalization:

1. Generalization across time—Also referred to as *maintenance,* or the durability and persistence of behavior change over time
2. Generalization across settings—Also referred to as *stimulus generalization,* or the extent to which behavior changes occur in settings other than the original training setting
3. Generalization across behaviors—Also referred to as *response generalization,* where changes in one behavior are accompanied by changes in other similar behaviors
4. Generalization across subjects—Where changes in the behavior of untreated subjects occur as a function of the treatment program.

Each of these types is relevant in programs for behaviorally disordered students, and procedures associated with each type will be presented and explained in more detail throughout this chapter.

STRATEGIES FOR PROMOTING GENERALIZATION

As we have focused more attention on the problem of generalization, we have gained more knowledge about how to achieve it. Much of this knowledge has accumulated from research efforts with handicapped students, specifically students with significant school adjustment problems. This section of the chapter will explain several techniques that can be used to facilitate generalization.

Before proceeding, however, it is important to note that there are very few short cuts to achieving generalized changes in behavior. It is very likely that ensuring generalization will require at least as much thought and effort (and probably more) as was required to obtain improvements in the treatment setting. In fact, Cooper, Heron, and Heward (1987) have stressed that planning for generalization should occur before the initial treatment program actually begins. This preimplementation planning would include identifying all the desired target behaviors, all the settings in which the desired target behaviors are to be performed, and all the behaviors required of all others in the generalization settings to support and maintain the improvement (Cooper et al., 1987).

Unplanned Generalization

In a seminal article, Stokes and Baer (1977) provided a comprehensive review and analysis of the research on generalization. They identified promising strategies for promoting generalization, several of which are discussed below. They also identified a "method" frequently used by both researchers and practitioners. They called this method the "train-and-hope" approach to promoting generalization.

An example of the train-and-hope method would be when a resource room teacher instructs a student in the skills needed for the regular classroom and then returns the student to the regular classroom, hoping that generalization will occur. If time allows, the teacher may occasionally check with the regular class teacher to monitor the student's progress. In this case, generalization has not been actively programmed. There were no systematic efforts to increase the probability that generalization would occur. The teacher hoped that the changes in behavior achieved in the resource room would automatically spill over into the regular classroom. While the train-and-hope method is sometimes successful (Alberto & Troutman, 1986), most of the time much more is needed.

Sequential Modification

This method refers to applying the same intervention procedures in every setting in which a change in behavior is desired. If there has been no generalization of treatment gains from a treatment setting to a generalization setting, the intervention that had been successfully implemented in the first setting would be introduced into the second setting.

For example, a student's on-task behavior in the resource room may have been successfully modified with the use of a token point system. However, the student has made little noticeable improvement in being on task in the regular classroom. Consequently, in collaboration with the regular classroom teacher, the special education teacher introduced the resource room token system into the regular classroom.

It may not always be possible or desirable to implement the exact intervention used in a treatment setting in the generalization setting. In fact, it is advisable to retain only those elements required to establish behavioral control. Technically, sequential modification is not an example of a strategy for programming for generalization because there is no "nontreatment" setting (Epps, Thompson, & Lane, 1985). However, if other generalization strategies have been attempted with little success, sequential modification should be tried. For some students, it may be necessary to use a modified version of an initially successful intervention for a long period in generalization settings. In general, however, sequential modification should not be used as a first choice among generalization programming strategies because of the considerable time required by two teachers to implement the same intervention twice (Epps et al., 1985).

Natural Contingencies of Reinforcement

Another method of promoting generalization of behavioral improvements is to teach behaviors that can be naturally reinforced in the gen-

Without a systematic plan for generalization, intervention efforts for behaviorally disordered students are unfinished.

eralization setting. This method has been called *trapping* reinforcement because certain behaviors (good social skills, for example) lead to increased reinforcement, which further helps to maintain the generalized behaviors (Baer & Wolf, 1970). In school, common natural contingencies of reinforcement would include grades, teacher approval, and peer reinforcement.

This method can be a very dependable and powerful means of producing generalized changes in behavior (Stokes & Baer, 1977). However, occasionally the existing contingencies in the generalization setting may need to be rearranged. That is, it may be difficult to identify appropriate student behaviors that are consistently reinforced by the teacher in some regular classrooms. Unfortunately, some teachers tend to ignore appropriate behavior and pay more attention to inappropriate behaviors. Similarly, other students in the classroom may pay too much attention to inappropriate behavior and not enough attention to appropriate behavior. When this happens, the natural maintaining contingencies may need to be rearranged to reinforce appropriate behavior more effectively. The teacher and class members may need to be prompted and coached by the special education teacher or consultant.

One variation of this method involves teaching students to actively recruit their own reinforcement from teachers. Teaching behaviorally disordered students to make comments such as, "Thank you for helping me with my math" or "How am I doing on this spelling assignment?" may elicit (i.e., trap) reinforcing comments from their often-surprised teachers. Behaviorally disordered students have been successfully taught to prompt teachers for assistance, praise teachers for providing help, and prompt teachers for approval on both their academic performance and classroom behavior (Morgan, Young, & Goldstein, 1983). These kinds of procedures should be used more frequently as part of a comprehensive program to facilitate the maintenance and generalization of treatment effects from special education settings to regular classrooms.

Students may also need to learn to recognize praise or encouragement when it is delivered (Graubard, Rosenberg, & Miller, 1974). Some intended classroom reinforcers may be very subtle (e.g., nonverbal messages), and students may not readily discriminate these subtleties as reinforcers. Therefore, teaching students to recognize them may increase the reinforcing potential of the natural environment.

Reprogramming the peer group in the regular classroom is a strategy employed by Walker and Buckley (1972) in a study investigating generalization and maintenance from a self-contained setting to a regular classroom. The peer group was encouraged to support the target student's efforts to behave appropriately and to ignore his disruptive behaviors. The student was allowed to earn points for appropriate social and academic behavior. When he had earned 100 points (approximately one week of appropriate behavior), the points were exchanged for a group activity reinforcer such as a film, a short field trip, or a class party. This strategy proved to be a very effective way to promote generalization from a self-contained setting to a regular classroom.

In programs for behaviorally disordered students, it is extremely important to assess the generalization setting (e.g., the regular classroom) to identify those behaviors that seem to be desired and important because they will be reinforced by the teacher. Teaching these students those behaviors to the level of fluency increases the likelihood that the newly acquired skills will be reinforced by the natural maintaining contingencies in the regular classroom.

Use a Sufficient Number of Teaching Examples

Generalization can be facilitated by using a number of different teaching examples that cover a range of possible response and stimulus conditions (Horner, Bellamy, & Colvin, 1984). As Baer (1981) said, "The most common mistake that teachers make, when they want to establish a generalized behavior change, is to teach one good example of it and expect the student to generalize from that example" (p. 17). Instead, what teachers should do is (a) teach the desired behavior in a variety of settings and under a variety of conditions and (b) teach a variety of different versions of the desired behavior (Cooper et al., 1987).

Two of the more common conditions that can be varied are settings and teachers. For example, a teacher may attempt to reduce the frequency of a student's noncompliance by taking a point away each time the student does not comply with a direction. By having the classroom aide, the school principal, and the playground supervisor involved in the same program, the teacher increases the likelihood that noncompliant behavior will decrease in other settings besides the classroom, lunchroom, and playground and with other people besides herself, the aide, the principal, and playground supervisor.

A technique closely related to using sufficient teaching examples is general case programming (Horner, Sprague, & Wilcox, 1982). General case programming emphasizes the importance of stimulus control and the role it plays in promoting generalization.

> From a stimulus control perspective, the applied problem is not one of generalizing behavior, but of bringing adaptive responses under the control of appropriate stimuli. . . . If a behavior does not occur in a novel setting, it may be because stimuli in that setting do not exert sufficient stimulus control over the response. If conditioned behaviors occur in inappropriate situations, it may be because training procedures have brought these behaviors under control of inappropriate stimuli or have not restricted the range of controlling stimuli. (Horner et al., 1984, p. 288)

The task then becomes one of systematically sampling the variety of stimulus and response situations in the settings where generalization is to occur and teaching those examples to students. When students can respond appropriately to a variety of different stimuli, the general case has been learned (Epps et al., 1985).

While used primarily with severely handicapped individuals (cf. Horner & McDonald, 1982; McDonnell, Horner, & Williams, 1984; Sprague & Horner, 1984), general case programming has potential applications in virtually any teaching/learning situation (Engelmann & Carnine, 1982). With behaviorally disordered students, for example, general case programming can be used when teaching compliance to teacher directions, certain social skills, and following lesson instructions.

Train Loosely

Tight control of many instructional variables is often essential when teaching new behaviors. However, as noted above, varying instructional conditions appears to facilitate generalization. Teachers should consider another method of promoting generalization, called *training loosely* (Stokes & Baer, 1977), when they encounter generalization problems and other transfer strategies have faltered. Baer (1981) has suggested that a teacher loosen teaching techniques by varying teachers, personal appearance, places, tone of voice, choice of words, time of day, reinforcers, arrangement of the physical environment, and even such variables as the temperature and noise level in the room. In so doing, it becomes "less likely that only one or a small group of stimuli will acquire exclusive control over the behavior and more likely that other settings where generality is desired will contain at least some of the stimuli present during training" (Cooper et al., 1987, p. 577).

Use Indiscriminable Contingencies

Once students have learned desirable behaviors, an effective way to maintain improved behavior is by making it difficult for them to distinguish which responses will be reinforced or when they will be reinforced. Because they are unpredictable, intermittent schedules of reinforcement may be efficient for maintaining behavior changes over the long term.

For example, delayed reinforcement in the form of a party at the end of a grading period may maintain improved behavior. Another example involves the use of colored marbles as tokens. Once a student has acquired a behavior, an opaque container containing six marbles is introduced. Five of the marbles are blue and one is red. When he earns reinforcement, the student chooses a marble without looking into the container. If he chooses a blue marble, he gets the reinforcer. Over time, however, more red marbles are added and a blue one is removed each time until, eventually, the student has a one-in-six chance of being reinforced. A very thin reinforcement schedule over the long term may be a desirable, cost-effective means of facilitating maintenance and generalization for some students.

Programming Common Stimuli

Making the training setting more like the generalization setting and the generalization setting similar to the training setting is a very powerful strategy for promoting generalization (Stokes & Baer, 1977). Programming common stimuli involves introducing various aspects of the regular classroom into the special education setting during training, as well as introducing various aspects of the special education setting into the regular classroom following training. Factors that might lend themselves to common programming include people, room arrangements, instructional materials, behavior management techniques, and classroom routines. For example, the physical design of the special education room can be made similar to the regular classroom. Desk type and arrangement, bulletin boards, and other furniture and equipment can resemble those of the regular classroom. The special education teacher can use the same instructional materials, give the same kinds of assignments, and follow similar grading procedures. Similarly, the regular classroom's rules and procedures can be used in the special classroom.

Elements from the special education setting can also be incorporated into the regular classroom. Walker and Buckley (1972) successfully used programming common stimuli as a generalization strategy for behaviorally disordered students in a self-contained classroom. They established as many common elements as possible between the successful special education program and the regular classroom. The common elements most involved were the academic curriculum materials and reinforcement system. Thus, a variation of the treatment model used successfully in special education was implemented in the regular classroom following the students' return. See Pointer 4.2 for another example of programming common stimuli from the special education setting to the regular classroom.

Epps et al. (1985) have developed a "Common Stimuli Form" used to gather information about aspects of a regular classroom that can be made part of the special education environment. Exhibit 4.1 summarizes the factors included in this checklist.

Teaching Skills Required in Mainstream Settings

Resource teachers often concentrate on improving only the academic skills of behaviorally disordered students. Similarly, teachers in self-con-

Pointer 4.2

PROGRAMMING GENERALIZATION USING "LUCKY CHARMS"

This study illustrates an effective and economical strategy to facilitate generalization from resource settings to regular classroom settings by programming common stimuli. Eight BD students (5 boys and 3 girls), aged 8 to 11 years, spent a portion of each day in a resource room designed to remediate academic and social/behavioral deficits. Observational data indicate that the students completed approximately 95% of their reading and math assignments while in the resource room, but only about 60% of the reading and math assignments required in the regular classroom.

Generalization was accomplished by establishing a "personalized discriminative stimulus" within the resource room for each student. The students were asked to bring a favorite object (the "lucky charm") from home to place on their work desk while in the resource room. Their teacher told them:

> I would like you to notice these things on my desk. I have a picture of my sister, my notebooks, my pencil holder, and other things I like to have around me when I work. Do your parents have their personal things around them where they work? Tonight I will visit you at your desk in the resource room so that you will have a reminder that your desk is a working place. This will become your lucky charm and will help remind you to do good work.

Items such as lipstick, medals, small family photos, and other assorted trinkets were identified by the students as their lucky charms.

Half of the students were then assigned to take their charms with them to their reading class in the regular classroom and the other half of the students were told to take their charms to their regular classroom math class. (This was done for experimental purposes.) They were told:

> You know your lucky charm really seems to help remind you to do your work. I'll bet if you took it to your reading class and kept it on your desk there it would remind you to work hard. You may take your lucky charms with you to your reading [or math] class today.

Overall, the results of the study suggested that taking the lucky charm to their regular classroom increased the performance of the eight students dramatically. Math performance improved from a mean performance of 41% prior to the introduction of the lucky charm to 94% after the students brought their lucky charms to the regular math classroom. Similarly, their reading performance improved from 46% to 94%. The authors concluded that transfer of academic skills was enhanced by the presence of stimuli in the regular classroom (e.g., "lucky charms") that had been previously associated with correct academic performance maintained by token reinforcement. Another possibility is that the lucky charms might have drawn the teacher's reinforcing attention to the students' performance.

Source: Drawn from "Programming Resource Room Generalization Using Lucky Charms" by T. Ayllon, C. Kuhlman, and W. J. Warzak, *Child & Family Therapy*, 1983, *4* (2/3), 61–67.

EXHIBIT 4.1 Programming common stimuli

Environmental Stimuli
- Class size
- Desk type
- Desk arrangement
- Teacher's desk location
- Bulletin board content
- Method of displaying student work
- Other people in classroom (e.g., aide, student teacher)
- Room dividers
- Study carrels
- Activity centers
- Other furniture
- Windows, carpet, pets
- Storage spaces
- Student desk decorations (e.g., stickers)

Instructional Materials
- Workbooks
- Textbooks
- Library books
- Games/puzzles
- Pencils, pens, crayons
- Paper
- Scissors, glue, paste

Teacher Behaviors and Instructional Methods
- Classroom rules
- Classroom routines
- Other classroom procedures
- Behaviors teacher reinforces
- Behaviors classmates reinforce
- Behaviors teacher dislikes
- Types of reinforcers used by teachers
- Schedules of reinforcement used
- Behavior reduction procedures used by teacher
- Daily schedule when subjects are taught
- Cooperative, competitive, individualistic goal structures

Instructional Media
- Chalkboard
- Overhead projector
- Charts/posters
- Films
- Audio tape
- Video tape
- Bulletin boards
- Filmstrips, records

Instructional Formats
- Instruction in whole class, small groups, individualized
- Teacher in front of class, at desk, circulates frequently
- Nature of practice assignments
- Students work independently or in groups
- Nature of verbal directions and questions
- Homework procedures
- Task completion expectations
- Who evaluates student work
- How work is evaluated
- Time given to complete assignments
- How students are graded
- Teacher use of cues, prompts (verbal, nonverbal)
- Nature of corrective feedback given to students
- Idiosyncratic verbal expressions of teacher

Source: Adapted from *Procedures for Incorporating Generalization and Maintenance Programming into Interventions for Special Education Students* by S. Epps, B. J. Thompson, and M. P. Lane, Des Moines: Iowa Department of Public Instruction, 1985, pp. 212–219. Used with permission.

tained classrooms for behaviorally disordered students may essentially ignore academic deficiencies and concentrate on improving social skills or classroom behavior. Neither of these approaches completely addresses the skills the students must have if they are to be successfully integrated into regular classroom programs. For success in regular classrooms, these students need three major types of skills: (a) social skills, (b) classroom behavior or survival skills, and (c) academic skills. They need appropriate instruction in each of these areas for successful integration.

Social Skills

The lack of appropriate social skills is a primary reason for the failure of behaviorally disordered students to succeed in regular classrooms. While their classmates have developed the ability to interact positively and to cope with peer pressures and demands, behaviorally disordered students have failed to do so.

Research indicates that unless they receive direct social skill training, these students will not exhibit improved social skills when they return to the regular classroom (Michelson & Mannarino, 1986). The assumption that exposure to normal peers will in and of itself facilitate the development of appropriate social skills has not been proved (Gresham, 1983). Thus, it is imperative that behaviorally disordered students receive specific training to prepare them to meet at least the minimal social demands of the regular classroom. If social skills training is omitted or not carried out systematically, students have little chance of succeeding in the regular classroom.

Classroom Behavior and Survival Skills

It is not surprising that appropriate classroom behavior is of great concern to regular teachers. Many of the classroom behaviors displayed by behaviorally disordered students significantly interfere with learning and a teacher's attempts to teach. Regular teachers have repeatedly identified a number of classroom behaviors as critical (Walker & Rankin, 1983). To be successful, students should:

1. Comply with teacher commands.
2. Follow established classroom rules.
3. Produce work of acceptable quality, given skill level.
4. Listen carefully to teacher instructions and assignment directions.
5. Behave appropriately outside the classroom.
6. Do seatwork assignments as directed.
7. Make assistance needs known appropriately.
8. Observe rules governing movement around the room.
9. Use classroom equipment and materials correctly.

10. Be flexible and adjust to different instructional situations.
11. Seek teacher attention at appropriate times.
12. Respond to conventional behavior management techniques.

Needless to say, the behavior of most behaviorally disordered students falls far short of these teacher expectations prior to intervention. Powerful behavior change procedures dealing directly with specific behavior excesses and deficits will typically be needed initially to produce needed improvements.

Academic Skills

Most behaviorally disordered students have significant academic deficiencies, which are another primary reason for their referral for special education services. A student with adequate academic skills is more likely to receive natural contingencies of reinforcement. Conversely, the absence of appropriate grade-level academic skills may lead to punishing contingencies that may further exacerbate the student's problems. To provide these students with the best possible chance for success, a strong academic program must also be included in the instructional program. (See chapter 5 for detailed information on academic instruction for behaviorally disordered students.)

Assessing Mainstream Classroom Expectations

An essential step in providing an effective instructional program is to assess the behavioral and academic expectations of the regular classroom, where the students will ultimately be expected to demonstrate their newly acquired skills. A socially valid special education program must be responsive to the expectations of the mainstreamed setting. However, until recently, little attention had been paid to assessing the expectations of regular classrooms.

Several methods can be used to assess the mainstream environment. For example, the SBS Inventory of Teacher Behavior Standards and Expectations (Walker & Rankin, 1983) can provide useful information about regular teachers' standards and expectations for students in their classrooms, including those who are behaviorally disordered. Teachers respond to this questionnaire by indicating the degree to which appropriate student behaviors are necessary for successful adjustment in their classes. They are also asked to indicate the degree to which they tolerate maladaptive or inappropriate student behaviors.

Similar information can be obtained by asking teachers about selected aspects of their classrooms. Questions could address the following aspects of the environment:

- Classroom rules—Especially rules governing out-of-seat behavior, talking aloud to teacher and classmates, going to the bathroom, obtaining permission, or requesting assistance from the teacher
- Free time rules—Expectations concerning student behavior when they are finished with their assigned work
- Classroom contingencies—Information about the system of reinforcers and punishers
- Daily classroom routines—Academic subject schedule, homework procedures, group versus individual academic work periods, transition time requirements

Ignoring the requirements of the regular classroom and not assessing the students' ability to demonstrate skills required for success in the mainstream classroom would very nearly insure a generalization failure. Because most teachers do not dramatically change their expectations to accommodate student differences, the attempt to reintegrate behaviorally disordered students without examining the expectations of the mainstream setting most often fails.

In addition, observational data on regular classroom peers can be used to determine a criterion level of appropriate classroom behavior. The handicapped students will need to reach that level for successful (i.e., within the normal range) classroom adjustment (Walker, 1979). To obtain a representative sample of appropriate behavior, the observer first needs to clarify the regular teacher's rules for the class. Judgments made during data collection as to whether behavior is appropriate or not should be based on the regular teacher's rules and requirements in that setting. By observing a random sample of regular classroom peers over a period, a teacher can calculate a percentage of appropriate behavior for the class as a whole. The special education teacher's aim is to exceed or at least equal this level of behavior before mainstreaming the student. The average level of appropriate behavior for the class as a whole can be used as a gauge against which to measure maintenance, deterioration, or need for further improvement of the student's behavior. Reasonable decisions can then be made regarding instruction or program adjustments for the student.

Teaching Self-Management Skills

This procedure involves teaching students to manage their own academic and social behavior. Commonly referred to as *self-control* or *self-management*, these strategies are among the more promising strategies for facilitating generalization. Because the use of self-management procedures with behaviorally disordered students has increased greatly in recent years, detailed information on it will be presented next.

What Is Self-Management?

The use of self-management procedures involves students' management and control of their own behavior through the application of behavioral principles. The objective of self-management programs is to gradually transfer as much control over behavior as possible from the teacher to the student himself or herself. The purpose is to eliminate as many external control techniques as possible (Rosenbaum & Drabman, 1979).

One of the advantages of teaching students to manage their own behavior is that they begin to depend less heavily on teachers for guidance, reinforcement, and control. Self-management strategies emphasize the student's role in behavior change. By becoming more aware of their own behavior, they may begin to better understand the potential long-term benefits of improved behavior (Frith & Armstrong, 1986). Self-management strategies are also thought to enhance the students' self-perceived competence (i.e., self-concept) because behavioral improvements are at least partially the result of their own efforts (Henker, Whalen, & Henshaw, 1980).

Another advantage is that behavioral improvements regulated by self-management procedures appear to be more resistant to extinction than improvements established by externally regulated procedures alone (Johnson, 1970; Kanfer & Duerfeldt, 1967; McLaughlin, 1976; Rosenbaum & Drabman, 1979). In regular classrooms, where teachers may be unwilling or unable to carry out systematic interventions, self-management strategies have been effective in maintaining increased appropriate classroom behavior for several weeks after treatment has been withdrawn (Epstein & Goss, 1978).

A student who can manage his or her own behavior probably requires less individual assistance, leaving the teacher more time to spend with other students who need assistance (O'Leary & Dubey, 1979). This approach to generalization and maintenance of improved behavior responds to teacher concerns regarding the time demands of having handicapped students in their classes (Workman & Hector, 1978).

Self-management strategies are portable (Henker et al., 1980) and can be employed in a variety of conditions because they rely mainly on students for implementation. In view of some of the practical problems related to generalization in classrooms, the advantages of providing students with training that is not specific to a behavior, a change agent, or a setting are evident. Thus, the appeal of self-management training as a viable solution to the problem of generalization and maintenance of treatment gains has recently increased considerably.

Types of Self-Management Training

A number of training strategies have been employed to teach students to control and manage their own behavior: self-assessment, self-recording, self-determination of reinforcement, and self-administration of reinforcement (Glynn, Thomas, & Shee, 1973); self-observation (Rosenbaum & Drabman, 1979); self-monitoring, self distraction, and self-punishment (O'Leary & Dubey, 1979); self-determined contingencies (Glynn, 1970); and self-instruction (Barkley, Copeland, & Savage, 1980). Rather than considering each of these strategies in detail separately, we have condensed them into three for more in-depth review in this section: self-monitoring, self-instruction, and self-reinforcement.

Self-Monitoring

An important component of self-management is the ability to monitor one's own behavior. Included under self-monitoring are such practices as self-recording, self-observation, self-assessment, and self-evaluation. Self-monitoring involves collecting data on either the quality or quantity of a specific behavior. Data collection systems typically used by students are relatively simple (see Exhibit 4.2). For example, students can monitor their own behavior through the use of event recording, time sampling, or analysis of permanent products (Alberto & Troutman, 1986). In event recording, the frequency of such behaviors as talking out or being out of seat could be recorded. Time-sampling procedures could be used by students to record if they were on-task when an intermittent audible "beep" sounded from a tape recorder. Permanent products such as completed math assignments can be qualitatively evaluated for accuracy and neatness.

Self-monitoring strategies have been successfully employed to modify classroom behavior by either increasing appropriate behaviors or decreasing inappropriate behaviors (Broden, Hall, & Mitts, 1971; Drabman, Spitalnik, & O'Leary, 1973; Glynn et al., 1973; Kneedler & Hallahan, 1981; Sagotsky, Patterson, & Lepper, 1978; Santogrossi, O'Leary, Romanczyk, & Kaufman, 1973; Sugai & Rowe, 1984; Turkewitz, O'Leary, & Ironsmith, 1975). They have also been used to improve academic skills and performance (Lovitt, 1973; Lovitt & Curtiss, 1969).

Self-recording has also been used successfully to increase on-task behavior and decrease disruptive behaviors with hyperactive students in regular classrooms. A study designed to examine the effectiveness of self-monitoring procedures in modifying on-task behavior (McLaughlin, Krappman, & Welsh, 1985) used a simple and inexpensive procedure in a self-contained classroom for students with learning and behavior problems. Each student was given a piece of paper divided into 20 squares. The students made a plus sign (+) in one of the squares each time they "thought about" whether they were working appropriately. Similarly, they were to put a minus sign (−) if they thought they were not working appropriately. The students also earned points exchanged for back-up reinforcers for the quality of their behavior. The students' on-task behavior

EXHIBIT 4.2   Examples of self-monitoring forms

_____
Name

_____
Date

ꟼꟼꟼ l

Put a mark down every time you talk out

_____
Date

+	+	−	−	+	+	−	+	−	+

−	+	−							

At the top of the page are several rows of squares. At different times during the period (whenever you think of it but don't fill them all in at the same time) put down a "+" if you were studying, a "−" if you weren't. If for example, you were ready to mark a square you would ask yourself if, for the last few minutes you had been study-ing and then you would put down a "+" if you had been or a "−" if you hadn't been studying.

Source: From "The Effects of Self-Recording on the Classroom Behavior of Two Eighth Grade Students" by M. Broden, R. V. Hall, and B. Mitts, *Journal of Applied Behavior Analysis,* 1971, *4,* 193, 196. Copyright © 1971 by the Society for the Experimental Analysis of Behavior, Inc. Used with permission.

increased significantly when they were recording their own behavior; it remained at very high levels over a relatively long period.

Self-monitoring is usually used with discrete behaviors that can be easily counted, though it has sometimes been used to keep track of thoughts or feelings. Safran and Safran (1984) developed a procedure for teaching elementary-aged behaviorally disordered students to monitor and recognize their moods. Words and pictures on a 5-point rating scale covered common feelings such as happy–sad, friendly–withdrawn, bored–interested, frustrated–relaxed, and nice–mean (see Exhibit 4.3). The meaning of each mood was taught by modeling examples to clarify subtle and not so subtle nuances. Students were taught through additional demonstration and practice how to select the rating that seems to reflect their mood at the time.

A possible application of mood chart and monitoring of moods by behaviorally disordered students might include a contingency management program to reinforce positive/adaptive moods. Another application would be establishing a regular time when teacher and student compare their perceptions (i.e., ratings) of the student's mood, discuss discrepancies, and identify possible precipitating events affecting the student's mood. They could also develop plans for improving the student's mood.

While this procedure seems to have potential for positive outcomes (e.g., personal awareness), you are cautioned to carefully evaluate its effects on the behavior of those students with whom it is used. While self-monitoring has been effective as a "first and only" intervention, the accumulated evidence seems to suggest that it is more prudently and effectively employed after a student's behavior has been brought under control with an externally imposed behavior management intervention. For example, a 6-year-old boy with severe conduct disorders and academic deficits was taught to evaluate his daily class assignments (Baer, Fowler, & Carden-Smith, 1984). Initially, the student's assignments were graded by a peer tutor. Responsibility for grading was then gradually shifted to the boy by having the tutor grade fewer assignments and having the student independently grade more of his assignments. Points were earned for accuracy (access to recess was the back-up reinforcer). It was necessary to also institute a response cost system to promote more accurate self-grading, and the boy earned bonus points for grading incorrect answers as errors. Task accuracy and on-task behavior substantially increased and disruptive behaviors decreased, and the improvements were maintained throughout all phases of the study. Observation indicated that the improvements did not generalize to other periods of the day when the self-grading procedures were not employed.

In another relevant study (Rhode, Morgan, & Young, 1983), six behaviorally disordered elementary-aged students were placed in a resource program where their highly disruptive and off-task behaviors were

EXHIBIT 4.3 Mood chart: How do you feel?

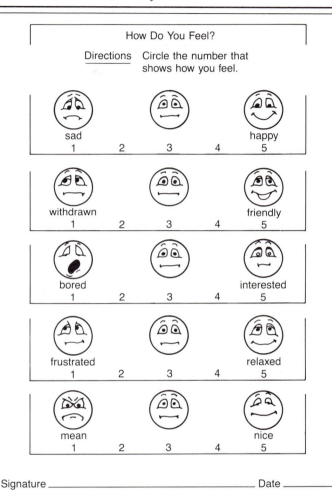

How Do You Feel?

Directions   Circle the number that
              shows how you feel.

sad   happy
1   2   3   4   5

withdrawn   friendly
1   2   3   4   5

bored   interested
1   2   3   4   5

frustrated   relaxed
1   2   3   4   5

mean   nice
1   2   3   4   5

Signature _____ Date _____

Source: From "The Self-Monitoring Mood Chart: Measuring Affect in the Classroom" by S. Safran and L. Safran, *Teaching Exceptional Children*, 1984, *16*, 173. Used with permission.

brought under control with a combination of treatment procedures emphasizing self-evaluation (a variation of self-monitoring). Rules for the program were introduced, discussed, and practiced. The teacher gave points for appropriate classroom behavior and correct academic work by using a rating scale where 5 = excellent, 4 = very good, 3 = average, 2 = below average, 1 = poor, and 0 = totally unacceptable (see Exhibit 4.4). Training sessions lasted an hour and were initially divided into four 15-minute intervals so points could be awarded and feedback given frequently.

EXHIBIT 4.4 Point card

Classroom Rules

1. Sit in your seat unless you have permission to leave it.
2. Do what your teacher asks promptly.
3. Unless you have permission to speak, talk only about your work.
4. Work when you are supposed to.
5. Do not bother or hurt others.

Back of Card

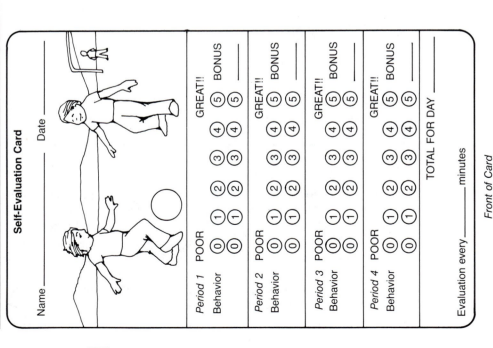

Self-Evaluation Card

Name _____ Date _____

Period 1	POOR					GREAT!!	
Behavior	⓪	①	②	③	④	⑤	BONUS
	⓪	①	②	③	④	⑤	—

Period 2	POOR					GREAT!!	
Behavior	⓪	①	②	③	④	⑤	BONUS
	⓪	①	②	③	④	⑤	—

Period 3	POOR					GREAT!!	
Behavior	⓪	①	②	③	④	⑤	BONUS
	⓪	①	②	③	④	⑤	—

Period 4	POOR					GREAT!!	
Behavior	⓪	①	②	③	④	⑤	BONUS
	⓪	①	②	③	④	⑤	—

TOTAL FOR DAY _____

Evaluation every _____ minutes

Front of Card

Source: From "Generalization and Maintenance of Treatment Gains of Behaviorally/Emotionally Handicapped Students from Resource Rooms to Regular Classrooms Using Self-Evaluation Procedures" by G. Rhode. Unpublished doctoral dissertation, Utah State University, 1981, p. 157. Used with permission.

When appropriate behavior increased and disruptive behaviors decreased to acceptable levels under the teacher-administered point system, students were taught to evaluate their own behavior using the same rating system. The teacher also continued to rate their work and behavior. The students would then compare their evaluations with the teacher's to determine if they matched. If a student's rating was within one point of the teacher's rating (higher or lower), the student kept the number of points he had given himself. If the two ratings matched exactly, the student earned an additional bonus point. If there was more than a one-point difference between ratings, no points were earned. When the students and teacher began to match ratings consistently, the comparisons were made less frequently, until the students were eventually rating themselves alone. However, the teacher continued to monitor the students' ratings and privately record her own ratings. If any student was awarding himself the maximum number of points when his actual behavior did not warrant it, the teacher could use an occasional "surprise" match to keep the students on their toes.

Once acceptable levels of appropriate behavior were established and students were accurately evaluating their own work and behavior in the resource program, the next goal was generalization. A modified version of the self-evaluation procedures was begun in the students' regular classrooms. The students rated themselves on the same behaviors using the same rating scale as in the resource room. At first, they evaluated themselves every 30 minutes, then every hour. After a few weeks, the point card and rating system were faded and students verbally evaluated themselves with their classroom teachers. Ultimately, the students' verbal self-evaluations were discontinued; instead, they were encouraged to "privately" evaluate their own behavior. Those students whose appropriate regular classroom behavior dropped below the 80% criterion for three consecutive days received brief booster sessions: Classroom rules were again reviewed, discussed, demonstrated, and practiced.

The results of this study show clearly that student behavior improved after self-evaluation procedures were taught in the resource room and that improved behavior generalized to and was maintained in the regular classrooms using a less intense version of the original procedure (Exhibit 4.5). For the group, the average appropriate behavior at the conclusion of the study was 54% higher in the regular classroom than it had been during baseline. Furthermore, the improvements in appropriate behavior for the subjects reached levels essentially equivalent to those of their classmates.

In this study, treatment gains generalized from a special education training setting to the regular classroom with the use of a modified, less intense form of the original intervention. The ultimate goal of the resource program was to reduce the requirements of the regular classroom teacher to a manageable level while still maintaining high levels of appro-

EXHIBIT 4.5   Appropriate behavior for the group of subjects and randomly selected peers for Phase I and Phase II

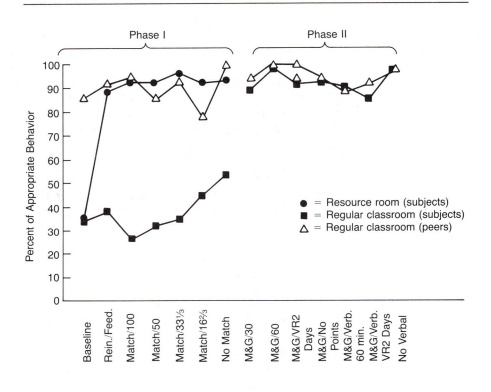

Source: From "Generalization and Maintenance of Treatment Gains of Behaviorally/Emotionally Handicapped Students from Resource Rooms to Regular Classrooms Using Self-Evaluation Procedures" by G. Rhode. Unpublished doctoral dissertation, Utah State University, 1981, p. 105. Used with permission.

priate classroom behavior. Although an intervention was used to promote generalization in the regular classroom, its cost in terms of teacher time and effort was clearly less than that of the initial intervention used in the resource room. Students in this study also evaluated their performance very accurately, matching the teacher's ratings about 90% of the time throughout the study. This finding is consistent with previous findings indicating that students are very capable of reliably monitoring their own behavior (Bolstad & Johnson, 1972). Interestingly, high levels of accuracy are not necessarily required to obtain positive changes in behavior (Rosenbaum & Drabman, 1979).

In summary, self-monitoring procedures hold substantial promise as a preferred practice for promoting generalization with behaviorally disordered students. To teach students to use self-monitoring procedures effectively, the following suggestions should be followed:

- *Define the behavior explicitly.* The more precisely a behavior is defined, the more likely it is that a student will be able to observe and record it accurately. . . . Viewing examples of specific behaviors on videotapes is particularly meaningful to most students.
- *Simplify behavior counting and recording.* The simpler the process, the more accuracy that can be expected.
- *Use time limits.* Students should not be expected to count behaviors over an indefinite period. Using a predetermined 15-, 30-, or 60-minute period is preferred.
- *Use teacher reliability checks.* Teachers should make unobtrusive reliability checks on an intermittent basis. Students achieving a given level of reliability (e.g., 80) should be rewarded.
- *Introduce the process early in the student's educational career.* If it is taught early in the child's educational career, the probability increases that self-monitoring can be used more successfully, and for more purposes, as the individual matures.
- *Practice the process.* The behavioral principles of teaching a skill to fluency levels may be as important in self-monitoring to generalization and maintenance as it is in other areas of functioning. (Frith & Armstrong, 1986, p. 146)

Self-Instruction

Another method of developing self-management skills is self-instruction. Self-instruction refers to the process of making "verbal statements to oneself which prompt, direct, or maintain behavior" (O'Leary & Dubey, 1979, p. 450). This strategy has been used with hyperactive children (Bornstein & Quevillon, 1976; Douglas, Parry, Marton, & Garson, 1976), aggressive children (Camp, Blom, Hebert, & vanDoorninck, 1977), and behaviorally disordered students (David & Hajicek, 1985; Kendall & Finch, 1978).

Sometimes referred to as *cognitive behavior modification* (Meichenbaum, 1977) or *cognitive behavior therapy* (Kendall & Braswell, 1985), self-instruction training owes its beginnings to the work of Donald Meichenbaum, who developed and tested a training program for impulsive children to "talk to themselves" as a means of developing self-control. The basic elements of the training program include the following procedural steps:

1. An adult model performed a task while talking to himself out loud (*cognitive modeling*);
2. The student performed the same task under the direction of the model's instructions (*overt, external guidance*);
3. The student performed the task while instructing himself aloud (*overt self guidance*).
4. The student whispered the instruction to himself as he went through the task (*faded, overt self-guidance*); and finally,
5. The student performed the task while guiding his performance via private speech (*covert self-instruction*). (Meichenbaum & Goodman, 1971, p. 116)

In teaching a child how to copy a complicated pattern of lines, the adult (i.e., teacher) first performed the task while providing the following model:

> Okay, what is it I have to do? You want me to copy the picture with the different lines. I have to go slowly and carefully. Okay, draw the line down, down, good; and then to the right, that's it; now down some more and to the left. Good, I'm doing fine so far. Remember, go slowly. Now back up again. No, I was supposed to go down. That's okay. Just erase the line carefully . . . Good. Even if I make an error I can go on slowly and carefully. I have to go down now. Finished. I did it! (Meichenbaum & Goodman, 1971, p. 117)

Most self-instructional programs employ the same pattern in teaching students how to first "think aloud" and, ultimately, just to themselves privately. The basic components of self-instructional procedures include:

1. *Problem definition:* "Let's see, what am I supposed to do?"
2. *Problem approach:* "I have to look at all the possibilities."
3. *Focusing of attention:* "I better concentrate and focus in, and think only of what I'm doing right now."
4. *Choosing an answer.* "I think it's this one. . ."
5. *Self-reinforcement:* "Hey, not bad, I really did a good job."
   or
   Coping statement: "Oh, I made a mistake. Next time I'll try and go slower and concentrate more and maybe I'll get the right answer." (Kendall & Braswell, 1985, p. 120)

The effects of a self-instructional package on overactive preschool boys' on-task behavior has been investigated (Bornstein & Quevillon, 1976). The self-instructional training package consisted of four types of verbalizations modeled by the teacher: (a) questions about the task (e.g., "What does the teacher want me to do?"), (b) answers to the questions about the task (e.g., "Oh, that's right, I'm supposed to copy that picture"), (c) self-instructions that guide the learner through the task (e.g., "OK, first I draw along here . . ."), and (d) self-reinforcement (e.g., "How about that; I really did that one well"). After the instructor modelled the task, the students performed the task while the experimenter verbalized aloud. The student then performed the task while talking aloud to himself with the teacher whispering softly in close proximity. Next the student performed the task while whispering the correct verbalizations while the teacher made lip movements but no sound. The student then performed the task while making lip movements only with no sound; finally the student performed the task with only covert self-instruction (e.g., talking to himself quietly).

This self-instructional package produced a dramatic effect on the on-task behavior of the three students. However, subsequent attempts to replicate these findings have been equivocal. For example, the same package used with second- and third-grade hyperactive students failed to produce changes in on-task behavior (Friedling & O'Leary, 1979), and using the same procedures with preschoolers failed to produce noticeable changes in on-task behavior (Billings & Wasik, 1985). These and other findings led Bornstein (1985) to state; "What then, does all of this mean? *Quite simply, it appears that self-instructional programs can be effective, although obviously they are not always effective*" (p. 70). (emphasis in original). He went on to say:

> Self-instructional training will probably be of great benefit to some, moderate benefit to others, and minimal or no benefit to yet a final grouping of individuals. Our job is to identify those variables that substantially affect the success of our treatment. (p. 71)

Another type of self-instruction is alternate response training. It involves learning another adaptive response to replace an undesirable behavior (Esveldt-Dawson & Kazdin, 1982). An example of alternate response training is the use of progressive muscle relaxation techniques to control anger. An application of alternate response training to students is the Turtle Technique (Robin, Schneider, & Dolnick, 1976). The Turtle Technique was developed to help teach highly aggressive elementary-aged students to manage their aggression using relaxation training and problem-solving techniques.

The Turtle Technique is introduced to students with the following analogy:

> Little Turtle was very upset about going to school. When he was there he got into trouble because he fought with his mates. Other turtles teased, bumped, or hit him. He then became angry and started fights. The teacher then punished him. One day he met the big old tortoise, who told him that his shell was the secret answer to many problems. The tortoise told Little Turtle to withdraw into his shell whenever he felt angry, and rest until he felt better. Little Turtle tried it the next day and it worked. He no longer became angry or started fights, his teacher now smiled at him, and he began to like school.

After the story is read to the students, the Turtle response is taught by demonstrating and practicing the following procedure: Pull your arms and legs in close to your body, lay your head on your desk, and imagine you are a turtle withdrawing into your "shell" by covering your head with your arms and hands. Students are taught, via demonstration and practice again, to "turtle" under four conditions: (a) when they believe an aggressive exchange is about to happen between them and other students, (b) when they are angry and think a tantrum or blow-up is imminent, (c) when the teacher tells them to turtle, and (d) when a peer tells them to turtle. The purpose of the first phase is to establish the turtle response as automatic through direct teaching and practice.

The second phase of the Turtle Technique is to teach students to relax. In learning relaxation, students are first shown how to alternately tense and relax various muscle groups. Once that is mastered, they are taught how to simply relax while in the turtle position. The final phase involves direct teaching and practice of problem-solving skills. Students are taught to generate a number of alternative coping strategies that they can use to deal with provocations that previously had resulted in aggressive responses. Students are also taught to evaluate the feasibility of the alternative coping responses by predicting the consequences of behaving in certain ways.

The Turtle technique illustrates the applications of alternative response training, specifically relaxation, to the problem of aggression. It is difficult to isolate the effects of relaxation alone on the development of more adaptive coping responses because other techniques (direct teaching, practice, positive reinforcement and feedback) were also used. In general, however, it is reasonable to conclude that the Turtle Technique and other, similar approaches are worthy of consideration in selecting interventions for very aggressive students.

The overall evidence concerning the effectiveness of self-instructional training with children, especially children with behavioral disorders, is inconclusive and inconsistent. Self-instruction has been effective in improving task performance in laboratory-like settings. However, its effectiveness in the classroom with aggressive students has not been convincing (Wilson, 1984). Still, efforts to identify promising applications of self-instructional training as a technique for programming generalization should continue. To increase the likelihood of successful applications of self-instructional approaches, the teacher should make sure that (a) correct self-instructions are reinforced, (b) self-instruction is used with behaviors or skills that have already been acquired to at least a moderate level of proficiency, (c) the self-instructions are, in fact, carried out, and (d) self-instruction is used in conjunction with self-monitoring or self-reinforcement procedures.

Self-Reinforcement

Self-reinforcement is potentially one of the most powerful types of self-management strategies. Self-reinforcement means that students reinforce themselves for appropriate behavior. Studies by Felixbrod and O'Leary (1974), Drabman et al. (1973), Turkewitz et al. (1975), and Rhode et al. (1983) provide practical guidelines for using self-reinforcement in the classroom.

1. Before using self-reinforcement, the student's behavior should be brought under control of a teacher-administered contingency management system.
2. Responsibility for reinforcement should be transferred from the teacher to the student gradually.

3. Students should be taught to reinforce themselves. Instruction, demonstration, practice, feedback, and teacher monitoring should be employed when teaching students to reinforce themselves.
4. Students should not be allowed to adopt lenient performance standards for reinforcement. Because higher or more stringent performance standards tend to be associated with greater levels of appropriate behavior, teachers should encourage students to select stringent criteria for reinforcement through modeling, prompts, and social reinforcement.
5. The self-reinforcement schedule should be gradually thinned to encourage maintenance of the behavior over time.

Another self-management strategy, self-punishment, is sometimes used in conjunction with a self-reinforcement program. Self-punishment involves applying aversive consequences contingent on the occurrence of a specific undesirable behavior. The most common form of self-punishment is response cost. Two studies examining student self-administered response cost found it effective when used in conjunction with self-reinforcement (Humphrey, Karoly, & Kirschenbaum, 1978; Kaufman & O'Leary, 1972).

As a general rule, it is not appropriate to use self-punishment as the foundation of a self-management program. The same undesirable side effects associated with externally administered punishment are present with self-punishment; that is, increased aggression, avoidance, cheating. In addition, self-punishment, when used alone, does not teach appropriate alternative behaviors.

As with other types of interventions that use punishment, teachers should carefully consider its advantages and disadvantages. Epps et al. (1985) have suggested the following questions be considered prior to implementing a response cost self-punishment procedure in the classroom:

1. Will the response cost, when combined with self-reinforcement, significantly contribute to behavior change or to generalization?
2. Is the student more likely to earn points than to lose them?
3. Is the self-administered response-cost procedure likely to cause the student to focus attention more on failure rather than on improvements?
4. Can the student implement a response-cost system on top of what (s)he is probably already doing, namely, self-recording and self-reinforcing? (p. 91)

Summary of Self-Management Procedures
The rationale underlying the use of self-management procedures with behaviorally disordered students is compelling. Self-management is one

way of achieving the ultimate educational goal of producing competent students who are self-reliant, responsible, and able to function independently and productively. Teaching behaviorally disordered students to manage their own behavior as a means of facilitating generalization of improved functioning from specialized treatment settings to the regular classroom has much intuitive and practical appeal.

However, as with so many other educational procedures, it is important that we not become overly enamored with a particular "innovation" before subjecting its effectiveness to rigorous scrutiny. Are self-management procedures effective in producing behavioral changes in behaviorally disordered students? How do self-management procedures compare in terms of efficacy to external control methods? Do self-management procedures promote generalization and maintenance of treatment gains with these students?

The evidence currently available suggests that we are not yet at the point where we can guarantee that self-management procedures are consistently superior to external control procedures or that self-management procedures are preferable to other procedures as a means of promoting generalization. The available evidence does suggest, however, that self-management procedures have produced promising results often enough that both continued rigorous empirical investigation and carefully implemented and monitored practical applications should be continued (Fowler, 1984).

As we have seen, there are procedures teachers can employ to maximize the effectiveness of self-management strategies with behaviorally disordered students. Students must be directly taught to use self-management procedures as opposed to simply being told to use them, and they must implement the procedures correctly to be effective (Baer, Fowler, & Carden-Smith, 1984).

Self-management is not a panacea. It is, however, a promising practice that can be successfully used with behaviorally disordered students as long as they receive high quality instruction on the use of the strategies, control is gradually faded from the teacher to the students, and there is continued surveillance by the teacher of the students' use of the self-management strategies.

MONITORING GENERALIZATION IN THE REGULAR CLASSROOM

Once new skills have been taught and the student has moved from a special education setting to a regular classroom, progress should be evaluated and monitored. Follow-up in the regular classroom is necessary to make certain that the new skills generalize to that setting and to deter-

Achieving generalization is not easy.

mine what program adjustments, additional instruction, and other fine tuning may be needed to insure that the newly learned skills are functional. In some cases, monitoring may be needed indefinitely, particularly for students whose problem behaviors are relatively severe and long-standing.

There are many ways to monitor and evaluate regular classroom performance. This assessment may be done by several different professionals, depending on the district, school, and personnel involved. Data may be collected by the regular teacher, the special education teacher, an aide, a volunteer, the student or ancillary personnel involved in the student's generalization program. The data may be formal or informal. The important point is that monitoring should be systematic, and, further, that the information obtained should be used to make decisions about whether the student's program should be continued as is or be altered in some way.

Formal Measures

Carefully structured formal observations usually yield the most specific and accurate information on student performance. Because formal observations are time-consuming, they cannot always be conducted by teachers while they are teaching. Thus, a third person is typically needed to conduct formal observations. Unfortunately, it can be difficult to find a third party observer to make regular classroom observations. In many cases, the special education teacher is not free to leave class to make the observations personally. Other potentially available sources—aides, university students, volunteer parents, psychologists, or social workers—may not always be available to draw on regularly either. Thus, formal observations may necessarily be fewer and less frequent than if the needed resources were readily available.

Several types of formal observations may provide helpful information for special education teachers fortunate enough to have the services of a third-party observer or the ability to structure their time to observe for themselves. For a general measure of appropriate and inappropriate classroom behavior, the recording system described in chapter 2 would be appropriate. When using this system, normative peer data can also be collected in the regular classroom, providing setting-specific data against which the behaviorally disordered students' performance can be compared. Positive and negative teacher interactions with the students may also be coded at the same time, adding another source of information about what is actually occurring in the regular classroom. Acceptable levels of appropriate behavior by the student indicate that the program is successful, while unacceptable or declining levels suggest that adjustments are needed. More specific data may be needed for problem areas.

Informal Measures

Informal measures are more commonly used because they are easier to implement and maintain within the framework of the regular classroom. Examples would include daily ratings by the regular teacher (e.g., a numerical rating of 1 to 5 or ratings of good, fair, poor) to describe student behavior and work for a specified period. Later in the student's program, ratings may decrease to weekly, biweekly or even less frequently. A simple form requesting information from the regular teacher may be delivered by the student or the special education teacher. More specific data may be obtained as needed. For example, regular teachers can keep frequency counts of classroom rules broken by students and of other discrete behaviors. Data such as citizenship marks the student earns each term can also indicate regular classroom performance.

Academic performance can also be monitored informally by the special education teacher. The teacher may examine daily assignments, completed homework, tests, timed drills, and grades and obtain feedback from the regular teacher on the student's academic performance. If the student's academic work is not acceptable in quality and quantity, the program can be adjusted to remediate specific problems.

The specificity and frequency of data obtained will depend upon the number and severity of the problem behaviors and the skill and willingness of those working with the student. In structuring a monitoring system, the special education teacher will need to be mindful of these considerations and constraints and yet still devise a system to provide a complete and accurate picture of the student's performance in terms of regular classroom demands.

A chart special education teachers can use to informally monitor generalization is provided in Exhibit 4.6. It is organized so that information can be collected in different settings, subject areas, and behaviors from several individuals.

Self-Monitoring of Generalization Strategies

The key to an effective generalization program is a teacher who is skilled and knowledgeable about generalization *and* who systematically implements the preferred practices and strategies reviewed in this chapter. Epps et al. (1985) developed a procedure teachers can use to monitor their own programming for generalization. The teacher self-monitoring procedure covers the major methods of programming for generalization —using natural contingencies of reinforcement, training sufficient examples, teaching loosely, using indiscriminable contingencies, general case programming, programming common stimuli, and teaching self-management skills. Teachers are instructed to monitor their own programming for generalization by recording every time they use a specific strategy. Exhibit 4.7 depicts self-monitoring data for the strategy of using natural contingencies of reinforcement. Each dot represents a separate instance of using a specific technique.

The primary purpose of this strategy is to let teachers determine whether they are actually using the preferred practices for promoting generalization. If the self-monitoring data indicate that specific strategies are being infrequently used, the teacher can reorient effort and actions to increase the frequency with which a specific strategy is used (Epps et al., 1985).

SUMMARY

Clearly, generalization of treatment effects is an issue of great importance in teaching behaviorally disordered students. Without effective procedures to promote generalization, a teacher's initial success in

EXHIBIT 4.6 Informal generalization probes

| KEY: | + Great (in top 3-5 students)* | − Poor (in bottom 3-5 students)* |
| | ✔ O.K. (any students between top 3-5 and bottom 3-5) | O Not Applicable |

*"Top" and "bottom" groups will vary depending on the class, setting, and activity.

Student's Name: _____

Settings:

Behaviors Dates:																
Assignments completed																
Assignments accurate																
Follows rules/directions																
Needs few reminders to start work																
Seeks teacher attention appropriately and not too often																
Does not talk out																
Does not get out-of-seat often																
Does not bother other students verbally																
Does not bother other students physically																
_____																
_____																
_____																
_____																
_____																

Source: Adapted from *Procedures for Incorporating Generalization and Maintenance Programming into Interventions for Special Education Students* by S. Epps, B. J. Thompson, and M. P. Lane, Des Moines: Iowa Department of Public Instruction, 1985, p. 227. Used with permission.

EXHIBIT 4.7 Teacher self-monitoring of generalization and maintenance techniques

Natural Contingencies of Reinforcement

Teacher _____ School _____

Dates _____ S-M Packet # _____

	M	T	W	TH	F
1. Observes regular-class environment	• •	•			
2. Interviews regular-class teacher	•				
3. Chooses easily trapped behavior	• • •	• • 1			
4. Reminds student to call attention to own appropriate behavior	• • • •	• •			
5. Teaches student to recognize reinforcement	• • •	• • •			
6. Rearranges natural environment (requests others to refrain from too much prompting or to reinforce a student)	• •				
7. Examines competing contingencies	•				

Source: Adapted from *Procedures for Incorporating Generalization and Maintenance Programming into Interventions for Special Education Students* by S. Epps, B. J. Thompson, and M. P. Lane, Des Moines: Iowa Department of Public Instruction, 1985, p. 231. Used with permission.

changing maladaptive behavior patterns and teaching more adaptive behavior patterns is a Pyrrhic victory. Without a systematic plan for generalization, an intervention effort is unfinished.

Fortunately, there is a set of preferred strategies available to teachers that, if carefully planned and implemented, will increase the probability that behavior change will generalize. As we have seen, there is a technology of generalization; our knowledge base of how best to promote generalization of treatment effects from special education to regular education continues to expand. The efficacy of engaging natural contingencies of reinforcement, programming common stimuli, and teaching multiple examples of the skill to be learned has been reliably demonstrated in research and practice. The promise of self-management strategies continues to energize researchers and practitioners who seek ways of more directly involving students in their own behavior change. Extending variations of the intervention program into the generalization setting and reprogramming the social environment hold great promise. The importance of the concepts associated with generalization has refocused our attention on the careful coordination and implementation of programs to teach students to survive and succeed in regular classroom environments.

These preferred practices tell us it is not easy to achieve generalization. Baer (1981) commented that an alternative title for his book *How to Plan for Generalization* might have been *How to **Try** for Generalization.* The importance of generalization and the effort to achieve it will be a continuing theme throughout the remainder of this text. Applications to academic instruction and social skills training, as well as issues concerning generalization in self-contained classrooms, resource programs, and regular classrooms, will be discussed in more detail in subsequent chapters.

REVIEW QUESTIONS

1. Explain the importance of generalization in programs for behaviorally disordered students.
2. Why is generalization so difficult to achieve?
3. Why is it important for the special education teacher to carefully observe in the regular classroom to which one of his or her students will soon be returned? What are the kinds of things that will be observed? What can the special educator do with that information prior to the student's return to the regular classroom?
4. You have just been hired as a generalization specialist in a medium-sized school district's program for behaviorally disordered students. Until now, the district has done very little active programming for generalization. Outline what you would attempt to establish as the basic strategy of a generalization programming effort in that district.
5. You are a resource teacher. One of your fourth-grade behaviorally disordered students, Joe, is in your room for 2 hours per day for academic instruction in reading and math. After a rough beginning, Joe's classroom behavior and academic skills have improved significantly *in your room.* However, few changes have been observed when he is in his regular classroom. In fact, Joe's fourth-grade teacher reports that, if anything, his behavior is worse now than it had been prior to starting in the resource room. What would you do? Describe the procedures you would implement to facilitate generalization.

6. Design a self-instructional procedure you could use with an aggressive student in an effort to decrease the frequency and intensity of aggressive responses.

REFERENCES

Alberto, P. A., & Troutman, A. C. (1986). *Applied behavior analysis* (2nd ed.). Columbus, OH: Merrill.

Ayllon, T., Kuhlman, C., & Warzak, W. J. (1983). Programming resource room generalization using lucky charms. *Child and Family Therapy, 4,* 61–67.

Baer, D. M. (1981). *How to plan for generalization.* Lawrence, KS: H. & H Enterprises.

Baer, D. M., Fowler, S. A., & Carden-Smith, L. (1984). Using reinforcement and independent grading to promote and maintain task accuracy in a mainstreamed class. *Analysis and Intervention in Developmental Disabilities, 4,* 157–169.

Baer, D. M., & Wolf, M. M. (1970). The entry into natural communities of reinforcement. In R. Ulrich, T. Stachnik, & J. Mabry (Eds.), *Control of human behavior* (Vol. 2). Glenview, IL: Scott, Foresman.

Barkley, R. A., Copeland, A. P., & Savage, C. (1980). A self-control classroom for hyperactive children. *Journal of Autism and Developmental Disorders, 10,* 75–89.

Billings, D. C., & Wasik, B. H. (1985). Self-instructional training with preschoolers: An attempt to replicate. *Journal of Applied Behavior Analysis, 18,* 61–67.

Bolstad, O., & Johnson, S. (1972). Self-regulation in the modification of disruptive classroom behavior. *Journal of Applied Behavior Analysis, 5,* 443–454.

Bornstein, P. H. (1985). Self-instructional training: A commentary and state of the art. *Journal of Applied Behavior Analysis, 18,* 69–72.

Bornstein, P. H., & Quevillon, R. P. (1976). The effects of a self-instructional package on overactive preschool boys. *Journal of Applied Behavior Analysis, 9,* 179–188.

Broden, M., Hall, R. V., & Mitts, B. (1971). The effect of self-recording on the classroom behavior of two eighth-grade students. *Journal of Applied Behavior Analysis, 4,* 191–199.

Camp, B., Blom, G., Hebert, F., & vanDoorninck, W. (1977). "Think aloud": A program for developing self-control in young aggressive boys. *Journal of Abnormal Child Psychology, 5,* 157–169.

Cooper, J. O., Heron, T. E., & Heward, W. L. (1987). *Applied behavior analysis.* Columbus, OH: Merrill.

Davis, R. W., & Hajicek, J. O. (1985). Effects of self-instructional training and strategy training on a mathematics task with severely behaviorally disordered students. *Behavioral Disorders, 10,* 211–218.

Douglas, V. I., Parry, P., Marton, P., & Garson, C. (1976). Assessment of a cognitive training program for hyperactive children. *Journal of Abnormal Child Psychololgy, 4,* 389–410.

Drabman, R. S., Hammer, D., & Rosenbaum, M. S. (1979). Assessing generalization in behavior modification with children: The generalization map. *Behavioral Assessment, 1,* 203–219.

Drabman, R. S., Spitalnik, R., & O'Leary, K. D. (1973). Teaching self-control to disruptive children. *Journal of Abnormal Psycholoigy, 82,* 10–16.

Engelmann, S., & Carnine, D. (1982). *Theory of instruction: Principles and applications.* New York: Irvington.

Epps, S., Thomas, B. J., & Lane, M. P. (1985). *Procedures for incorporating generalization and maintenance programming into interventions for special education students.* Des Moines: Iowa Department of Public Instruction.

Epstein, R., & Goss, C. M. (1978). A self-control procedure for the maintenance of nondisruptive behavior in an elementary school child. *Behavior Therapy, 9,* 109–117.

Esveldt-Dawson, K., & Kazdin, A. E. (1982). *How to use self-control.* Lawrence, KS: H & H Enterprises.

Felixbrod, J. J., & O'Leary, K. D. (1974). Self-determination of academic standards by children: Towards freedom from external control. *Journal of Educational Psychology, 66,* 845–850.

Fowler, S. A. (1984). Introductory comments: The pragmatics of self-management for the developmentally disabled. *Analysis and Intervention in Developmental Disabilities, 4,* 85–89.

Friedling, C., & O'Leary, S. (1979). Effects of self-instructional training on second and third-grade hyperactive children: A failure to replicate. *Journal of Applied Behavior Analysis, 12,* 211–219.

Frith, G. H., & Armstrong, S. W. (1986). Self-monitoring for behavior disordered students. *Teaching Exceptional Children, 18,* 144–148.

Glynn, E. L. (1970). Classroom applications of self-determined reinforcement. *Journal of Applied Behavior Analysis, 3,* 123–137.

Glynn, E. L., Thomas, J. D., & Shee, S. M. (1973). Behavioral self-control of on-task behavior in an elementary classroom. *Journal of Applied Behavior Analysis, 6,* 105–113.

Graubard, P. S., Rosenberg, H., & Miller, M. B. (1974). Student applications of behavior modification to teachers and environments or ecological approaches to social deviancy. In E. A. Ramp & B. L. Hopkins (Eds.), *A new direction for education: Behavior analysis.* Lawrence, KS: Support for Development Center for Follow Through.

Gresham, F. M. (1983). Social skills assessment as a component of mainstreaming placement decisions. *Exceptional Children, 49,* 331–336.

Henker, B., Whalen, C. K., & Henshaw, S. P. (1980). The attributional contexts of cognitive intervention strategies. *Exceptional Educational Quarterly, 1,* 17–30.

Horner, R. H., Bellamy, G. T., & Colvin, G. T. (1984). Responding in the presence of nontrained stimuli: Implications of generalization error patterns. *The Journal of the Association for Severe Handicaps, 9,* 287–295.

Horner, R. H., & McDonald, R. S. (1982). Comparison of single instance and general case instruction in teaching a generalized vocational skill. *Journal of the Association for the Severely Handicapped, 7,* 7–20.

Horner, R. H., Sprague, J., & Wilcox, B. (1982). Constructing general case programs for community activities. In B. Wilcox & G. T. Bellamy, *Design of high school programs for severely handicapped students.* Baltimore: Paul H. Brookes.

Humphrey, L. L., Karoly, P., & Kirschenbaum, D. S. (1978). Self-management in the classroom: Self-imposed response cost versus self-reward. *Behavior Therapy, 9,* 592–601.

Johnson, S. M. (1970). Self-reinforcement versus external reinforcement in behavior modification with children. *Developmental Psychology, 3,* 147–148.

Kanfer, F. H., & Duerfeldt, P. H. (1967). Effects on retention of externally or self-reinforced rehearsal trials following acquisition. *Psychological Reports, 21,* 194–196.

Kaufman, K. F., & O'Leary, K. D. (1972). Reward, cost, and self-evaluation procedures for disruptive adolescents in a psychiatric hospital school. *Journal of Applied Behavior Analysis, 5,* 293–309.

Kendall, P. C., & Braswell, L. (1985). *Cognitive-behavioral therapy for impulsive children.* New York: Guilford.

Kendall, P. C., & Finch, A. J., Jr. (1978). A cognitive-behavioral treatment for impulsivity: A case study. *Journal of Consulting and Clinical Psychology, 46,* 110–118.

Kneedler, R. D., & Hallahan, D. P. (1981). Self-monitoring of on-task behavior with learning disabled children: Current studies and directions. *Exceptional Education Quarterly, 2,* 73–82.

Lovitt, T. C. (1973). Self-management projects with children with behavioral disabilities. *Journal of Learning Disabilities, 6,* 138–150.

Lovitt, T. C., & Curtiss, K. A. (1969). Academic response rate as a function of teacher- and self-imposed contingencies. *Journal of Applied Behavior Analysis, 2,* 49–53.

McDonnell, J. J., Horner, R. H., & Williams, J. A. (1984). Comparison of three strategies for teaching generalized grocery purchasing to high school students with severe handicaps. *Journal of the Association for Persons with Severe Handicaps, 9,* 123–133.

McLaughlin, T. F. (1976). Self-control in the classroom. *Review of Educational Research, 46,* 631–663.

McLaughlin, T. F., Krappman, V. F., & Welsh, J. M. (1985). The effects of self-recording for on-task behavior of behaviorally disordered special education students. *Remedial and Special Education, 6,* 42–45.

Meichenbaum, D. H. (1977). *Cognitive-behavior modification: An integrative approach.* New York: Plenum Press.

Meichenbaum, D. H., & Goodman, J. (1971). Training impulsive children to talk to themselves: A means of developing self-control. *Journal of Abnormal Psychology, 77,* 115–126.

Michelson, L., & Mannarino, A. (1986). Social skills training with children: Research and clinical applications. In P. S. Strain, M. J. Guralnick, & H. M. Walker (Eds.), *Children's social behavior: Development, assessment, and modification*. New York: Academic Press.

Morgan, D. P., Young, K. R., & Goldstein, S. (1983). Teaching behaviorally disordered students to increase teachers' praise and attention in mainstreamed classrooms. *Behavioral Disorders, 7*, 265–273.

O'Leary, S. G., & Dubey, D. R. (1979). Applications of self-control procedures by children: A review. *Journal of Applied Behavior Analysis, 12*, 449–465.

Rhode, G., Morgan, D. P., & Young, K. R. (1983). Generalization and maintenance of treatment gains of behaviorally handicapped students from resource rooms to regular classrooms using self-evaluation procedures. *Journal of Applied Behavior Analysis, 16*, 171–188.

Robin, A., Schneider, M., & Dolnick, M. (1976). The turtle technique: An extended case study of self-control in the classroom. *Psychology in the Schools, 13*, 449–453.

Rosenbaum, M. S., & Drabman, R. S. (1979). Self-control training in the classroom: A review and critique. *Journal of Applied Behavior Analysis, 12*, 467–485.

Safran, S., & Safran, J. (1984). The self-monitoring mood chart: Measuring affect in the classroom. *Teaching Exceptional Children, 16*, 172–175.

Sagotsky, G., Patterson, C. J., & Lepper, M. R. (1978). Training children's self-control: A field experiment in self-monitoring and goal-setting in the classroom. *Journal of Experimental Child Psychology, 25*, 242–253.

Santogrossi, D. A., O'Leary, K. D., Romanczyk, R. G., & Kaufman, K. F. (1973). Self-evaluation by adolescents in a psychiatric hospital school token program. *Journal of Applied Behavior Analysis, 6*, 277–287.

Sprague, J. R., & Horner, R. H. (1984). The effects of single instance, multiple instance and general case training on generalized vending machine use by moderately handicapped students. *Journal of Applied Behavior Analysis, 17*, 273–278.

Stokes, T. F., & Baer, D. M. (1977). An implicit technology of generalization. *Journal of Applied Behavior Analysis, 10*, 349–367.

Sugai, G., & Rowe, P. (1984). The effect of self-recording on out-of-seat behavior of an EMR student. *Education and Training of the Mentally Retarded, 19*, 23–28.

Turkewitz, H., O'Leary, K. D., & Ironsmith, M. (1975). Generalization and maintenance of appropriate behavior through self-control. *Journal of Consulting and Clinical Psychology, 43*, 577–583.

Vaughn, S., Bos, C. S., & Lund, K. A. (1986). . . . But they can do it in my room: Strategies for promoting generalization. *Teaching Exceptional Children, 18*, 176–180.

Wahler, R. G., Berland, R. M., & Coe, T. D. (1979). Generalization processes in child behavior change. In B. B. Lahey & A. E. Kazdin (Eds.), *Advances in clinical child psychology* (Vol. 1). Boston: Allyn & Bacon.

Walker, H. M. (1979). *The acting out child: Coping with classroom disruption.* Boston: Allyn & Bacon.

Walker, H. M., & Buckley, N. K. (1972). Programming generalization and maintenance of treatment effects across time and across settings. *Journal of Applied Behavior Analysis, 5,* 209–224.

Walker, H. M., Hops, H., & Johnson, S. M. (1975). Generalization and maintenance of classroom treatment effects. *Behavior Therapy, 6,* 188–200.

Walker, H. M., & Rankin, R. (1983). Assessing the behavioral expectations and demands of less restrictive settings. *School Psychology Review, 12,* 274–284.

Wilson, R. (1984). A review of self-control treatments for aggressive behavior. *Behavioral Disorders, 9,* 131–140.

Workman, E. A., & Hector, M. A. (1978). Behavioral self-control in classroom settings: A review of the literature. *Journal of School Psychology, 16,* 227-236.

5 Teaching Academic Skills To Behaviorally Disordered Students

Stan C. Paine
Lynne Andersen-Inman
University of Oregon

After completing this chapter, you should be able to

- *List the goals of academic instruction for behaviorally disordered students.*
- *Describe the assumptions underlying the approach to teaching academic skills discussed in this chapter.*
- *Explain the essential elements of the direct instruction and opportunity-to-respond approaches to teaching academic skills.*
- *Discuss the relationship between academic deficits and behavior problems in behaviorally disordered students.*
- *Identify preferred practices in teaching academic tool subjects to behaviorally disordered students.*
- *Identify preferred practices in teaching content area subjects.*
- *Describe procedures for reinforcing academic performance.*
- *Identify ways in which teachers can maximize time use in the classroom.*
- *Define transenvironmental programming and explain its relationship to teaching academic skills to behaviorally disordered students.*

An often troubling area of concern for teachers of behaviorally disordered students is the academic curriculum. So much attention and energy is devoted to managing disruptive behaviors and dealing with emotional crises that the questions of what the students should be taught and how they should be taught are not afforded the careful consideration they are due.

The approaches to be discussed in this chapter represent preferred practices for teaching academic skills to behaviorally disordered students that have been validated through extensive research in recent years. This research, conducted with "hard-to-teach" students, has much to tell us about how to succeed. We will distill this research into a set of preferred practices and describe these practices in some detail. The first part of the chapter reviews the basic goals and underlying assumptions of academic programming. Next, the characteristics of a direct instruction approach to academic instruction are described. The content of the academic curriculum is covered in the following section, including specific recommendations for instructional programming. The last section of the chapter offers important recommendations related to reinforcing academic skills and maximizing available time.

GOALS AND ASSUMPTIONS OF ACADEMIC INSTRUCTION

As has already been discussed, when a behavior problem interferes with a student's school success or with the success of other students, educators should try to eliminate the problem behavior and replace it with more productive behaviors. However, we believe that this behavior intervention should be done in the context of actively teaching the student academic skills. Hence, the focus with behaviorally disordered students is first to provide them with high quality, responsive academic instruction and second to manage their behavior while promoting academic success. The assumption is that if students' academic successes are maximized, their behavior problems are minimized. Students with long histories of problem behaviors will undoubtedly continue to display inappropriate behavior, even with highly structured academic programming. However, without a high quality academic program and a gradual improvement of academic skills, even the most sophisticated behavior management program will not lessen or eliminate school behavior problems on a long-term basis.

The approach to academic instruction presented in this chapter has four goals:

1. To achieve at or above grade level in all academic areas
2. To behave in accordance with school rules and expectations at all times and in all settings
3. To produce change and academic success that will be rated acceptable by the students as well as by their peers, teachers, administrators, and parents
4. To achieve widespread and durable behavioral improvements and academic success

These goals might seem overly ambitious. To set the goals any lower, however, would be to deprive the student of the opportunity for real success in school and to deprive teachers of the accomplishment of knowing that they can succeed in teaching even the most difficult students. Thus, a viable program for behaviorally disordered students consists of interventions that focus on behavioral and social excesses and deficits and sufficiently improves academic skills to enable them to be successfully integrated, from the perspective of academic curriculum, on a full-time basis.

The approaches to teaching academic skills presented in this chapter rest on several important assumptions:

1. Behaviorally disordered students want to succeed in school. This might not always be apparent, but it is relatively safe to conclude that they would rather succeed than fail.

2. Behaviorally disordered students can succeed in school if they are given sufficient structure. Structure includes everything from rules to reinforcers, from praise to points, from time management to teacher expectations. Given enough structure in the initial stages of intervention, students will succeed.
3. Teaching behaviorally disordered students academic skills is very similar to teaching other students academic skills. It requires a curriculum, a teaching method, and an evaluation system. These students learn much like other students. The teaching/learning process is essentially the same; it is only the intensity of the process that may vary.
4. To enable behaviorally disordered students to experience long-term success, the structure that is so important to their early success must eventually be faded.

These assumptions will be expanded upon in the discussion that follows.

DIRECT INSTRUCTION AS A PREFERRED PRACTICE

What is the best method for teaching academic skills to behaviorally disordered students? A simple answer to this question is that there is no single, best method; the task is too complex. There is, however, a collection of assumptions, procedures, and practices available that generally seem to be effective in meeting the challenge of teaching academic skills to these students. This collection has been called by many different, but closely related, terms.

Two approaches that can be used to teach academic skills to behaviorally disordered students will be discussed in this chapter. These are *direct instruction* and its off-shoot, *opportunity-to-respond*. Both represent contemporary research in education. Rather than describe these two approaches independently, we will describe their similarities and differences within the context of eight basic functions of instruction: origin of the approach; the philosophy and assumptions of the approach; the goals of instruction; the content of instruction (the curriculum); use of time with respect to instruction (including scheduling and time efficiency); classroom organization and instruction delivery; behavior management; and measurement, monitoring, and evaluation of instruction. These issues are summarized for each of the two approaches in Exhibit 5.1.

Although these approaches are related, neither of them can stand alone in providing most effectively for the educational needs of behaviorally disordered students. The most promising strategy incorporates the best elements of each approach. Both terms—direct instruction and opportunity-to-respond—will be used in the discussion of how these students should be taught.

Origins

Direct instruction grew out of the work of two groups of researchers, one working on compensatory education and the other on teacher effectiveness. The former group developed the methods of direct instruction in the late 1960s as part of Project Follow Through (the public school sequel to Project Head Start). As developed in Project Follow Through, direct instruction was a structured educational approach designed to provide academic instruction to economically disadvantaged children (Becker, Engelmann, Carnine, & Rhine, 1982). The second group of researchers (e.g., Rosenshine, 1976) proposed *direct instruction* as the name for a collection of teacher practices found to be closely related to student achievement.

The opportunity-to-respond approach is closely related to direct instruction. In fact, it is a direct outgrowth of the teacher effectiveness research. The initial research focused on the time students spend working, called students' *on-task behavior* (Broden, Bruce, Mitchell, Carter, & Hall, 1970). This work was then expanded by Rosenshine (1976) to include allocated and engaged time—the proportion of classroom time in which students are actively engaged in the lesson the teacher provides for them. Then, Greenwood, Delquadri, and Hall (1983) took this line of research one step further and proposed the concept of opportunity-to-respond, or the opportunities students have within an instructional period to participate actively in the lesson.

Although neither of these efforts directly focused specifically on the academic needs of behaviorally disordered students, both approaches are well-suited for use with these students, many of whom require compensatory education and effective teaching to improve their academic functioning to grade level (Strain, Cooke, & Apolloni, 1976). What these students generally need is a structured education, which is what the direct instruction and opportunity-to-respond approaches provide.

Philosophy and Assumptions

Direct instruction makes three basic assumptions: all students can be taught, teachers and administrators are responsible for student learning, and there is a promising approach available that can be used to teach academic skills to hard-to-teach students (Association for Direct Instruction, 1982). The starting point in the opportunity-to-respond approach is that student learning depends, in part, on the number of response opportunities the student has (Greenwood, Dinwiddie, Terry, Wade, Stanley, Thibadeau, & Delquadri, 1983). These assumptions might seem self-evident, but they differ considerably from common practice.

First, direct instruction does not allow hard-to-teach students to be cast aside as unteachable. When a teacher does not use an effective, reliable teaching approach, it is perhaps easier to conclude after an initial, unsuccessful effort that the student cannot be taught. It is more accurate

EXHIBIT 5.1   Direct instruction versus opportunity-to-respond

Element	Direction Instruction	Opportunity-to-Respond
Origin Philosophy/ Assumptions	1. All students can be taught 2. Teachers are responsible for student learning 3. There is a viable technology available to teachers	Student learning depends in part on their response opportunities in the instructional process
Goals Basic goal	Efficient acquisition, long-term information recall, and generalized skill use	Increase student achievement by increasing academic response opportunities
Approach	Extended practice, cumulative review, integration, mastery criteria, distributed practice	Control of activities provided to students; added tutorial time for additional practice
Curriculum Principles	Principles of instructional design as described in Engelmann and Carnine (1982)	Materials must require active student responding at an appropriate level of difficulty
Materials	Developmental, remedial, and microcomputer series and program	None
Scheduling and Time Use Emphasis	Matching time allocation to instructional priorities; addresses need to do more in less time so that skill deficits can truly be remediated	Maximizing the number of chances each student has for active responding in a given period
Strategies	Small group instruction with unison responding, rapid instructional pacing, effective use of aides, peers, and volunteers	Uses formats that maximize student responding; uses parent and peer tutoring
Classroom Organization and Instructional Delivery (management of antecedent events) Instruction	Uses empirically derived collection of techniques for instructional delivery (see Carnine & Silbert, 1979)	Identifies discrete strategies (e.g., peer/parent tutoring) for increasing opportunity to respond in a practice format; deals less directly with teaching new material

EXHIBIT 5.1 *continued*

Element	Direction Instruction	Opportunity-to-Respond
Classroom organization	Accounts for most of the antecedents of student behavior (e.g., physical environment, rules, schedule, use of human resources) (see Paine et al., 1983)	Assesses various instructional and practice formats for their adequacy in promoting response opportunities

Behavior Management (management of consequences)

Element	Direction Instruction	Opportunity-to-Respond
For correct (appropriate) behavior	Uses a variety of motivational devices (praise, point systems, challenges, game-like structures) to promote student interest and hard work	Uses positive consequences to motivate students
For incorrect (inappropriate) behavior	Uses specific correction procedures for student errors rather than ignoring or punishing them (sees errors and misbehavior as indicating need for more instruction, not as student defiance or lack of ability)	Uses positive correction procedures to remediate errors

Measurement, Monitoring and Evaluation

Element	Direction Instruction	Opportunity-to-Respond
Type	Uses both accuracy and frequency measures	Primarily uses frequency measures
Short-term	Probes students' ability within lessons, at the end of lessons, and on biweekly continuous progress tests in each curriculum area; also does error analysis on daily worksheets to determine where more instruction is necessary	Typically measures daily student performance
Long-term	Uses standardized achievement tests	Uses standardized achievement tests

to conclude that some procedures, especially those that are somewhat loose or unstructured, frequently cannot help some students. This is not to say that some teachers cannot teach; it is to say that the strength of the approach must match the difficulty any student presents. Direct instruction assumes that all students can be taught.

Second, teachers (and administrators) are responsible for student learning. This position is quite different from one that suggests that students alone are responsible for their own learning. Students have definite responsibilities and must play a role in their own learning, but teachers are primarily responsible for ensuring that students actually learn. This means that students cannot be blamed when they do not learn. Teachers are still responsible and must find another way to get through to the students. Administrators are responsible for ensuring that teachers carry out their responsibility and for helping them learn to do so.

Third, there is an effective technology of teaching available to educators. It is the technology of direct instruction, and it will be described below.

Finally, student learning depends on active participation. The lecture method, for example, even with some discussion, does not provide sufficient response opportunities for all students. Even many individualized approaches, such as extensive use of student workbooks, while providing more response opportunities, typically do not provide the sufficient, timely feedback necessary for effective learning. Direct instruction and opportunity-to-respond provide frequent response opportunities for all students, with corrective feedback as necessary, to ensure that learning takes place.

Goals and Approaches

The basic goal of direct instruction is to develop academic skills with widespread and long-lasting utility. It takes direct aim at academic skill levels that will truly serve the student well, enabling students to recall information and apply academic skills across a wide variety of settings, materials, and situations. The goal of opportunity-to-respond is to increase student learning by increasing the number of response opportunities available.

Direct instruction teaches for durability and carry-over of academic skills in several ways. First, it introduces new material according to a set of instructional principles (Engelmann & Carnine, 1980) (see "Curriculum," below) that virtually assures that students understand the material. Second, it provides extensive practice of previously introduced material (Engelmann, 1982), and it schedules this practice carefully over time so that it is distributed across various contexts, situations, and times. Third, direct instruction uses cumulative review and integration of material, in which newly learned material is integrated into previously learned content (cf. Carnine & Silbert, 1979). Fourth, the approach uses mastery criteria, in which high standards are set and maintained as the teacher invests whatever time and effort are necessary to ensure that students reach proficiency before ending instruction on a skill (Bloom, 1976). Finally, teachers frequently present practice opportunities at unpredictable times and in unexpected places to build widespread utility into students' skill levels. A student should be able to recall a bit of information or use a skill upon demand. Random presentation of response opportunities helps to promote this ability (cf. Silbert, Carnine, & Stein, 1981).

The opportunity-to-respond approach is a daily process for achieving longer-term gains. Opportunity-to-respond increases response opportunities by controlling the activities provided to students, by adding turtorial time for additional practice (called *firm-up time* in direct instruction), and by conducting daily and weekly probes on target behaviors to ensure that continuous progress is taking place (Greenwood, Delquadri, & Hall, 1983). These probes are very similar to direct instruction's daily check-outs and biweekly continuous progress tests (Becker et al., 1982). These assessment practices are described more fully in the section on monitoring, measurement, and evaluation.

Curriculum

The principles upon which direct instruction programs are based include rules for teaching various kinds of concepts and operations. These rules govern the selection and sequencing of teaching examples to generate faultless, efficient instructional presentations. *Faultless* means instructional presentations that communicate one (and only one) interpretation of the information, controlling for other possible interpretations the learner might otherwise make and, thus, preventing many student errors (Engelmann, 1980). *Efficient* means instructional sequences that are as concise as possible without sacrificing clarity. Further detail on the importance and content of these instructional design principles, which make direct instruction curriculum materials unique, can be found in a volume by Engelmann and Carnine (1980) entitled *Theory of Instruction.*

Direct instruction curriculum materials include developmental series in reading, language, spelling, handwriting, creative writing, mathematics, and content area (science and social studies) knowledge systems. They also include remedial series in reading, spelling, and mathematics and microcomputer software for computer-assisted instruction. Exhibit 5.2 lists direct instruction curriculum materials currently available from commercial publishers. Opportunity-to-respond does not use an independent curriculum. Instead, it employs a teacher's materials and focuses on what the teacher does to maximize response opportunities while using those materials.

Text continues on p. 212

EXHIBIT 5.2 Direct instruction curriculum materials

Program	Population	Overview	Publishers
Reading Mastery A basal reading sheet series intended for grades 1 through 6.			
Reading Mastery I Distar Reading	Preschool and primary students	Teaches basic decoding and comprehension skills. Students learn how to read letters, words, and stories, both aloud and silently. Students also answer literal comprehension questions about their readings. (160 lessons)	SRA
Reading Mastery II Distar Reading	Primary students who read at about a 2.0 level	Expands basic reading skills. Students learn strategies for decoding difficult words and for answering interpretive comprehension questions. Also teaches basic reasoning skills, such as using rules and completing deductions. (160 lessons)	SRA
Teach Your Child to Read in 100 Easy Lessons	Parents teaching average preschool and primary students (first-grade level)	A slightly accelerated version of Reading Mastery I. (100, rather than 160, lessons)	Simon & Schuster
Reading Mastery Fast Cycle I & II	Preschool and primary students of average or above-average age ability (first- and second-grade level)	Accelerates material presented in Reading Mastery I and II. (170 lessons)	SRA
Reading Mastery III	Primary students who read at about 3.0 level	Emphasizes reasoning and reference skills. Students apply rules in a wide variety of contexts and learn how to interpret maps, graphs, and time lines. Also teaches new vocabulary and complex sentence forms. (140 lessons)	SRA

EXHIBIT 5.2 *continued*

Program	Population	Overview	Publishers
Reading Mastery IV	Intermediate students who read at about a 4.0 level	Emphasizes problem-solving and reading in the content areas. Students evaluate problems and solutions, learn facts about the world, and complete research projects. Continues to introduce new vocabulary and sentence forms. (140 lessons)	SRA
Reading Mastery V	Intermediate students who read at about a 5.0 level	Emphasizes literary skills. Students read novels, short stories, biographies, and poetry, as well as expository selections. Students analyze characters, settings, plots, and themes. Students also learn how to infer the main idea and how to predict word meaning from context. (120 lessons)	SRA
Reading Mastery VI	Intermediate students who read at about a 6.0 level	Teaches a wide range of literary, reasoning, and writing skills. Students interpret figurative language, analyze arguments, and complete writing assignments. The readings include a number of classic novels, stories, and poems. (120 lessons)	SRA
Reading Mastery I Spelling Book	Students in Reading Mastery I who have reached lesson 50	Emphasizes writing sounds, short phonetic words, a few short irregular words, and short sentences. (110 lessons)	SRA

EXHIBIT 5.2 *continued*

Program	Population	Overview	Publishers
Reading Mastery, *continued*			
Reading Mastery II Spelling Book	Students in Reading Mastery II between lessons 1 and 85	Emphasizes spelling common sound combinations such as *ar, al, sh, th,* and *wh,* phonetic words, some irregular words, and simple sentences. (79 lessons)	SRA
Direct Instruction Spelling Programs A basal reading series intended for grades 1 through 6.			
Reading Mastery I Spelling Book	Students in Reading Mastery I who have reached lesson 50	Emphasizes writing sounds, short phonetic words, a few short irregular words, and short sentences. (110 lessons)	SRA
Reading Mastery II Spelling Book	Students in Reading Mastery II between lessons 1 and 85	Emphasizes spelling common sound combinations such as *ar, al, sh, th,* and *wh,* phonetic words, some irregular words, and simple sentences. (79 lessons)	SRA
Spelling Mastery Level A	Second-grade or older students	Emphasizes a basic *phonemic* spelling strategy and the memorization of a set of high-utility *irregular words.* (60 lessons)	SRA
Spelling Mastery Level B	Third-grade or older students	Teaches advanced *phonemic* spelling strategies, high-utility *irregular words,* and the integration of all spelling skills into related language arts activities, with emphasis on writing skills. (140 lessons)	SRA

EXHIBIT 5.2 *continued*

Program	Population	Overview	Publishers
Spelling Mastery Level C	Fourth-grade or older students	Teaches a few hundred morphographs, a small set of useful structural spelling rules, and the integration of these spelling skills in a variety of writing and proofreading activities. (140 lessons)	SRA
Spelling Mastery Level D	Fifth-grade or older students	Teaches *advanced morphographs* and spelling rules, substantially increases ability to perform independently, and broadens the association of spelling and other language arts, especially writing skills and word meanings. (140 lessons)	SRA
Spelling Mastery Level E	Sixth-grade student–adults	Emphasizes *advanced morphographs* and spelling rules, substantially increases ability to perform independently, and broadens the association of spelling and other language arts, especially writing skills and word meanings. (140 lessons)	SRA
Corrective Spelling Through Morphographs	Fourth-grade students–adults	Teaches 650 morphographs and the principles for combining them, thereby enabling students to spell thousands of words, including most words on the complete Dolch word list and most commonly misspelled high school and college words. (140 lessons)	SRA

EXHIBIT 5.2 *continued*

Program	Population	Overview	Publishers
Direct Instruction Language Arts Program			
Distar Languages: A basal language series for preschool through grade 3.			
Distar Language I	Preschool and primary	Teaches the language of instruction used in school along with word knowledge, the foundations for logical thinking, and oral language skills. (160 lessons)	SRA
Distar Language II	Primary students	Teaches the language foundation for reading comprehension, with emphasis on reasoning skills, following directions, and the meanings of words and sentences. (160 lessons)	SRA
Distar Language III	Primary students	Focuses on the analysis of sentences, both spoken and written. Includes consideration of information communicated and mechanics, consolidated in writing exercises. (160 lessons)	SRA
Expressive Writing I	Elementary or secondary students who write 20 words per minute and read at middle third grade level or above	Teaches sentence-writing skills, paragraph-writing skills, and editing techniques. (50 lessons)	C.C. Publications
Expressive Writing II	Students who have completed Expressive Writing I or read at a fourth-grade level, can write in cursive, and can write and punctuate simple declarative sentences.	Teaches the student to write, punctuate, and edit compound sentences, sentences with dependent clauses, direct quotes in dialogue form, and sentences that list things. (45 lessons)	C.C. Publications

EXHIBIT 5.2 *continued*

Program	Population	Overview	Publishers
Cursive Writing Program	Third- and fourth-grade students or older students who are poor in cursive skills	Teaches the student who has already mastered manuscript writing how to form letters, create words, write sentences, and write faster and more accurately. (140 lessons)	C.C. Publications
Your World of Facts I	Third- through fifth-grade students or remedial students with beginning third-grade reading skills	Teaches the facts and relationships taught in science and social studies programs. Using the facts learned, the students can better understand their texts. Level I teaches 10–20 facts and relationships on 25 topics. (40 lessons)	C.C. Publications
Your World of Facts II	Third- through fifth-grade students with beginning third-grade reading skills	Level II teaches hundreds of facts and relationships of climate and vertebrates. (45 lessons)	C.C. Publications

Corrective Reading
A remedial reading series for students in grades 4 through 12 and for adults who have not mastered decoding and comprehension skills

Decoding Strand

Corrective Reading: Decoding A (Word-Attack Basics)	Fourth-grade students–adults	Emphasizes basic skills: identifying sounds, rhyming, sounding out, and word and sentence reading. (60 lessons)	SRA
Corrective Reading: Decoding B (Decoding Strategies)	Fourth-grade students–adults	Emphasizes critical letter and word discriminations, letter combinations, and story reading with comprehension questions. (140 lessons)	SRA

EXHIBIT 5.2 *continued*

Program	Population	Overview	Publishers
Corrective Reading, *continued*			
Corrective Reading: Decoding C (Skill Applications)	Fourth-grade students–adults	Emphasizes advanced decoding skills: word build-ups, affixes, vocabulary, story reading with comprehension questions, and outside reading applications. (140 lessons)	SRA
Comprehension Strand			
Corrective Reading: Comprehension A (Thinking Basics)	Fourth-grade students–adults	Emphasizes oral language skills: deductions, inductions, analogies, vocabulary building, and inferences. (60 lessons)	SRA
Corrective Reading: Comprehension B (Comprehension Skills)	Fourth-grade students–adults	Emphasizes literal and inferential skills, reading for information, writing skills, following sequenced instructions, analyzing contradictions, and learning information. (140 lessons)	SRA
Corrective Reading: Comprehension C (Concept Applications)	Fourth-grade students–adults	Emphasizes advanced comprehension applications: survival skills, reading for information, analyzing arguments, and reasoning. (140 lessons)	SRA
Mathematics Modules: Basic Fractions	Fourth- through twelfth-grade students	Teaches addition, subtraction, and multiplication of fractions and whole numbers for fractions, and finding equivalent fractions. (55 lessons)	SRA

EXHIBIT 5.2 *continued*

Program	Population	Overview	Publishers
Mathematics Modules: Fractions, Decimals, and Percents	Fourth- through twelfth-grade students	Teaches addition, subtraction, multiplication, and division of fractions, mixed numbers, and decimals. Also teaches reducing improper fractions, writing decimals or percents for fractions, writing fractions or percents for decimals, and writing fractions or decimals for percents. (70 lessons)	SRA
Mathematics Modules: Ratios and Equations	Fourth- through twelfth-grade students	Teaches ratios, rate and distance problems, logical simple analysis, and story problems. (60 lessons)	SRA

Direct Instruction Mathematics Programs
Distar Arithmetic: A basal arithmetic series for preschool grade 2.

Distar Arithmetic I	Preschool and primary students	Emphasizes beginning problem solving strategies for addition, subtraction, and stories. (160 lessons)	SRA
Distar Arithmetic II	Primary students	Emphasizes advanced problem-solving strategies for addition with carrying, multiplication, fractions, column subtraction, and complex story problems. (160 lessons)	SRA

Corrective Mathematics: A remedial series in basic mathematics for grades 3 through 12 and adults who have not mastered basic skills.

Corrective Mathematics: Addition	Third- through twelfth-grade students	Teaches basic facts, addition of two or more numbers with and without carrying, and story problems. (65 lessons)	SRA

EXHIBIT 5.2 *continued*

Program	Population	Overview	Publishers
Direct Instruction Mathematics Programs, *continued*			
Corrective Mathematics: Subtraction	Third- through twelfth-grade students	Teaches basic facts, subtraction with and without borrowing, and story problems. (65 lessons)	SRA
Corrective Mathematics: Multiplication	Third- through twelfth-grade students	Teaches basic facts, multiplication with and without carrying, and story problems. (65 lessons)	SRA
Corrective Mathematics: Division	Third- through twelfth-grade students	Teaches basic facts, long division with and without remainders, and story problems (65 lessons)	SRA

Source: Descriptions of these direct instructions materials were taken from the publishers' catalogs (SRA, Simon & Schuster, C.C. Publications). The information was compiled by Patty Willis, Department of Special Education, Utah State University. Used with permission.

Scheduling and Time Use

Another characteristic of direct instruction and opportunity-to-respond is the emphasis placed on determining instructional priorities within the school year, then allocating time to these priorities. Most educators say that reading, writing, and arithmetic are their highest priorities, but their classroom schedules do not always reflect this. In one study (Paine, 1982), teachers were found to devote the largest share of time to language arts activities, as would be expected, but they often devoted the second largest block of time to either lunch and recess or to organizational time (roll call, lining up, taking lunch and milk counts, reward time). Clearly, if too much time is spent on these nonacademic activities in class, insufficient time is left for academic pursuits. As a result, learning suffers (Berliner, 1979; Rosenshine, 1979). Direct instruction and opportunity-to-respond clearly acknowledge that, if students' deficits are to be remediated significantly, teachers must accomplish more with their students in the same or less time than usual (Becker et al., 1982). Otherwise, time will continue to pass by without sufficient progress; academic gaps will widen, not narrow.

Direct instruction contains a number of elements designed to maximize available teaching time. Most importantly, it allocates significantly more time to academic instruction. It also advocates the use of (a) small group instruction with unison responding, to give each student the greatest possible number of response opportunities (Fink & Sandall, 1977), (b) rapid pacing of instructional presentation to maintain student attention and increase the amount of material covered in a lesson (Carnine, 1976), and (c) available "person-power" in the classroom to provide additional individualized practice and feedback. Opportunity-to-respond accomplishes this efficiency by focusing primarily on instructional formats that maximize student responding and, like direct instruction, by using available people as tutors to provide extra academic response time (e.g., Delquadri, Greenwood, Stretton, & Hall, in press).

Classroom Organization and Instructional Delivery

Most behavior management procedures focus primarily — if not exclusively — on the consequences of student behavior. Direct instruction and opportunity-to-respond address consequences, but they also place considerable emphasis on antecedents (or setting events) as important influences on what students do. Managing the antecedents of student behavior is a preventive approach to instruction and student discipline (Paine, Radicchi, Rosellini, Deutchman, & Darch, 1983). It takes place at the levels of instruction and classroom organization.

Management of antecedent events in instruction includes several of the components mentioned earlier: grouping students into small units, maintaining a brisk instructional pace, calling for unison student response, and providing instructions. At the level of classroom organization, it includes arranging the physical environment, establishing and maintaining classroom rules, formulating and adhering to an academically oriented schedule, and making good use of any help available in the classroom (Paine et al., 1983). Opportunity-to-respond evaluates levels of responding under a variety of classroom formats, including teacher lecture, discussion periods, question-and-answer periods, independent seatwork, and peer tutoring (Greenwood, Delquadri, & Hall, 1983). Those activities that produce the highest levels of student response are recommended. Activities that provide few or no opportunities for active student participation, such as the lecture method, are discouraged — at least for students who need carefully structured learning.

Behavior Management

Behavioral approaches to education use reward systems to strengthen or maintain correct academic responses and appropriate classroom conduct. Positive motivational strategies are a basic element of both direct instruction and opportunity-to-respond. The motivational procedures used most often in direct instruction are teacher praise, point systems, challenges, and game-like structures for academic tasks. Opportunity-to-respond makes frequent use of team competition, group consequences, and other forms of social structure. It also features rewards for getting material correct on the first attempt as a bonus for academic accuracy (Delquadri, Whorton, Elliot, Greenwood, & Hall, 1981).

Most behavioral approaches react to student errors or inappropriate behavior with extinction, time-out, or mild punishment. This is another area where direct instruction and opportunity-to-respond differ. They typically react to these situations with positive correction and reteaching procedures. This practice is based on the philosophy that problems in student performance or conduct do not mean that the student is stupid, lazy, rude, or inconsiderate; they simply indicate the need for more teaching. While many educators might believe that student errors or problem behavior must be suppressed (a punitive approach), direct instruction and opportunity-to-respond focus instead on increasing the correct or appropriate form of the behavior (an educative approach).

Measurement, Monitoring, and Evaluation

Direct instruction uses both accuracy and frequency measures in short-term evaluation. Opportunity-to-respond primarily uses frequency measures. Accuracy measures are appropriate when a student is first learning a skill; the student must first learn to be correct before learning to be fast in working a new type of arithmetic problem, for example. Later, when the student has become quite accurate on the new skill, attention can be shifted to speed (how *fast* the student can work the problems correctly). At this point, frequency measures become more important, for they measure how much of something the student can do in a given period.

Both approaches also measure several process variables. For example, opportunity-to-respond measures academic responding mastery levels. Research has shown that responding during 50 to 70% of academic session time with 75 to 80% mastery levels can lead to high achievement (Greenwood et al., 1983).

On a short-term basis, direct instruction and opportunity-to-respond use several types of measures to keep track of student performance and to evaluate teaching. Skills that are currently being taught are assessed both within lessons and at the end of each lesson every day. In opportunity-to-respond, a quiz is given each week to ensure that student learning is progressing on schedule (Greenwood et al., 1983). In direct instruction, a quiz is given every 2 weeks to make sure that the student has learned the recently taught skills before going on in the program (Becker et al., 1982). These biweekly tests, called *continuous progress tests,* are keyed to the instructional programs so that, if the student misses one skill, the teacher knows where to go in the previous lessons to brush up on that skill. These tests are generally provided for each of the initial direct instruction programs. Direct instruction also calls for an error analysis of students' daily written work to determine where more instruction might be necessary.

Direct instruction and opportunity-to-respond both use standardized achievement tests at least once each year (in the spring) and preferably twice a year (fall and spring). The achievement tests tell how many months of growth a student has experienced in 9 or 10 months of school. One month's growth for each month of instruction is considered average. However, with programs like direct instruction or opportunity-to-respond, it is often possible to achieve 1½ or 2 months growth per month of instruction or even more (Maggs & Morath, 1976).

While achievement tests are important for evaluating the instructional program across subject areas and time, they are insufficient to manage a responsive learning environment, because they only provide feedback to the teacher once or twice a year. If a student does poorly in a subject, it is often too late to do anything about it by the time the teacher receives the information. This is why the weekly or biweekly tests are important. They allow a teacher to correct students' errors almost immediately, a critical element in effective education.

CURRICULUM CONTENT

The last section of this chapter discussed how teachers can effectively facilitate the acquisition of academic skills by employing direct instruction. This section addresses the content of the academic curriculum—the nature of the skills taught, rather than the methods for teaching them. Although this distinction works well conceptually, in actual practice it is often difficult to separate the two. This section will address three different academic curricular domains: (a) academic tool subjects, (b) content area subjects, and (c) academic survival skills. Each of these subsections will describe the types of skills taught, discuss why they should be taught to behaviorally disordered students, and make recommendations for how to teach them.

Academic Tool Subjects

When the word "academics" is used, it usually refers to such skills as reading, writing, and 'rithmetic—the three R's. These skill domains are called *academic tool subjects;* i.e., the basic academic skills used as tools to learn other skills.

Research indicates that behaviorally disordered children are often seriously delayed in acquiring these basic academic skills. Yule and Rutter (1968), for example, found a high incidence of reading retardation in a group of these children. From a sample of 126 maladjusted children aged

9 to 11, Yule and Rutter found more than ⅓ of the 44 children labeled *antisocial* were at least 4 years behind their predicted reading age. Others have found similar relationships between behavioral disorders and academic underachievement. Wright (1974) found that 53.2% of 47 conduct-disordered boys in regular third-grade classes were underachievers; another 17% were low achievers. In other words, more than 70% had reading problems.

In addition, it seems that the academic deficiencies of behaviorally disorderd children are not limited to reading. Glavin and Annesley (1971) examined the learning problems of 130 behaviorally disordered children referred to a resource room. Approximately 81% were found to be underachieving in reading; approximately 72% were underachieving in arithmetic. It is interesting to note that, in this study, Glavin and Annesley found no significant differences in the academic problems of conduct-disordered children as compared to withdrawn children, unlike the findings of previous research (Yule & Rutter, 1968).

It is quite evident from these studies that these children are very likely to have academic problems in addition to their behavior problems. For more seriously disturbed children in more restrictive settings (self-contained classrooms, private residential treatment programs, state institutions), the likelihood is even greater (Stainback & Stainback, 1980). Skill deficiencies in the basic tool subjects of reading and arithmetic have a major impact on students' self-esteem, their relationships with peers, and their chances for success in later life.

The potential impact of school failure is, in fact, so great that many educators and researchers have suggested that the primary problem for behaviorally disordered students may be academics, not behavior (Critchley, 1968; Mangers, 1950; Rutter & Yule, 1970). Two lines of investigation support this interpretation: (a) studies where reading difficulties were found to emerge prior to students' behavior problems and (b) studies where behavior problems have been found to be situation-specific, i.e., to appear only in particularly stressful settings such as school. Other educators and psychologists (Dreikurs, 1954) argue that academic problems are the result of social and emotional maladjustment, not the cause of it.

Two recent studies have attempted to address this issue. McMichael (1979) examined the behavior of 198 boys upon entering school and compared it with their reading achievement in the first 2 years of school. She found that significantly more poor readers had been either antisocial or neurotic upon entering school than had fair to good readers. Stott (1981) also found that early maladjustment was a predictor of poor academic achievement. Perhaps as important was the finding that the severity of the behavior problems did not seem to increase as a result of school failure. These two studies suggest that, though some children may develop antisocial behavior in response to learning problems, there may also be some students who enter school with both behavioral problems and cognitive delays. Thus, the origins of their behavioral and academic problems may lie outside the school, not within it.

It has often been said that "nothing can be learned until their behavior or emotional problems are satisfactorily resolved." This attitude has persisted for a long time in the field of behavior disorders. Contemporary attitudes about the role of academic instruction in the education of behaviorally disordered students are reflected in the following statement:

> Although emotionally disturbed children usually require training in social behavior and appropriate classroom behavior, this cannot be the sole objective of a viable intervention program—they must be able to meet the minimal academic performance criteria to succeed in less restrictive educational environments. Although social interventions sometimes take precedence over academic interventions, a major advantage of an emphasis on improving academic proficiency is that it strengthens behavior that competes with problem behavior while building skills that will be valued and reinforced outside the immediate training situation. In general, evidence from classroom studies suggests that academic proficiency cannot be assumed to develop as a consequence of improvements in a child's social behavior; it must be planned as part of a total intervention program for the child. (Polsgrove & Nelson, 1982, p. 189)

Whatever the relationship between behavioral disorders and academic achievement, the fact that large percentages of students with behavior problems also have learning problems is not as relevant as the issue of what can be done to eliminate them—or at least minimize their effect on student academic performance. The following paragraphs will briefly outline the content of an academic tool skills curriculum in reading and mathematics and then offer some suggestions for teaching these skills.

Reading

As discussed previously, the reading achievement levels of many behaviorally disordered students are significantly below their actual grade placement levels. These reading problems will detrimentally affect students' performance in other areas of the curriculum as well. Thus, reading is the academic tool skill with which teachers will be most concerned.

The organization, management, and implementation of the reading program should follow the principles of effective teaching discussed throughout this text. The principles emphasize actively teaching the content to be learned, ensuring high rates of success, providing ample practice opportunities, and monitoring student performance and progress. Above all else, according to *Becoming a Nation of Readers: The Report of the Commission on Reading* (Anderson, Hiebert, Scott, & Wilkinson, 1985), effective teachers of reading create "literate environments" for students where reading is treated as a high priority activity and the instructional program is well-paced, stimulating, and reinforcing.

Carnine and Silbert (1979) have amplified these suggestions with the following guidelines for designing and implementing reading programs for skill-deficient students:

- *Extra instruction.* The more deficient a student is in reading, the greater the amount of instruction the student should receive.
- *Early remediation.* The sooner remediation begins, the more likely the student can be helped.
- *Careful instruction.* The more severe the student's deficit, the more careful the instruction must be.
- *Well-designed program.* The greater the student's deficit, the more they will benefit from a well-designed program that teaches essential skills.
- *Rapid progression.* The more deficient a student is in reading skills, the more quickly she must progress through the program.
- *Motivation.* The more highly motivated a remedial reader is, the greater the student's progress and success. (pp. 50–51)

Samuels (1986) suggested that good classroom teaching of basic skills has much in common with good athletic coaching. Good teachers and good coaches motivate, increase skills to mastery, and provide plenty of practice.

There are many excellent instructional programs and materials in reading from which the teacher can choose. For example, one program was developed by the Exemplary Center for Reading Instruction (ECRI) in Salt Lake City. The ECRI program is a total language arts program designed to supplement existing basal instruction. Using a highly structured, teacher-directed, mastery learning approach, ECRI incorporates the principles of effective instruction (i.e., a demonstration–prompt–practice instructional paradigm) by structuring reading instruction into three time periods each day: (a) "skills time," where new skills are directly taught by the teacher, (b) "practice time," where students apply the skills independently with teacher guidance and monitoring, and (c) "backup skills time," involving instruction in other language arts areas such as handwriting and spelling (Reid, 1986).

There seems to be a gap between what we know about effective teaching of reading and what actually happens to students in reading programs. For example, it has been estimated that students spend up to 70% of the time allocated to reading instruction in independent practice or unsupervised seatwork activities, and most of that time is spent working on workbooks and skill sheets (Anderson et al., 1985). This is, by far, the largest share of all the time allocated to reading instruction. According to the National Commission on Reading, too much time is devoted to an activity that does not have a strong relationship to increases in reading proficiency:

> In the all too typical classroom, too much of the precious time available for reading instruction is given over to workbook and skill task sheets and students invest only the most perfunctory level of attention in the tasks. For these problems, teachers and school administrators are responsible . . . . Workbook and skill sheet tasks should be pared to the minimum that will actually contribute to growth in reading. (p. 76)

The practice of assigning workbook activities or skill sheets is relatively common in special education, but it should be drastically reduced if students are to receive quality education. There is a big difference between keeping students busy or occupied and providing quality instruction. As Schloss and Sedlak (1986) stated, "merely assigning work is not teaching" (p. 286).

The interested reader is encouraged to consult additional sources for information on effective strategies and instructional materials for teaching reading (see, for example, Askov & Otto, 1985; Carnine & Silbert, 1979; Robinson & Good, 1987; Wallace, 1981). Remember, however, that all instructional materials, no matter how well designed and well sequenced, are useless without a conscientious, skillful teacher—the key ingredient to successful remediation (Wallace & Kauffman, 1986).

Mathematics

Most behaviorally disordered students who have reading problems will also have problems in mathematics. Teaching mathematics requires the application of the same active teaching behaviors and lesson formats that have been stressed throughout this book. Group instruction led by the teacher, with clear demonstrations, brisk pacing, high student success rates, and ample opportunities for guided practice with careful teacher monitoring of learner progress are the essential ingredients (Good & Grouws, 1979).

In the design and implementation of a mathematics program for behaviorally disordered students, mastery of basic computational skills will be one of the most important areas. Students who have not mastered the basic skills will have great difficulty with higher-level skills and concepts. Clearly, then, an important instructional activity for developing mastery of basic facts is drill and practice. However, recent research advises that drill and practice will not be useful if students have not first developed automaticity — the rapid, effortless, and errorless recall of basic math facts (Hasselbring, Goin, & Bransford, 1987). Before standard paper-and-pencil or computer-assisted drill-and-practice activities are used, Hasselbring et al. suggest that teachers use the following instructional strategies: (a) assess current level of automaticity, (b) build on existing knowledge by working on only a small set of facts at a time, and (c) use challenge times to reduce retrieval time to around one second per problem.

Care must be taken to ensure that computation skills are not over-emphasized to the virtual exclusion of other important skills and concepts (Sedlak & Fitzmaurice, 1981). A total mathematics curriculum should include the following areas in addition to basic computation skills: problem-solving ability, basic mathematics concepts and terms, understanding and use of measurement and money, and practical application of mathematics skills and concepts to daily life (Bartel, 1986). There is ample evidence to suggest that teaching students to compute word problems is an often neglected aspect of school mathematics programs (Peters & Lloyd, 1987). However, directly teaching strategies for solving word problems does have a positive effect on students' ability (Stein, 1987).

An exhaustive review of specific mathematics instructional programs that can be used with behaviorally disordered students is beyond the scope of this chapter. The interested reader is referred to excellent reviews of the topic (Bartel, 1986; Sedlak & Fitzmaurice, 1981; Silbert et al., 1981; Wallace & Kauffman, 1986).

Content Area Subjects

Academic instruction involves more than the acquisition of basic skills such as reading, writing, and arithmetic. The behaviorally disordered child, like any other child, needs to acquire knowledge about the world—its past, its present, and its prospects for the future. The tool subjects discussed above are tools for accessing and manipulating this information. Like all other tools, they are useless unless applied to a problem. Reading, for example, has no value as a skill unless used to acquire information that someone has previously written down. This information is referred to as the "content," and the topics under which this content falls are referred to as "content-area subjects." Some examples are science, social studies, health, music, and art. At the secondary level, many of these subject areas are broken into several courses, each with a narrower focus. Science, for example, may be taught as "biology," "chemistry," and "physics." Similarly, social studies might be offered as "world history," "civics," or even "anthropology."

How should behaviorally disordered students be taught the information normally presented in content-area subjects? Related to this question is another one: To what extent should instruction in content-area subjects be a priority concern? In the absence of any empirical evidence to serve as a guideline, this question must be answered on the basis of common sense recognizing instructional constraints. For students with severe behavior disorders, primary emphasis should probably be placed on eliminating inappropriate behaviors and providing instruction in basic academic and self-help skills. For students whose behavioral problems are milder or less frequent, an expanded curriculum can be considered.

Students who have been placed in a self-contained special education classroom for behaviorally disordered students are less likely to receive instruction in content-area subjects than those who have been mainstreamed into regular classes. The assumption underlying placement in a self-contained class is that the student's behavioral and academic deficiencies are so severe that only full-time attention and remediation from a specially trained teacher will result in improvement. The goals for these students are to eliminate the behaviors that prevent a less restrictive placement and to remediate academic deficits to the maximum extent possible. These endeavors alone are time consuming and require considerable instructional planning. For one teacher to provide content-area instruction to a wide range of students in a self-contained classroom is usually impossible and probably an inappropriate use of time. Although some teachers in self-contained classrooms for the behaviorally disordered do teach content-area subjects, their purpose is usually more to provide practice opportunities for other skills (behavioral as well as academic) than to promote acquisition of specific information.

Instruction in content-area subjects is most appropriate for students who receive all or part of their education in regular classrooms. Although some of these students will also receive special education assistance in a setting such as a resource room, the focus of that instruction is usually on academic tool subjects. This brings us to the original question: How should behaviorally disordered students be taught content-area subjects? For those students who do not have accompanying academic deficiencies, content-area instruction can be provided with minimal alteration of the normal curriculum. Attention should be paid to the students' need for structure and behavioral contingencies but little curriculum modification is required.

Unfortunately, however, the majority of behaviorally disordered students, even those in regular classrooms, are seriously delayed academically. To teach these students content-area subjects effectively often requires modification of the curriculum and of the procedures students use to demonstrate that they have acquired the targeted knowledge. Described below are three types of recommended modifications.

Modify Reading Assignments

Acquisition of knowledge in a content-area subject often depends upon reading a textbook or some other written material. Although this may be a reasonable approach for most, behaviorally disordered students will probably find the experience frustrating. To promote success with reading assignments for these students (and to avoid the behavior problems that often erupt when frustration sets in), teachers can try one or more of the following suggestions for making written material more accessible.

1. *Develop reading guides.* A reading guide is like a road map to what an author has written. By developing reading guides, a teacher can direct attention to the main ideas in an assignment and help sort out the array of details used to support these ideas. For students whose reading ability is significantly below the text's difficulty level, a guide that walks the reader through the text paragraph by paragraph (or page by page) is usually the most appropriate. When developing this type of reading guide, a teacher can paraphrase what the author has written, using familiar vocabulary; indicate paragraphs that can be skipped; summarize several key ideas; and help the student answer questions posed by the author throughout the text. It is also helpful if the reading guide directs the student's attention to any important graphic aids in the assigned reading (graphs, flow charts, diagrams, etc.) and assists the student to interpret the information they present. For students whose reading ability is closer to the difficulty level of the text, this much structured assistance may not be necessary. Other types of reading guides might then be considered. For example, a three-level guide can be used to help students comprehend the author's message at more than the literal level. This type of reading guide has students answer questions at all three levels of comprehension: the literal level (what the text actually says), the interpretive level (what this information means), and the applied level (how this information can be used). For reading assignments organized along some underlying principle (e.g., cause and effect, time sequence), it is often helpful to develop reading guides that help students grasp these relationships. Called *pattern guides*, this form of reading guide can be used effectively to help behavior disordered students recognize the organization of written material they are asked to read and to manipulate the author's ideas in a meaningful way. For a more detailed explanation of the various types of reading guides teachers have found useful (and numerous examples), see Vacca's excellent book, *Content Area Reading* (1981).

2. *Highlight the text with marking pens.* An alternate way to provide assistance to poor readers is to develop and use a marking system on the reading passage assigned. With marking pens of different colors, the teacher can indicate (by underlin-

ing or highlighting) the sentences that convey main ideas and those that provide supporting details. It is also possible to indicate which paragraphs should be read very carefully and which can be skimmed or skipped. By providing this assistance, a teacher is giving the student a strategy for attacking a reading assignment and learning the content presented. Although easier to implement than reading guides, a marking system also has its disadvantages. Students may become dependent on the various markings added by the teacher and find reading passages without these prompts extremely difficult. The answer to this problem is, of course, to eventually fade the use of the marking system or alternate marking passages with reading guides. Other disadvantages can be eliminated by buying textbooks especially for a given student (this is much cheaper than hiring a teacher consultant when the student blows up because reading assignments are too difficult) or photocopying needed passages if a variety of materials are used. When using a textbook marking system, it is important to remember to explain to a student what each color means and how these markings can be helpful in comprehending the passages assigned. Guided practice is usually necessary at the beginning; without it, the effort expended in marking the text is often wasted.

3. *Put the reading passage on tape.* Taping a reading assignment can be an effective means of circumventing students' poor reading skills in content-area subjects. Many behaviorally disordered students have the conceptual ability to acquire the knowledge presented in content-area textbooks but not the requisite reading skills. By putting a reading assignment on tape, a teacher can capitalize on a student's strengths while minimizing the impact of deficient skills. Deshler and Graham (1980) have made the following recommendations for teachers who want to use taped materials. (a) Avoid recording the entire chapter or unit verbatim. Not only does extensive verbatim recording require too much time to tape, but the resulting tape takes a long time to listen to. Attention and motivation can be maintained by paraphrasing less important material, and shorter tapes will facilitate repeated listening. Exceptions are, of course, reading selections such as poems and short stories, both of which usually need to be heard in their entirety. (b) Have students follow along in the text while listening. Most students benefit from having visual as well as auditory input; in addition, they may improve their reading skills by doing so. This suggestion necessitates the next recommendation. (c) Use a marking system to indicate which paragraphs are recorded

verbatim, which are paraphrased, and which are deleted. The student will then know when to read along with the tape and when to sit back and listen. (d) Take advantage of one-to-one communication to teach text usage and study skills. One of the reasons that many behaviorally disordered students are unable to use textbooks independently is lack of knowledge of how the material is organized and how to search through a passage for requested information. Teachers can help students acquire these skills if, when recording, they include directions on how to use headings and subheadings, how to interpret accompanying illustrations and graphs, how to differentiate main and supporting ideas, and how to skim through a text to find answers to questions. A final recommendation grows out of the research on effective teaching. (e) Take advantage of the tape's flexibility to provide students with advance organizers, comprehensive questions interspersed throughout the text, and summaries of key concepts and ideas. All of these suggestions can improve reading comprehension and can easily be incorporated into a tape.

4. *Rewrite selected materials.* To accommodate students' low reading abilities, it is sometimes useful to rewrite selected portions of a reading assignment. Selections to be rewritten should be chosen carefully, with an eye for the instructional purpose behind teaching any given content. Rewriting textbook passages and other written materials is time consuming and should, therefore, be reserved for reading selections that do not lend themselves to any of the other techniques. Adapting curriculum materials by rewriting them assumes that reading selections are composed of multiple ideas or concepts and that some of these concepts are more important than others (Coleman, 1979). Altering the difficulty of a reading passage by rewriting it is a process of (a) deemphasizing or deleting the less important concepts, (b) simplifying the passage's sentences, and (c) choosing more familiar vocabulary whenever possible. Technical terms that are retained in the simplified material should be underlined or highlighted in some way and meanings should be taught before the selection is read. Although somewhat time consuming, the task of rewriting content-area materials is not actually difficult; some teachers have found that their students are quite adept at it. Peers are more likely to be in touch with the vocabulary of their classmates, as well as their entry level of knowledge on any given subject. By allowing them to use a microcomputer for the task and exempting them from taking tests on any material rewritten, a

teacher can easily create the necessary motivation to get volunteers.

5. *Provide alternative reading materials.* Another strategy for accommodating low reading skills is to provide alternative materials from which students can acquire the targeted content-area knowledge. The goal with this strategy is to find materials on a lower reading level than the text normally used. Dillner and Olson (1977) identified two different methods for doing this. The first possibility, labeled *multilevel, single materials approach,* is to locate and use instructional materials produced by the same publisher but written at different levels of difficulty. A single textbook, for example, might be written at the third-, fifth-, and seventh-grade reading levels. A teacher using this textbook for a fifth-grade class might order the third-grade level for underachieving students and the seventh-grade level for advanced students with more sophisticated reading skills. Unfortunately, only a few textbooks have editions at several levels of difficulty. An alternate method, then, is to adopt the *multilevel, multiple materials approach.* When using this technique the teacher uses written materials at a variety of difficulty levels, but they have been written by different authors and are usually available from different publishers. To use this technique effectively, of course, it is important that instructional goals have been clearly identified and the various materials integrated with these goals.

Modify Written Assignments

As students get older, there is an accompanying increase in teachers' tendency to use written assignments to encourage them to apply the ideas learned and to evaluate the acquisition of targeted knowledge. Underachieving behaviorally disordered students are often deficient in the skills needed to complete these assignments, resulting in frustration, poor performance, and even refusal to work. By modifying written assignments, teachers can encourage low-performing students to perform at their best while at the same time getting a much more accurate picture of their knowledge acquisition. Described below are three types of modifications that teachers have found effective.

1. *Shorten the assignment.* Students with a history of frustration and failure are often immobilized when faced with a long list of comprehension questions to answer or a lengthy paper to write. A written assignment can sometimes be made more manageable by breaking it into sections or selecting only some of the questions for responses. Instead of having these

students write a single, long research paper, it might be more appropriate to assign two shorter papers, each with a more narrow focus.

2. *Alter the response mode.* Because of poor writing and spelling skills, many behaviorally disordered students can't respond appropriately to written assignments, even when shortened. Modifying assignments for these students may require altering the manner in which they are asked to respond, i.e., the response mode. Some possible alternatives to writing answers on paper are (a) responding orally into a tape recorder, (b) designing an art project representing the relationship of concepts learned, (c) presenting information to the class in a dramatic form (puppets, role play), (d) taking oral quizzes, and (e) using a microcomputer with a word-processing program that corrects for spelling errors.

3. *Provide increased assistance.* Written assignments can often be made easier for low-performing behaviorally disordered students by providing the assistance needed to compensate for their skill deficits. Assistance can be in the form of prompts and aids on the written assignment or help from peers or the teacher. Comprehension questions, for example, can be made easier if students are directed to critical passages with page numbers written beside each question. Another helpful technique is to simplify worksheets containing several response formats by rewriting sections all in the same format. Sometimes adding more explicit and simpler directions will have a positive impact on students' ability to do an assignment. A technique Nichols (1980) found useful for improving the quality of assignments such as essays, summaries, and book reviews was the use of paragraph frames. Designed to provide students with needed structure for organizing their ideas, the paragraph frames comprise a standardized set of sentence beginnings appropriate for a given content-area assignment. The students complete the sentences, sometimes adding their own. In doing so, they produce a well-organized, intelligible essay. Use of these aids resulted in "coherent efforts from previously uncooperative students" (Nichols, 1980, p. 231) and passing grades in all their subjects. Using peers as tutors and having students do some assignments in groups can also provide needed assistance.

Modify the Listening Situation

It is not unusual to find that behaviorally disordered students also have difficulty following a lecture or some other oral presentation in class. The teacher's organizational framework for a lecture is not always apparent to these students, who soon get lost in the detail. Following verbal directions for in-class projects may also be a problem. The following suggestions will assist these students, as well as their classmates, to acquire information from classroom listening situations.

1. *Provide a structured overview.* Structured overviews are graphic displays of key terms to be used in a lecture or encountered in a reading assignment. The words can be technical vocabulary that a teacher intends to teach or terms representing critical concepts that will be discussed. By providing students with a visual display of how these terms are related, the teacher shares with the student an organizational framework for comprehending and recalling the information presented. A structured overview can be developed before a lecture and presented as a handout, or it can be developed gradually on the board as the lecture unfolds.

2. *Provide a lecture outline.* Another strategy is to give students an outline of the material to be covered. The outline can be in standard outline form or in the form of a listening guide calling for student input. Both require advanced planning by the teacher and willingness to follow a predetermined organization when talking. The benefits, of course, are significant. Not only will low-performing students be able to acquire important information, they will also learn appropriate note-taking skills and probably be less disruptive.

3. *Use visual and auditory props.* Many low-performing students have difficulty listening because the content seems to be very abstract. Anything a teacher can do to increase the concreteness of a listening situation will help these students attend to what is being said and acquire the targeted knowledge. Various visual and auditory props can accomplish this. Some examples are manipulative materials (maps, models, lab work), demonstrations, and audio-visual aids (pictures, charts, tapes, films, overhead transparencies).

4. *Break up the listening period into sections.* Some students find following a verbal presentation for an entire class period very difficult. They lose track of the main theme and the examples used to support it. Candler and Green (1982) have suggested breaking the listening situation into several shorter sections, each with a summary at the end. For example, a 30-minute lecture might be broken into five or six sections. Each section focuses on a few main ideas that are summarized before going on to the next section.

Three general strategies and numerous specific suggestions for modifying the curriculum so that low-performing behaviorally disorderd students can succeed in content-area classes have just been described. All have been tried by teachers and are practical. It is important to ask, however, if curriculum modification works. Does the time and effort involved actually result in improved academic performance? Edwards (1980) explored the effects of curriculum modification using 23 behaviorally disordered fourth graders in four different regular classrooms. Students in two of these classrooms went through a modified curriculum for a 6-week social studies unit while students in the other two classes were taught using traditional procedures. Curriculum modification consisted of adaptation of content-area materials to meet students' instructional reading levels, modification of existing workbook materials, provisions for corrective feedback, and self-graphing. Results support the use of curriculum modification for these students. As a group, the students receiving the modified curriculum scored significantly higher on unit achievement measures than students receiving the traditional approach. In addition to improved academic achievement, there were also significant differences between the two groups in the number of deviant behaviors observed during classroom instruction. Not only did curriculum modification seem to improve academic success, it also seemed to reduce the students' deviant behavior.

Academic Survival Skills

Success in school requires that students master a variety of behaviors that, technically, cannot be classified as basic academic skills. These behaviors, however, facilitate the acquisition of academic skills or make it possible for a student to indicate that targeted skills or knowledge have been acquired. Known as *academic survival skills,* these behaviors are prerequisites for academic success (see Exhibit 5.3).

The specific nature of these academic survival skills varies as a function of grade level. In the primary grades, for example, important academic survival skills seem to be following directions, paying attention to the teacher, and raising a hand to answer questions. At the intermediate level these skills continue to be important but others are added. They include talking about academic material with the teacher, interacting with peers about academic material, attending to task during independent work, and handing in legible written assignments. At the secondary level students must do all of these plus acquire a variety of study and test-taking skills to survive in the increasingly difficult curriculum.

Many academic survival skills have been found to be correlated with academic achievement. Cobb (1970, 1972), for example, found a consistent relationship between students' performance on achievement tests and the extent to which first and fourth graders exhibited such skills as

EXHIBIT 5.3 Survival skills and competing behaviors

Survival Skills	Competing Behaviors
Looking at teacher or academic work	Looking around or look away from teacher or task
Following teacher's directions immediately (4–5 seconds)	Engaging in behaviors other than those specified by the teacher, e.g., continuing previous task, refusing to comply, being out-of-seat, talking to peers, pushing desks or chairs, hitting peers
Working (writing, coloring, reading, etc.) on appropriate task	Engaging in other behaviors—talking to peers about other than academics, working on wrong material, not working, putting head on desk, getting out-of-seat, destroying materials
Volunteering information in response to teacher questions by raising hand	Talking aloud, talking without permission, talking at times designated inappropriate by teacher
Talking to teacher about academic matters	Talking to teacher about unrelated off-task matters; talk-outs, complaints, refusals, "That's not fair"
Talking to peers about academics or assigned task	Talking to peers about other matters

Source: Adapted from *Program for Academic Survival Skills: Consultant Manual* by C. R. Greenwood, H. Hops, J. Delquadri, and H. M. Walker, 1977, Eugene: Center at Oregon for Research in the Behavorial Education of the Handicapped.

paying attention to the teacher, following instructions, and volunteering to answer questions in class. The importance of this last skill was supported by the work of Shipman and her colleagues (1976). In an examination of variables affecting the achievement of children with low socioeconomic status, Shipman found that inhibition in responding to questions and hesitancy to attempt a response when questions became more difficult were two predictors of low achievement.

Behaviorally disordered students are often deficient in the extent to which they demonstrate these and other academic survival skills. Many have spent large portions of their school careers in highly structured settings. In these placements, instruction is carefully controlled by the teacher and systematic reinforcement programs are often used to increase student responding. To survive in less restrictive and less structured settings, students need to acquire the academic survival skills that will help them meet teachers' expectations and achieve academically. Unfortunately, the traditional curriculum makes little provision to teach students the essential academic survival skills. This is probably because most nonhandicapped students are perceptive enough to recognize the demands of the classroom and academically capable enough to meet these demands without intervention.

Behaviorally disordered students often lack academic survival skills.

Attempts to facilitate the acquisition of academic survival skills for handicapped and other low-performing students have taken one of two major approaches: the behavior management approach and the direct instruction approach. Representative of the first was the work of researchers at the Center at Oregon for Research in the Behavioral Education of the Handicapped (CORBEH). In a series of studies investigating the effects of reinforcement on academic survival skills, they found, for example, that contingent reinforcement resulted in a 24% increase in the use of survival skills by low-performing first graders and a corresponding 28% increase in reading achievement (Cobb & Hops, 1973). Both gains were maintained when the children were tested 4 to 6 weeks later. These studies led to the development of the Program for Academic Survival Skills (PASS) (Greenwood, Hops, Delquadri, & Walker, 1977), a well thought-out and extensively field-tested intervention program designed to increase the proportion of time that all students in a class spend engaged in six classroom survival skills. (See chapter 7 for an extended discussion of this program.)

As effective as this program is, there are limitations on the extent to which reinforcement alone can facilitate the acquisition of academic survival skills. For skills that are not in a student's behavioral repertoire, no amount of reinforcement will put them there. It is often necessary to teach these skills first, after which behavior management can be used to increase the frequency of use or promote their transfer to other educational settings.

Silverman, Zigmond, and Sansone (1981) found this instructional approach to be effective in teaching adolescents the survival skills needed in regular classes. Their School Survival Skills Curriculum used three phases (presentation, practice, and mastery) to teach three strands of skills: behavior control, teacher-pleasing behaviors, and study skills. Use of the curriculum resulted in more student interactions with peers as well as with adults.

The potential of academic survival skill training to affect academic performance makes attention to this domain extremely important. Academic survival skills, because they are not based on specific content, can be useful in a variety of settings, both currently and in the future. The time spent providing students with the academic survival skills needed to succeed in classrooms is a wise investment because they will be able to use these skills throughout their school careers.

ADDITIONAL CONSIDERATIONS

This chapter has attempted to provide a basic framework and some specific suggestions for teaching academic skills to behaviorally disordered students. This section will discuss several additional important aspects of an effective academic program. They are reinforcement for academic performance, scheduling time, and transenvironmental programming.

Academic Reinforcement

A problem that teachers of behaviorally disordered children face every day is how to motivate their students and how to increase or maintain their skills over time. As explained in chapter 3, the general strategy for motivating students and increasing or maintaining their behavior is reinforcement. Seldom do we question the necessity for reinforcing students or the validity of the reinforcers we give them. However, teachers should ask several important questions to ensure that they are getting the most value out of the reinforcers they use and that their reinforcement is not getting in the way of their goals for their students.

Because reinforcement time competes with academic learning and practice time as distinct activities, it can sometimes work against the goal of maximizing academic learning time. We once knew a teacher who was very committed to insuring that his students were well motivated. He developed an elaborate point system, and he spent considerable time dispensing points, allowing students to count and exchange their points, and providing them time to partake of the reinforcers they had selected. Just to make sure that the students remained motivated, this process was conducted twice daily, in the morning and again in the afternoon. Although this teacher was very well intentioned, he was spending nearly an hour each day implementing his motivational system—much, too much time, time that could have been spent in academic practice, review, or new instruction.

This is not to say that teachers should not take time to motivate their students, only that motivating students does not need to take *much* time. Similarly, time spent in reinforcement need not be play time. It can be academic learning time if academic tasks are provided and structured in such a way that they are actually entertaining (Taffel & O'Leary, 1976).

There are several ways to make even the most routine academic tasks come alive. Information can be reviewed or skills practiced on a microcomputer. Classwide peer tutoring can be arranged so that students take turns drilling each other on spelling words, math facts, or vocabulary. Older students or community volunteers can be brought in for this purpose, also. Test-like situations can even be fun. The key seems to be competition, between individuals or teams or against a criterion score or one's own best score, scorekeeping, feedback, standings and statistics, and other game-like elements (Harris & Sherman, 1973). If a way can be found to impose a game-like structure, even the most mundane tasks can be made enjoyable.

Once educational games or activities have been structured for the students, the next task lies in using them as reinforcers. Of course, a teacher would never want to deprive students of regularly scheduled instructional or practice time, but the amount of academic activities available can actually be increased, dependent on a certain level of performance in other academic tasks. Thus, if a student particularly enjoys science projects or reading, these activities can be used as reinforcers for other tasks on which the student has more difficulty or less interest (Gallant, Sargeant, & Van Houten, 1980). Academic reinforcers need not comprise the entire reinforcement menu, but they provide a surprisingly enjoyable motivational alternative that will help both teacher and students reach academic goals.

Another reinforcement issue not yet addressed is what to reinforce. In classroom context, there are basically two choices: reinforce student conduct (e.g., in seat, on task) or academic performance (e.g., assignments completed, percentage correct). Although it is certainly possible to reinforce both conduct and performance, it is helpful to have a central focus. This communicates to the student what the teacher considers to be most important.

Research done in this area to date has been quite clear: Focus first on academic performance, then on behavior if it is still necessary (e.g., Hay, Hay, & Nelson, 1977). This recommendation stems from a series of studies comparing the relative effectiveness of reinforcing students' work-related behaviors or their academic output. The research is quite consistent in concluding that both strategies are successful in improving the behaviors upon which the contingencies rest. Reinforcement for appropriate behavior promotes appropriate behavior; reinforcement for academic performance enhances academic performance. The real advantage of one approach over the other can be seen when the effects of reinforcing one type of behavior on the other type are examined. When teachers reinforce conduct, conduct improves, but academic performance does not usually improve as a by-product (Broughton & Lahey, 1978). When academic skills are reinforced, both academics and conduct improve (Ayllon, Layman, & Burke, 1972; Ayllon & Roberts, 1974).

This one-way spillover effect — from academics to conduct but not from conduct to academics — suggests that teachers should focus first on improving academic performance. This will communicate to students that producing good work is what is most important. Then, if students' academic performance improves but their conduct still falls short of expectations, contingencies focusing directly on conduct can be added. This approach should take advantage of any possible spillover effects, making the most efficient use of teacher time and programming efforts.

Time Use

Time is one of the most underused resources available to teachers. Several different dimensions of time can influence teaching success. For example, the following variables contribute positively to student academic performance: (a) the number of days in the school year and the number of hours in the school day (National Commission, 1983); (b) the manner in which those hours are allocated to various curriculum areas and the extent to which students are required to actively participate during the lesson (Greenwood, Dinwiddie, Terry, Wade, Stanley, Thibadeau, & Delquadri, 1983).

Several basic rules emerge from what is known about using time to the best advantage in schools. First, make sure that the vast majority of available instructional time is devoted to the highest priority subjects — generally reading, math, writing, and spelling in the lower grades, content-area skills in the upper grades, and social behavior or conduct at all grade levels for behaviorally disordered students. Second, make sure that this schedule is faithfully followed. A good schedule is no good if it is not followed. Third, control the disruptions the students encounter. Make sure the students are under control; then make sure outsiders are under control. Leave a sign and a note pad outside the classroom door to discourage people from interrupting unless it is a true emergency. Fourth, "teach up a storm" during the available time. Make every minute count. Use every available opportunity to review a previously taught skill or check on a student whose academic error was corrected earlier. Use volunteers or peer tutors to maximize the amount of instruction each student receives. Fifth, challenge students, praise them, and provide them with frequent feedback (Van Houten, 1980). Keep them motivated. Establish ongoing games or contests with an academic focus. Sixth, in short, maximize students' opportunities to respond actively, to do so with gusto, and to receive positive and corrective feedback for their efforts. These strategies have the potential to generate much more learning out of the available time than might be thought possible.

Transenvironmental Programming

Behaviorally disordered students are often removed from regular education settings to provide systematic behavior management and intensive academic instruction. It is important to remember that, even though a child is removed from a given classroom, that placement remains the arrangement of choice toward which special education should be directed. In other words, removal is justified only when the provisions outside the regular class will lead to improved success for the student when back inside that setting. This statement embodies the spirit of least restrictive alternative; in so doing, it provides guidelines for making necessary decisions about academic curriculum and methodology.

Programming for handicapped students, whether academic or behavioral, should be geared toward maximizing each student's successful performance in an educational setting that is less restrictive than the current placement. To do this effectively, special educators need to adopt a data-based decision-making approach that systematically prepares a student for the academic and behavioral demands of the target environment. Anderson-Inman (1981, 1986) has suggested an approach called *transenvironmental programming* to fill this need.

Transenvironmental programming is an organizational construct for a process composed of four steps. Its purpose is to promote successful academic or behavioral adjustment in a targeted educational setting that is less restrictive than a student's current placement. The following four procedures are used to achieve this goal:

1. Identify, via observation and interview, the skills necessary for success in the target environment.
2. Provide instruction in the training environment to students who are deficient in the skills identified.
3. Incorporate into the training specific strategies for promoting the transfer of skills from the training environment to the target environment.

Behaviorally disordered students can succeed in school if they are given sufficient structure.

4. Evaluate the success of this instruction by monitoring student performance in the target environment.

Although none of these steps is a radical departure from current educational theory, they are seldom put into operation systematically. Decisions regarding what and how behaviorally disordered students should be taught in special education are often made in a vacuum. Seldom are the decisions based on information about the expectations and performance demands of the target setting; rarely are efforts made to promote the transfer of learned skills to less restrictive environments. Although considerable research has shown that much of human behavior is situation-specific (Mischel, 1968) and, therefore, does not transfer to new settings automatically, this fact is seldom considered when providing special education assistance. For a more detailed discussion of the transenvironmental programming process and its implications for teaching academic skills to behaviorally disordered students, the reader is referred to Anderson-Inman (1981, 1986; Anderson-Inman, Walker, & Purcell, 1984).

SUMMARY

This chapter has reviewed current developments in teaching academic skills to behaviorally disordered students. The importance of establishing academic skills instruction as a high priority area of instruction was stressed. Although there is no single, best method for teaching academic skills, a combination of two instructional approaches—direct instruction and opportunity to respond — holds great promise. Both approaches emphasize the importance of structure, carefully programmed instruction, feedback, and systematic monitoring of student progress. Above all, each assumes that *all students can be taught.*

Specific recommendations for teaching academic tool subjects and content area subjects were also provided. A common theme throughout all the recommendations is that more potent, more structured, and more direct instructional interventions are required to remediate the academic deficiencies of these students successfully. The relationship between academic performance and classroom behavior problems was also discussed. The efficacy of focusing intervention efforts on academic problems because of the spillover effects to behavior problems was explained. Also reviewed were strategies for maximizing the time available for academic instruction. Finally, specific procedures for implementing a transenvironmental programming approach were also recommended.

REVIEW QUESTIONS

1. Explain how a teacher can "make every minute count" in the academic program.
2. Do you agree with the contention that too much time is spent by students completing skill sheets or workbook assignments as a seatwork activity? The next time you are in a classroom during reading instruction, pay attention to how time is spent and the nature of the instructional activities.
3. React to the following statement about behaviorally disordered students: "Nothing can be learned until their behavioral and emotional problems are satisfactorily resolved." Do you agree or disagree? Why?
4. Visit a curriculum or instructional materials library and review several of the materials identified in Exhibit 5.2. Examine the teacher's manuals. In what ways do the materials incorporate the principles and practices of effective instruction discussed in this chapter?
5. How can an academic intervention also be a behavioral intervention? Why is it generally more effective to focus reinforcement on academic performance instead of conduct?

REFERENCES

Anderson, R. C., Hiebert, E. H., Scott, J. A., & Wilkinson, I. A. G. (1985). *Becoming a nation of readers: The report of the commission on reading.* Washington, DC: National Institute of Education.

Anderson-Inman, L. (1981). Transenvironmental programming: Promoting success in the regular class by maximizing the effect of resource room instruction. *Journal of Special Education Technology, 4*(4), 3–12.

Anderson-Inman, L. (1986). Bridging the gap: Student-centered strategies for promoting the transfer of learning. *Exceptional Children, 52,* 562–572.

Anderson-Inman, L., Walker, H. M., & Purcell, J. (1984). Promoting the transfer of skills across settings: Transenvironmental programming for handicapped students in the mainstream. In W. Heward, T. Heron, D. Hill, & J. Trap-Porter (Eds.), *Focus on behavior analysis in education.* Columbus, OH: Merrill.

Askov, E. N., & Otto, W. (1985). *Meeting the challenge: Corrective reading instruction in the classroom.* Columbus, OH: Merrill.

Association for Direct Instruction. (1982). The direct instruction philosophy. *Direct Instruction News, 1*(2), 16.

Ayllon, T., Layman, D., & Burke, S. (1972). Disruptive behavior and reinforcement of academic performance. *The Psychological Record, 22,* 315–322.

Ayllon, T., & Roberts, M. (1974). Eliminating discipline problems by strengthening academic performance. *Journal of Applied Behavior Analysis, 7,* 71–76.

Bartel, N. R. (1986). Teaching students who have reading problems, In D. D. Hammill & N. R. Bartel, *Teaching students with learning and behavior problems* (4th ed.). Boston: Allyn & Bacon.

Becker, W., Engelmann, S., Carnine, D., & Rhine, R. (1982). The direct instruction model. In R. Rhine (Ed.), *Encouraging change in America's schools: A decade of experimentation.* New York: Academic Press.

Berliner, D. (1979). Tempus educare. In P. Peterson & H. Walberg (Eds.), *Research on teaching: Concepts, findings, and implications.* Berkeley, CA: McCutchan.

Bloom, B. S. (1976). *Human characteristics and school learning.* New York: McGraw-Hill.

Broden, M., Bruce, C., Mitchell, M., Carter, V., & Hall, R. (1970). Effects of teacher attention on attending behavior of two boys at adjacent desks. *Journal of Applied Behavior Analysis, 3,* 205–211.

Broughton, S., & Lahey, B. (1978). Direct and collateral effects of positive reinforcement, response cost, and mixed contingencies for academic performance. *Journal of School Psychology, 16,* 126–136.

Candler, A. C., & Green, C. (1982). The handicapped learner in the secondary social studies class. *American Secondary Education, 12*(1), 23–24.

Carnine D. (1976). Effects of two teacher presentation rates on off-task behavior, answering correctly, and participation. *Journal of Applied Behavior Analysis, 9,* 199–206.

Carnine, D., & Silbert, J. (1979). *Direct instruction reading.* Columbus, OH: Merrill.

Cobb, J. A. (1970). *Survival skills and first grade academic achievement.* Report No. 1. Eugene: Center at Oregon for Research in the Behavioral Education of the Handicapped.

Cobb, J. A. (1972). Relationship of discrete classroom behavior to fourth grade academic achievement. *Journal of Educational Psychology, 63,* 74–80.

Cobb, J. A., & Hops, H. (1973). Effects of academic survival skill training on low achieving first graders. *Journal of Educational Research, 67,* 108–113.

Coleman, L. J. (1979). Using readability data for adapting curriculum materials. *Education and Training of the Mentally Retarded, 14,* 163–169.

Critchley, E. M. R. (1968). Reading retardation, dyslexia, and delinquency. *British Journal of Psychiatry, 115,* 1537–1547.

Delquadri, J., Greenwood, C., Stretton, K., & Hall, R. (in press). The peer tutoring spelling game: A classroom procedure for increasing opportunity to respond and spelling performance. *Education and Treatment of Children.*

Delquadri, J., Whorton, D., Elliot, M., Greenwood, C., & Hall, R. (1981). *The Juniper Gardens classroom peer tutoring program for oral reading.* Kansas City: University of Kansas, Juniper Gardens Children's Project.

Deshler, D. D., & Graham, S. (1980). Tape recording educational materials for secondary handicapped students. *Teaching Exceptional Children, 12,* 52–54.

Dillner, M. H., & Olson, J. P. (1977). Adapting content area materials to students' reading ability. In J. P. Olson & M. H. Dillner (Eds.), *Personalizing reading instruction in middle, junior, and senior high schools.* New York: Macmillan.

Dreikurs, R. (1954). Emotional predispositions to reading difficulties. *Archives of Pediatrics, 71,* 339–353.

Edwards, L. L. (1980). Curriculum modification as a strategy for helping regular classroom behavior disordered students. *Focus on Exceptional Children, 12*(8), 1–11.

Engelmann, S. (1980). Toward the design of faultless instruction: The theoretical basis of concept analysis. *Educational Technology, 20*, 28–36.

Engelmann, S., & Carnine, D. (1980). *Theory of instruction: Principles and applications.* New York: Irvington.

Fink, B., & Sandall, S. (1977). *A comparison of one-to-one and small group instructional strategies on a word identification task by developmentally disabled preschoolers.* Eugene: University of Oregon, Direct Instruction Follow Through Project.

Gallant, J., Sargeant, M., & Van Houten, R. (1980). Teacher-determined and self-determined access to science activities as a reinforcer for task completion in other curriculum areas. *Education and Treatment of Children, 3*, 101–111.

Glavin, J. P., & Annesley, F. R. (1971). Reading and arithmetic correlates of conduct-problem and withdrawn children. *Journal of Special Education, 5*, 213–219.

Good, T., & Grouws, D. (1979). The Missouri mathematics project: An experimental study of fourth grade classrooms. *Journal of Educational Psychology, 71*, 355–362.

Greenwood, C., Delquadri, J., & Hall, R. (1983). *Opportunity to respond and student academic performance.* Kansas City: University of Kansas, Juniper Gardens Children's Project.

Greenwood, C., Dinwiddie, G., Terry, B., Wade, L., Stanley, S., Thibadeau, S., & Delquadri, J. (1983). *Experimental analysis of the achievement effects produced by low vs. high opportunity to respond instruction.* Kansas City: University of Kansas, Juniper Gardens Children's Project.

Greenwood, C. R., Hops, H., Delquadri, J., & Walker, H. M. (1977). *Program for academic survival skills: Consultant manual.* Eugene: Center at Oregon for Research in the Behavioral Education of the Handicapped.

Harris, V., & Sherman, J. (1973). Use and analysis of the "good behavior game" to reduce disruptive classroom behavior. *Journal of Applied Behavior Analysis, 6*, 405–417.

Hasselbring, T. S., Goin, L. I., & Bransford, J. D. (1987). Developing automaticity. *Teaching Exceptional Children, 19*, 30–33.

Hay, W., Hay, L., & Nelson, R. (1977). Direct and collateral changes in on-task academic behavior resulting from on-task versus academic contingencies. *Behavior Therapy, 8*, 431–441.

Maggs, A., & Morath, P. (1976). The effects of direct verbal instruction on intellectual development of institutionalized moderately retarded children: A two-year study. *Journal of Special Education, 1976, 10*, 257–264.

Mangers, A. R. (1950). Effect of mental and educational retardation on personality development of children. *American Journal of Mental Deficiency, 55*, 208–212.

McMichael, P. (1979). "The hen or the egg?" Which comes first—antisocial emotional disorders or reading disability? *British Journal of Educational Psychology, 49,* 226–238.

Mischel, W. (1968). *Personality and assessment.* New York: John Wiley.

National Commission on Excellence in Education. (1983). *A nation at risk: The imperative for educational reform.* Washington, DC: Author.

Nichols, J. N. (1980). Using paragraph frames to help remedial high school students with written assignments. *Journal of Reading, 24,* 228–231.

Paine, S. (1982). *Time, teaching, and student achievement in 55 elementary school classrooms: Data summary and management recommendations.* Eugene: University of Oregon, Direct Instruction Follow Through Project.

Paine, S., Radicchi, J., Rosellini, L., Deutchman, L., & Darch, C. (1983). *Structuring your classroom for academic success.* Champaign, IL: Research Press.

Peters, E., & Lloyd, J. (1987). Effective mathematics instruction. *Teaching Exceptional Children, 19,* 30.

Polsgrove, L., & Nelson, C. M. (1982). Curriculum intervention according to the behavioral model. In R. L. McDowell, G. W. Adamson, & F. H. Wood (Eds.), *Teaching emotionally disturbed children.* Boston: Little, Brown.

Reid, E. R. (1986). Practicing effective instruction: The Exemplary Center for Reading Instruction approach. *Exceptional Children, 52,* 510–519.

Robinson, R., & Good, T. L. (1987). *Becoming an effective reading teacher.* New York: Harper & Row.

Rosenshine, B. (1976). Classroom instruction. In N. Gage (Ed.), *The psychology of teaching methods: Seventy-fifth yearbook of the National Society for the Study of Education.* Chicago: University of Chicago Press.

Rosenshine, B. (1979). Content, time, and direct instruction. In P. Peterson & H. Walberg (Eds.), *Research on teaching: Concepts, findings, and implications.* Berkeley, CA: McCutchan.

Rutter, M., & Yule, W. (1970). Reading retardation and antisocial behavior—The nature of the association. In M. Rutter, J. Tigard, & K. Whitmore (Eds.), *Education, health, and behavior.* London: Longman.

Samuels, S. J. (1986). Why children fail to learn and what to do about it. *Exceptional Children, 53,* 7–16.

Schloss, P. J., & Sedlak, R. A. (1986). *Instructional methods for students with learning and behavior problems.* Boston: Allyn & Bacon.

Sedlak, R. A., & Fitzmaurice, A. M. (1981). Teaching arithmetic. In J. M. Kauffman & D. P. Hallahan (Eds.), *Handbook of special education.* Englewood Cliffs, NJ: Prentice Hall.

Shipman, V. C. (1976). *Notable early characteristics of high and low achieving black low-SES children.* Princeton, NJ: Educational Testing Services.

Silbert, J., Carnine, D., & Stein, M. (1981). *Direct instruction mathematics.* Columbus, OH: Merrill.

Silverman, R., Zigmond, N., & Sansone, J. (1981). Teaching coping skills to adolescents with learning problems. *Focus on Exceptional Children, 13*(6), 1–20.

Stainback, S., & Stainback, W. (1980). *Educating children with severe maladaptive behaviors.* New York: Grune & Stratton.

Stein, M. (1987). Arithmetic word problems. *Teaching Exceptional Children, 19,* 33–35.

Stott, D. H. (1981). Behavior disturbance and failure to learn: A study of cause and effect. *Educational Research, 23,* 163–172.

Strain, P., Cooke, T., & Apolloni, T. (1976). *Teaching exceptional children: Assessing and modifying social behavior.* New York: Academic Press.

Taffel, S., & O'Leary, K. (1976). Reinforcing math with more math: Choosing special academic activities as a reward for academic performance. *Journal of Educational Psychology, 68,* 579–587.

Vacca, R. T. (1981). *Content area reading.* Boston: Little, Brown.

Van Houten, R. (1980). *Learning through feedback: A systematic approach for improving academic performance.* New York: Human Sciences Press.

Wallace, G. (1981). Teaching reading. In J. M. Kauffman & D. P. Hallahan (Eds.), *Handbook of special education.* Englewood Cliffs, NJ: Prentice-Hall.

Wallace, G., & Kauffman, J. M. (1986). *Teaching students with learning and behavior problems* (3rd. ed.) Columbus, OH: Merrill.

Wright, L. S. (1974). Conduct problem or learning disability. *Journal of Special Education, 8,* 331–336.

Yule, W., & Rutter, M. (1968). Educational aspects of childhood maladjustment: Some epidemiological findings. *British Journal of Educational Psychology, 38,* 7–9.

6 Teaching Social Skills to Behaviorally Disordered Students

After completing this chapter, you should be able to

- *Define* social skills.
- *List social skills commonly taught to behaviorally disordered students.*
- *Explain the importance of teaching social skills.*
- *Describe basic instructional methods used in teaching social skills.*
- *Describe procedures used to facilitate generalization of social skills training.*
- *Identify the basic design and common teaching elements of several commercially available social skills training programs.*
- *Discuss criteria to be used in selecting social skills training programs.*
- *Describe procedures for integrating social skills training into a program for behaviorally disordered students.*

Behaviorally disordered children lack social skills. In fact, inability to build or maintain satisfactory relationships with peers and teachers is one of their key identifying characteristics (Bower, 1969). And, unfortunately, a growing body of literature suggests that an individual's repertoire of social skills has profound implications for nearly every facet of life — in school, on the job, in the community, and at home.

Despite the central importance of social skills, only recently has social skills training been recognized as a necessary part of the basic school curriculum. Researchers have now begun to systematically address ways to improve social skills. The results of these efforts have been very promising. Social skills training has been found to be effective in improving peer-to-peer interaction skills and social acceptance of behaviorally disordered students (Cartledge & Milburn, 1986; Gresham, 1981; Hops, 1982; Schneider & Byrne, 1985).

The attention given to social skills training stems from the recognition that people without good social skills are more likely to have problems as children and are more likely to encounter serious difficulties in adjustment in adulthood (Bornstein, Bellack, & Hersen, 1977; Roff, 1961). Children who lack social skills are often rejected or neglected by their peers. The cumulative effect of years of rejection or neglect may be a significant deleterious impact on emotional well-being, self-concept, and confidence, as well as academic competence and vocational skills. The resulting adjustment problems—poor mental health, dropping out of school, juvenile delinquency — may produce a tremendous handicap for the individual and a potentially heavy burden for society.

The purpose of this chapter is to examine relevant issues concerning social skills training for behaviorally disordered students. How to teach social skills constitutes the primary focus of the chapter. Also included will be discussion of those social skills commonly taught. Basic techniques that facilitate generalization will be described. The chapter concludes with suggestions for integrating social skills training into the overall instructional program for behaviorally disordered students.

SELECTING SOCIAL SKILLS

Social skills are those interpersonal behaviors that allow an individual to interact with others successfully. More specifically, social skills are verbal and nonverbal behaviors a person uses to interact with others so that the encounter is mutually beneficial and reinforcing. The decision concerning which social skills to teach is neither simple nor straightforward; this is an area that has been closely examined, but few conclusive answers have been found. As Strain (1982) has said, "While we know a great deal about tactics for producing changes in exceptional children's social behaviors, the *content* of instruction remains a major, unresolved issue" (p. vi). This section of the chapter will briefly review several methods that have been used to select social skills for training programs. Target behaviors from representative programs will also be identified.

One approach that has been used to identify social skills is a *competence-correlates* approach (Asher & Taylor, 1982). In this approach, skills associated with peer social acceptance are identified through sociometric and observational procedures. The more frequent social behaviors of children who are liked by their peers are then targeted for intervention. Careful tracking and recording of children's social behavior in natural settings can provide detailed information about specific skills related to social competence (Foster & Richey, 1979). However, in addition to its being expensive and time-consuming, a potential limitation of validation through naturalistic observation is that there seems to be no clear relationship between the frequency of children's social interactions and their acceptance by their peers. Some well-liked children interact infrequently, while some unpopular children have high rates of social interaction.

The child's developmental level is also an important consideration in identifying social skills for training (Strain, Odom, & McConnell, 1984). Social behaviors that are developmentally appropriate for primary-aged or preschool children may not be appropriate for older students. Similarly, behaviors considered appropriate for older students may require skills beyond the capabilities of younger students. This is especially true in communication skills and language.

Gresham (1983) has suggested that the concept of *social validity* be seriously considered in selecting social skills for intervention. One aspect of social validity, social significance, asks whether the goals of a training program are important or valuable to significant others in the person's everyday environment. Obviously, it would be a critical mistake to teach social skills that are considered insignificant or superfluous by the child's associates. Another aspect of social validity, social importance, examines the effects of social skills training. The basic question here asks whether learning new social skills makes a difference in the individual's overall functioning. Thus, socially important behaviors for children in training programs would seem to include behaviors that lead to increased acceptance by peers and adults, improved school adjustment, and improved overall mental health (Gresham, 1986).

Walker and Rankin (1983) developed the *Teacher Social Behavior Standards and Expectations* questionnaire to help determine which specific social skills teachers deemed important for students. Other researchers have used a similar approach, using parents, court workers, mental health professionals, and other adult lay people to identify target social skills. A potential shortcoming is that this approach may provide an adults-only view of children's behavior. That is, while the skills identified may be important to adults, they may not be as important or relevant to the child's peers.

Most social skills researchers and training program developers have targeted skills for instruction by (1) reviewing the literature to identify key social skills that discriminate between socially competent and incompetent children, (2) reviewing social skills taught in existing training programs, and (3) logically analyzing the skills handicapped children need to satisfactorily cope and adjust in school (Walker, McConnell, Holmes, Todis, Walker, & Golden, 1983). Exhibit 6.1 lists skills taught in several social skills training programs. While none of the curricula are exactly the same, there is considerable similarity across programs. The skills identified in the exhibit are clearly related to the goal of helping students establish and maintain satisfactory peer relationships by exhibiting prosocial interaction skills positively correlated with peer acceptance and school success.

TEACHING SOCIAL SKILLS

The procedures reviewed in this section share many characteristics of the direct and systematic teaching approaches identified as preferred practices in earlier chapters. Demonstration–prompt–practice teaching formats are used in most programs. Guided and controlled practice of student learning activities, which has a high probability of student success, is also incorporated. Careful preassessment and continuous monitoring of student progress are built in, as is independent practice activities (e.g., homework) to facilitate generalization of newly acquired skills.

Goldstein (1981) captured the essence of the direct instruction approach with the following definition of *social skills training:*

> Social skills training is the planned, systematic teaching of the specific behaviors needed and consciously desired by the individual in order to function in an effective and satisfying manner, over an extended period of time, in a broad array of positive, negative, and neutral interpersonal contexts. The specific teaching methods which constitute social skills training directly and jointly reflect modern psychology's social learning theory and education's pedagogic principles and procedures. (p. 162)

He continued by stating that social skills training is

> a behavioral approach, designed to enhance the overt actions of the trainee, in contrast to those psychotherapeutic and educational interventions which seek to alter the individual's beliefs about himself, or self-understanding, in the (typically vain) hope that somehow behavior change will follow. (pp. 162–163)

The fact that many training programs follow a direct teaching/behavioral approach is not based on whim and fancy. Instead, the direct instruction teaching methods used have been derived from research studies indicating that certain procedures are more effective than others in teaching social skills to children (see, for example, Clarke, Caldwell, & Christian, 1979; Cooke & Apolloni, 1976; Kiburz, Miller, & Morrow, 1984; Madson et al., 1980; Strain, Shores, & Kerr, 1976; Walker, Hops, & Greenwood, 1984). These effective instructional methods include instructions and rationales, modeling, concept teaching, role-playing, rehearsal, and practice, coaching, and contingent reinforcement.

Instructions and Rationales

Teaching social skills is easier when the learners are informed about what they are to be taught and why it is important to learn the skill. Not informing a child or being vague (e.g., "I'm going to teach you how to be nice") may confuse the child and lead to misinterpretation about the purpose of the training (Stocking, Arezzo, & Leavitt, 1980).

The purposes of providing instructions and rationales are to (a) concisely state what specific skills are to be taught, (b) explain the rationale for teaching a particular skill (i.e., how it will help them be more successful in daily interactions), and (c) provide some examples of the particular skill to be taught. Students are told specifically what skills and subskills they will be learning (e.g., "Today we're going to learn how to make requests"). A definition of the behavior and an example may then follow: "A request is asking for something that we want, or asking someone to do something. For example, would you give me a ride home?"

Students are also provided with a reason for learning the new skill. The rationale typically gives an example of how one can be more successful in interacting with peers and adults because of the skill. The teacher

EXHIBIT 6.1   Representative social skill curriculum sequences

ACCEPTS (Walker, McConnell, Holmes, Todis, Walker, & Golden, 1983)	ASSET (Hazel, Schumaker, Sherman, & Sheldon-Wildgen, 1981)	GETTING ALONG WITH OTHERS (Jackson, Jackson, & Monroe, 1983)

I. CLASSROOM SKILLS
  – Listening to the teacher
  – When the teacher tells you to do something
  – Doing your best work
  – Following the classroom rules
 	
II. BASIC INTERACTION
  – Eye contact
  – Using the right voice
  – Starting
  – Listening
  – Answering
  – Making sense
  – Taking turns talking
  – Questioning
  – Continuing
 	
III. GETTING ALONG
  – Using polite words
  – Sharing
  – Following the rules
  – Assisting others
  – Touching the right way
 	
IV. MAKING FRIENDS
  – Grooming
  – Smiling
  – Complimenting
  – Expressing anger
  – Making friends
 	
V. COPING
  – When someone says "no"
  – When someone teases you
  – When someone tries to hurt you
  – When someone asks you to do something you can't do
  – When things don't go right
	1. Giving positive feedback
	2. Giving negative feedback
	3. Accepting negative feedback
	4. Resisting peer pressure
	5. Problem-solving
	6. Negotiations
	7. Following instructions
	8. Conversation
		1. Introducing
		2. Following directions
		3. Giving and receiving positive feedback
		4. Sending an "I'm interested" message
		5. Sending an ignoring message
		6. Interrupting a conversation
		7. Joining a conversation
		8. Starting a conversation and keeping it going
		9. Sharing
		10. Offering to help
		11. Compromising
		12. Asking for clear directions
		13. Problem solving
		14. Using positive consequences
		15. Giving and receiving a suggestion for improvement
		16. Handling name-calling and teasing
		17. Saying "no" to stay out of trouble

EXHIBIT 6.1 *continued*

SOCIAL SKILLS IN THE CLASSROOM (Stephens, 1978)	SKILLSTREAMING THE ELEMENTARY SCHOOL CHILD (McGinnis & Goldstein, 1984)

ENVIRONMENTAL BEHAVIORS
Care for the environment
Dealing with an emergency
Lunchroom behavior
Movement around environment

INTERPERSONAL BEHAVIORS
Accepting authority
Coping with conflict
Gaining attention
Greeting others
Helping others
Making conversation
Organized play
Positive attitude toward others
Playing informally
Property: Own and others'

SELF-RELATED BEHAVIORS
Accepting consequences
Ethical behavior
Expressing feelings
Positive attitude toward self
Responsible behavior
Self-care

TASK RELATED BEHAVIORS
Asking and answering questions
Attending
Classroom discussion
Completing tasks
Following directions
Group activities
Independent work
On-task
Performing before others
Quality work

I. CLASSROOM SURVIVAL SKILLS
  1. Listening
  2. Asking for help
  3. Saying thank you
  4. Bringing materials to class
  5. Following instructions
  6. Completing assignments
  7. Contributing to discussions
  8. Offering help to an adult
  9. Asking a question
  10. Ignoring distractions
  11. Making corrections
  12. Deciding on something to do
  13. Setting a goal

II. FRIENDSHIP-MAKING SKILLS
  14. Introducing yourself
  15. Beginning a conversation
  16. Ending a conversation
  17. Joining in
  18. Playing a game
  19. Asking a favor
  20. Offering help to a classmate
  21. Giving a compliment
  22. Accepting a compliment
  23. Suggesting an activity
  24. Sharing
  25. Apologizing

III. SKILLS FOR DEALING WITH FEELINGS
  26. Knowing your feelings
  27. Expressing your feelings
  28. Recognizing another's feelings
  29. Showing understanding of another's feelings
  30. Expressing concern for another
  31. Dealing with your anger
  32. Dealing with another's anger
  33. Expressing affection
  34. Dealing with fear
  35. Rewarding yourself

IV. SKILL ALTERNATIVES TO AGGRESSION
  36. Using self-control
  37. Asking permission
  38. Responding to teasing
  39. Avoiding trouble
  40. Staying out of fights
  41. Problem solving
  42. Accepting consequences
  43. Dealing with an accusation
  44. Negotiating

V. SKILLS FOR DEALING WITH STRESS
  45. Dealing with boredom
  46. Deciding what caused a problem
  47. Making a complaint
  48. Answering a complaint
  49. Dealing with losing
  50. Showing sportsmanship
  51. Dealing with being left out
  52. Dealing with embarrassment
  53. Reacting to failure
  54. Accepting no
  55. Saying no
  56. Relaxing
  57. Dealing with group pressure
  58. Dealing with wanting something that isn't mine
  59. Making a decision
  60. Being honest

may also ask for one or two examples from the students to further emphasize that the skills are functional and important.

It is important to remember that the teacher does not always have to be the sole source of information. Students can analyze the nature of the skills to be taught and the reasons for learning them (Kelly, 1982). In the introduction, it is important to be brief and to the point. Too much elaboration (i.e., excess teacher talk) causes students to lose interest and hinders rather than facilitates learning. State the skill precisely, give the rationale, present the rules and examples, and move on.

Modeling

The work of Albert Bandura (1977) on modeling as a treatment for behavioral excesses and deficits has been the basis for incorporating it into many social skills training programs. Essentially, modeling can be used to teach new skills, inhibit inappropriate behaviors, and encourage behaviors that are currently inhibited.

Modeling can be accomplished using film or videotape, audiotape, live demonstrations, mental imagery, puppets, and books. Because each of these formats has relative advantages and disadvantages, the following factors should be kept in mind when choosing a format (Eisler & Frederiksen, 1980):

1. The desired behavior must be accurately and unambiguously presented.
2. It should be possible to present the same model when requested later.
3. The model should be versatile enough to adapt to changing conditions in the learners, the training context, or generalization settings.
4. The time, effort, and cost required to produce and use the models are also major considerations.

Some social skills training programs include either filmed, videotaped, or audiotaped modeling vignettes. While these programs may be repeatable, their accuracy, versatility, and costs may not be satisfactory. Live models are versatile and cost-effective, but may not be accurate or repeatable.

What may be more important than the specific format is identifying those factors that significantly affect the degree of learning. Specifically, according to Goldstein (1981), the probability that a child will learn from a model increases when (a) the model is viewed as highly skilled or expert, of high status or same sex, age, and race as the learner, gives the overall appearance of friendliness and helpfulness, and receives reinforcement for the behavior being modeled; (b) the actual modeling sequence is clear and detailed, progressing from least difficult to most difficult behaviors; and (c) the lesson is repetitive, free of extraneous details, and uses more than one model. Goldstein also pointed out that modeling is a "necessary but insufficient" component of social skills training. Modeling can show a child what to do but more instruction is needed for the child to actually perform the skills.

Concept Teaching

Concept teaching involves presenting the critical and irrelevant attributes of a concept (i.e., social skill) and assessing whether the student can discriminate between *examples* and *nonexamples* of the concept (Engelmann & Carnine, 1982). The social skills tutoring component of the PEERS program (Hops et al., 1978), a program for socially withdrawn children, uses concept teaching procedures. The trainer first describes the relevant attributes of the concept; for example, "The first *two* things we do in starting to play with someone are find someone to play with and call their name." The trainer then demonstrates the concept by giving examples and providing nonexamples of the concept. Finally, the trainer assesses the student's understanding by providing examples and nonexamples of the concept that the student must correctly discriminate. The examples and nonexamples may be presented live by the teachers or through mediated methods such as videotapes. Again, used alone, concept teaching would not be sufficient for significantly changing a student's social behaviors. The PEERS program, for example, also includes modeling, behavioral rehearsal and practice, and contingent reinforcement.

Role-Playing/Behavior Rehearsal and Practice

Role-playing and behavior rehearsal techniques have been widely used in clinical and other therapeutic settings. In role-playing/behavior rehearsal, the individual rehearses how to behave in given situations that have caused or may cause difficulty. This exercise is usually conducted under the guidance of a teacher, who may initially model an appropriate response and also provide prompts, coaching, and feedback during the rehearsal.

Role-playing/behavior rehearsal and practice provide the learner with an opportunity to "try his wings" under the teacher's watchful eye before using the skill in the real world. Behavior rehearsal also gives the teacher an opportunity to assess progress and provide corrective feedback as required (Eisler & Frederiksen, 1980).

Role-playing/behavior rehearsal and practice may be structured, unstructured, or some combination of the two (Kelly, 1982). In a structured behavior rehearsal, the teacher presents students with a situation from a pool of vignettes related to a specific social skill. In unstructured behavior rehearsal, the vignettes to be rehearsed are drawn from situations directly related to a student's novel circumstances and may in fact be suggested by the student.

For any skill to be acquired and mastered, whether it be decoding words, playing the piano, or kicking field goals, one of the key predictors of success is the amount and quality of practice time devoted to that particular skill. That is why role-playing and behavior rehearsal and practice are prominent in most social skills training programs. Few studies have examined the use of role-playing/behavior rehearsal and practice alone as a social skills training program with handicapped students. Usually, these techniques are employed along with other instructional procedures such as modeling, concept teaching, contingent reinforcement, and coaching.

Coaching

Coaching involves verbally instructing children by focusing on relevant cues, concepts, and rules. For example, in training socially isolated elementary-aged children, Oden and Asher (1977) conducted a series of training sessions in which the children were taught concepts of how to play with other children by emphasizing the presentation of rules and standards of conduct, given an opportunity to practice the new behaviors with a peer, and given feedback on their behavior by the coach. According to Cartledge and Milburn (1986), coaching is most useful when it is used during behavioral rehearsal and practice.

Contingent Reinforcement

To teach social skills effectively, teachers must know when and how to praise, ignore, and give students corrective feedback (see Pointer 6.1). Although the systematic application of contingent reinforcement is critical to the overall success of social skills training, a token reinforcement system will also probably be needed to promote acquisition and maintenance with behaviorally disordered students.

Token reinforcement procedures have three general functions: (a) to help the student initially acquire the targeted social skills, (b) to facilitate maintenance and generalization of newly acquired skills to other settings and times, and (c) if necessary, to control behavior during the training sessions. The token reinforcement system should incorporate the following preferred practices.

1. The ultimate goal should be to bring a student's behavior under the control of natural consequences (e.g., social praise, approval, surprise rewards).

Pointer 6.1

HOW TO GIVE CORRECTIVE FEEDBACK

During social skills instruction, when a child makes an incorrect response or does not give any kind of response, the teacher should provide corrective feedback. Corrective feedback should be instructional and nonaversive. Corrective feedback should lead directly to the student giving a correct response where previously he or she had failed. Corrective feedback should be accompanied by praise for the corrected performance.

Corrective feedback involves an instructional procedure known as "model-lead-test." The steps involved in the model-lead-test procedure are:

1. The teacher *models* the correct response.
2. The teacher *leads* the student through the correct response.
3. The teacher *tests* the student by again asking for the correct response.

If the student responds correctly to the original task, the teacher should praise the student. If the student responds incorrectly again, the teacher should recycle the student through the model-lead-test procedure.

The following example illustrates the use of the model-lead-test procedure in a social skills lesson.

Situation
Student has just completed practicing how to "say nice things" to a peer.

Model
Teacher: Very good, Billy. You said that Tommy was nice in helping you with your math. You need to remember to make eye contact and use the right tone of voice, though. Here, watch me do it. (Teacher models behavior using same role-playing example.)

Lead
Teacher: Now do it with me.
(Teacher may coach the student by reminding him to make eye contact and to use the right tone of voice.)

Test
Teacher: Great! Now do it with Tommy the same way.
Teacher provides feedback. If not done correctly, teacher takes Billy through the sequence again. If done correctly, the teacher may give Billy another role-playing situation to test for generalization.

2. The simplest and least complex token system should be used whenever possible. As a general rule, a more intense system is likely to be needed at the beginning of training. As students progress, they can move to a less intense system.
3. The ultimate goal of any social skills training program is to produce lasting, positive changes in the students' social behavior. The token system should be designed with careful attention to the goal of long-term maintenance of improved skills.
4. Student behavior is the most critical element in assessing whether token systems are appropriate and effective. Careful, frequent monitoring of student progress is essential.

Experience has shown that behaviorally disordered students need carefully implemented, systematic programs to help them acquire social skills. However, not every student requires the same level of intensity to benefit from social skills training. Some may require a relatively simple system consisting of teacher social reinforcement and contingent free time. Others may benefit from the more structured approach of a contingency contract. A program of even greater intensity may be required for some especially deficient or disruptive students. The next section shows how these behavior management principles have been incorporated in selected programs.

GENERALIZATION OF SOCIAL SKILLS TRAINING

Social skills *can* be learned and demonstrated under the controlled circumstances of a classroom. However, social skills that have been successfully rehearsed and practiced in the classroom still ultimately must transfer to other times, places, situations, and people. A significant problem in social skills training has been that the student often does not have the same level of skill *outside* the classroom (Schloss, Schloss, Wood, & Kiehl, 1986).

One of the major reasons for this failure to generalize is that the training programs have not adequately programmed for generalization (see Pointer 6.2). A big mistake, made too often, is to assume that generalization will occur naturally or spontaneously (again, the train-and-hope approach). There are a number of procedures that should be implemented to encourage generalization. This section of the chapter will first review several general suggestions. How homework can be used to promote generalization will be discussed and followed by an explanation of how to involve the peer group in generalizing behavior improvements.

Pointer 6.2

SOCIAL SKILLS TRAINING WITH CHILDREN: PROCEED WITH CAUTION

A study by Berler, Gross, and Drabman (1982) is an excellent illustration of the current state of the art in generalizing social skills training. Three elementary-age learning disabled children received training consisting of coaching, modeling, behavior rehearsal, and feedback. The target social skills were eye contact and appropriate verbal behavior.

The subjects' progress was determined by gains made on three dependent measures: performance on a role-play test, observation of their interactions in free play settings, and sociometric ratings. When compared to three learning disabled children in a control group, the group that received social skills training only did significantly better on the role-play test. There were no significant differences on the free play or sociometric measures.

In other words, as the authors candidly admit, the social skills training the subjects received was of little value because the "gains" did not generalize to real-life situations and acceptance by their peers did not improve.

Note, however, that there were problems specific to the conduct and design of this study that prevented more favorable results. For example, the teachers did not provide feedback to the children about their social interactions in the generalization settings. Problems with the design of the observation instrument may have also obscured gains. Finally, errors in the initial selection of skills to be trained may have influenced the results.

These problems are frequently found in experimental studies of social skills training. The authors are correct in warning practitioners not to latch on to social skills training as a panacea for curing the problems of socially incompetent children. We, too, agree that social skills trainers should proceed with caution.

Basic Considerations

The procedures identified below are strongly recommended for any social skills training program.

- Teach behaviors that will maximize success and minimize failure. Selecting socially valid behaviors is critical.
- Make the training realistic. Use relevant examples and non-examples. Role-play and rehearsal activities should reflect what actually happens in students' lives.
- Make sure students learn the skills in the classroom training part of the program. They are more likely to master the skills if they have lots of supervised practice opportunities.

- Extend practice by providing homework assignments. Homework assignments allow the students to practice outside the training situation.
- Require a self-report following a homework assignment. Reinforcement should be programmed into the homework assignment to provide positive consequences for (a) the accuracy of the self-report and (b) the achievement of homework assignments. If the student fails to do the assignment or the self-report is inaccurate, the teacher should use problem-solving/positive practice procedures before the next lesson.
- Program the natural environment to support performance of the targeted skills. Teachers, other school personnel, peers, and parents must help reinforce and prompt the newly learned social skills.
- For more difficult cases, the teacher may need to go the extra mile to facilitate generalization, and gradually transfer stimulus control. That is, the teacher actually follows the student into a variety of nontreatment settings to prompt, coach, correct, and reinforce the targeted skills. The teacher would then fade out and other individuals in the environment would take over this role.
- Fade special reinforcement programs to approximate the reinforcement schedules in real life.
- Teach self-management skills the student can use to help maintain the improved social behaviors (see chapter 4).
- Use periodic booster shots if a student's behavior deteriorates or as a preventive measure. The student would be recycled to the appropriate lesson or to specially designed booster sessions.

Homework Assignments

Another way to program for generalization is through homework assignments, which are a very common component that reflects the emphasis on practice in the acquisition of social skills. Typically, homework is incorporated into social skills training at the end of a training session. The teacher assigns each student an individual homework assignment. The assignment may be determined by student suggestions at the end of the lesson, or the teacher may develop assignments related to the day's topic or skill. For example, in a lesson on sharing and helping, a homework assignment might be to keep track of the number of times students helped someone else over the next 24 hours. The homework assignment might involve assigning a student a specific person to share something with during the next recess.

Social skills training is effective when the students can demonstrate improved social behavior outside the training situation.

Following these guidelines can increase the value of homework assignments.

1. Be sure the response requirements of the homework assignment are spelled out in sufficient detail. Check to make sure students understand what they are to accomplish.
2. Make sure students have already demonstrated that they can perform the skill. If not, break the skill down into manageable proportions. Homework assignments should provide success, not failure.
3. Begin with small homework assignments and gradually increase their size, complexity, and difficulty.
4. If students do not know how to monitor their own performance, teach, reteach, or prompt as necessary. Practice self-monitoring with students.
5. Elicit from students a public commitment to complete the homework assignment.
6. Monitor compliance with as many other sources as possible (other teachers, principals, peers).
7. Practice assignments with students. Have the students actually rehearse the response(s) required in the homework assignment.
8. Simply completing homework assignments should be reinforced, as should successful completion.
9. Before presenting any new lesson material, begin each training session with a review. The teacher and students should briefly discuss the previous day's instruction, reviewing specific lesson rules and then homework assignments. Reinforce students who completed assignments. If a student has not completed an assignment, assign a similar task or proceed with a new homework assignment. Depending on group size, a good review should take only 7 to 8 minutes, after which the lesson begins where the previous day's lesson concluded.

Involving Peers

Increasingly, research and development projects on social skills training with handicapped students have focused on the need to involve both the student and peers. The basic rationale for involving peers is intuitively simple. To enhance social reciprocity (i.e., a positive social response that is met by a similar positive response), peers should be used to model and prompt appropriate social behavior from behaviorally disordered students. Failing to systematically involve peers in social skills training may be an important underlying reason for the weak generalization and maintenance often seen (Strain et al., 1984). As Strain et al. have said,

> While social skills training may teach the handicapped child skills that are necessary for social acceptance in the new classroom . . . we have no guarantee that regular education peers will exhibit the same behaviors to the handicapped child. In fact, it is possible that regular education peers may directly reduce the generalization of the handicapped child's new skills by ignoring — or even overtly punishing — attempts by the handicapped child to engage in new, not yet perfected, social behaviors. (p. 23).

Involving peers as an integral part of the training program has the added advantage of maintaining a sense of normalcy in typical peer-to-peer interactions. That is, teachers interrupt the natural flow of social interaction when they provide reinforcement and prompt handicapped students while they are playing (Strain & Fox, 1981). Peer-mediated interventions promote prosocial behavior more normally and unobtrusively (Strain et al., 1984).

Peers have proven to be effective behavior change agents in facilitating positive social interactions. They have been used to initiate social interactions, to model appropriate behavior, to reinforce behavior, and to provide feedback (Gresham, 1981; Kerr & Nelson, 1983; Strain & Fox, 1981). The most promising approach is peer social initiation. In this strategy, peers are taught to initiate and engage in positive social interactions with targeted students in much the same way the target students are taught social skills. Commonly taught skills include sharing, organizing play, and offering assistance. Peers are taught these behaviors by the teacher using a demonstration–guided practice–feedback instructional paradigm very similar to the steps reviewed earlier. The teacher may then use additional coaching and prompting to elicit social initiations in actual play situations with the targeted student(s).

While peer social initiation has been used primarily with preschool children, it has also been used successfully with elementary-aged behaviorally disordered students (Strain & Odom, 1986). Evaluation data suggest that it has produced no negative effects and some positive effects for the normal peer confederates (Strain & Odom, 1986).

A REVIEW OF SELECTED
SOCIAL SKILLS PROGRAMS

In the last few years, there has been a dramatic increase in the number of commercially available social skills training programs appropriate for use with behaviorally disordered students. Developers of these programs recognized the need to package the training procedures and materials so as to substantially increase the probability of effective replication and dissemination. This section of the chapter will briefly review five programs that have been successful with behaviorally disordered students. Following this review will be a section offering recommendations for selecting an appropriate program.

Getting Along with Others

Getting Along with Others: Teaching Social Effectiveness to Children (Jackson, Jackson, & Monroe, 1983) provides training in 17 core social skills (see Exhibit 6.1) to students in either school or community-based therapeutic settings such as mental health clinics. The authors underline a bias toward an instructionally oriented program in describing their approach to teaching social skills:

> The most straightforward treatment is to simply *tell* the person what to do in situations defined as problematic; *show* the person how to do it; and to have the person *practice* the new skill before having to use it in real life. (Jackson et al. 1983, p. vii)

This tell–show–practice model of social skills training is just another variation on the basic direct instruction approach.

While the program stresses that any naturally occurring teacher–student interaction is an opportunity to teach social skills, it also provides an instructional format for small group direct instruction. The authors suggest that the groups consist of six to eight children meeting twice weekly for 17 two-hour sessions. Alternative scheduling formats are also suggested for schools with time constraints.

A training session consists of the following activities: free play for completing homework, review of homework, relaxation training, presentation of new skills, snack time, activity time, home notes (see Exhibit 6.2) and written homework assignments. The program provides the teacher scripts to use to demonstrate and coach progressive muscle relaxation exercises and lesson scripts to use to teach a new skill. The lesson components are introduction of new skill, role-play appropriate example, ask children to identify skill components, role-play inappropriate example, ask children to role-play, ask children to give positive feedback to others for role-playing, ask children for rationales, and reality check.

The reality check is an important portion of the lesson. Students are asked to consider what they would do if they met with peer rejection after using the social skills they had just learned. This example illustrates how the reality check is introduced in *Getting Along with Others:*

Teacher 1: *Sometimes you might try really hard to* handle name-calling and teasing, *and this might happen.* I'm on the playground, and another kid is calling me names.

Teacher 2: You're stupid and ugly and no fun to play with, and I hate you!

EXHIBIT 6.2 A home note

Skill 3: Giving & Receiving Positive Feedback
Home Note

Name _____ Instructors _____

During today's lesson we practiced giving Positive Feedback to someone when he/she does something we like and receiving Positive Feedback when someone says something nice about what we did.

Today's Objectives			**Target Behaviors**	
To give positive feedback, did the child:				Score
	Yes	No	A. _____	_____
1. Use a pleasant face and voice?	____	____	B. _____	_____
2. Look at the person?	____	____	C. _____	_____
3. Tell the person exactly what he/she liked about what the person did?	____	____	D. _____	_____
4. Tell the person right after it was done?	____	____	E. _____	_____

To give positive feedback, did the child:

Yes　No

1. Use a pleasant face and voice?
2. Look at the person?
3. Tell the person exactly what he/she liked about what the person did?
4. Tell the person right after it was done?

To receive positive feedback did the child:

5. Use a pleasant face and voice?
6. Look at the person?
7. Acknowledge the feedback by saying "Thanks" or "You're Welcome"?

Score using this scale:
1 = Completely satisfied
2 = Satisfied
3 = Slightly satisfied
4 = Neither satisfied nor dissatisfied
5 = Slightly dissatisfied
6 = Dissatisfied
7 = Completely dissatisfied

The best thing your child did today in social skills was _____
_____
_____

- -

Parents — Please Complete This Section & Return
Skill 3: Giving and Receiving Positive Feedback

Name _____

The following objectives and target behaviors refer to those named above. Please mark or score your child in these areas and have him/her return this bottom section with your signature to the next social skills group.

Did your child meet the objectives of today's lesson at least once this week?

	Yes	No
Objective 1	____	____
Objective 2	____	____
Objective 3	____	____
Objective 4	____	____
Objective 5	____	____
Objective 6	____	____
Objective 7	____	____

Score your child on his/her target behaviors, using the 1–7 scale above:

Target　Behavior　A _____
Target　Behavior　B _____
Target　Behavior　C _____
Target　Behavior　D _____
Target　Behavior　E _____

Parent Signature _____ Date _____

Source: From *Getting Along With Others: Teaching Social Effectiveness to Children* by N. F. Jackson, D. A. Jackson, and C. Monroe, 1983, Champaign, IL: Research Press. Used with permission.

Teacher 1: (takes a deep breath, stays calm, looks away, maintains pleasant face) I'm thinking, "I'm all right; I'm calm; I don't need to get mad."

Teacher 2: I wish you'd get lost! You nerd. [heckling continues]

Teacher 1: *You just did everything right to* handle name-calling and teasing. *What should you do if this happens to you?* [children respond or are prompted]

To cope with situations like this, students are taught to relax, ignore, walk away, initiate to someone else, and "keep a good attitude." By rehearsing potential responses, students learn to use adaptive coping responses.

The program has been extensively field-tested in mental health clinic settings, special education classes, and regular classes. The primary measures of success were gains on a Consumer Satisfaction Scale, completed by parents, teachers, and psychologists, and on a standardized problem behavior checklist. When implemented properly, the program produced positive changes in students' social skills. The authors have pointed out, however, that children with very minor or very severe problems and children whose problems were primarily motivational were not as successful in the program as children who had clear skill deficits in the areas targeted.

The PEERS Program

PEERS, an acronym for Procedures for Establishing Effective Relationship Skills, is designed for use with socially withdrawn, elementary-aged children (Hops et al., 1978). The major goal is to increase the amount of time the children spend interacting with their peers. It is designed to be implemented by a teacher-consultant (i.e., a consulting teacher, resource teacher, school psychologist, social worker) who works with the regular classroom teacher to implement the components of the program. PEERS, which takes about 2 months to complete, involves direct instruction in specific social skills, a peer-pairing arrangement, a recess point system, and a self-report for establishing and maintaining appropriate social behaviors over time.

The teacher consultant provides direct instruction in specific social skills to the withdrawn child and a nonwithdrawn classmate. The social skills taught include initiating interactions (starting), responding to initiations from peers (answering), maintaining interactions (keeping it going), being positive with peers (saying something nice), and playing appropriately (cooperating).

During the peer-pairing phase, the child interacts with a different classmate each day in a 10-minute structured classroom activity arranged by the teacher. Also called a *joint-task activity,* it has built-in opportunities for turn-taking and verbal interaction between students. Joint-task activities include some that are academically related (e.g., flashcards) and some that are nonacademic (e.g., games). The teacher supervises the pair and provides descriptive praise for appropriate social behavior. Not answering questions, playing alone, not joining in when invited, and not talking to peers do not earn points. The points the child earns are exchangeable for a group reward to be shared by all the classmates at the end of the day.

Each day, prior to recess, the entire class selects a reward from several listed by the teacher (e.g., 5- to 10-minute extra recess, games, movie, records, stories). Three or four special helpers are selected to insure that the withdrawn child will have an opportunity to interact and earn points. The special helpers are asked to engage the child in a specific activity during recess. The teacher also coaches the children how and when to talk with and play with the child. The payoff to the special helpers is the group activity reward they are helping the child earn for the class.

Immediately preceding recess, the teacher gives the child a pep talk during which the child is prompted and coached about the number of points needed for the reward, the reward selected, the special helpers, and the child's task to earn points. If the child earns the number of points required for the group reward, the accomplishment is announced to the class immediately after recess. If the child fails to earn enough points for the group reward, the consultant provides immediate feedback and may also do a little coaching. The child also takes the point card home every day to show his or her parents, who have already been asked to praise the child for these accomplishments and to demonstrate enthusiasm for any progress.

The self-report component of the program requires the child to give a verbal report to the teacher about the play activities during recess periods. The child is rewarded for accurately reporting social behavior. The accuracy of the report is verified by the peer helper, who also confirms or disconfirms the child's performance. Requiring only about 2 to 3 minutes after each recess, the self-report is designed to facilitate maintenance and generalization of skill improvements.

The PEERS program has been found to be effective in improving the frequency and quality of the socially withdrawn child's social behaviors (Hops, Walker, & Greenwood, 1979; Paine et al., 1982). However, the gains have not been conclusively demonstrated to be durable, which is a not-uncommon finding among social skills programs.

ACCEPTS

The *ACCEPTS Social Skills Curriculum* (Walker, McConnell, Holmes, Todis, Walker, & Golden, 1983) is designed to facilitate the social behavioral competencies of handicapped students that are essential for a successful adjustment to the behavioral demands and expectations of regular class teachers. There are 28 skills taught, organized in five major areas: Classroom Skills, Basic Interaction Skills, Getting Along, Making Friends, and Coping Skills (see Exhibit 6.1). The main elements of the program include a placement test, a 9-step instructional procedure, daily lesson scripts, a videotape containing examples and nonexamples of the skills, role-play tests to assess skill acquisition, and behavior management procedures for encouraging and strengthening skill acquisition.

The ACCEPTS instructional sequence is based upon principles of direct instruction. It provides daily lesson scripts following the instructional steps outlined below.

Step 1: *Definition and guided discussion*
Teacher defines skill and checks for understanding; discussion and examples of how skill is used.

Step 2: *Positive examples*
Appropriate skill application is modeled (either by videotape or teacher demonstration); discussion.

Step 3: *Negative examples*
Inappropriate skill application is modeled (either by videotape or teacher demonstration); discussion.

Step 4: *Review and restate skill definition*

Step 5: *Positive example*
Appropriate skill application is modeled (either by videotape or teacher demonstration); discussion.

Step 6: *Activities*
Teacher models additional examples of appropriate skill application; students role-play and practice examples of skill application.

Step 7: *Positive example*
Appropriate skill application is modeled (either by videotape or teacher demonstration); discussion.

Step 8: *Criterion role-plays*
Students role-play and practice examples of skill application; teacher rates quality of student performance; teacher reteaches if necessary.

Step 9: *Informal contracting*
Teacher gives each student a homework assignment to be completed before next lesson; students give verbal commitment to complete homework.

Behavior management procedures are included to facilitate generalization of the skills to natural settings. The procedures consist of an individual point system for classroom skills and a combined individual-group point system for peer-to-peer playground behavior. Both point systems award points to increase adaptive behaviors and take away points for maladaptive behaviors.

During recess, the teacher rates social participation during each of three equal time intervals. If the student has interacted appropriately with peers for at least half the interval, a point is awarded. The two most recently taught social skills and a previously taught skill are targeted. The teacher awards a point for correct performance of each skill during recess, and rates the overall skill level at the end of the recess. The points the student earns are exchanged for extra free time shared with the peers with whom the student interacted. The teacher also coaches the child before, during, and after recess. In the ACCEPTS program, coaching includes prompting, priming, and praising. (Priming involves giving specific suggestions or instructions to the child regarding when, what, and where interactions with peers should occur.)

The ACCEPTS program has been field-tested with handicapped children in self-contained classrooms. In one study (Walker, McConnell, Walker, Clarke, Todis, Cohen, & Rankin, 1983), three groups of children were randomly assigned to either the entire ACCEPTS program (skills training and behavior management), skills training only, or a control condition. The results clearly favored the experimental groups over the control group on all measures. Subsequent studies have confirmed these results (Walker, McConnell, Walker, Clarke, Todis, Cohen, & Rankin, 1983). However, the improvements did not last as long as desired. To address this problem, the authors recommend implementing the program over a much longer period and using low-cost variations of the procedures as needed after the formal program has been completed.

Teaching Social Skills to Handicapped Children and Youth: Programs and Materials

Teaching Social Skills to Handicapped Children and Youth: Programs and Materials (Morgan, Young, Likins, Cheney, & Peterson, 1983) was developed for use with mildly and moderately handicapped children. This program, which also emphasizes direct instruction, contains four instructional packages, each of which contains four to five separate lessons:

- Basic social interaction skills (eye contact, getting someone's attention, voice volume and tone)
- Conversation skills (starting, keeping it going, making comments/asking questions, positive feedback, dealing with unresponsiveness)
- Being positive (invitations to play, sharing, helping, praising, encouraging, being polite)
- Assertiveness skills (for adolescents)

The program materials include step-by-step lesson guides for the teacher, assessment materials, a teacher's manual containing background information as well as directions, a behavior management program, and videotapes to help students learn to discriminate between appropriate and inappropriate social behavior. Each lesson has four components: introduction, discrimination training, role-play and practice, and homework.

The purpose of discrimination training is to teach students to discriminate between examples and nonexamples of the social skills taught in the lesson. A series of videotaped examples and nonexamples of each of the skills is presented. In each example, the relevant attributes of the social skills are modeled and the irrelevant attributes (e.g., settings, individuals, situations) are varied. For example, one situation for sharing might show two children in their classroom sharing crayons during an art project while another might present three neighborhood children taking turns on a new bike. In the nonexamples, the irrelevant attributes are again varied, but some of the key attributes have been intentionally left out. For example, a student wants to share with another child but does not make eye contact or talk loud enough. Each lesson has approximately 20 scenes.

This program uses a point system consisting of three phases. The first phase involves a token reinforcement program where students are taught to evaluate their own behavior and to award themselves points based on their evaluation. The Social Skills Point Card (see Exhibit 6.3) is used to rate the quality of the student's social skills performance. Initially, points are awarded by the social skills teacher and at least one other person who comes into contact with the student outside the training session (e.g., the child's regular teacher, a counselor, parents). Then, following a carefully programmed sequence, students are taught to evaluate their own behavior and to record their ratings on the point card. The student carries around the point card throughout the day. Thus social behavior can be systematically evaluated and reinforced outside the training session. Back-up reinforcers are initially provided in exchange for points every day. Eventually the student is required to work for longer and longer periods before receiving back-up reinforcement.

The second phase, contingency contracting, is less intense than the first phase because the student's behavior has improved. Self-evaluation is still emphasized. The third phase of the program is the maintenance agreement. The primary intent of this phase is to use social reinforcement, occasional surprise rewards, and continued student self-evaluation to maintain improvements. Booster training sessions are used if the student's improved social behavior begins to deteriorate.

These materials have been field-tested under controlled conditions to assess and improve their effectiveness (Cheney, 1983; Likins, 1983;

EXHIBIT 6.3   Social skills point card

		Rating					Points
I.	**Social skills lessons**						
	A. Paid attention	1	2	3	4	5	_____
	B. Worked hard	1	2	3	4	5	_____
	C. Followed directions	1	2	3	4	5	_____
	D. Demonstrated new skills	1	2	3	4	5	_____
	E. Completed homework	1	2	3	4	5	_____
II.	**Demonstrating new social skills** **in other places**						
	A. Classrrom	1	2	3	4	5	_____
	B. Lunch	1	2	3	4	5	_____
	C. Recess	1	2	3	4	5	_____
	D. Home	1	2	3	4	5	_____
	E. Other	1	2	3	4	5	_____

Ratings: 5 = Excellent
           4 = Good
           3 = Adequate
           2 = Poor
           1 = Terrible
The point card used with students is printed on a 5″ x 8″ card.

Source: From *Teaching Social Skills: Assessment Procedures, Instructional Methods, and Behavior Management Techniques* by D. Morgan and K. R. Young, 1984, Logan: Utah State University, Department of Special Education. Used with permission.

Peterson, 1981). Results from all three studies indicated that they were effective in increasing appropriate social interaction.

Skillstreaming the Elementary School Child

The curriculum of *Skillstreaming the Elementary School Child: A Guide for Teaching Prosocial Skills* (McGinnis & Goldstein, 1984) contains five content areas: dealing with feelings, classroom survival skills, alternatives to aggression, friendship-making skills, and dealing with stress. Within these general areas, 60 specific social skills, such as saying thank you, asking for help, apologizing, dealing with anger, responding to teasing, and handling group pressure, are taught (see Exhibit 6.1).

The program's instructional procedures are based on the premise that it is not enough to simply tell students that their behavior is inappropriate; they need additional instruction to learn what to do as well as what not to do. Using a structured learning approach, the teacher provides instruction that gives students:

1. Specific steps to learn to proficiency, with actual examples to illustrate
2. Practice on these steps in simulated, real-life situations

3. Feedback on how they have performed these steps
4. Practice in real-life situations
5. Approval for successful acquisition of the skill

This program relies on the same basic instructional techniques as the other programs — modeling, role-playing and practice, corrective feedback, generalization training, and reinforcement. Supplementary materials are also provided. For example, there are assessment forms for the teacher to use, student self-assessment forms, homework report forms, contracts, self-monitoring forms, cue cards, and award certificates. A similarly structured related program for adolescents is also available (Goldstein, Sprafkin, Gershaw, & Klein, 1980).

Which Social Skills Program Should You Use?

The programs reviewed in this section represent only a few of the programs available for use with behaviorally disordered students. In addition, there are several excellent programs designed primarily for adolescents that have not been included in this review. Examples include *ASSET* (Hazel, Schumaker, Sherman, & Sheldon-Wildgen, 1981) and *Aggression Replacement Training: A Comprehensive Intervention for Aggressive Youth* (Goldstein & Glick, 1987). Recently a few programs for moderately and severely retarded students have also become more available; an example is *Stacking the Deck* (Foxx & McMorrow, 1983).

The availability of so many social skills training programs poses a dilemma for teachers. How do you know which one to use? Schumaker, Pederson, Hazel, and Meyen (1983) have outlined five important questions to ask in selecting a program. First, does the program promote social competence? Second, how well does the program accommodate the students' learning characteristics? Specifically, the program should:

- Be simple and easy to understand, with low readability levels and a minimum of required writing.
- Provide for the discrimination of significant social cues and the acquisition of problem-solving skills.
- Be programmed for a minimum of student failure and provide reinforcement for each successful step toward mastery.
- Provide the student with strategies for acquiring the skills.
- Provide procedures for assuring, as well as measuring, the generalization of learned skills to naturally occuring situation.
- Provide motivation for the learners to set and accomplish social goals once a social skill has been acquired. (Schumaker et al., 1983, p. 3).

Third, does the program specifically target important deficits the students typically display? That is, special problems should be addressed by the program. Fourth, does the program provide training in situations as well as specific skills to facilitate generalization? An effective program should teach strategies for deciding not only how to demonstrate specific skills but also what skills are appropriate for what conditions and situations. Finally, does the program incorporate effective instructional methods? Schumaker et al. specifically identify modeling, practice, transfer of training, and reinforcement and corrective feedback as key methods.

In a similar vein, Stowitschek and Powell (1980) analyzed training materials using the Social Materials Analytic Review Technique (SMART). Their criteria, based on findings from previous research on social skills training with handicapped students, are particularly noteworthy. For example, one category of questions examined the extent to which the target student's peers were involved in the program's instructional procedures. Another question asked if the program had been field-tested and validated for effectiveness. A review of 75 different programs revealed that relatively few reflected the research on children's social development or included elements of systematic instruction that research had previously identified as being important. Their most important finding was that almost two-thirds of the programs reported no field-test data that could be used to assess their effectiveness.

Combining the recommendations and criteria discussed above, we can develop an informal checklist. Among the most important questions to be asked are:

1. Does the program teach socially valid behaviors?
2. Does the program use instructional procedures known to be positively associated with student learning and achievement?
3. Does the program ensure that students are interested and motivated?
4. Does the program include specific procedures for facilitating generalization and maintenance of skills?
5. Does the program include plans to involve socially skilled peers?
6. Does the program provide sufficient directions to teachers?
7. Has the program been adequately field-tested to determine its effectiveness?

In the absence of a consumer's guide to social skills training programs, the classroom teacher will probably be the person responsible for determining the extent to which various programs meet these standards. Fortunately, there are a number of programs available that yield affirmative answers to each of these questions. It is unlikely, however, that any single program will be completely appropriate for all possible students or teaching situations. The best decision would be to acquire several programs and mix, match, and adapt them, as appropriate, to fit a particular instructional situation.

INTEGRATING SOCIAL SKILLS TRAINING IN THE CLASSROOM

Earlier sections of this chapter have described the basic procedures used in teaching social skills and reviewed specific available programs. An important issue not yet addressed is how to integrate social skills training into the on-going classroom program for behaviorally disordered students. This section discusses some difficulties encountered in implementing social skills training. We will then make specific recommendations for integrating social skills training into the overall program.

Despite recent attention and effort, social skills training is still not widespread in our schools. Even in special education programs, social skills may be viewed as a frill in the curriculum (Reiser, 1987). Several factors help explain the current status of social skills training. One is the contemporary drive for excellence in education, which emphasizes academic proficiency over social proficiency. *A Nation at Risk* (National Commission on Excellence in Education, 1983) stressed the need to improve school discipline and student control, but did not address the need for improving social skills training. Improving social skills cannot be equated with improving school discipline. It appears as if the development of prosocial behaviors remains part of the school's hidden curriculum (Cartledge & Milburn, 1978).

While the proper role of social skills training in schools remains a topic of concern and debate, it is likely that other factors — such as the time available to teach social skills — significantly affects the extent to which it is implemented (Cartledge & Milburn, 1986). Both regular and special education teachers regularly express their concern that they have an ever-expanding curriculum to teach without more instructional time. Furthermore, teachers are reluctant to accept special intervention strategies that appear to require a great deal of extra time (Witt & Martens, 1983).

It is clear that more effort must be devoted to changing the perception of social skills training from a time-consuming frill to an essential aspect of the special education curriculum for behaviorally disordered students. It is not enough to rely on the evidence linking social skills to overall school or postschool adjustment. A concentrated effort to highlight the importance of social skills training for all students — especially behaviorally disordered students — is critically needed. It is in this framework that we make the following recommendations for integrating social skills into the classroom program:

- Social skills training must be a high priority within the school's program for behaviorally disordered students. It should have a priority equal to academic instruction.

Social skills training is an integral part of a total intervention program.

- Teachers and other school personnel responsible for implementing social skills training programs should have the necessary training and resources to enable them to implement social
  skills training effectively. A well-designed program will quickly
  become ineffective if the person responsible for it is not
  skilled. Special education training programs addressing social
  skills should be available to preservice and inservice teachers
  of behaviorally disordered students.
- Sufficient instructional time must be allocated to social skills
  training so that students have the opportunity to learn. Direct
  training should occur regularly throughout the school year. At
  a minimum, social skills training should occur at least once a
  week, and three to four times a week would be ideal. The
  length of the training sessions will vary with the age of the

students being taught. For younger students, about 20 to 30 minutes per session is recommended; for older students 30- to 45-minute sessions are appropriate. (These guidelines refer to the time devoted to direct instruction.)

- Social skills training should be a collaboration among all personnel involved in the students' program. The teacher (i.e., self-contained classroom teacher, resource room teacher, consulting teacher) should be the person primarily responsible for running the social skills program. Related services personnel (such as school psychologists or social workers) may team-teach with the teacher but, in our judgment, should not be the primary teacher. Regular teachers with behaviorally disordered students part-time or full-time and school administrators should also be informed about and involved in the program. This will facilitate generalization of improvements from the training setting to natural settings. Parents should be involved as well.

- Social skills training should not be confined to a 30-minute period three times per week. Based on what we know about generalization, teachers and other school personnel should seize every opportunity available to teach social skills by being alert to situations where coaching and feedback can be given. The teaching interaction (Pointer 6.3) is very well-suited to the incidental teaching of social skills.

- Student progress and growth in social skills should be monitored in the same way progress in other, more traditional areas of the curriculum is measured. Careful and continuous evaluation of the program's effectiveness is perhaps the most important guarantee of improving the students' social skills. Observations in nontraining situations, self-reports, and behavioral checklists can all be used to document improvements and to change the training program.

SUMMARY

In this chapter we have pointed out the importance of social skills training for behaviorally disordered children. We have identified the social skills children need to establish positive peer relationships and described some of the work done in this area.

The instructional procedures most often incorporated in social skills training programs were also described: instructions and rationales, modeling, concept teaching, role-playing/behavior rehearsal and practice, coaching, and contingent reinforcement. Typically these instructional procedures are combined in a multifaceted package. The proce-

Pointer 6.3

THE TEACHING INTERACTION

The teaching interaction is a 10-step procedure designed to facilitate the incidental teaching of social skills. Originally formulated during the early developmental work on the Teaching Family Model, a group home program for adjudicated youth, teaching interactions may be used to teach a new social skill, strengthen weak social skills, or intervene during an inappropriate occurrence of a social skill (Jackson et al., 1983). The 10 steps in a teaching interaction are:

1. Make a positive approach to indicate that teacher is interested and concerned about student's problems. May be a friendly greeting or other expression of warmth.
2. Describe inappropriate behavior and clearly indicate what has been done inappropriately or incorrectly.
3. Describe appropriate behavior to be performed instead. This description should be very detailed, if necessary.
4. Give rationale for appropriate behavior, focusing on potential future consequences (positive and aversive) for behaving appropriately.
5. Demonstrate appropriate behavior by modeling correct and incorrect example of the social skills being taught.
6. Practice the social skill in a behavior rehearsal format.
7. Provide feedback during practice (include praise and corrective feedback).
8. Provide additional practice to refine skills further.
9. Provide additional praise for accomplishments.
10. Give a homework assignment requiring student to practice skill in another setting, at another time, or with other people.

A shortened version of the teaching interaction has been developed by Jackson et al. for the *Getting Along with Others* program. This version consists of five steps:

1. Interrupt the inappropriate behavior by *saying something positive* related to the situation.
2. Ask the child for an *alternative way of behaving*. If the child doesn't know, *verbalize* or *model* one and have the child repeat it.
3. Ask the child to *practice* the appropriate behavior.
4. Give the child *positive feedback* for *any* improvement.
5. Give the child *homework*.
   (p. 34)

The best opportunity to conduct a teaching interaction is when the student has just done something socially inappropriate and the teacher can devote about 5 minutes to just that student without ignoring other students. In reality, the time required for this very abbreviated lesson is quite brief.

dures encourage active learner involvement in a relatively novel and positive instructional environment. There is really nothing fancy or complicated about these procedures. They are quite basic teaching strategies that are effective in a variety of contexts.

The overall effectiveness of a social skills training program is ultimately measured by how well and for how long students demonstrate improved behaviors outside the training situation. That is, do students' social skills and interactions improve, qualitatively and quantitatively, in real-life situations—the playground, the cafeteria, school bus, neighborhood, community? This is an often difficult and sometimes elusive goal, but it is not impossible. It does require attention, effort, and patient persistence.

Several commercially available social skills training programs were also reviewed, and recommendations were made concerning the choice of a program(s) to use. Guidelines for implementing social skills training regularly and consistently in programs for behaviorally disordered students were offered.

There are still many things that we do not yet know about social skills and behaviorally disordered students. Why are some children rejected or neglected and not others? Which social skills should be taught to which children? Which combination of methods works best for which children and what types of problems? What needs to be done to produce durable improvements in the social skills of behaviorally disordered students?

Clearly, there is still much to be learned. Yet the fields of psychology and special education have made great strides. Social skills training for behaviorally disordered students is not a panacea; it is not likely to result in instant or dramatic cures. However, the results to date suggest that systematic instruction in social skills should be an integral part of a total intervention program whose aim it is to produce a more adaptive, well-adjusted person.

REVIEW QUESTIONS

1. Define *social validity*. What is the role of social validity in selecting social skills to be taught to behaviorally disordered students?
2. What are the advantages of involving nonhandicapped peers in a social skills training program for behaviorally disordered students? Are there any disadvantages?
3. What is the purpose of providing nonexamples of social skills in teaching a particular skill? Wouldn't providing examples only be more efficient and reasonable?
4. You are beginning to implement a social skills training program in your class. How will you monitor student progress? What will be your criteria for success?

5. Review the skills from the programs listed in Exhibit 6.1. How many of the skills appear in all of the programs? What are the most frequently taught social skills? Are there any skills unique to a specific program?
6. Obtain review copies of the social skills programs reviewed in this chapter. Using the guidelines suggested, which program(s) would you select for use in your classroom? Justify your response.
7. Conduct a simulated teaching interaction with one of your peers. Arrange for another person to observe you.

REFERENCES

Asher, S., & Taylor, A. (1982). Social outcomes of mainstreaming: Sociometric assessment and beyond. In P. S. Strain (Ed.), *Social development of exceptional children*. Rockville, MD: Aspen Systems Corp.

Bandura, A. (1977). *Social learning theory*. Englewood Cliffs, NJ: Prentice-Hall.

Berler, E. S., Gross, A. M., & Drabman, R. S. (1982). Social skills training with children: Proceed with caution. *Journal of Applied Behavior Analysis, 15*, 41–53.

Bornstein, M. R., Bellack, A. S., & Hersen, M. (1977). Social skills training for unassertive children: A multiple baseline analysis. *Journal of Applied Behavior Analysis, 10*, 183–195.

Bower, E. M. (1969). *Early identification of emotionally handicapped children in school* (2nd ed.). Springfield, IL: Charles C Thomas.

Cartledge, G., & Milburn, J. F. (1978). The case for teaching social skills in the classroom: A review. *Review of Educational Research, 48*, 133–156.

Cartledge, G., & Milburn, J. F. (Eds.). (1986). *Teaching social skills to children: Innovative approaches* (2nd ed.). New York: Pergamon Press.

Cheney, D. (1983). *The effects of mediated social skills training on the social behavior of behaviorally disordered adolescents*. Unpublished masters' thesis, Utah State University.

Clark, H. B., Caldwell, C. P., & Christian, W. P. (1979). Classroom training of conversational skills and remote programming for the practice of these skills in another setting. *Child Behavior Therapy, 1*, 139–160.

Cooke, T. P., & Apolloni, T. (1976). Developing positive social-emotional behavior: A study of training and generalization effects. *Journal of Applied Behavior Analysis, 9*, 65–78.

Eisler, R. M., & Frederiksen, L. W. (1980). *Perfecting social skills: A guide to interpersonal behavior development*. New York: Plenum Press.

Engelmann, S., & Carnine, D. (1982). *Theory of instruction*. New York: Irvington.

Foster, S. L., & Ritchey, W. L. (1979). Issues in the assesment of social competence in children. *Journal of Applied Behavior Analysis, 17*, 625–633.

Foxx, R. M., & McMorrow, M. J. (1983). *Stacking the deck: A social skills game for retarded adults*. Champaign, IL: Research Press.

Goldstein, A. P. (1981). Social skills training. In A. P. Goldstein, E. G. Carr, W. S. Davidson II, & P. Weher (Eds.), *In response to aggression: Methods of control and prosocial alternatives.* New York: Pergamon Press.

Goldstein, A. P., & Glick, B. (1987). *Aggression replacement training: A comprehensive intervention for aggressive youth.* Champaign, IL: Research Press.

Goldstein, A. P., Sprafkin, R. P., Gershaw, N. J., & Klein, P. (1980). *Skillstreaming the adolescent.* Champaign, IL: Research Press.

Gresham, F. M. (1981). Social skills training with handicapped children: A review. *Review of Educational Research, 51,* 139–176.

Gresham, F. M. (1983). Social skills assessment as a component of mainstreaming placement decisions. *Exceptional Children, 49,* 331–336.

Gresham, F. M. (1986). Conceptual issues in the assessment of social competence in children. In P. S. Strain, M. J. Guralnick, & H. M. Walker (Eds.), *Children's social behavior: Development, assessment, and modification.* New York: Academic Press.

Hazel, J. S., Schumaker, J. B., Sherman, J. A., & Sheldon-Wildgen, J. (1981). *Asset.* Champaign, IL: Research Press.

Hops, H. (1982). Social skills training for socially isolated children. In P. Karoly & J., M. Steffen (Eds.), *Advances in child behavior analysis and therapy, Vol. 2: Intellectual and social deficiencies.* New York: Gardner Press.

Hops, H., Fleischman, D. H., Guild, J., Paine, S., Street, A., Walker, H. M., & Greenwood, C. R. (1978). *Program for establishing effective relationship skills (PEERS): Consultant manual.* Eugene: University of Oregon, Center at Oregon for Research in the Behavioral Education of the Handicapped.

Hops, H., Walker, H. M., & Greenwood, C. R. (1979). PEERS: A program for remediating social withdrawal in school. Behavioral systems for the developmentally disabled. In L. A. Hammerlynck (Ed.), *School and family environments.* New York: Bruner/Mazel.

Jackson, N. F., Jackson, D. A., & Monroe, C. (1983). *Getting along with others: Teaching social effectiveness to children.* Champaign, IL: Research Press.

Kelly, J. A. (1982). *Social skills training: A practical guide for interventions.* New York: Springer.

Kerr, M. M., & Nelson, C. M. (1983). *Strategies for managing behavior problems in the classroom.* Columbus, OH: Merrill.

Kiburz, C. S., Miller, S. R., & Morrow, L. W. (1984). Structured learning using self-monitoring to promote maintenance and generalization of social skills across settings for a behaviorally disordered adolescent. *Behavior Disorders, 10,* 47–55.

Likins, M. (1983). *The effects of mediated social skills training on the positive interactions of handicapped elementary students.* Unpublished masters' thesis, Utah State University.

Madson, J. L., Esveldt-Dawson, K., Andrasik, F., Ollendick, T. H., Petti, T., & Hersen, M. (1980). Direct, observational, and generalization effects of social skills training with emotionally disturbed children. *Behavior Therapy, 11,* 522–531.

McGinnis, E., & Goldstein, A. P. (1984). *Skillstreaming the elementary school child.* Champaign, IL: Research Press.

Morgan, D. P., Young, K. R., Likins, M., Cheney, D., & Peterson, T. J. (1983). *Teaching social skills to handicapped childern and youth: Programs and materials.* Logan: Utah State University, Department of Special Education.

National Commission on Excellence in Education. (1983). *A nation at risk.* Washington, DC: U.S. Department of Education.

Oden, S. L., & Asher, S. R. (1977). Coaching children in social skills for friendship making. *Child Development, 48,* 496–506.

Paine, S. C., Hops, H., Walker, H. M., Greenwood, C. R., Fleischman, D. H., & Guild, J. J. (1982). Repeated treatment effects: A study of maintaining behavior change in socially withdrawn children. *Behavior Modification, 6,* 171–199.

Peterson, T. J. (1981). *Effectiveness of social skills training in teaching conversation skills to handicapped elementary age children.* Unpublished masters' thesis, Utah State University.

Reiser, J. (1987). *A survey of social skills training implementation variables among special education teachers.* Unpublished masters' project, Utah State University.

Roff, M. (1961). Childhood social interactions and young adult bad conduct. *Journal of Abnormal and Social Psychology, 63,* 333–337.

Schloss, P. J., Schloss, C. N., Wood, C. E., & Kiehl, W. S. (1986). A critical review of social skills research with behaviorally disordered students. *Behavioral Disorders, 12,* 1–14.

Schneider, B. H., & Byrne, B. M. (1985). Children's social skill training. A meta-analysis. In B. H. Schneider, K. H. Rubin, & J. E. Ledingham (Eds.), *Children's peer relations: Issues in assessment and intervention.* New York: Springer-Verlag.

Schumaker, J. B., Pederson, C. S., Hazel, J. S., & Meyen, E. L. (1983). Social skills curricula for mildly handicapped adolescents: A review. *Focus on Exceptional Children, 16,* 1–16.

Stephens, T. M. (1978). *Social skills in the classroom.* Columbus, OH: Cedars Press.

Stocking, S. H., Arezzo, D., & Leavitt, S. (1980). *Helping kids make friends.* Allen, TX: Argus Communications.

Stowitschek, J. J., & Powell, T. H. (1980). *Materials for teaching social skills to handicapped children: An analytic review.* Technical report No. 50. Logan: Utah State University, Developmental Center for Handicapped Persons.

Strain, P. S. (1982). Preface. In P. S. Strain (Ed.), *Social development of exceptional children.* Rockville, MD: Aspen Systems Corp.

Strain, P. S., & Fox, J. J. (1981). Peer as behavior change agents for withdrawing classmates. In B. B. Leahey & A. E. Kazdin (Eds.), *Advances in clinical child psychology* (Vol. 4). New York: Plenum Press.

Strain, P. S., & Odom, S. L. (1986). Peer social initiations: Effective intervention for social skills development of exceptional children. *Exceptional Children, 52,* 543–551.

Strain, P. S., Odom, S. L., & McConnell, S. (1984). Promoting social reciprocity of exceptional children: Identification, target behavior selection, and intervention. *Remedial and Special Education, 5,* 21–28.

Strain, P. S., Shores, R. E., & Kerr, M. M. (1976). An experimental analysis of "spillover" effects on social interaction among behaviorally handicapped preschool children. *Journal of Applied Behavior Analysis, 9,* 31–40.

Walker, H. M., Hops, H., & Greenwood, C. R. (1984). The CORBEH research and development model: Programmatic issues and strategies. In S. Paine, T. Bellamy, & B. Wilcox (Eds.), *Human services that work.* Baltimore: Paul H. Brookes.

Walker, H., McConnell, S., Holmes, D., Todis, B., Walker, J., & Golden, N. (1983). *The Walker Social Skills Curriculum.* Austin, TX: ProEd.

Walker, H. M., McConnell, S., Walker, J. L., Clarke, J. Y., Todis, B., Cohen, G., & Rankin, R. (1983). Initial analysis of the Accepts curriculum: Efficacy of instructional and behavior management procedures for improving the social adjustment of handicapped children. *Analysis and Intervention in Developmental Disabilities, 3,* 105–127.

Walker, H. M., & Rankin, R. (1983). Assessing the behavioral expectations and demands of less restrictive settings. *School Psychology Review, 12,* 274–284.

Witt, J. C., & Martens, B. K. (1983). Assessing the acceptability of behavioral interventions. *Psychology in the Schools, 20,* 510–517.

7 Teaching Behaviorally Disordered Students in the Regular Classroom

After completing this chapter, you should be able to

- *Provide a rationale for teaching behaviorally disordered students in the regular classroom.*
- *Explain the concept of shared responsibility between regular and special education.*
- *Describe preferred practices for establishing classroom rules.*
- *Explain the potential effects of teacher attention and approval and teacher expectations on behaviorally disordered students.*
- *Discuss the purpose and basic procedures of the PASS program and assertive discipline.*
- *Identify the common elements in group behavior management programs.*
- *Describe several surface management techniques.*
- *Describe the hero procedure, the CLASS program, and the RECESS program.*
- *Discuss several cautions in using behavior management strategies in regular classrooms.*
- *Identify several basic instructional considerations used in managing academic instruction for behaviorally disordered students in the regular classroom.*
- *Describe essential features of several approaches to peer tutoring.*
- *Explain the purpose and operation of a school-based teacher support group.*

The foundation of an effective and responsive continuum of services for behaviorally disordered students is the regular classroom. Almost half of all behaviorally disordered students receiving special education are taught in the regular classroom for at least part of the school day. Regular classroom teachers play a pivotal role in determining the quality of services offered to these students. Involved in the initial referral and assessment process, they are often an integral component of any special interventions developed. The academic curriculum often must be modified. Home–school intervention programs may need to be coordinated and monitored by regular teachers. Even though teachers often receive assistance from support personnel such as the school psychologist, social worker, resource teacher, or consulting teacher, a regular teacher still needs considerable skill to effectively teach behaviorally disordered students.

The purpose of this chapter will be to explain and describe preferred practices for teaching behaviorally disordered students in regular classrooms. It has been written with two audiences in mind: regular teachers who teach BD students in their classrooms and special education teachers who work with regular classroom teachers. The chapter covers group and individual behavior management strategies, guidelines for academic instruction, recommendations concerning peer-tutoring strategies, and ideas for working with support personnel.

SHARING THE RESPONSIBILITY FOR TEACHING BEHAVIORALLY DISORDERED STUDENTS

The regular classroom is the preferred placement for all handicapped students, including behaviorally disordered students, for many reasons. As PL 94-142 clearly states, regular classrooms are the least restrictive of all possible educational environments for many handicapped students, including the behaviorally disordered. Furthermore, efficacy studies comparing self-contained special classes to regular classes indicate that self-contained placements may be inferior for many handicapped students (Carlberg & Kavale, 1980). That is, handicapped students in regular classrooms do better in achievement and overall adjustment than similar students in self-contained special education classrooms.

Third, as we have seen, the problems encountered in generalizing improvements from more restrictive settings such as self-contained classes suggest a more prudent approach: It may be preferable to deal with problem behaviors in the setting where the problems occur. As Walker (1979) has said, *"What you teach is what you get, and where you teach it is where you get it"* (p. 298). In other words, if you can avoid the problem of generalized behavior change, do so. If you can improve behavior by intervening at the source of the problem, you eliminate the need for removing a student from the mainstream. A student who must be removed from the regular classroom should be returned as quickly as possible.

Finally, in recent years there has been an increasing awareness of certain conceptual, philosophical, and structural flaws in the basic purpose and design of special education programs (Bickel & Bickel, 1986; Reynolds & Wang, 1983; Reynolds, Wang, & Walberg, 1987). Problems include lack of coordination among those responsible for providing services, which leads to inefficient and fragmented programs where responsibility is diffused. According to Reynolds and his colleagues (1987), "The result is extreme disjointedness, which also leads to excesses of proceduralism, including the tedious, costly, and scientifically questionable categorizing of students and programs" (p. 392). Renewed calls for restructuring and merging special education and regular education are being heard with increasing frequency (Lilly, 1987; Reynolds et al., 1987; Stainback & Stainback, 1984; Wang & Birch, 1984).

Madeline Will (1986), Assistant Secretary for Special Education and Rehabilitative Services in the U.S. Department of Education, has called for a concerted effort to remove the barriers between regular and special education preventing the full integration of handicapped students:

> The predominant instructional strategy for dealing with the problems of students with learning difficulties is, in fact, an administrative one. It is to remove these students from the regular class and to place them in a resource room or special class — in common educational jargon, the "pullout approach." This approach is backed by a storehouse of good intentions — but its effectiveness is often limited by the obstacles described above. Although for some students the "pullout approach" may be appropriate, it is driven by a conceptual fallacy: that poor performance in learning can be understood solely in terms of deficiencies in the student rather than deficiencies in the learning environment.
>
> The logic of the approach works this way: A student is performing poorly as a learner; we can even measure the gap between him and his peers. Because his peers are performing acceptably in the same environment, the trouble must be with the student. If we remove him from the regular classroom to a special program to work on his problems, we can remediate the problem and return the student to the original placement.
>
> The major flaw in this argument is the premise that to improve student performance we always have to create a new educational environment. Recent experience has shown there is an alternative. This is to adapt the regular classroom to make it possible for the student to learn in that environment. By doing this — by delivering service far more often than is now common in the regular classroom — we can avoid the obstacles to educating students with learning problems posed by special programs.
>
> The belief has emerged over the past two decades that regular education has little responsibility and expertise to help children with learning problems, particularly those children who can qualify for a special program. In fact, as more children have been served through these special programs, regular education has had fewer and fewer incentives to do so. Therefore, it is not surprising that regular education has not learned how to serve these children in the way that special programs have. Nor has regular education learned the teaching techniques, curricula strategies and other competencies that special programs have developed and used successfully over the years. The challenge is to take what we have learned from the special programs and begin to transfer this knowledge to the regular education classroom. This challenge is not only to transfer knowledge, it is also to form a partnership between regular education and the special programs and the blending of the intrinsic strengths of both systems. (pp. 10–12)

In the last section of this chapter, we address a couple of approaches that have been used successfully to put these lofty goals into operation.

BASICS OF CLASSROOM MANAGEMENT

The skills required to teach behaviorally disordered students in the regular classroom effectively do not significantly differ from the skills required to teach all students. The primary objective is to keep all students productive by maximizing the time spent on relevant and meaningful academic work. The focus of classroom management is on preventing behavior problems by creating an environment where they are less likely.

A study conducted by Larivee (1985) identified teaching behaviors and classroom conditions positively associated with academic achievement gains and social/emotional benefits in mildly handicapped students in regular classrooms. The results were basically consistent with previous teacher effectiveness research conducted with nonhandicapped students. The most effective teachers

1. Managed an organized and efficient learning environment;
2. Maximized student time on academic tasks and minimized time spent on noninstructional activities;
3. Provided students with tasks that allowed them to be successful;
4. Used active, or direct, teaching procedures a great deal of time with groups of students;
5. Were responsive to students needing support for learning or behavioral difficulties; and
6. Had high expectations for student achievement and behavior.

Success with mainstreamed handicapped students did not have a negative effect on nonhandicapped students in the same room. In fact, success with mainstreamed students was positively associated with success with nonhandicapped students as well.

Another important aspect of classroom management for behaviorally disordered students is *structure* (Haring & Phillips, 1962; Hewett, 1968). Why do these students require structure? Many of them have had unpredictable and inconsistent lives, with few rules inconsistently enforced. Structure provides predictability and consistency that, in turn, may provide a sense of security for students. Structure diminishes frustration, and thus limit-testing and need for coercion. A structured classroom has clearly stated and consistently followed classroom rules, procedures, routines, and contingencies. The more consistently implemented they are, the more structured the classroom. The next section will focus on three basic aspects of a structured classroom: classroom rules, teacher praise and attention, and teacher expectations.

Establishing Classroom Rules

While classroom rules do not guarantee appropriate classroom behavior (Greenwood, Hops, Delquadri, & Guild, 1974; Madsen, Becker, & Thomas, 1968), they are very important in effective classroom management. Clearly stated rules convey to students their teacher's expectations. More importantly, they define the relationship between student behavior and its consequences and help guide and direct both student and teacher behavior. Classroom rules are not a time-honored tradition to be routinely established and then forgotten. Instead of "rules are made to be broken," the emphasis should be on "rules are made to be followed" (Paine, Radicchi, Rosellini, Deutchman, & Darch, 1983). There are several preferred practices teachers should follow in establishing classroom rules.

- *Set as few rules as needed to cover the essentials.* Too many rules may cause problems for both teacher and students. When there are too many rules, there may be lax enforcement simply because there are too many different rules to track. Generally, four to six rules should be sufficient for most classrooms. Exhibit 7.1 shows an example of common classroom rules.
- *Develop situation-specific rules for frequent events.* Cover the following common situations: getting out of seat (sharpening pencils, going to the bathroom or drinking fountain, getting materials), talking to peers, obtaining permission, using free time (what students do when work is completed), and requesting assistance from the teacher.
- *State rules clearly.* Students are not likely to understand what is expected of them if rules are vague. While teachers may think everyone knows what a rule means, some rules are open to different interpretation. The resulting confusion and uncertainty will likely lead to inconsistent enforcement. Teachers should state rules in clear and observable terms. For example, "Respecting the rights of others" might become "When someone else is talking, let him finish before interrupting," "Look at the teacher when she is talking to the class," "When the teacher tells you to do something, do it right away," or "Ask permission before borrowing someone else's property."
- *Provide examples and nonexamples of the rules.* To insure that students clearly understand the rules, give examples and nonexamples of what they mean. For the rule, "When the teacher asks you to do something, do it right away," students could be given examples and nonexamples of what it means to "do it right away." Students could generate their own examples and nonexamples, too. Providing practice in discriminating rule-

EXHIBIT 7.1   Common classroom rules

1. Be polite and helpful.
2. Respect other people's property (keep the room clean and neat, pick up litter, return borrowed property, do not write on desks, do not use another person's things without permission).
3. Don't interrupt the teacher or other students when they are speaking.
4. Do not hit, shove, or hurt others.
5. Obey all school rules.

Source: Adapted from *Classroom Management for Elementary Teachers* by C. M. Evertson, E. T. Emmer, B. S. Clements, J. P. Sanford, and M. E. Worsham, 1984, Englewood Cliffs, NJ: Prentice-Hall.

following from rule-breaking is especially important when there is some measure of doubt in the way rules are stated.

- *State rules positively.* In general, state what students *should do* instead of what they *should not do.* For example, instead of "No yelling," a more positively stated rule would be "Talk in a moderate tone of voice." "No looking around" could be stated "Keep your eyes on the teacher or your work." However, stating rules positively may occasionally result in awkward or imprecise statements. "No hitting" communicates intent more clearly than does "Keep your hands to yourself." Similarly, "No swearing" may be preferable to "Use appropriate language." An example of carrying this guideline to an extreme is "Keep your saliva in your mouth" to explain that spitting is against the rules (Alberto & Troutman, 1986).
- *Post the rules.* Public posting of rules in a prominent location reminds students and the teacher.
- *Actively involve students in developing rules.* Rules developed by students are probably as effective as rules developd solely by teachers (Dickerson & Creedon, 1981; Felixbrod & O'Leary, 1973; Lovitt & Curtiss, 1969), though student-developed rules tend to be more stringent. Teachers should carefully guide students to decide if the rules are reasonable, enforceable, and deal with essential behaviors.
- *Teach the rules to students.* Simply telling students is not the most effective way to ensure that they will understand and follow them. If the behaviors addressed in the rules are important, they are worth some time for active and systematic teaching. Teaching rules involves demonstrating and modeling, discrimination training, rehearsal and guided practice, corrective feedback, and reviews.

Establishing reasonable rules, providing an understandable rationale for their selection, teaching the rules to students, and consistently enforcing them are critical elements of effective classroom management.

Teacher Attention and Praise

One of the most powerful methods for managing student behavior is teacher attention. Teacher attention in the form of verbal and nonverbal approval and praise is highly valued by most students, especially in the elementary grades. It sometimes seems as if they will do whatever they need to do to get it. Teacher attention is so important and potent that O'Leary and O'Leary (1977) stated: "When a child is not learning or behaving productively, there are many ways of changing the child's behavior, *but systematic teacher attention should be either the first procedure tried or a central component of other procedures*" (p. 55, emphasis added).

The evidence on the powerful effects of teacher attention is unequivocal. In a classic study, Madsen and his colleagues (1968) systematically varied the attention of two elementary school teachers and studied the effects on the classroom behavior of their students. They concluded that showing approval for appropriate behaviors, in combination with ignoring inappropriate behaviors, was very effective in reducing disruptive classroom behaviors. These findings have been replicated several times (Cantrell, Stenner, & Katzenmeyer, 1977; Drabman & Lahey, 1974; Good, Ebmeier, & Beckerman, 1978).

Despite the empirical evidence concerning teacher attention and praise, many teachers do not consistently or systematically use contingent attention to promote student learning. Observational studies of teacher–student interactions indicate that teachers attend to inappropriate and undesirable student behaviors much more frequently than to appropriate behaviors (Thomas, Presland, Grant, & Glynn, 1978; Thompson, White, & Morgan, 1982; Walker & Buckley, 1973; Walker, Hops, & Fiegenbaum, 1976; White, 1975). When interactions between teachers and students with significant behavior problems are analyzed, more interactions are negative than positive and the teacher uses more critical reprimands (Walker, 1979). Behaviorally disordered students are virtual experts at gaining attention from their teachers with their inappropriate behavior. Even though the attention may be negative, the student receives a disproportionate amount of teacher attention. The *amount* of attention appears to be important, not necessarily the quality of attention.

Behaviorally disordered students can be very cunning in attracting teacher attention by displaying a repertoire of tricks that coerce the teacher into responding negatively in the attempt to regain control. The inappropriate behavior may be unintentionally reinforced by the teacher's negative attention. Some teachers think they need to crack down on misbehavior so the students won't think they can do anything they please. Unfortunately, the more the teacher cracks down, the more likely it is that the inappropriate behavior will increase. For some extreme cases, contingent teacher attention and praise may not be sufficient to produce significant changes in behavior. More intensive interventions, such as those described later in this chapter, may be needed.

Under certain circumstances, teacher praise might be counterproductive. Brophy (1981) found that praise is more effective when it is spontaneous and genuine, a reaction to actual student accomplishment or effort, than when it is overly gushy or effusively theatrical praise for mere conformity or minor achievements. Students see through attempts to manipulate their behavior artificially with praise that is random and unenthusiastic. For most students in regular classrooms (including behaviorally disordered students), the contingent use of genuine teacher attention and praise is very effective.

Teacher Expectations

The importance and relevance of teacher expectations has already been discussed (Walker & Rankin, 1983). Research has demonstrated convincingly that teachers' expectations affect how they respond to students. Teacher behaviors that can indicate differential treatment of low and high achievers include (Good & Brophy, 1987):

- Not waiting as long for low achievers to answer
- Criticizing low achievers more often for failure
- Praising low achievers less frequently for success
- Generally paying less attention to low achievers and interacting with them less frequently
- Calling on low achievers less frequently to answer questions
- Demanding less from low achievers
- Giving high achievers the benefit of the doubt in grading tests or papers in borderline cases more often than low achievers
- Less friendly interaction with low achievers, i.e., less frequent smiling and other nonverbal indicators of support

An appropriate expectation would be that all students progress at a realistic pace through an instructional program designed according to their individual needs. One of the biggest mistakes a teacher can make is not to expect a student to behave appropriately in the classroom *because he or she is behaviorally disordered*. This kind of thinking will likely result in an increase in the student's current level of inappropriate behavior and may create the undesirable situation where inappropriate behavior is excused, accepted, or reinforced.

GROUP BEHAVIOR MANAGEMENT STRATEGIES

When implemented consistently from the beginning of the school year, the basic classroom behavior management strategies are effective in promoting productive and positive learning environments. However, in some classrooms, where students are often off-task and disruptive, more powerful intervention strategies may be needed to improve the learning atmosphere. Several behavior management programs designed for use with disruptive classes are reviewed in this section.

Program for Academic Survival Skills

As mentioned in chapter 5, the Program for Academic Survival Skills (PASS) (Greenwood, Hops, Delquadri, & Walker, 1977) is a behavior management program designed to increase academic survival skills (i.e., following classroom rules such as working on assignments, following directions, attending to teacher, talking appropriately) of all the students in the class. The goal of PASS is to increase survival skills of an entire group of students to 80% and maintain that level throughout the year. While PASS involves all students in a class, it specifically targets students who are most deficient in academic survival skills.

PASS is implemented by the classroom teacher with the assistance of a consultant (consulting teacher, resource teacher, school psychologist) in five stages: preliminary assessment, teacher baseline, full program, program fade-out, and maintenance. In the preliminary assessment phase, the consultant observes in the teacher's classroom to determine if PASS would be useful. In general, if these observational data indicate that the group's survival skills fall below 50%, PASS would be beneficial. The second stage of the program, teacher baseline, involves observations of the group's survival skills during the one or two daily academic periods (often reading and math) when the program is to be in effect. The teacher observes and records group survival skills using a clocklight to record the cumulative time students display their survival skills and to signal the students that their behavior is appropriate.

The full program phase begins with the teacher presenting the classroom rules to the students. The teacher continues to use the clocklight to record and signal the amount of time all members of the group are following the classroom rules at the same time. If even one student breaks a rule, the light is turned off and the clock stops. Consequences in the form of group activity rewards (e.g., a 5- to 15-minute game, story, extra recess, movie) are provided if previous peformance improves. Initially, the rewards are provided immediately after a daily goal has been achieved. After the group's survival skill rate reaches 80% for 3 consecutive days, the frequency and immediacy of the reward is thinned to every other day. Eventually the class must work for five consecutive 80% periods before earning a reward.

The program fade-out and maintenance stages of PASS are designed to remove major components while maintaining improved group survival skills. The clocklight, the PASS rules, and the group rewards are systematically and gradually faded while the teacher continues to use attention and approval to maintain the improvements. The teacher makes random, occasional observations with a stopwatch to check if the group's survival skills are maintaining at or very near the 80% level.

There is much more to PASS than merely learning to operate the clocklight while teaching a class full of students. The teacher's contingent use of attention and praise is critical. The clocklight is an effective signalling and cueing device; it is not an effective reinforcer. There are four basic praising tactics used in the PASS program:

1. Group callout praise for the entire class or group—"Good going, class! You're all following the rules and the clocklight is on."
2. Callout praise for an individual student so all can hear—"I see Steven getting right to work."
3. Quiet private praise of just one child—Teacher gives child a pat on the back and says, "You're working quietly, Sally."
4. Callout praise to prompt the correct survival skill for a child demonstrating inappropriate classroom behavior—"Mike and George are sure helping—they're writing their spelling words."

The goal is to use at least one type of praise at least once a minute during a PASS instructional session. Teachers are also taught to scan the classroom by moving and looking around, or spot checking to see what students are doing. Teachers who are successful with PASS must be continuously aware of what each and every student in the class is doing at any given time and then must be able to quickly decide if the classroom rules are being followed and, hence, whether to keep the clock running and light turned on.

The program has comprehensive user's manuals for the consultant (Greenwood, Hops, Delquadri, & Walker, 1977) and the classroom teacher (Greenwood, Delquadri, Hops, & Walker, 1977) that describe the procedures in depth. It has been extensively field-tested (Greenwood et al., 1974; Greenwood, Hops, & Walker, 1977; Greenwood et al.,1979), with results indicating that it is a powerful package capable of producing significant improvements in student behavior and maximizing student engaged time.

Assertive Discipline

Assertive discipline is an approach intended to help teachers take charge in their classrooms. Developed by Lee and Marlene Canter (1976), assertive discipline is both a philosophy of classroom management (i.e., discipline) and a set of very specific strategies to help teachers deal con-structively with student misbehavior while maintaining a positive and productive learning environment. The underlying philosophy begins with the premise that teachers have certain rights in their classrooms:

1. The right to establish a classroom structure and routine that provides the optimal learning environment in light of your own strengths and weaknesses.
2. The right to determine and request appropriate behavior from the stu-dents which meet your needs and encourage the positive social and educational development of the child.
3. The right to ask for help from parents, the principal, etc., when you need assistance with a child. (Canter & Canter, 1976, p. 2)

Students, too, have the rights to:

1. Have a teacher who is in a position to and will help the child limit his inappropriate self-disruptive behavior,
2. Have a teacher who is in the position to and will provide the child with positive support for his appropriate behavior, and
3. Choose how to behave and know the consequences that will follow. (Canter & Canter, 1976, p. 8)

The rights of teachers and the rights of students are not incompatible. They can best be met by a classroom management system that empha-sizes clear expectations and consistent follow-through, implemented assertively, not hostilely or aggressively, by the teacher.

For the teacher, the essence is to use assertive response styles, as opposed to hostile and aggressive styles or distinctly nonassertive styles. An assertive response style involves doing things like saying no without feeling guilty, giving and receiving genuine compliments, standing up for one's own feelings and desires when pressured by others, placing de-mands on others without feeling uncomfortable, and influencing the behavior of students without yelling and threatening (Charles, 1985). Exhibit 7.2 illustrates the differences between assertive, hostile, and nonassertive response styles of teachers.

Learning to set limits and to follow through are two critical class-room management skills stressed by assertive discipline. The first steps in setting limits are establishing classroom rules, communicating the rules to students, and making sure they understand the rules. Teachers often need to remind students of the classroom rules continually, using a procedure called *verbal limit-setting*. In verbal limit-setting, the teacher requests specific behavior in one of the following ways: by using hints or prompts ("Everyone should be looking at me right now"), sending I-messages ("I want you to go to your seat now"), asking questions ("Would you stop talking now and start working?"), or issuing demands ("Sit down now"). To enhance the impact of these tactics, teachers should

EXHIBIT 7.2 Differences between assertive, hostile, and nonassertive response styles of teachers

---

Situation: Third-grade classroom whose students frequently push, shove, and eventually fight when lining up to go to recess and lunch.

Nonassertive Response: The teacher walks up to the children and states, "I don't know what's wrong with you children. You're pushing and shoving again. You children need to learn how to line up like good boys and girls. Now I want you all to try to do so."

Hostile Response: The teacher walks up to the children who were pushing and grabs them and roughly yanks them to the back of the line. Once they are at the end of the line she angrily states, "You push and shove others, I'll push and shove you!"

Assertive Response: The teacher firmly tells the children, "Stop pushing and shoving." To back up her words, she makes all the children who were pushing and shoving go to the back of the line.

(a) always make eye contact when interacting with students, (b) use hand gestures to emphasize the verbal message (not hostile gestures such as shaking or pointing a finger), (c) use the student's name, and (d) occasionally use physical contact (e.g., hand on shoulder) when talking to convey both sincerity and control.

Another recommended verbal limit-setting strategy is the *broken record.* This strategy is for students who refuse to comply, arguing about or denying their misbehavior after the teacher has requested new behavior. In these situations, the teacher should ignore the student's arguments and denials and, instead, simply preface any response with either "That's not the point . . .," or "I understand but . . .," and then repeat the original hint, I-message, question, or demand to the student until he or she complies (up to a maximum of three times). The broken record is designed to let teachers remain calm but insistent when enforcing classroom rules and limits, without being affected by the student's coercive or manipulative behaviors.

Following through on the set limits is the most important aspect of assertive discipline. The operating guideline underlying following through is the principle of giving students choices. Students are informed that they can choose what happens to them as a consequence of their behavior. They can choose pleasant consequences as a result of appropriate behavior or unpleasant consequences as a result of inappropriate behavior.

Teachers are encouraged to *make promises, not threats.* According to the Canters, a promise is a "vow of affirmative action," whereas a threat is a "statement or expression of intention to hurt or punish." The promises a teacher makes are basically a system of consequences and contingencies for appropriate and inappropriate behavior. Time-out, loss of privilege or activity, after-school detention, intervention by school principal, and a call or note sent home to parents are a recommended hierarchy of unpleasant consequences. In some cases, systematic exclusion may be needed for severe problem behavior. Assertive discipline also emphasizes the use of *positive assertions* (i.e., positive reinforcement) as consequences for appropriate student behavior. Social praise, special awards and privileges, notes or calls to parents, and edibles are used to reinforce and increase desirable classroom behaviors.

Assertive discipline has many support materials available for teachers, school administrators, and parents that explain its underlying principles and describe in some detail how to implement a program in a single classroom or an entire school. An important shortcoming is that most of the reports concerning its effectiveness are anecdotal in nature; few controlled studies have been conducted. Those studies that have been reported, however, do indicate that this program can be practical in the classroom (Mandlebaum, Russell, Krouse, & Gonter, 1983).

Other Packaged Classroom Management Programs

There are other behavior management programs that can be used classwide in the regular classroom. Many of these programs involve a token economy or point system where individual students, as well as the entire class, earn rewards for their appropriate behavior. Three such programs will be briefly reviewed: the Timer Game, the Practice Skills Mastery Program, and the Good Behavior Game.

The Timer Game

The original Timer Game study (Wolf, Hanley, King, Lachowicz, & Giles, 1970) reduced the amount of time a group of low-achieving fourth-grade students were out of their seats. A timer clock was placed in the front of the classroom and set to go off every 20 minutes, on the average, throughout the day; the range of the intervals varied between just a few minutes and a maximum of 40 minutes. When the clock sounded, the teacher would scan the room to see who was in their seats and working, and those students received points and social reinforcement. Then the clock would be reset and students would resume working. The points were exchanged for backup reinforcers (snacks, candy, field trips).

The Timer Game has been replicated in many classrooms since the first study. Various timing devices have been used, with kitchen timers probably the most common. The basic game can be modified in other ways as well. For example, instead of using the game throughout the day, it can be scheduled during times when student behavior is the worst or when it is most important that students work appropriately. The target behaviors can vary from being out of seat to other inappropriate behaviors (e.g., talking) to appropriate behaviors (e.g., working on assignment). Students can also be taught to monitor their own behavior with a timing device, which can eventually save the teacher a great deal of time and teach students important self-management skills.

Practice Skills Mastery Program

The Practice Skills Mastery Program (Erken & Henderson, 1976) is a variation of the Timer Game using audiotapes to signal when students are eligible to receive token reinforcement for appropriate behavior. The program includes six audiotapes with ½-second beep tones at variable intervals; the six tapes contain 25, 20, 15, 10, 5, and 3 beeps respectively. First, classroom rules and expectations, usually for on-task behaviors, are specified and explained, and the tape is started. Each time a beep sounds, the teacher scans the classroom to determine who is following the rules, calls the names of the students to receive points, and determines the number of points to be awarded. In a large class, the students are divided into smaller groups and each member of the smaller group must be following the rules when the beep sounds for everyone to receive points. If one student continually penalizes the group by persistent off-task behavior, he or she is dropped from the group and treated as a group of one. At the end of an instructional period, the students count their points and add them to their own accounts in the token economy to be traded for a variety of backup reinforcers.

The Practice Skills Mastery Program consists of a package of materials including (a) a teacher's manual, (b) the six audiotapes, (c) a pay board (a chart used to publicly display points earned by individual students), (d) pay schedule cards with variable schedules for awarding points, and (e) student pay sheets to record the points. The program's effectiveness has been validated in a variety of settings (Henderson, Jenson, & Erken, 1986; Henderson, Jenson, Erken, Davidsmeyer, & Lampe, 1986), indicating that it is effective for promoting on-task behavior, thus increasing the probability of academic achievement. In addition, it prompts teachers to observe and reinforce appropriate student behavior systematically.

The Good Behavior Game

The Good Behavior Game (Barrish, Saunders, & Wolf, 1969) is so versatile that it can be used in regular classrooms, resource rooms, and self-contained classrooms (Kosiec, Czernicki, & McLaughlin, 1986). Target behaviors, the time in which the game is in effect, backup reinforcers, and make-up of teams can be easily varied (see Pointer 7.1). Instead of

Pointer 7.1

USING GROUP CONSEQUENCES TO ELIMINATE DISRUPTIVE CLASSROOM BEHAVIOR

The behavior problem of concern was the Naughty Finger (specifically, the extended middle finger) waved in the air by certain students while in the classroom. Not only was the Naughty Finger a problem, but so was the accompanying verbal commotion (tattling, teasing, and other exclamations). The teacher decided that the problem needed to be eliminated and, because the effects of the Naughty Finger spread across virtually all students in the classroom, a group contingency would be appropriate. The teacher developed the following plan:

1. The teacher put 10 cards numbered 1 through 10 in a desk calendar bracket at the front of the classroom.
2. The students were told that they would be able to earn a special 10-minute recess at the end of the day. They were also told that if the Naughty Finger was seen or if any talk about the Naughty Finger was heard, one of the cards would be flipped. This would mean that they would have 1 less minute of recess for each flipped card.
3. The normal classroom schedule was followed. Whenever the teacher saw or heard about the Naughty Finger, a card was immediately flipped and the students were briefly told why.
4. Just before the end of the day, the teacher would tell the students how much time they had earned for extra recess and would reinforce them for improvements from previous days.

The procedure was very successful in reducing the frequency of the Naughty Finger and related problem behaviors. Although this procedure was developed in a self-contained classroom of mildly retarded students, it is adaptable for application in regular classrooms as well. The basic strategy can also be used for a variety of inappropriate behaviors as well.

Source: Drawn from "A Tactic to Eliminate Disruptive Behaviors in the Classroom: Group Contingent Consequences" by S. I. Sulzbacher and J. E. Houser, 1968, *American Journal of Mental Deficiency, 73,* 88–90.

keeping track of the number of misbehaviors (e.g., talk-outs, out of seat), the teacher could count the number of appropriate behaviors of each team. Another variation to increase the precision of the frequency counts would be to use a signaling device (kitchen timer or audio tape) to help the teacher keep track of the group's behavior.

Common Elements among the Group Management Programs

The classroom behavior management programs just reviewed — the PASS program, Assertive Discipline, the Timer Game, the Practice Skills

Mastery Program, and the Good Behavior Game—share several characteristics that contribute to their effectiveness. First, they place a premium on teacher awareness of students' behavior at virtually all times. In an earlier chapter, this ability was referred to as *with-itness*. With-it teachers constantly move and circulate among their students, scanning the entire group and simultaneously making contact with individuals. Second, the contingent use of teacher attention and approval for appropriate student behavior is extremely important in these programs.

These programs are often used correctively to improve a less-than-desirable classroom atmosphere. However, they also can be used preventively. That is, the teacher behaviors required for successful implementation—with-itness, movement, contingent attention and approval, consistency—are often found in classrooms where students work well and are not often disruptive. Those same teacher behaviors typically result in orderly, business-like, and supportive classrooms where student efforts and achievements are maximized.

INDIVIDUAL BEHAVIOR MANAGEMENT STRATEGIES

Many behaviorally disordered students will respond to the group behavior management strategies described in the last section with an increase in appropriate behavior and a decrease in inappropriate behavior. However, these strategies will not always be powerful enough to produce significant changes in some students. For these students, individual interventions will be required. This section reviews several effective strategies for intervention with individual behaviorally disordered students.

Surface Management Techniques

Not all inappropriate behaviors require sophisticated or elaborate behavior management strategies. Some respond to quick teacher action to nip a problem in the bud by redirecting the student into more productive and appropriate ways of behaving. Consider the following strategies recommended for managing inappropriate classroom behavior (Evertson, Emmer, Clements, Sanford, & Worsham, 1984):

1. For off-task behavior, redirect attention by calmly and firmly calling the student's attention to the task. ("Sammy, the assignment is to complete all the problems on the page.")
2. When repeating directions or redirecting attention, make eye contact with the student.
3. Provide reminders and prompts.
4. Tell the student to stop misbehaving and to begin a constructive activity.

In a similar vein, Long and Newman (1980) identified *surface management techniques* for behaviors that do not require full-blown intervention programs.

- *Planned ignoring* — Sometimes it is better to ignore misbehavior than to pay attention to it, especially when student misbehaviors seem designed to get the teacher's goat. By withholding attention, teachers reduce the chance that the inappropriate behavior will occur in the future. They also reduce the possibility of continual confrontations over relatively harmless infractions. Usually planned ignoring is the preferred practice when the inappropriate behavior does not last long, is not likely to spillover onto other students, and is relatively minor, and where reacting to it would interrupt the flow of instruction in the classroom (Evertson et al., 1984). Examples that meet these criteria would include occasionally calling out during a discussion, brief whispering and talking between students during work time, and brief periods of inattentiveness.
- *Signal interference* — This technique involves using nonverbal signals to communicate disapproval for inappropriate behavior or to prompt appropriate behavior. Gestures, eye contact, and facial expressions can be effectively used to stop misbehavior in its earliest stages.
- *Proximity control* — Whether intentionally or unintentionally, every teacher uses this strategy to control student misbehavior. Proximity control means moving close to the student who is misbehaving and, if needed, placing a hand on the student's desk or shoulder. By being near the student, the teacher exerts a calming and steadying influence, enabling the student to redirect attention to the task.
- *Tension decontamination through humor* — All teachers need a sense of humor, not only for their own mental health and stability but for its potential for behavior management. Long and Newman (1980) used the following vignette as an example of tension decontamination through humor:

  As soon as I entered the room two students who had remained in the room during the playground period informed me that Stella and Mary had a fight in the girls' restroom and were at present being seen by the principal. Since both of these girls are good pupils and are well liked by the class, I imagined that they and the class were wondering what I would do when the two girls returned to the room. Fifteen or 20 minutes elapsed before the girls returned. They entered and took their seats and the room became very quiet. I closed my book, looked at one of the girls and said in a rasping voice of a fight announcer, "And in this corner we have Stella, weighing 78 pounds." Everyone laughed. The tension vanished and we proceeded with our work.

- *Support from routine*—This relatively straightforward and simple strategy involves developing and maintaining a routine schedule of daily and weekly events and activities. A routine provides students with much-needed predictability and consistency.
- *Direct appeal to value areas*—The direct appeal is a specific request for a student to stop misbehaving and start behaving appropriately.
- *Removing seductive objects*—Many students enjoy bringing toys, sports equipment, and other miscellaneous paraphernalia with them to school. These objects create a potentially powerful distraction. Student attention will be directed towards the playthings as opposed to the task at hand, unless the teacher is aware of them and takes steps to remove them.

There is nothing magical about these surface behavior management techniques, nor is there anything particularly new about them. The key to handling relatively minor inappropriate behavior is to handle it promptly, calmly, and firmly before it spreads and becomes more intense. When behaviorally disordered students become "wound up," more serious problems usually occur, disrupting the learning environment. These techniques are effective preventive measures that can redirect students into more productive ways of behaving while maintaining a positive learning climate in the classroom.

Individual Token Systems and Contingency Contracts

The problem behaviors of some students may be too frequent, too severe, or too persistent to use basic group management strategies or surface management techniques. Teachers need more powerful and more direct interventions to manage these students. In this situation, individualized token reinforcement programs or contingency contracts should be considered.

Token reinforcement programs are often recommended as an intervention in regular classrooms (Kerr & Nelson, 1983; Lovitt, 1978; Walker & Buckley, 1974; Walker & Shea, 1984). Before beginning a token reinforcement system, a teacher must make several very important decisions: (a) identify target behaviors, (b) select backup reinforcers and fines, (c) set prices for backup reinforcers, (d) set wages (tokens awarded or taken away for specific target behaviors), and (e) design a system for monitoring tokens earned and spent.

Contingency contracting is another effective intervention (Rutherford & Polsgrove, 1982). Contracting is particularly appropriate in regular classrooms when only one or two students need special interventions. Contracts can be highly individualized and are relatively easy to implement and monitor (Hall & Hall, 1982).

Two variations on the basic contingency contract are verbal contracting and home–school contracts. In verbal contracts, the teacher and student strike a daily verbal agreement concerning some aspect of the student's behavior; e.g., "If you don't hit anyone this morning, you may have an extra milk at lunch" (Walker & Shea, 1984). Verbal contracts are appropriate for students whose problems are relatively mild and who will probably respond to what is essentially a very low-key intervention. In home–school contracts, the same procedures are recommended. However, the student's parents also sign the contract and may provide the reinforcers. Home–school contracts can help extend the impact of the intervention to the home and increase communication and cooperation between teachers and parents.

Specific examples of a token system, contracts, and home–school contracts are provided in chapters 9 and 10. The systems described there can easily be implemented in regular classrooms.

The Hero Procedure

Some regular teachers may object to providing one or two students with opportunities to earn special privileges and other rewards. Their concerns are usually expressed as follows: "Why should misbehaving students have the chance to earn rewards while the well-behaved students in the class do not?" It isn't difficult to understand why a teacher would ask this question.

Several alternative procedures can mitigate the potentially demoralizing effect of singling out behaviorally disordered students for "special" treatment. The backup reinforcer for a student with a contingency contract or a token reinforcement program may be that the student earns an activity or some other special prize for the entire class. This procedure is known as the *hero procedure.*

One of the first applications of the hero procedure (Patterson, 1965; Patterson, Shaw, & Ebner, 1969) was developed for use with Karl, a hyperactive, elementary-aged student. The basic intervention consisted of (a) reinforcing Karl with candy on a variable-interval schedule for appropriate on-task behavior and (b) having Karl share the candy earned with his classmates at the end of a work session. The procedures were presented to Karl's classmates as follows:

> Karl has some trouble with sitting and that makes it hard for him to
> learn some things. This box sitting on his desk is a "work box." Each

time the light flashes, it tells him that he has been sitting still and working. When he sits still, he earns candy for himself and for the rest of you.
When he is finished, the counter will tell us how much candy he has
earned. He can pass it out to the rest of you at the end of the class
period. If you want him to earn a great deal of candy, don't pay any
attention to him when he makes noise, gets out of his chair or walks
around the room. (Patterson et al., 1969, p. 20)

Hero procedures have two primary benefits: They provide more powerful backup consequences in the form of increased peer approval and support for appropriate behavior, and they help to eliminate peer attention to
inappropriate classroom behavior (Greenwood & Hops, 1981). However
teachers need to be especially watchful to ensure that the peer group is
providing support and approval for appropriate behavior and ignoring the
inappropriate behavior of the hero. Here we review two programs that involve the hero procedure.

The CLASS Program
The CLASS (Contingencies for Learning Academic and Social Skills) Program is a packaged intervention program designed to produce rapid and
significant changes in the classroom behavior of students who act out
(Hops, Beickel, & Walker, 1976). A consultant (consulting teacher, resource teacher, school psychologist, school social worker) must be available to help the classroom teacher use CLASS.

The program is divided into two phases. The first phase, lasting
5 days, requires the consultant to be very involved in the classroom. During the second phase, lasting about 25 days, the regular teacher runs the
program with the support and guidance of the consultant. The intervention procedures use a red/green point card, a 5-inch square card made of
heavyweight construction paper. On the green side of the card (see
Exhibit 7.3) are the target behaviors for the student, a place to record
points earned, and a place for the teacher and parents to indicate their
involvement every day. On the red side of the card are the behaviors that
result in removal from the classroom and a place to record points lost for
not following the classroom rules (i.e., the target behaviors). The
red/green point card is also used to signal the student. When the green
side is showing, it tells the student that behavior is appropriate and he or
she is eligible to earn points. When the red side is shown, it says that the
behavior is inappropriate.

The red/green point card is used extensively during the early stages
of the program. During the first 5 days, the consultant operates the point
card while sitting or standing near the student. The student is reinforced
on a variable interval schedule, starting with a VI30-second on the first
day and extending to a VI6-minute by the fifth day. Thus, the student has
an opportunity to earn 40 points on the first day (that is, 2 points per

EXHIBIT 7.3 Class program red/green point card

POINTS LOST

Session 1   Session 2

Removed from class for:

1. Hurting or attempting to hurt another person.
2. Destroying or stealing property.
3. Continual disobedience to a staff member.
4. _____
5. _____
6. _____

Red Side

Child's Name _____ Date _____

1. Talk in a moderate tone.
2. Follow teacher's instructions.
3. Remain in seat except when school work requires being out of seat.
4. Talk, work, and play at proper times with classmates.
5. Attend to teacher and work.
6. _____
7. _____
8. _____

S1. Points Possible _____ Need _____ Earned _____
S2. Points Possible _____ Need _____ Earned _____

Session 1 Time _____   Session 2 Time _____

Earned: _____ points required for home privilege.
Did not earn:

Teacher's signature _____

School privilege _____

Parent's signature _____

Home privilege _____

Green Side

Source: *From CLASS: Contingencies for Learning Academic and Social Skills—Manual for Consultants* by H. Hops, S. L. Beickel, and H. M. Walker, 1976, Eugene: Center at Oregon for Research in the Behavioral Education of the Handicapped. Used with permission.

minute on a VI30″ schedule) for a 20-minute work session but, by the fifth day, the maximum number of points possible is 5 (a VI6′ schedule) for a 30-minute work session.

To earn a reinforcer, the student must obtain 80% of the total number of points possible for each work session; for example, 32 points on the first day, 4 points on the fifth day. If the student is successful, a group activity reinforcer such as a game or free time is earned for the whole class. However, the student also receives an individual reinforcer at home from the parents each day criterion is met. The home reward might be staying up an extra 30 minutes at night, a bedtime story, an ice cream cone, extra outside play time, or a special trip or activity. Later in the program, when the student has to behave appropriately for longer periods of time and the delay between reinforcements is longer, larger rewards are available (perhaps dinner out with the family, a movie, a special toy or game, a party for friends). In addition to points and the group and individual backup reinforcers, social praise is paired with the points by both the consultant and the teacher.

In the second phase of the program, the classroom teacher operates the red/green point card. By the program's 10th day, the student is working all day to earn enough points for a larger group reinforcer and the individual reinforcer from home. From day 8 through day 20, points are awarded on a VI10-minute reinforcement schedule; the 80% criterion is still in effect. The teacher continues to provide social reinforcement with points. By the last 2 weeks of the program (Day 21 to Day 30), the points and backup reinforcers have been faded, and the teacher continues to praise once every 10 minutes.

Detailed manuals and support materials provide background information and specific directions for both the consultant and the classroom teacher (Hops et al., 1976; Hops, Fleischman, & Beickel, 1976). The CLASS program has been extensively field-tested and has proven effective in producing dramatic and relatively long-lasting gains in the behavior of acting-out children in the regular classroom (Hops et al., 1978; Walker & Hops, 1976; Walker et al., 1976).

The RECESS Program

RECESS (Reprogramming Environmental Contingencies for Effective Social Skills), designed for use with socially aggressive/negative students, is relatively complex. Compared to normal students, socially negative/aggressive students have much higher rates of the following types of behaviors: (a) disturbing other children (teasing, provoking fights), (b) responding to teasing with angry, aggressive behavior, (c) arguing, (d) displaying physical aggression toward objects or persons, (e) speaking to others in an impatient or grouchy tone of voice, and (f) saying uncomplimentary or unpleasant things to other children (Walker et al., 1978).

The primary goals of RECESS are to reduce the frequency of socially negative/aggressive behaviors and to increase appropriate peer-to-peer social interactions. The students are taught that there is only one rule to follow — Rule Number One:

BE POLITE AND COOPERATIVE

- Talk politely. (Don't be grouchy in any way.)
- Be helpful and considerate of others.
- Cooperate with your classmates.
- Wait for your turn.
- Ask permission before borrowing.
- Don't boss or pester other children.
- Don't take things that don't belong to you.
- Don't grab things away from other people.
- Don't hit, shove, push, or hurt others in any way.

RECESS is very similar to a social skills training program in that many of the procedures are actually carried out on the playground. However, because socially negative/aggressive students frequently misbehave in the classroom, intervention procedures are included for the classroom as well.

The basic intervention program consists of four components: direct social skills training, a response-cost point system for the playground and classroom, contingent adult praise for appropriate social behavior, and both group and individual backup reinforcers for appropriate behavior. RECESS is divided into four phases: recess only, classroom extension, fading program components, and program maintenance. The first three phases require approximately 40 school days, while the maintenance phase may be in effect indefinitely.

With the response-cost point system, the student starts off with one point for every 5 minutes of recess time. In other words, for a 30-minute lunch recess, the student starts with six points. A point is subtracted each time the student breaks a rule or is socially negative/aggressive. The task for the student is to retain as many points as possible by being polite and cooperative with others and by following the playground rules. In the classroom extension, the student earns access to recess by behaving appropriately in the classroom between recess periods (see Exhibit 7.4). The student earns backup reinforcers (group and individual) as follows:

1. If the student keeps all points during at least two out of three recess periods during a single day, the class earns a group activity reward at the end of the day.
2. The points the student earns during the day at school can be exchanged at home for an individual reward.
3. Points earned can also be saved for a larger group activity reward every 5 to 7 days, depending on the quality of the student's behavior.

EXHIBIT 7.4 Recess classroom extension point card and rules

Instructions for Classtime

A. Praise (record on wrist counter):
   1. After each recess, praise child for points retained and bonus points added.
   2. During classtime, praise child every 5-10 minutes for appropriate behavior.
   3. At end of each classtime, praise child for classtime points retained and bonus points added.
B. Bonus Points: If the child is extra thoughtful or handles a difficult situation admirably, give a bonus point and praise the child.
C. Point Losing: Subtract 1 point each time a classroom rule is broken. Tell the child as soon as possible (see rules on clipboard).
D. Missing Recess: If all the *regular* points are lost for a particular time block, have the child miss the next recess (does not apply for the last time block).
E. Timeout: If an additional rule is broken after all of the points have been lost in a given time block, have the child sit in a timeout area for 10-15 minutes.
F. Send-Home: If child acts up during timeout, or if a fourth timeout is necessary on a given day, have the child sent home (or employ the alternate procedure).
G. Rewards Before End of Day:
   1. Happy Face Poster: Draw in 1 facial feature for each regular point retained and bonus points* added.
   2. Take-Home Tickets: Give 1 take-home ticket for every points (regular or bonus*). Ticket fractions are o.k., if marked.
   3. Daily Group Reward: Have child draw a surprise card if at least two recesses show no points lost.
H. Happy Face Poster: Arrange for an extra special group reward when the poster is filled.
I. Record Keeping: Keep Daily Record Form up-to-date.
J. Review Manual: Review the teacher's manual for program implementation details.
   . Bonus point minimum = 2
   Bonus point maximum for credit = ___ (1/4 of the total points available for a day)

Recess and Classtime

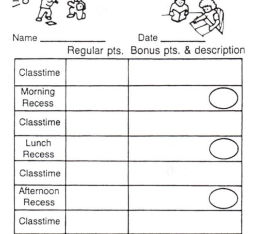

Name _____   Date _____

	Regular pts.	Bonus pts. & description
Classtime		
Morning Recess		⃝
Classtime		
Lunch Recess		⃝
Classtime		
Afternoon Recess		⃝
Classtime		

Instructions for Recess Supervisors

A. Praise: Give praise frequently during each recess (at least 1 each 5 minutes). Keep tally in circle provided. Initial tally at end of recess.
B. Bonus Points: If child is extra thoughtful or handles a difficult situation admirably, give a bonus point, till the child and, if possible, jot down a brief description.
C. Point Losing: Cross out 1 point for every rule broken. Tell child as soon as possible (see rules on clipboard).
D. Timeout: If all the *regular* points are lost during a given recess, have the child sit out for the duration of that recess (bonus points are not lost). If child does not cooperate with this, inform the teacher or consultant.

Instructions for Classroom Teacher on Back

Source: From *RECESS—Reprogramming Environmental Contingencies for Effective Social Skills—Manual for Consultants,* by H. M. Walker, A. Street, B. Garrett, J. Crossen, H. Hops, and C. R. Greenwood, 1978, Eugene: Center at Oregon for Research in the Behavioral Education of the Handicapped. Used with permission.

In RECESS, a consultant is responsible for the initial phases of the program, prepares the classroom teacher and playground supervisor to operate the program, and oversees and coordinates its overall operation. The classroom teacher is responsible for providing group activity rewards at school and managing the classroom extension. The consultant trains the playground supervisor to manage the response-cost system during recess periods after the second week of the program. The student's parents are responsible for providing individual rewards, including social reinforcement, based on school behavior. The student's peers are also influential intervention agents who actively reinforce and support the student's improved social and classroom behavior.

The effectiveness of RECESS has been carefully documented (Walker, Hops, & Greenwood, 1981). It is a very comprehensive program requiring close coordination, a significant investment of energy and effort, and careful attention to details. However, as Walker et al. indicate, RECESS is only as complex as necessary to produce positive changes in the behavior of socially negative/aggressive students.

Cautions in Using Behavior Management Strategies

The strategies discussed in this section assume that teachers will implement the procedures consistently and correctly. However, even the most carefully designed and implemented programs do not always work. For a variety of reasons, results may not always be as clear or as quick as planned and hoped for. Often, the detours and delays are unavoidable and could not have been foreseen even with proper planning. What is important is that teachers become adept at identifying potential difficulties. The following factors are signs of potential problems (Morris, 1985; Harris & Kapche, 1978):

- Inconsistency in the application of reinforcement contingencies
- Vaguely defined target behaviors
- Progress not monitored; data on student progress not collected or charted
- Too many behavior problems targeted for intervention at once; expecting too much too soon
- Inadequate and ineffective backup reinforcers
- Inadequate delivery of reinforcement; too long a delay between performance and actual reinforcement; schedules of reinforcement too long
- Inadequate preparation prior to program
- Lack of knowledge and understanding regarding the operation of the program or the underlying principles
- Lack of strategies to promote generalization
- Failure to fade out token systems

It is better to try to increase appropriate behavior than to just decrease inappropriate behavior.

- Failure to pair social reinforcement with token reinforcement
- Failure to adjust the token economy
- Giving up if first attempts are unsuccessful

In addition to troubleshooting potential problems, teachers should also keep in mind several basic principles:

- It is easier to increase behavior than to decrease it. When selecting target behaviors, choose appropriate behaviors to increase. Increasing an appropriate behavior involves the contingent application of positive reinforcement; decreasing misbehavior, of necessity, involves the contingent application of aversive consequences. Of course, with a severe problem, it may be necessary to design a program combining both positive reinforcement of appropriate behavior and mild aversive consequences for inappropriate behavior.
- We have found one of the primary ingredients of successful interventions with behaviorally disordered students in regular classrooms is the teacher's willingness and ability to prepare carefully before beginning the program. Knowing what is to be done, when it is to be done, how it is to be done, and even why it is to be done can save time in the long run and result in benefits to both student and teacher.

- Teachers implementing behavior management programs must also expect the program to succeed. A failure or a less-than-desirable outcome should be viewed as an *implementation problem,* not as a student problem or as a fundamental flaw in the principles underlying the behavior management program. With this approach, a teacher will analyze the program, locate the flaws, make adjustments, and try again.
- Inherent in each of these suggestions is the assumption that student performance data are of paramount importance. The teacher must monitor student performance by regularly and systematically collecting data, chart the data, and decide whether to continue the intervention as designed or change it to improve performance.

Many teachers—regular and special educators alike—commenting on behavior management programs say something like, "Oh, I've tried that before . . . it didn't work! I'm not going to try it again!" Whether a particular behavior management program worked or did not work is not the issue. Instead of bemoaning the fact that a program was unsuccessful (if, in fact, it was), the teacher should systematically analyze the program by troubleshooting high probability problem areas and trying again. The ability and willingness to *try again* are hallmarks of an effective teacher.

MANAGING ACADEMIC INSTRUCTION

As discussed throughout this text, most behaviorally disordered students have academic skills deficits. Therefore, they will require extra help and specialized assistance with academic subject areas. The extent and nature of their academic deficits, however, may be no greater than the academic deficits of other, nonbehaviorally disordered students in the same class. What distinguishes them from their academically deficient classmates is that they may display much more exaggerated inappropriate behavior if their academic needs are not effectively addressed. The behavior management strategies discussed earlier in this chapter will be ineffective if the students' academic instruction is poorly programmed. Some low achievers may suffer in silence; most behaviorally disordered students will not. This section of the chapter will explore ways in which the academic needs of these students can be met in the regular classroom.

Basic Instructional Considerations

Teachers who effectively meet the academic instruction needs of all their students should also be able to meet the academic instruction needs of behaviorally disordered students. Teaching large numbers of students in regular classrooms necessitates many decisions. What is to be taught, when it is to be taught, to whom it will be taught, what materials will be used, and how instruction will occur are just a few obvious questions addressed by teachers committed to meeting the instructional needs of all students (Mercer, 1987).

All regular classroom teachers adjust to meet the instructional needs of their students. Probably the greatest challenge to a teacher's organizational and management skills is discovering effective ways to manage individual differences in academic skills and content. However, truly individualizing instruction is not always the best solution; organizational and management difficulties can result in a hodge-podge program for all students. When a teacher is faced with the task of teaching academic skills to 25 different students, many of whom are performing significantly below grade level, the highest priority should be to organize the day so that there is enough time available for students who require more intensive instruction.

There are several practical guidelines for teachers developing specific procedures to accommodate behaviorally disordered students' academic needs:

- Involve all students in the instructional program, especially during whole group instructional lessons. Do not exclude or ignore certain low-achieving students from a lesson because they may not understand or may not be able to answer questions.
- Seat students with academic problems closer to the teacher, or at least closer to the classroom's center of active teaching. This will enable the teacher to monitor these students more closely. In addition, the teacher's proximity will help control student attention and prevent misbehavior.
- Make sure directions for assignments are clear and understood. Check to determine whether students understand the directions. Provide both auditory and visual directions for students who may need extra help following directions.
- Use a variety of instructional arrangements in physically organizing the classroom for academic instruction (see Exhibit 7.5).
- Do not provide too much independent seatwork time for low-achieving behaviorally disordered students. It is unlikely they will behave appropriately for much longer than 20-minute stretches when unsupervised. Instead, use short instructional sessions, with frequent checks for understanding, corrective feedback, and reteaching sessions if needed. In general, it is better to cover a little bit of content thoroughly than a lot of content quickly with these students (Evertson et al., 1984).

EXHIBIT 7.5   Instructional arrangements in the regular classroom

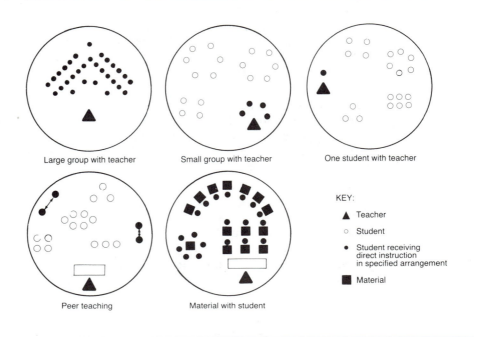

Source: From *Teaching Students With Learning Problems* by C. D. Mercer and A. R. Mercer, 1985, Columbus, OH: Merrill, p. 78. Used with permission.

- Maximize the reciprocal relationship between academic performance and disruptive behavior. That is, instead of focusing on the students' disruptive behaviors, target the improvement of academic skills as the top priority for intervention. (See Pointer 7.2.)
- Provide plenty of feedback on academic and social performance. (See Pointer 7.3.)

Peer-Tutoring Strategies

The students themselves are often a neglected extra set of hands for regular classroom teachers. Historically, teachers have informally involved certain students as teachers' helpers or teachers' assistants in routine clerical or tutoring jobs. Recently structured peer-tutoring programs have been used with increasing frequency by teachers in a variety of instructional contexts. To date, the effects on academic achievement, social relationships, and classroom behavior have generally been positive (see Exhibit 7.6).

Pointer 7.2

ELIMINATING DISCIPLINE PROBLEMS BY STRENGTHENING ACADEMIC PERFORMANCE

The subjects of this investigation were five fifth-grade boys (in a class of 38 students!) who were highly disruptive to the entire classroom because they got out of their seats, talked out, and moved around too much. Instead of designing an intervention program to reduce the disruptive behavior by using aversive consequences, the researchers devised a plan to focus on the students' academic behavior. The intervention consisted of the following components:

1. The students' performance in reading was selected as the behavior to be reinforced. Immediately following small reading groups, the students were assigned follow-up seatwork activities in their reading workbooks involving vocabulary and comprehension skills. The tasks, which were to be completed individually, usually required from 15 to 20 minutes.

2. To strengthen task completion and accuracy, a point system was implemented for the five students. Students were awarded points for scores of 80% or higher on completed assignments; more points were awarded for assignments that

were 100% accurate and complete. No points were awarded for incomplete assignments or for assignments less than 80% accurate. The backup reinforcers included access to game room, extra recess time, being an assistant teacher, a weekly movie, a good work letter sent home, being ball captain, being classroom helper, and so on.

The results confirmed that, when academic responses were reinforced, disruptive behaviors decreased. Before intervention, the boys' accuracy on academic assignments averaged 40 to 50% and their disruptive behavior averaged 40 to 50%. By the end of the study, their accuracy had increased to an average of 85% and disruptive behaviors had decreased to a 5%.

The most important lesson to be learned from this study concerns the myth that, with disruptive students, teachers must first make them sit still and be quiet so they will learn. Instead, this study showed that a better approach would be to "teach them better and then they will sit still and be quiet." While severe behavior problems may still require aversive measures, the emphasis should be on increasing desired academic responses.

Source: Drawn from "Eliminating Discipline Problems by Strengthening Academic Performance" by T. Ayllon and M. D. Roberts, 1974, *Journal of Applied Behavior Analysis, 7,* 71–76.

Pointer 7.3

PUBLIC POSTING: A PERFORMANCE FEEDBACK SYSTEM

Public posting improves academic performance by posting student performance data in clear public view so that all students in the class have easy access to feedback (VanHouten, 1979). Initially developed in response to objections to token reinforcement programs, public posting requires less time, is less expensive, is more amenable to promoting generalized behavior change, and is as effective as token reinforcement (VanHouten, 1980). Public posting has been used in math, reading, instruction following, and story writing.

Student performance data can be posted in a variety of ways. The best results are obtained when the data are posted on a large chart where all students can see it. Each student's daily performance (e.g., number of problems computed correctly, words read correctly per minute, percentage of instructions followed, positive comments said to others) as well as their best performance to date can be posted (see the chart).

In addition to individual scores, the class' total score should be computed daily. This activates a sense of spirit, unity, and shared goals among students in the class.

Why is public posting effective? It seems as if public posting of individual scores on a chart provides students with discriminative stimuli that serve as social norms; further, low-achieving students typically seem to benefit the most from public posting in terms of improved performance. Public posting also helps to teach students to reinforce and to encourage themselves. An excellent resource for learning more about public posting is *Learning through Feedback: A Systematic Approach for Improving Academic Performance* (VanHouten, 1980).

Task _____ _____ _____

Name	Best Score	Best Score	Best Score
Best Team Total			

Source: From *Learning through Feedback: A Systematic Approach for Improving Academic Performance* by R. VanHouten, 1980, New York: Human Sciences Press, p. 96. Used with permission.

EXHIBIT 7.6   Peer tutoring

Research Finding:	**Students tutoring other students can lead to improved academic achievement for both student and tutor and to positive attitudes toward coursework.**

Comment: Tutoring programs consistently raise the achievement of both the students receiving instruction and those providing it. Peer tutoring, when used as a supplement to regular classroom teaching, helps slow and underachieving students master their lessons and succeed in school. Preparing and giving the lessons also benefits the tutors themselves because they learn more about the material they are teaching.

Of the tutoring programs that have been studied, the most effective include the following elements:
- Highly structured and well-planned curricula and instructional methods
- Instruction in basic content and skills (grades 1–3), especially in arithmetic
- A relatively short duration of instruction (a few weeks or months)

When these features were combined in the same program, the students being tutored not only learned more than they did without tutoring, they also developed a more positive attitude about what they were studying. Their tutors also learned more than students who did not tutor.

Source: From *What Works: Research About Teaching and Learning,* 1986, Washington, DC: U.S. Department of Education.

Several structured peer-tutoring programs have been developed that have particular applicability to behaviorally disordered students in regular classrooms. These programs are classwide peer tutoring, team-assisted individualization, and cooperative learning strategies. Each will be reviewed briefly below. In addition, we will present several other potentially useful peer involvement strategies.

Classwide Peer Tutoring

The classwide peer-tutoring system was developed at the Juniper Gardens Children's Project at the University of Kansas (Delquadri, Greenwood, Whorton, Carta, & Hall, 1986). The system was developed and has been refined to increase the students' opportunities to actively and meaningfully respond to instruction in regular classes. Earlier observational studies indicated that many students, especially those behind academically, had very few opportunities to respond on academic tasks during the course of a typical school day (Greenwood, Delquadri, & Hall, 1984). Thus, classwide peer tutoring was conceived as a means by which students could have significantly more opportunities to respond on academic tasks—spelling, vocabulary, math facts, oral reading, and comprehension skills.

Classwide peer-tutoring systems are relatively easy to implement in the regular classroom. The basic arrangements are as follows:

1. A period of approximately 30 minutes per day is required. Each student receives 10 minutes of tutoring and tutors for 10 minutes, and 5 to 10 minutes are spent counting points and posting results.
2. Tutor–tutee pairs for the week are randomly selected each Monday. The pair sit next to or across from each other. They begin a 10-minute session with one as tutor and the other as tutee when the teacher sounds a signal to begin. If the task is reading, the tutor monitors the tutee's oral reading, corrects errors, and awards two points for each sentence correctly read. The tutor also requires the tutee to correct reading errors; the tutee receives one point for each error corrected. Similar procedures are followed in spelling and math sessions. At the end of 10 minutes, the roles are reversed. Tutor becomes tutee, and vice versa.
3. During tutoring sessions, the teacher circulates among the students and awards bonus points for correct tutoring behavior. The teacher also divides the class into two teams (e.g., rows 1 and 2 versus rows 3 and 4).
4. At the end of the second 10-minute session, each student counts the number of points earned as both tutor and tutee and calls out the grand total when the teacher calls his or her name. The teacher records the point totals for each student in one of two team columns on a chart posted in front of the class. The teacher tallies the total number of points earned by each team and announces the winning team for that day. Each week the composition of the two teams changes.
5. At the end of each week, usually on Friday, the teacher may conduct a more intensive assessment of each student's progress on the skills from that week.

An important part of the success of the classwide peer-tutoring system is the time initially invested in training students to be effective tutors. The teacher carefully explains and demonstrates each major procedure entailed in the actual tutoring session. Error correction procedures and the point system are carefully reviewed and demonstrated.

Supervised practice opportunities, with corrective feedback, are also an integral part of training.

This system has been extensively field-tested and the results are very positive and encouraging (Delquadri, Greenwood, Stretton, & Hall, 1983; Greenwood et al., 1984). The data strongly suggest that, in addition to academic achievement gains, cooperative peer relations are enhanced (Kohler, Richardson, Mina, Dinwiddie, & Greenwood, 1985).

Cooperative Learning Strategies

Cooperative learning strategies are a method of promoting social acceptance between handicapped and nonhandicapped students in mainstreamed settings (Johnson & Johnson, 1986). Consider the following scene:

> At the door of the classroom Carl stopped and glanced anxiously at the busy hum of students clearing their desks in preparation for math. The special education teacher escorting Carl to the classroom turned and looked intently at the child, a trace of anxiety appearing on her face also as she took Carl by the hand and entered the classroom. Carl unobtrusively slipped into a desk at the back of the classroom as the special education teacher chatted for a moment with the regular teacher. (Johnson, R., & Johnson, D. W., 1980, p. 9)

The questions Carl might have been asking himself—Will I be liked? Will I be rejected? Will I be ignored?—are at the heart of the mainstreaming challenge (Johnson, R., & Johnson, D. W., 1980).

Cooperative learning strategies stand in marked contrast to the individualistic or competitive learning strategies that predominate in most classrooms. Cooperative learning strategies create a pattern of positive interaction and perceptions and feelings of mutual concern and friendliness among students (Johnson, D. W., & Johnson, R., 1980). The procedures used to implement this approach are as follows (Johnson, D. W., & Johnson, R., 1980, 1986):

- Before a lesson, identify both the academic objectives and the cooperative learning objectives (i.e., interpersonal cooperative skills) to be taught and stressed.
- Decide on the size of the groups, composition of groups, how long the group will function (week, month, semester, year), and the classroom's physical arrangements (generally, arranging student chairs in a circle is preferred).
- Assign roles to group members (e.g., summarizer, checker, accuracy coach, elaboration seeker); convey to group members that their task is collaborative and that they, in essence, will sink or swim together.

- Explain the learning task and cooperative goal structure to students. The assignment may involve a variety of academic curriculum areas. The cooperative goal structure usually entails (a) a group goal, (b) criteria for success, (c) an understanding that all group members receive the same grade, (d) an awareness of the cooperative learning skills for the particular task, and (e) a reminder that it is desirable to assist other groups in the classroom.
- Monitor and intervene, if necessary, as students work collaboratively. Provide assistance on the academic task or collaboration skills.
- Evaluate individual student learning, group products, and individual and group cooperative learning/collaboration skills.

More extensive directions and examples of how to implement cooperative learning strategies may be found in Johnson and Johnson (1975, 1984) and Johnson, Johnson, Holubec, and Roy (1984).

Team-Assisted Individualization

Team-assisted individualization (TAI) strategies are concerned with promoting the social acceptance and academic achievement of mainstreamed handicapped students by combining cooperative learning strategies and individualized instruction (Slavin, Madden, & Leavey, 1984). TAI involves heterogeneous cooperative learning groups working on individualized mathematics content units. The main features of TAI are as follows (Slavin, 1984):

1. *Teams*—Four- or five-member teams composed of high-, average-, and low-achieving boys and girls, including handicapped students. Teams change every month or so.
2. *Assessment*—Students are given a placement test and placed appropriately in the math program based on the results.
3. *Instructional materials*—Students work on individualized math curriculum materials in the areas of addition, subtraction, multiplication, division, numeration, decimals, fractions, word problems, and introductory algebra. These materials are organized into instruction sheets, skill sheets with 20 problems each, check-out tests, final tests, and answer sheets.
4. *Team-study method*—Work in the teams proceeds as follows:
   - Pairs or triads of students locate the unit they are currently working on and give the answer sheets to another student in the working group.
   - Students read the instructions, asking partners for assistance if necessary, and complete the first four problems on the skill sheet. The student then asks his or her partner to

correct them using the answer sheet. If all four problems are correct, the student goes on to the next skill sheet. If one or more problems are incorrect, the student continues on the skill sheet until four consecutive problems are completed correctly.

- At any time during this stage, if students have trouble with the operations, they are encouraged to seek assistance from within their team before requesting help from the teacher.

- After a student has completed four problems in a row correctly, the check-out test is taken and corrected by a team member. A score of 80% is required before the final test may be taken. Additional practice may be recommended by the teacher if the 80% score is not achieved on the first check-out.

- Final tests are obtained from one of the three student monitors appointed each day, usually a member of a different team, who also scores the final test.

5. *Team scores and recognition* — The teacher computes a weekly score for each team. The score is based on the average number of units completed by each member and scores on the final test. Depending on team performance, attractive *Super-team* or *Greatteam* certificates may be presented to qualifying teams.

6. *Teaching groups* — The teacher conducts instructional sessions with students from different teams who are placed at about the same point in the curriculum to introduce new concepts, operations, and skills.

7. *Homework* — Students have brief homework assignments 4 days a week.

8. *Facts test* — Timed basic facts tests (multiplication and division) are given by the teacher to all students twice each week.

9. *Group-paced units* — Every fourth week, the teacher conducts large group instructional sessions with all students over content areas not included in the individualized units.

TAI has successfully improved the social acceptance, classroom behavior, and mathematics achievement of mildly handicapped students (Madden & Slavin, 1983a, 1983b; Slavin, 1984; Slavin et al., 1984). Furthermore, TAI has beneficial effects for the nonhandicapped students involved.

Summary
Interventions that involve peers in teaching social skills and fostering the social adjustment of behaviorally disordered students were discussed in chapter 6. Peers have also been used as monitors to reduce inappropriate

behaviors and increase appropriate social and classroom behaviors of behaviorally disordered students (Carden-Smith & Fowler, 1984; Dougherty, Fowler, & Paine, 1985; Fowler, 1986). In some instances, serving as a peer monitor has also benefited the monitors, some of whom have been behaviorally disordered students.

It is clear from the descriptions of the three structured peer-tutoring programs and other effective applications of peer-mediated intervention strategies (cf. Strain, 1984) that teachers have at their disposal a potentially valuable, yet untapped, resource. As with any other effective instructional practice, however, the benefits cannot be realized without careful planning and preparation before implementation and close supervision and monitoring after implementation. Peer tutoring is not a complete solution, nor is it the only solution, to the problems of meeting the academic needs of behaviorally disordered students in regular classrooms. Based on the positive effects demonstrated to date, however, peer tutoring seems to be a preferred practice that should be part of any approach to improving the overall adjustment of these students in regular classrooms.

BUILDING-BASED SUPPORT TEAMS

Another promising source of support to regular teachers is the building-based support team,

> a school-based problem-solving group whose purpose is to provide a vehicle for discussion of issues related to specific needs of teachers or students and to offer consultation and follow-up assistance to staff. The team can respond to staff needs in a variety of ways. It can provide immediate crisis intervention, short-term consultation, continuous support, or the securing of information, resources, or training for those who request its service. (Stokes, 1981, p. 3)

The primary benefits of this approach are the increased skills and confidence acquired by regular classroom teachers and improved learning and adjustment of the students who are the focus of the support team's activities.

A widely known and implemented building-based support team model is the Teacher Assistance Team (Chalfant, Pysh, & Moultrie, 1979). The Teacher Assistance Team helps teachers cope with students who have learning or behavior problems. The composition of the Teacher Assistance Team varies from school to school, though there is usually a core group of regular teachers, the referring teacher, a special education teacher, and occasionally the student's parents. The Teacher Assistance Team (a) helps teachers develop strategies for effectively dealing with classroom learning and adjustment problems, (b) provides direct assistance for teachers who are having a hard time using recommendations from special education personnel, and (c) helps teachers obtain assistance from special educators.

Clearly, the concept of a building-based support team is a preferred practice. Regular classroom teachers can solicit advice and support concerning problems they are having with students with learning and behavior problems.

Support teams can also help teachers with prereferral interventions. A prereferral intervention is a systematic strategy, implemented in the regular classroom and evaluated for its effectiveness, used before a student is formally referred for special education (Graden, Casey, & Christenson, 1985). The need for prereferral interventions has grown out of the serious concern about the large number of referrals for special education and the evidence that most students referred are eventually classified and placed in special education programs. Estimates are that 3 to 5% of school-aged children are referred for special education annually; of those, 92% are formally evaluated; of those, 73% are declared eligible for and receive special education (Algozzine, Christenson, & Ysseldyke, 1982; Sevcik & Ysseldyke, 1986).

The prereferral intervention model was proposed by Graden and colleagues (1985). The goal of the model is to provide intervention assistance to regular classroom teachers, and thus reduce inappropriate referrals for formal assessment and inappropriate and unnecessary placements in pull-out special education programs. Initiatives such as prereferral intervention strategies can be very effective in providing quick, responsive support to regular classroom teachers.

WORKING WITH SUPPORT PERSONNEL

Behaviorally disordered students in regular classrooms are often taught for at least a portion of the day by a special education teacher in addition to a regular classroom teacher. This type of arrangement often raises the question of "ownership." That is, who is ultimately responsible for the handicapped student? The answer is that the regular classroom teacher and the special education teacher (resource teacher, resource teacher/consultant, consulting teacher) are jointly responsible for the student's program. While specific responsibilities may differ, the goal for both teachers is to teach the student in a way that promotes maximum growth and does not leave either teacher with the feeling that the responsibility is his or hers alone.

When special educators and regular teachers work together, their success often hinges on the communication between them. The special educator who "knows it all," or acts as if the regular teacher knows very little, is not likely to be asked another time. Collaboration is a success only when the teachers view each other as skilled and dedicated professionals with individual strengths and teaching styles. The next chapter discusses a collaborative consultation approach between special education and regular education.

SUMMARY

Increasing numbers of behaviorally disordered students are taught in regular classrooms. When faced with the challenge of teaching behaviorally disordered students, the regular classroom teacher's primary responsibility is really no different than it is with "normal" students: to prevent behavior problems by maximizing the amount of time students spend engaged in appropriate educational activities and working productively.

To accomplish this goal requires the systematic application of sound behavior management practices and strategies for modifying the academic curriculum. This chapter explained several group and individual behavior management strategies and programs and stressed the importance of the academic curriculum by reviewing several approaches (notably peer tutoring) that teachers can implement to promote the academic achievement of behaviorally disordered students.

Teaching behaviorally disordered students in regular classrooms requires the teacher and other support personnel to share responsibility for the successful integration of these students. Building-based support teams and other prereferral support systems were discussed as examples of ways regular classroom teachers can be helped to provide quality educational programs to behaviorally disordered students.

REVIEW QUESTIONS

1. You overhear a regular classroom teacher talking with a colleague about a behaviorally disordered student in his class. The teacher says, "Well, the kid can't really help how he behaves . . . he's behaviorally disordered!" How could you respond?
2. Specify a set of classroom rules for a regular classroom of the fourth graders. Follow the guidelines and examples discussed in this chapter. Next, outline a procedure you would use to teach the rules to your students.
3. Research indicates that many teachers attend to inappropriate classroom behaviors more than appropriate behaviors. Why do you think this happens? What are the long-term consequences of this pattern for students? What can be done to modify teacher behavior in this instance?
4. You have been asked to make a presentation at your school's next faculty meeting. The topic is: "Sharing Responsibility for Teaching Behaviorally Disordered Students." Prepare an outline of what you will say.

5. Is it fair to nonhandicapped students to involve them in peer-tutoring programs? What would you say to a parent of a nonhandicapped student who complained to you about your involving that parent's child in a classwide peer-tutoring program which also included "special education kids"?

REFERENCES

Alberto, P. A., & Troutman, A. C. (1986). *Applied behavior analysis for teachers* (2nd ed.). Columbus, OH: Merrill.

Algozzine, B., Christenson, S., & Ysseldyke, J. (1982). Probabilities associated with the referral to placement process. *Teacher Education and Special Education, 5,* 19–23.

Barrish, J., Saunders, M., & Wolf, M. (1969). Good behavior game: Effects of individual contingencies for group consequences on disruptive behavior in a classroom. *Journal of Applied Behavior Analysis, 2,* 119–124.

Bickel, W. E., & Bickel, D. D. (1986). Effective schools, classrooms, and instruction: Implications for special education. *Exceptional Children, 52,* 489–500.

Brophy, J. (1981). Teacher praise: A functional analysis. *Review of Educational Research, 51,* 5–32.

Canter, L., & Canter, M. (1976). *Assertive discipline: A take-charge approach for today's educator.* Los Angeles: Lee Canter and Associates.

Cantrell, R., Stenner, A., & Katzenmeyer, W. (1977). Teacher knowledge, attitudes, and classroom teaching correlates of student achievement. *Journal of Educational Psychology, 69,* 172–179.

Carden-Smith, L. K., & Fowler, S. A. (1984). Positive peer pressure: The effects of peer monitoring on children's disruptive behavior. *Journal of Applied Behavior Analysis, 17,* 213–227.

Carlberg, C., & Kavale, K. (1980). The efficacy of special versus regular class placement for exceptional children: A meta-analysis. *Journal of Special Education, 14,* 295–309.

Chalfant, J. C., Pysh, M., & Moultrie, R. (1979). Teacher assistance teams: A model for within-building problem solving. *Learning Disabilities Quarterly, 2,* 85–96.

Charles, C. M. (1985). *Building classroom discipline: From models to practice.* (2nd ed.). New York: Longman.

Delquadri, J. C., Greenwood, C. R., Stretton, K., & Hall, R. V. (1983). The peer tutoring spelling game: A classroom procedure for increasing opportunity to respond and spelling performance. *Education and Treatment of Children, 6,* 225–239.

Delquadri, J. C., Greenwood, C. R., Whorton, D., Carta, J. J., & Hall, R. V. (1986). Classwide peer tutoring. *Exceptional Children, 52,* 535–542.

Dickerson, E. A., & Creedon, C. F. (1981). Self-selection of standards by children: The relative effectiveness of pupil-selected and teacher-selected standards of performance. *Journal of Applied Behavior Analysis, 14,* 425–433.

Dougherty, B. S., Fowler, S. A., & Paine, S. C. (1985). The use of peer monitors to reduce negative interaction during recess. *Journal of Applied Behavior Analysis, 18,* 141–153.

Drabman, R. S., & Lahey, B. B. (1974). Feedback in classroom behavior modification: Effects on the target and her classmates. *Journal of Applied Behavior Analysis, 7,* 591–598.

Erken, N., & Henderson, H. (1976). *Practice skills mastery program.* Logan, UT: Mastery Programs.

Evertson, C. M., Emmer, E. T., Clements, B. S., Sanford, J. P., & Worsham, M. E. (1984). *Classroom management for elementary teachers.* Englewood Cliffs, NJ: Prentice-Hall.

Felixbrod, J. J., & O'Leary, K. D. (1973). Effects of reinforcement on children's academic behavior as a function of self-determined and externally imposed contingencies. *Journal of Applied Behavior Analysis, 6,* 241–250.

Fowler, S. A. (1986). Peer-monitoring and self-monitoring: Alternatives to traditional teacher management. *Exceptional Children, 52,* 573–581.

Good, T., Ebmeier, H., & Beckerman, T. (1978). Teaching mathematics in high and low SES classrooms: An empirical comparison. *Journal of Teacher Education, 29,* 85–90.

Good, T. L., & Brophy, J. E. (1987). *Looking in classrooms.* (4th ed.). New York: Harper & Row.

Graden, J. L., Casey, A., & Christenson, S. L. (1985). Implementing a prereferral intervention system: Part I. The model. *Exceptional Children, 51,* 377–384.

Greenwood, C. R., Delquadri, J. C., & Hall, R. V. (1984). Opportunity to respond and student academic performance. In W. L. Heward, T. E. Heron, D. S. Hill, & J. Trap-Porter (Eds.), *Focus on behavior analysis in education.* Columbus, OH: Merrill.

Greenwood, C. R., Delquadri, J., Hops, H., & Walker, H. (1977). *PASS teacher manual: Group management of academic related behaviors.* Eugene: Center at Oregon for Research in the Behavioral Education of the Handicapped.

Greenwood, C. R., Dinwiddie, G., Terry, B., Wade, L., Stanley, S. O., Thibadeau, S., & Delquadri, J. C. (1984). Teacher- versus peer-mediated instruction: An ecobehavioral analysis of achievement outcomes. *Journal of Applied Behavior Analysis, 17,* 521–538.

Greenwood, C. R., & Hops, H. (1981). Group-oriented contingencies and peer behavior change. In P. S. Strain (Ed.), *The utilization of classroom peers as behavior change agents.* New York: Plenum Press.

Greenwood, C. R., Hops, H., Delquadri, J., & Guild, J. (1974). Group contingencies for group consequences in classroom management: A further analysis. *Journal of Applied Behavior Analysis, 7,* 413–425.

Greenwood, C. R., Hops, H., Delquadri, J., & Walker, H. M. (1977). *PASS consultant manual: Group management of academic related behaviors.* Eugene: Center at Oregon for Research in the Behavioral Education of the Handicapped.

Greenwood, C. R., Hops, H., & Walker, H. M. (1977). The program for academic survival skills: Effects on behavior and achievement. *Journal of School Psychology, 15,* 25–35.

Greenwood, C. R., Hops, H., Walker, H. M., Guild, J. J., Stokes, J., Young, K. R., Keleman, K. S., & Willardson, M. (1979). Standardized classroom management program: Social validation and replication studies in Utah and Oregon. *Journal of Applied Behavior Analysis, 12,* 235–253.

Hall, R. V., & Hall, M. C. (1982). *How to negotiate a behavioral contract.* Lawrence, KS: H & H Enterprises.

Haring, N. G., & Phillips, E. L. (1962). *Educating emotionally disturbed children.* New York: McGraw-Hill.

Harris, A., & Kapche, R. (1978). Problems of quality control in the development and the use of behavior change techniques in public school settings. *Education and Treatment of Children, 1,* 43–51.

Henderson, H. S., Jenson, W. R., Erken, N. F., Davidsmeyer, P. L., & Lampe, S. (1986). Variable interval reinforcement as a practical means of increasing and maintaining on-task behavior in classrooms. *Techniques, 2,* 217–229.

Henderson, H. S., Jenson, W. R., & Erken, N. F. (1986). Using variable interval schedules to improve on-task behavior in the classroom. *Education and Treatment of Children, 9,* 250–263.

Hewett, F. M. (1968). *The emotionally disturbed child in the classroom.* Boston: Allyn & Bacon.

Hops, H., Beickel, S. L., & Walker, H. M. (1976). *CLASS program for acting-out children: Manual for consultants.* Eugene: Center at Oregon for Research in the Behavioral Education of the Handicapped.

Hops, H., Fleischman, D., & Beickel, S. L. (1976). *CLASS program for acting-out children: Manual for teachers.* Eugene: Center at Oregon for Research in the Behavioral Education of the Handicapped.

Hops, H., Walker, H. M., Fleischman, D., Nagoshi, J., Omura, R., Skinrud, K., & Taylor, J. (1978). CLASS: A standardized in-class program for acting-hut children. II. Field test evaluations. *Journal of Educational Psychology, 70,* 636–644.

Johnson, D. W., & Johnson, R. (1975). *Learning together and alone: Cooperation, competition, and individualization.* Englewood Cliffs, NJ: Prentice-Hall.

Johnson, D. W., & Johnson, R. T. (1980). Integrating handicapped students into the mainstream. *Exceptional Children, 47,* 90–98.

Johnson, D. W., & Johnson, R. (1984). Classroom learning structure and attitudes toward handicapped students in mainstream settings: A theoretical model and research evidence. In R. Jones (Ed.), *Special education in transition: Attitudes toward the handicapped.* Reston, VA: Council for Exceptional Children.

Johnson, D. W., & Johnson, R. (1986). Mainstreaming and cooperative learning strategies. *Exceptional Children, 52,* 553–561.

Johnson, D. W., Johnson, R., Holubec, R. E., & Roy, P. (1984). *Circles of learning.* Alexandria, VA: Association for Supervision and Curriculum Development.

Johnson, R., & Johnson, D. W. (1980). The social integration of handicapped students into the mainstream. In M. C. Reynolds (Ed.), *Social environment of the schools.* Reston, VA: Council for Exceptional Children.

Kerr, M. M., & Nelson, C. M. (1983). *Strategies for managing behavior problems in the classroom.* Columbus, OH: Merrill.

Kohler, F. W., Richardson, T., Mina, C., Dinwiddie, G., & Greenwood, C. R. (1985). Establishing cooperative peer relations in the classroom. *The Pointer, 29,* 12–16.

Kosiec, L. E., Czernicki, M. R., & McLaughlin, T. F. (1986). The good behavior game: A replication with consumer satisfaction in two regular elementary school classrooms. *Techniques, 2,* 15–23.

Larrivee, B. (1985). *Effective teaching for successful mainstreaming.* New York: Longman.

Lilly, M. S. (1987). Lack of focus on special education in literature on educational reform. *Exceptional Children, 53,* 325–326.

Long, N. J., & Newman, R. G. (1980). Managing surface behavior of children in school. In N. J. Long, W. C. Morse, & R. G. Newman (Eds.), *Conflict in the classroom: The education of emotionally disturbed children* (4th ed.). Belmont, CA: Wadsworth.

Lovitt, T. C. (1978). *Managing inappropriate behaviors in the classroom.* Washington, DC: Council for Exceptional Children.

Lovitt, T. C., & Curtiss, K. A. (1969). Academic response rate as a function of teacher and self-imposed contingencies. *Journal of Applied Behavior Analysis, 2,* 49–53.

Madden, N. A., & Slavin, R. E. (1983a). Cooperative learning and social acceptance of mainstreamed academically handicapped students. *Journal of Special Education, 17,* 171–182.

Madden, N. A., & Slavin, R. E. (1983b). Mainstreaming students with mild academic handicaps: Academic and social outcomes. *Review of Educational Research, 53,* 519–569.

Madsen, C. H., Becker, W. C., & Thomas, D. (1968). Rules, praise, and ignoring: Elements of elementary classroom control. *Journal of Applied Behavior Analysis, 1,* 139–150.

Mandlebaum, L. H., Russell, S. C., Krouse, J., & Gonter, M. (1983). Assertive discipline: An effective classwide behavior management program. *Behavioral Disorders, 8,* 258–264.

Mercer, C. D. (1987). *Students with learning disabilities* (3rd ed.). Columbus, OH: Merrill.

Morris, R. J. (1985). *Behavior modification with exceptional children: Principles and practices.* Glenview, IL: Scott, Foresman and Company.

O'Leary, K. D., & O'Leary, S. G. (1977). *Classroom management: The successful use of behavior modification* (2nd ed.). New York: Pergamon Press.

Paine, S., Radicchi, J., Rosellini, L., Deutchman, L., & Darch, C. (1983). *Structuring your classroom for success.* Champaign, IL: Research Press.

Patterson, G. R. (1965). An application of conditioning techniques to the control of a hyperactive child. In L. P. Ullman & L. Krasner (Eds.), *Case studies in behavior modification.* New York: Holt, Rinehart and Winston.

Patterson, G. R., Shaw, D. A., & Ebner, M. J. (1969). Teachers, peers and parents as agents of change in the classroom. In A. M. Benson (Ed.), *Modifying deviant social behaviors in various classroom settings.* Eugene: University of Oregon, Report No. 1.

Reynolds, M. C., & Wang, M. C. (1983). Restructuring "special" school programs: A position paper. *Policy Studies Review, 2,* 189–212.

Reynolds, M. C., Wang, M. C., & Walberg, H. J. (1987). The necessary restructuring of special and regular education. *Exceptional Children, 53,* 391–398.

Rutherford, R. B., & Polsgrove, L. J. (1982). Behavioral contracting with behaviorally disordered and delinquent children and youth: An analysis of the clinical and experimental literature. In R. B. Rutherford (Ed.), *Monograph in behavioral disorders: Severe behavior disorders of children and youth.* Reston, VA: Council for Children with Behavioral Disorders.

Sevcik, B. M., & Ysseldyke, J. E. (1986). An analysis of teachers' prereferral interventions for students exhibiting behavioral problems. *Behavioral Disorders, 11,* 109–117.

Slavin, R. E. Team assisted individualization: Cooperative learning and individualized instruction in the mainstreamed classroom. *Remedial and Special Education, 5,* 33–42.

Slavin, R. E., Madden, N. A., & Leavey, M. (1984). Effects of cooperative learning and individualized instruction on the social acceptance, achievement, and behavior of mainstreamed handicapped students. *Exceptional Children, 50,* 434–443.

Stainback, W., & Stainback, S. (1984). A rationale for the merger of special and regular education. *Exceptional Children, 51,* 102–111.

Stokes, S. (Ed.). (1981). *School-based staff support teams: A blueprint for action.* Bloomington: Indiana University; National Inservice Network.

Strain, P. S. (Ed.). (1984). *The utilization of classroom peers as behavior change agents.* New York: Plenum Press.

Thomas, J. D., Presland, I. E., Grant, M. D., & Glynn, T. L. (1978). Natural rates of teacher approval and disapproval in grade-7 classrooms. *Journal of Applied Behavior Analysis, 11,* 91–94.

Thompson, R. H., White, K. R., & Morgan, D. P. (1982). Teacher-student interaction patterns in classrooms with mainstreamed mildly handicapped students. *American Education Research Journal, 19,* 220–236.

VanHouten, R. (1979). The performance feedback system: Generalization of effects across time. *Child Behavior Therapy, 1,* 219–236.

VanHouten, R. (1980). *Learning through feedback: A systematic approach for improving academic performance.* New York: Human Sciences Press.

Walker, H. M. (1979). *The acting-out child: Coping with classroom disruption.* Boston: Allyn & Bacon.

Walker, H. M., & Buckley, N. K. (1973). Teacher attention to appropriate and inappropriate behavior: An individual case study. *Focus on Exceptional Children, 5,* 5–11.

Walker, H. M., & Buckley, N. K. (1974). *Token reinforcement techniques: Classroom applications for the hard to teach child.* Eugene, OR: E-P Press.

Walker, H. M., & Hops, H. (1976). Increasing academic achievement by reinforcing direct academic performance and/or facilitative non-academic responses. *Journal of Educational Psychology, 68,* 218–225.

Walker, H. M., Hops, H., & Fiegenbaum, E. (1976). Deviant classroom behavior as a function of combination of social and token reinforcement and cost contingency. *Behavior Therapy, 7,* 76–88.

Walker, H. M., Hops, H., & Greenwood, C. R. (1981). RECESS: Research and development of a behavior management package for remediating social aggression in the school setting. In P. S. Strain (Ed.), *The utilization of classroom peers as behavior change agents.* New York: Plenum Press.

Walker, H. M., & Rankin, R. R. (1983). Assessing the behavioral expectations and demands of less restrictive settings: Instruments, ecological assessment procedures, and outcomes. *School Psychology Review, 12,* 274–284.

Walker, H. M., Street, A., Garrett, B., Crossen, J., Hops, H., & Greenwood, C. R. (1978). *RECESS: Manual for consultants.* Eugene: Center at Oregon for Research in the Behavioral Education of the Handicapped.

Walker, J., & Shea, T. M. (1984). *Behavior management: A practical approach for educators* (3rd ed.). Columbus, OH: Merrill.

Wang, M. C., & Birch, J. W. (1984). Effective special education in regular classes. *Exceptional Children, 50,* 391–398.

White, M. A. (1975). Natural rates of teacher approval and disapproval in the classroom. *Journal of Applied Behavior Analysis, 8,* 367–372.

Will, M. C. (1986). *Educating students with learning problems—A shared responsibility.* Washington, DC: U.S. Department of Education, Office of Special Education and Rehabilitative Services.

Wolf, M. M., Hanley, E. L., King, L. A., Lachowicz, J., & Giles, D. K. (1970). The timer-game: A variable interval contingency for the management of out-of-seat behavior. *Exceptional Children, 37,* 113–117.

8 Teaching Behaviorally Disordered Students in Resource Room Programs

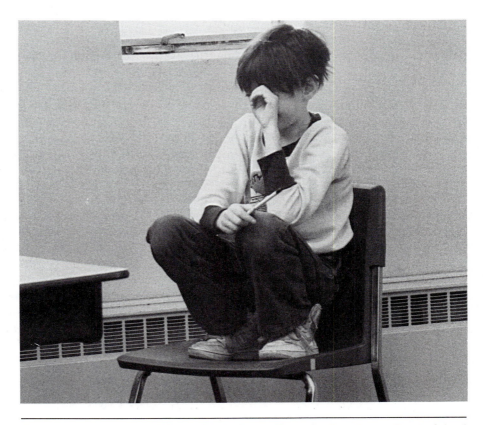

This chapter was written with Ginger Rhode, Special Education Coordinator, Granite School District, Salt Lake City, Utah.

After completing this chapter, you should be able to

- *Identify the purpose of a resource room program.*
- *Identify several functions that should not be performed by resource programs.*
- *Describe several types of resource programs.*
- *Explain the nature of the resource teacher's role.*
- *Explain the advantages and disadvantages of the resource program approach to service delivery for behaviorally disordered students.*
- *Describe ways the resource program can support the regular classroom program in academic skills, classroom behavior, and social skills.*
- *Define teacher consultation.*
- *Explain the purpose of teacher consultation.*
- *Describe the process of teacher consultation.*
- *Describe methods used to promote generalization of improvements from the resource program to the regular classroom.*

T eaching all behaviorally disordered students full-time in the regular classroom is not necessarily the best idea. Some students may require more intensive intervention. A frequently employed alternative for providing special education services to behaviorally disordered students is the resource room. Generally, students in resource programs have fewer and less intense behavioral and social problems and academic deficiencies than students in self-contained classes (Coleman, 1986). Behaviorally disordered students are placed in resource rooms to improve their academic and behavioral functioning while maintaining them in regular classrooms for most of the day.

This chapter first provides an overview of the resource room approach by describing several distinct types of resource programs, the role of the resource teacher, the effectiveness of resource programs, and some advantages and disadvantages of this approach. The nature of the curriculum and instructional approaches used will be reviewed in the next section. Special attention will be devoted to two related topics in the last part of the chapter: the consultative role of the resource teacher and methods of promoting generalization of improvements from the resource program to the regular classroom.

WHAT IS A RESOURCE ROOM PROGRAM?

A concise one- or two-sentence description of resource room programs is very difficult to construct. Resource room programs take many different and varied shapes, not only among the states but also between schools in the same school district (Friend & McNutt, 1984). According to Friend and McNutt (1984), the resource room model is the most widely used alternative to the regular education classroom. Typically, teachers are required to be certified in the areas of exceptionality to be served, and the programs are categorical or multicategorical in nature. They usually have recommended time parameters for students' attendance, though the time varies from a minimum of 3 hours a week to a general maximum of up to, but not more than, half the school day. Harris and Schutz (1986) have stated that a common ingredient is "support," which they define as:

> a comprehensive concept that is provided by resource programs in many different ways: support is assessment and placement at an appropriate instructional level; support is counseling, encouraging, and caring; support is the reinforcement of progress in the smallest increments; support is consulting with teachers, parents, social workers, and others who influence the life of the handicapped child. Support activities create and maintain an educational environment in which handicapped students can learn and grow to the fullest extent possible while benefiting from association with their peers and participating in a full school program. (pp. 11–12)

While the actual shape and form of resource room programs are many and varied, there are several functions that may be but should *not* be considered attributes of these programs (Weiderholt, Hammill, & Brown, 1986):

1. The resource program is not a tutoring program primarily designed to help students complete their assignments from the regular classroom.
2. The resource program is not a study hall where students independently work on regular classroom assignments or homework.
3. The resource program is not a dumping ground for students who are annoyances in the regular classroom and, in general, make life unpleasant for the regular teacher.

The rest of this section will briefly review the various types of resource programs and the role of the resource teacher. Also covered is the effectiveness of this approach and some of its advantages and disadvantages.

Types of Resource Programs

There are at least six different types of resource programs that serve behaviorally disordered students: the categorical, the multicategorical, the noncategorical, the itinerant, the helping/crisis teacher, and the resource/consulting teacher models.

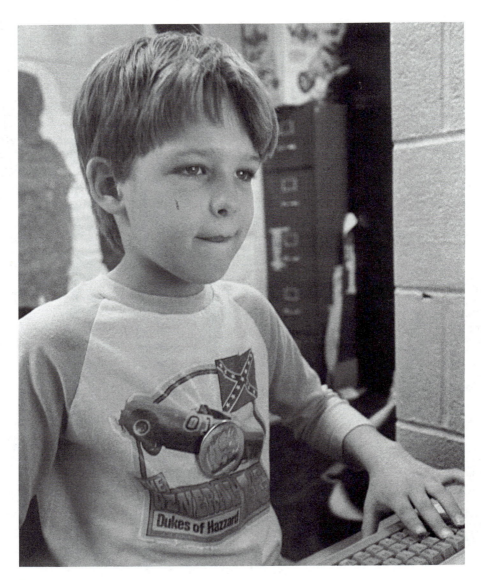

The basic purpose of the resource program is to provide supportive instructional services.

Categorical Resource Program

In this program, students are served according to their identified handicapping condition (i.e., mentally retarded, learning disabled, behaviorally disordered). An assumption is that the educational needs of students are similar because of their common handicapping condition. A disadvantage relates to teacher certification requirements; school districts must establish separate resource programs for each major area of handicap (e.g., a resource program for behaviorally disordered students, another program for learning disabled students, and yet another one for mentally retarded students).

Multicategorical Resource Program

In this approach, two or more handicapping conditions are served in the same program but at different times. For example, only behaviorally disordered students are scheduled during the first hour of the day, learning disabled students during the second, mentally retarded students during the third hour, and so on (a heterogeneous program serves ostensibly homogeneous groups of students). Another type of multicategorical model would be to teach at one time a mix of students who have been grouped according to instructional needs (Weiderholt et al., 1986). This model can be used where the district cannot support a categorical program. Problems may arise, however, in finding teachers certified to teach students with more than one handicapping condition.

Noncategorical Resource Programs

Students receiving services in a noncategorical program may or may not be classified as handicapped. That is, the noncategorical resource program may serve some students who have been officially classified as handicapped and some students who have not. Favored by regular and special educators alike (Gickling, Murphy, & Malloy, 1979), with this model students who need support services for learning or behavior problems may receive help based on their educational needs regardless of their classifications. However, this type of program cannot rely strictly on state categorical special education funds, because many of the students served are not classified as handicapped.

The Itinerant Resource Program

The itinerant resource program is mobile. That is, the resource teacher travels to more than one school, carrying necessary supplies and materials. An itinerant resource program may be any one of the previous three types. This model is appropriate in districts where there are too few handicapped students in each school to warrant individual programs. The disadvantages here are numerous, including a significant amount of time lost in traveling, difficulty of transporting materials, lack of adequate facilities at schools where services are provided, scheduling difficulties, difficulty in forming relationships with other school personnel who are at the same school every day, and less frequent instructional sessions for students (Cohen, 1982).

Helping Teacher/Crisis Teacher Program

Another model for delivering services to behaviorally disordered students was designed and implemented in the late 1960s in Michigan. Originally conceptualized by William Morse, the crisis teacher, or helping teacher as it later came to be called, was a teacher whose assignment was to work with behaviorally disordered students by responding when they were "in crisis" and also helping with both academic and emotional problems for all children (Morse, 1976). The underlying intent of this model was to make available a "therapeutic alternative" for students whose behavior had deteriorated to the point where they could no longer be taught in the regular classroom. Sometimes the helping teacher managed crises by providing a cooling-off period. At other times, the helping teacher conducted life-space interviews with students. The helping teacher also saw students regularly for academic or behavioral instruction. While the helping teacher model, per se, is not frequently employed in schools today, many of its general purposes are directly applicable to the resource room program model as it is currently known.

The Resource/Consulting Teacher Model

This model combines the resource room program model with the consulting teacher model (Idol, Paolucci-Whitcomb, & Nevin, 1986) of special education service delivery. The resource/consulting teacher provides direct and indirect services to handicapped students. Direct services are provided in traditional resource room settings, and indirect services are provided by working with regular teachers in areas such as performance assessment, behavior management, and academic programming. The resource/consulting teacher model is an emerging promising practice in special education today and has much to offer in meeting the educational needs of behaviorally disordered students. The last section of this chapter will be devoted to a more in-depth discussion of the role and function of the resource/consulting teacher for these students.

The Resource Teacher's Role

Harris and Schutz (1986) provided the following comprehensive description of the many functions of the resource teacher:

1. Establish, monitor, and coordinate screening and referral processes to ensure all handicapped children within a school or school district are identified.
2. Establish, monitor, and coordinate procedures to ensure due process regulations related to special education are fully implemented.
3. Evaluate, acquire, administer, and interpret a variety of assessment instruments and strategies.
4. Develop individual educational plans and monitor their evaluation.
5. Provide direct instruction to individual students and small groups related to academic deficits.
6. Provide direct instruction to individual students and small groups related to needed social skills.

7. Consult with classroom teachers regarding academic and behavioral problems of students in their classrooms.
8. Consult with parents regarding their child's programs, progress, and ways they might assist the school, or the school might assist them.
9. Maintain working relationships with related community schools, services, and agencies that may have relevance to the needs of handicapped students or their families.
10. Acquire a full knowledge of other supportive and potentially supportive programs in the school or school district and use such services as needed.
11. Design and coordinate or provide in-service training for the educational needs of handicapped students. (pp. 12–13)

As can be seen, the resource teacher has many important roles to fill. The resource teacher is expected to help identify, assess, and place eligible handicapped students. The resource teacher also provides direct instruction in academic and behavioral skills. The consultative role, mentioned above, may include inservice training of regular classroom teachers.

However, role conflict may be a serious problem for resource teachers (D'Alonzo & Wiseman, 1978). Resource teachers may think that what they are actually doing is not what they should be doing. One survey of resource teachers indicated that their biggest concerns were (a) unclear role descriptions, (b) lack of time to consult and work with regular classroom teachers, and (c) diverse and sometimes inappropriate expectations by regular classroom teachers and administrators for resource teachers (McLoughlin & Kelly, 1982).

The Effectiveness of Resource Programs

Relatively few well-controlled experimental studies have evaluated the effectiveness of resource programs since this model became common. In a review of 17 studies conducted in the late 1960s and early 1970s, Sindelar and Deno (1978) compared the effectiveness of resource programs and full-time regular classroom placement. Because of methodological shortcomings in the studies, they were unable to arrive at definitive conclusions. In general, however, the results of the more carefully designed experiments suggested that resource room programs were more effective than regular classrooms in increasing academic achievement of behaviorally disordered[1] and learning disabled students. The effects on social/emotional behaviors were not established.

Why, then, in the absence of conclusive data, have resource programs flourished over the last 15 years? First, public policy is not always

[1]The studies analyzed in this review that included only behaviorally disordered students as subjects included Glavin, Quay, Annesley, and Werry (1971), Quay, Glavin, Annesley, and Werry (1972), and Glavin (1973; 1974).

shaped or determined by empirical evidence. That is, a program does not always have to be clearly effective or the best alternative available to be widely adopted. The available evidence suggests that handicapped students do at least as well in resource programs as they do in regular classrooms. When combined with the fact that segregated, self-contained settings are highly restrictive and that regular classroom programs may not be prepared to effectively accommodate the needs of behaviorally disordered students, resource rooms seem to be a "logical" choice for service delivery. However, in view of the resource program's apparent current popularity, there still remains a pressing need for carefully designed studies documenting its effectiveness.

Advantages and Disadvantages of Resource Programs

Despite a lack of empirical data conclusively demonstrating effectiveness, resource programs have several attractive features. Weiderholt and his colleagues (1986) have summarized some of the more salient advantages:

- Students benefit from special education while remaining in the mainstream much of the school day.
- More students can be helped by a resource program than by a self-contained classroom.
- The resource teacher can serve as an information clearinghouse and expert consultant to the entire school staff, as well as to parents.
- Severe learning and behavior problems may be prevented through early intervention in resource programs.
- With more mildly and moderately handicapped children served by resource programs, self-contained classes can be reserved for students with severe learning and behavior problems.
- Resource teachers can be advocates for their students with regular teachers and building administrators.
- Most handicapped students can be served in neighborhood schools.

The resource program model is not without its faults, however. In addition to the weaknesses of the different types of programs already discussed, there are several other important potential disadvantages:

- Inappropriate programming for behaviorally disordered students is frequent. This happens when the resource teacher focuses exclusively on academic problems while ignoring the behavioral or social problems the students have in the regular classroom.

- Lack of coordination with regular classroom teachers can diminish the overall effectiveness of resource programs. Unfortunately, some resource room teachers fail to establish close working relationships with regular teachers as a fundamental aspect of their roles. This problem may be attributed to the background and orientation of the resource teacher. Administrative inertia and the attitudes and skills of regular teachers can also significantly contribute.
- Assigning behaviorally disordered students to resource programs for most of the school day is an inappropriate circumvention of the intent of the model. When students are "mainstreamed" only for lunch, recess, and physical education, the resource program essentially becomes a self-contained classroom.
- Too many students may be placed in a resource program with one teacher. The maximum number of students served by one resource teacher is usually specified by state rules and regulations (e.g., Utah allows 35 students to be served by one resource teacher). The recommended number of students is approximately 20 (Gickling et al., 1979; Reger, 1973; Weiderholt et al., 1986). Resource teachers are often tempted to accept more than the allowable number of students into their programs. While those who exceed the limit may think that a student and, perhaps, the student's teacher are being helped, no one is truly being helped because there is much to do with each student and only a finite amount of time in which to do it.

It has been said that "the resource room is not the solution for all the ills of special education" (Hallahan & Kauffman, 1986, p. 125). Until something better comes along, however, it appears as if it has staying power (Friend & McNutt, 1984). Strategies to overcome the disadvantages of resource programs need to be developed and evaluated. How to maximize the advantages and minimize the disadvantages in ways that benefit behaviorally disordered students will be addressed in the remainder of this chapter.

MODEL RESOURCE PROGRAMS FOR BEHAVIORALLY DISORDERED STUDENTS

An effective resource program remediates students' academic and social deficits that interfere with successful adjustment in the regular classroom. Two model programs that have successfully served behaviorally disordered students are briefly reviewed below.

Resource Homeroom for Students with Behavior and Learning Problems

A homeroom-type setting has been used to serve elementary-aged students with behavior and learning problems who required support services for more than the typical one or two resource periods a day (Demers, 1981). Students were referred for behaviors such as shouting, screaming, spitting at teachers, hitting and kicking peers, stealing, damaging property, being out-of-seat, and throwing tantrums. The students required careful, day-long monitoring by either the resource teacher or her aide. At first students left their special homeroom only for art, P.E., and music, but as their skills improved to the level of the regular teachers' middle groupings for academic content areas, students went to the regular class for those areas.

In the special homeroom, rules were defined and consequences explained. A token reinforcement system was established in which students were expected to earn at least 100 points per day. Points were earned by meeting expectations in the homeroom and regular class. Regular class teachers helped set point values and criteria to be met in their classrooms. Prelabeled point slips for classes students attended each day were given to the teachers. At the end of each class period, teachers circled the number of points the students had earned according to the criteria; pertinent comments were also added. After each class, students returned their point slips to the homeroom aide, who recorded the number of points earned and provided immediate feedback and reinforcement. Whenever the number of points earned or the regular teacher's comments indicated problems, the aide immediately notified the homeroom teacher, who intervened to prevent further deterioration in student performance.

Lunch and recess were also awarded point values and monitored carefully. Certain behaviors (e.g., fighting, swearing, being disrespectful, being late to class, skipping class) resulted in a loss of points earned that day. Especially positive behaviors (e.g., kind deeds, very neat papers, being on time for class) could earn extra points.

At the beginning and end of each day, all students were scheduled into the homeroom for discussion, sharing, and pep talks. Students were also asked to evaluate their own and other students' school day before leaving for home. Students who earned at least 100 points and received a good evaluation for the day received a small treat or sticker; those who met criteria all week also received a special "Friday Treat." Extra points over 100 could be spent for free-time activities in the homeroom. Additional motivators such as lunch with the teacher at a fast-food restaurant could also be earned for helpful, kind behavior.

Using this system, the students' disruptive behavior in their regular classes decreased in frequency by 80%. Task completion rose from 38%

during baseline to 98% during the first quarter. Clearly, the homeroom resource program with continuous day-long monitoring has potential for serving students with similar instructional needs.

Santa Monica Resource Specialist Program

The student as a learner and readiness for academic skills and regular classroom functioning are emphasized in Santa Monica's Resource Specialist Program (Hewett & Taylor, 1980). Hewett and Forness (1977) first described readiness in terms of four basic abilities needed for successful regular class functioning in the Madison School Plan. The basic abilities taught by the resource specialist are:

1. Paying attention, following directions, following classroom rules, and participating
2. Academic abilities, including neatness, correctness, and subject matter
3. Functioning in different instructional situations in the regular classroom (e.g., working independently, in small groups, when the teacher is giving directions to the class)
4. Responding to regular classroom consequences (e.g., grades, social reinforcement, intrinsic satisfaction)

The student spends a maximum of a half-day in the resource program, which uses a checkmark system whereby the student may exchange a completed "recognition" card for 15 minutes of free time or other reinforcers. Occasionally, edibles are used as reinforcers if they appear to be necessary. A student can earn a maximum of five checkmarks at a time for academic performance and classroom behavior. Checkmarks are awarded every 15 to 20 minutes, with the resource specialist providing meaningful feedback on academic performance and behavior as they are awarded.

This program appears to have the requisite components for improving behavior and academic work in the resource room. The resource room approximates the regular classroom in expectations, instructional materials, and instructional situations. While this approach does help students acquire the skills they need in regular classrooms, research suggests that specific programming of those abilities in the regular classroom is still likely to be needed.

These two examples of resource programs for behaviorally disordered students are representative rather than exhaustive. In considering model programs, a teacher may choose to adopt an entire program or adapt components from several to meet the needs of the students and the local service patterns. Examining published literature is also helpful and effective in dealing with special circumstances, unforeseen problems, and fine-tuning resource room programs.

CURRICULUM AND INSTRUCTION IN THE RESOURCE PROGRAM

The overriding purpose of the resource program is to support the instructional program the student receives in the regular classroom. This purpose is fulfilled by providing assistance in specific academic and behavioral areas (e.g., reading, math, social skills) above and beyond the regular program.

The ultimate goal of the resource program is successful full-time integration of handicapped students in the regular classroom. To achieve this goal, the curriculum and instruction offered must focus on teaching critical academic and behavioral skills. Thus, social skills and peer relations, classroom survival skills and independent work habits, and academic skills form the foundation of the curriculum and instruction used with behaviorally disordered students in the resource room.

Of course, this purpose and goals represent an ideal that is not always realized. Instead of supporting the regular classroom program, the resource program's curriculum and instructional program often actually supplant the regular classroom's curriculum and instructional program (Coleman, 1986). That is, a student may receive all of his or her reading instruction, for example, in the resource room instead of the regular classroom.

The question of whether to supplement or to supplant the regular program is one of the more difficult issues addressed by resource teachers. There are no firm guidelines, nor is there any hard evidence clearly pointing to preferred strategies. We recommend that the curriculum and instructional methods used in the resource program should supplement those used in the regular classroom. This does not mean, however, that the resource teacher is essentially a "super tutor," helping the student complete work assigned but not completed in the regular class. Nor should the resource teacher be expected to teach concepts or skills that should have been taught in the regular classroom but were not because of the student's poor academic survival skills or other inappropriate behaviors or because of the regular teacher's inability to spend extra time with the student.

Other approaches that are more comprehensive and effective than tutoring are available in resource programs. One promising approach is to design and implement effective instructional programs in as many curriculum areas as needed in both the regular classroom and the resource program itself. If at all possible, the student should receive as much of the regular curriculum as possible within the regular class. If there are performance problems, the resource teacher can modify the regular instructional program in several ways (Weiderholt et al., 1986). First, if the problem is related to classroom behavior ("won't do" as opposed to "can't do"), the resource teacher can develop and implement a behavior management system to increase appropriate behaviors. In other cases, the teacher may need to modify selected elements of the instructional program, such as additional practice activities or special instructions. In still other cases, the resource teacher may adapt certain tasks related to the area of instruction, for example, homework or independent seatwork activities. Successful extensions of the resource program into the regular classroom obviously require close communication and coordination between the resource teacher and the regular classroom teacher. The last section of this chapter addresses these issues in more detail.

Regardless of the success or failure of the curriculum and instructional modifications implemented in the regular classroom, the resource instructional program should emphasize direct teaching of those critical academic and social/behavioral skills the students need to improve their chances for successful adjustment. Careful attention must be paid to allocating sufficient time for instruction in the resource program, using direct instructional tactics, and making sure that students are learning while they are in the resource program.

Sadly, this may not always be the case. In a study investigating differences in allocated time and engaged time in regular and resource classrooms (Thurlow, Ysseldyke, Graden, & Algozzine, 1983), eight learning disabled students were observed to determine how they spent their time. There were more opportunities for meaningful instruction available in the resource program (i.e., more time was allocated for instruction). However, there were no significant differences in engaged time. In fact, the overall amount of engaged time in both settings was very low. We mention this study as a reminder that special education programs ought not to be called *special* unless and until quality instructional programming is intentionally and consistently implemented. As Vallecorsa, Zigmond, and Henderson (1985) said, "Time is a limited resource in special education classrooms . . . it is essential that students spend their time working on the 'right things' " (p. 23).

The remaining section of this chapter will provide a brief overview of the two areas of primary concern in resource programs: (a) the academic curriculum and associated instructional procedures and (b) classroom behaviors and social skills curriculum and associated instructional procedures.

Academic Curriculum

An often-troubling area of concern to resource teachers of behaviorally disordered students is the academic curriculum. What should these students be taught? How should they be taught? A resource teacher's background and experience may not have adequately prepared him or her to effectively teach academic skills. That is, the teacher's preservice training program may have emphasized managing disruptive behavior and de-emphasized teaching academic skills. And the converse may also be true; i.e., training may have emphasized teaching academic skills and de-emphasized behavior management skills, social skills training, and techniques for modifying disruptive behaviors. Obviously neither extreme is appropriate. Resource programs that emphasize behavior and social skills and ignore academic skills or programs that emphasize academic skills and ignore social skills and classroom behaviors are not at all adequate.

The organization, management, and actual implementation of the resource room academic program should follow principles and recommendations discussed in chapter 5. Selecting appropriate instructional materials requires careful consideration; materials must be compatible with those used in the regular classroom, though they can be different. There are several excellent programs designed for this purpose (see chapter 5). Another approach would be to select a program that can be used as a supplement to the regular class program. For an expanded discussion of the academic instructional program in the resource program, see *The Special Education Resource Program: Rationale and Implementation* (Harris & Schutz, 1986).

Classroom Behavior and Social Skills Curriculum

Most behaviorally disordered students are initially referred to special education because of behavioral excesses and deficits in classroom behavior and social skills. Assuming the reason for referral was valid, the student should be exposed to a curriculum and corresponding instructional methods developed with these kinds of targets in mind. As we have seen, a key determinant of overall success and adaptation in the regular classroom is appropriate classroom behavior and social skills (Cartledge & Milburn, 1978; Greenwood, Hops, & Walker, 1977).

The basic approach here is similar to the approach recommended for the academic curriculum. That is, the resource program should be a support system for the regular classroom teacher, with interventions to modify the existing program and improve the student's performance in the regular classroom. In addition, the student's specific behavioral or social deficits and excesses should be directly addressed within the resource room itself.

Classroom Behavior
Being off-task, failing to complete tasks, being out of seat, and not complying with teacher directions are likely to be significant problems of behaviorally disordered students in regular classrooms. Consequently,

these behaviors—classroom survival skills—should be key target behaviors. Some students who frequently misbehave in regular classrooms may behave more appropriately in the resource program because of the lower teacher-student ratio and the concomitant increase in teacher proximity and supervision. However, a very structured behavior management program is still needed in the resource program. This program should have, as a minimum, the following features:

1. Class rules governing student conduct while in the resource program
2. A group behavior management program and contingencies
3. Individual behavior management programs and contingencies
4. An individual behavior management program that extends into the regular classroom

Many of the techniques and procedures discussed in the chapters on behavior management and self-contained classrooms can be implemented in the resource program. Specific procedures that extend the impact of the resource program's classroom behavior curriculum to the regular classroom are discussed under "Promoting Generalization."

Social Skills

Social skills curricula and instructional methods were reviewed in detail in chapter 6. To implement social skills training in the resource program, the teacher must make several decisions.

1. *What skills and behaviors will be targeted?* The teacher must assess the students' individual characteristics and needs before choosing the target behaviors. Fortunately, there are a number of social skills curricula and training programs available from which to choose. The target behaviors will be determined by the particular training program(s). Thus, all students receiving social skills training may be taught the same skills as a group, with special emphasis given to the unique needs of individual students.
2. *Who should be included in social skills training?* All students directly served in the resource program should receive social skills training. If the program is multicategorical and serves learning disabled or mentally retarded students along with behaviorally disordered students, they should be involved in social skills training as well. As discussed in chapter 6, most handicapped students, as well as many nonhandicapped students, display social skills deficits and could profit from systematic training.
3. *How often should social skills training occur?* To be useful and effective, social skills training should be scheduled at least

EXHIBIT 8.1   Skills taught in the transition curriculum

Skill	When Taught 5th Grade	6th Grade
Academic Skills		
1. Reading for the purpose of content comprehension (Deemphasis on decoding)		
1.1 Paraphrasing/Summarizing		
1.1.1 Oral paraphrasing	x	
1.1.2 Written paraphrasing/Taking notes from text	x	
1.2 Text analysis		x
Self-Management/Study Skills		
2. Listening		
2.1 Following oral directions	x	
2.2 Notetaking from lectures		x
3. Self-Management		
3.1 Planning Work Time		
3.1.1 Planning time use at school	x	
3.1.2 Planning study time at home	x	x
3.1.3 Organization of materials		x
3.2 Record-Keeping Techniques		
3.2.1 Assignment record keeping	x	
3.2.2 Assignment completion	x	
3.2.3 Self-evaluation of assignments before submission		x
4. Test Taking		
4.1 Test preparation		x
4.2 Test taking		x
Social/Adaptive Behavior		
5. Interactive Learning		
5.1 Appropriate questioning	x	
5.2 Interpreting feedback	x	
5.3 Group discussion skills		x
General Orientation to Junior High School Setting		x

Source: From "Preparing Dysfunctional Learners to Enter Junior High School: A Transitional Curriculum" by S. M. Robinson, C. T. Braxdale, and S. E. Colson, 1985, *Focus on Exceptional Children, 18*(4), 5. Used with permission.

three times a week for at least 20 to 30 minutes per session. These minimum requirements should not pose major scheduling problems. For example, if six students are scheduled to spend an hour a day in the resource program, approximately 30 to 40 minutes of that time could be designated for academic instruction; the remaining time could be reserved for social skills training. Conceivably, there may be another group of students who are scheduled into the resource room for 30 minutes every day for social skills training only.

It is also extremely important to remember that social skills training will not be effective without systematic training for generalization of those skills to nontraining settings. Chapter 4 explained these procedures in detail. "Promoting Generalization" will briefly review selected procedures for generalizing academic and social/behavioral improvements from the resource setting to the regular classroom.

A Transitional Curriculum

A recent development for resource programs is the "transitional curriculum," designed to bridge the gap between elementary school and middle or junior high school for many handicapped students (Robinson, Braxdale, & Colson, 1985). The underlying rationale is based on the nature and number of changes elementary students face when they enter middle/junior high school — bigger schools, more teachers, more classmates, unfamiliar instructional formats, different expectations. The transitional curriculum prepares students for these changes and facilitates successful adjustment and achievement.

The transitional curriculum offers training in compensatory skills and learning strategies (i.e., learning how to learn). The curriculum is organized in four separate but related areas: academic skills, self-management and study skills, social skills and adaptive behavior, and general orientation to junior high school. Exhibit 8.1 describes in more detail the targeted skills. The program is typically implemented during the last 2 years of elementary school.

The resource room is the logical setting for implementing the transitional curriculum. The instructional methods used were developed by Deshler and his colleagues at the University of Kansas Institute for Research on Learning Disabilities (Deshler, Alley, Warner, & Schumaker, 1981). These methods are very similar to the basic effective instructional practices discussed throughout this text.

SPECIAL CONSIDERATIONS FOR RESOURCE PROGRAM TEACHERS

There are a number of nuts-and-bolts issues that resource teachers must address. Chief among those is the issue of scheduling. Use of classroom aides and the physical design of the classroom are two other important issues.

Scheduling

Resource teachers often complain that heavy caseloads and lack of time are their greatest barriers to effective programming. If a resource teacher has responsibility for 35 pupils (not an uncommon caseload) and sees each pupil for an average of two subject areas per day (some students will require only one period, others as many as three or four), teachers who teach all day are actually responsible for teaching 70 students daily! This is equivalent to about 12 students per resource period.

Scheduling a heavy caseload requires a great deal of creativity and organization. However, other aspects of the resource teacher's role must also be considered before students are scheduled. For example, what other functions happen during the day? Testing students, consulting with parents and other school personnel, observing current pupils and new referrals in other classrooms and settings, recording student performance, filling out required forms, and completing other paperwork are but a few of the tasks requiring regularly scheduled time.

Most teachers find it necessary to schedule one or more class periods every day to complete all of these tasks. The time of day during which these activities are scheduled (i.e., end of day, consecutive, one in the morning and one in the afternoon) will depend on the nature of the tasks, availability of students, and the time required. The time allotted must be weighed against needed instructional time, considering the way in which students will be grouped and scheduled for services.

Occasionally the resource teacher will have very little influence on how students are scheduled. In some secondary schools, particularly, students may be scheduled by the main office (possibly by computer) so that they have the most "convenient" overall schedule. In these cases, the resource teacher may have a very heterogeneous group of students each class period with few common instructional needs. In some cases, larger schools with several resource teachers deal with this difficult situation by having each resource teacher teach only one or two subjects. The resource teachers pool all the students assigned to them for each period and reassign students on the basis of more homogeneous educational needs. Thus, several resource subjects can be taught each hour, as needed.

The resource teacher is at a distinct disadvantage if he or she does not have the cooperation of the school principal and regular teachers in scheduling students. It is often necessary to schedule students by hand, giving resource time a higher priority than other scheduling needs. Grouping students effectively is extremely important if they are to gain from their time in the resource program.

The most common method of scheduling elementary-school students is by current level of performance in core subjects. Thus, students of different grade levels and with different handicapping conditions may be scheduled for instruction together if their instructional needs in a particular subject, such as reading, are similar.

In addition to assessing the academic skills that will be taught, the teacher must assess classroom behavior and social skills of behaviorally disordered students. Data on these behaviors can be analyzed so that students with similar behavioral needs can also be grouped for instruction in these areas. When feasible, students with similar behavior needs can be scheduled together for social and behavior instruction only; they can be included in academic skill groups if classroom behavior skills can be integrated with academic instruction. Another option is to use a resource period for training in specific classroom behavior and social skills and to continue to emphasize and reinforce newly trained skills in academic periods in the regular class. In this way, generalization of newly acquired behavioral skills is also encouraged.

Most resource teachers today teach six or seven class periods per day. The basic schedule outlined by Hawisher (1975) seems workable for many classrooms:

8:00– 9:00	Pre-School Planning
9:00– 9:45	Group A
9:30–10:15	Group B
10:00–10:45	Group C
10:30–11:45	Planning Time
11:45–12:30	Lunch
12:30– 1:15	Group E
1:15– 2:00	Group F
2:00– 2:45	Group G
2:15– 3:10	Post-School Planning (p. 39)

This schedule permits planning, consulting, or assessment at three different times during the day, for a total of almost 3 hours daily. Seven different instructional groups are scheduled for 45 minutes each, which is adequate for most subjects.

Even though a resource teacher may try to establish a schedule that takes all of the demands for time into account, it is unlikely the perfect schedule will ever be created. By experimenting and adjusting as needed, however, teachers can usually draw up a workable schedule. Of course, once a schedule is workable, chances are that the expectations and constraints under which the teacher works will change, necessitating additional schedule adjustments.

Recruiting and Using Classroom Aides

Obviously, the resource teacher's capabilities increase as the amount of instructional assistance increases. In some cases, school districts provide a full- or part-time instructional or clerical aide. But most resource teachers are on their own unless they team teach with other resource teachers or recruit their own aides.

For the teacher willing to put in the time and effort to recruit aides, the benefits can be great. An excellent source of aides is the local PTA. Members live in the neighborhood for easy access, have children in the same school, and may be sufficiently interested in the overall well-being of the school to volunteer regularly. These aides can be trained to collect observational data, tutor individuals or small groups of students, and provide clerical assistance. In one instance a resource teacher found a PTA volunteer data collector willing to work regularly. The PTA volunteer was so enthusiastic about her job and the importance of the special education services being provided that she began recruiting her friends to help. The group organized themselves to provide regular assistance, even finding their own substitutes when needed.

The aides also served an excellent public relations role with the rest of the school (including their own children) and the neighborhood. Two of the volunteers were also regular playground supervisors. During their time as special education aides, their attitudes toward behaviorally disordered students changed drastically. These supervisors became advocates for these students on the playground, cooperating with teacher management strategies and providing follow-up assistance with regular classroom mainstreaming efforts.

Similarly, local universities and colleges may be able to provide psychology, regular education, and special education students to assist the resource teacher. Active recruiting by resource teachers can often help here, too, in establishing ties with preprofessional programs. Most preservice teachers are required to spend time in classrooms as part of their training. Because course grades may be tied to performance in the schools, preservice teachers are generally reliable and responsible aides. Senior citizens are another sometimes-overlooked source of classroom assistance. Foster grandparents have served in many useful capacities in school programs.

As described in chapter 7, peers can also be helpful. Same-age peers who have already mastered material being taught can help their peers with drill and practice. Same-age peers from the regular classroom or peers assigned to the resource room can be equally helpful. Likewise, older students in the school may be selected to help younger students or serve as aides to the resource teacher.

Of course, for any aide program to be functional, the aides must be trained. Time initially invested here will yield benefits later. To use aides as data collectors, for example, the teacher must train them initially, make reliability checks, and provide ample opportunity for the aides to ask questions and discuss issues that have surfaced. Clerical assistants may need to be trained in specific filing procedures, paper grading policies, recording and monitoring strategies, and use of duplicating equipment. Tutors and instructional aides require even more training to learn the proper use of the curriculum materials they will use, along with correction and feedback procedures and positive reinforcement techniques. Meeting student needs more effectively and relieving some of the work of a heavy student caseload, however, seem to be good reasons to spend time recruiting and training paraprofessional help.

Physical Design of the Resource Room

The physical design of the resource room will depend upon the size, shape, location, and limitations of the room itself as well as the budget available for furnishing it. Resource rooms may take almost any form. Examples include (a) a standard-size regular classroom, (b) a portable unit outside the main school building but on the school grounds, (c) a converted storage closet, (d) a room shared with another resource teacher, (e) the school stage, (f) the music room, with tiers for choral and musical groups, or (g) a room that happens to be empty during a given class period. One junior high resource teacher reported having to move from room to room six times daily, carrying her materials with her in a box as she traveled!

Few resource teachers, it seems, have the luxury of designing an ideal classroom; they often must make the best use of the assigned space. Furnishings, or the lack thereof, seem to be obtained similarly, by making use of what is available or can be collected over a period of years.

TOWARD A CONSULTATIVE ROLE FOR THE RESOURCE TEACHER

It should be clear by now that an effective resource program is very dependent on a close, mutually supportive alliance between the resource teacher and regular classroom teachers. Without such a partnership, the resource program runs the risk of becoming just a pull-out program. In this case it is not likely that students' gains will generalize or that they will eventually return to the regular classroom full-time. For this reason, the consultative role of the resource teacher has been discussed with increasing frequency in recent years as a key to successful mainstreaming (Idol et al., 1986).

Teacher consultation is the process whereby special education personnel (consulting teachers, resource teacher/consultants, resource teachers, school psychologists) collaborate with regular classroom teachers to plan, implement, and evaluate intervention programs designed to improve the academic, social, and behavioral functioning of handicapped students, including the behaviorally disordered (Idol et al., 1986). Consultation with regular classroom teachers has several distinctive characteristics: (a) the special education consulting teacher does not provide direct instructional service to students; (b) all individuals involved are assumed to have the expertise to collaborate and to share responsibility for designing and implementing effective instructional programs; (c) all individuals willingly participate in consultation activities; and (d) consultation is oriented toward problem solving; the primary goal is to resolve classroom learning problems (Idol, 1986).

Implemented correctly, special education consultation with regular education concerning behaviorally disordered students, as well as other mildly handicapped students, is an effective and preferred practice (Idol-Maestas & Ritter, 1985; Knight, Meyers, Paolucci-Whitcomb, Hasazi, & Nevin, 1981; Nelson & Stevens, 1981; Paolucci-Whitcomb & Nevin, 1985). Pointer 8.1 gives an example of the type of intervention consulting teachers can develop and implement in the regular classroom.

Yet the evidence suggests that only a few resource teachers are prepared and willing to serve as consultants. It is also clear that resource teachers do not spend much of their time—perhaps 5%—consulting with regular classroom teachers (Evans, 1980; Sargent, 1981; Speece & Mandell, 1980). Whether this is because they have been inadequately trained (Idol-Maestas & Ritter, 1985) or because administrators do not provide enough time to consult (Aloia, 1983), there is a strong basis for concluding that close, collaborative working relationships between regular teachers and special education resource teachers simply do not exist (Speece & Mandell, 1980).

A number of models have been proposed (Deno & Mirkin, 1977; Idol-Maestas, 1983; Jenkins & Mayhall, 1976) to bridge the gap between the resource program and the regular classroom. In these models, the resource teacher provides direct instructional services to students in the resource program; indirect services (i.e., consultation) are provided within the regular classroom. The important difference between this model and the traditional model of the pull-out resource teacher is that indirect services are clearly specified and sufficient time is set aside for consultation. We strongly recommend that no less than 25% of the resource teacher's time be allocated to consultation; 40 to 50% would be preferable. According to a recent report by the National Task Force on School Consultation (Idol, 1986), a 50/50 split between direct and indirect service would translate into approximately 10 students being served via direct services and approximately 18 students through indirect services, for a total "caseload" of 28 students. A full-time (100%) consultant would be expected to carry a caseload of around 40 students.

The indirect services provided by the resource teacher involve planning, developing, implementing, managing, and monitoring intervention programs to improve the learning and behavior of behaviorally dis-

Pointer 8.1

SOME PRACTICAL ADVICE ON BEING A CONSULTANT

A lot of special educators are frustrated doctors. We like to be able to give advice, prescribe procedures. It makes us feel good to be "experts," to know The Answer. We tend to use impressive terms like *hyperkinesis, dyspraxia,* and *strephosymbolia* not for what they communicate about the student, but for what they communicate about ourselves: that we are, in fact, a special breed of teacher. . . .

We often feel that we are the only ones who really understand the nature and needs of the exceptional child (after all we took a course with just that title!). We see the regular teacher as unacceptable for "our" special kids. While these feelings are all too justified, they are rarely very productive. By thinking of yourself as the only hope for the special child you are building a barrier between your program and the rest of the school. Furthermore, by helping regular teachers abdicate their responsibility you are keeping them from growing, from expanding their capabilities in needed directions. . . .

You are neither the expert who is going to tell Mrs. Smith what to do, nor her aide, helping her by doing her job for her. You need to foster a cooperative relationship with the regular teacher, where you can function as two equals, each bringing your unique skills and perspective to the situation. . . .

The first rule for consultants is to *listen.* It seems like a simple notion, but it usually makes the difference between an effective and an ineffective helper. Being a good listener is not just polite, it's smart. By giving Mrs. Smith a chance to talk freely about the problem you are doing two positive things: helping her relieve her anxiety about the situation, thereby making her more receptive to your ideas, and gathering valuable information — her view of the problem.

Be on alert for attempts to get you to do things for the convenience of the system, rather than for the benefit of the children. Don't let Mrs. Smith tell you that she will not teach Johnny because she doesn't have time. (You'll hear this one at least twice a day!) Help her to find time, to realize that it is her responsibility to teach Johnny unless she has a contract that allows her to teach only the kids she wants to, and to see that by expanding her skills now, she will do a better job with her whole class, and with other "problem learners" that she might have in coming years.

Source: From "The Special Educator as Consultant: Some Strategies" by M. D. Montgomery, 1978, *Teaching Exceptional Children, 10,* pp. 110–112. Used with permission.

ordered students in the regular classroom. When working with regular teachers, the consultant should follow these operational guidelines to ensure optimal results (Idol-Maestas, 1983):

- Establish a referral system for use by regular classroom teachers to request assistance from the resource teacher.
- Pinpoint, define, and prioritize the problem behaviors (academic or social) in a meeting between the resource teacher and the regular classroom teacher.
- Design a system to collect preliminary data on the problem behaviors for use by the regular classroom teacher.
- Have the regular classroom teacher collect baseline data on the problem behaviors, with the resource teacher serving in a supportive role.
- Assess academic skills using curriculum-based assessment procedures.
- Hold a meeting to discuss the assessment results and baseline data and to plan an intervention strategy.
- Demonstrate and practice the intervention strategy with the regular classroom teacher prior to actual implementation with the student.
- Continue to collect data every day on the targeted behaviors.
- Graph the data and make decisions about modifications in the program based on results.

These guidelines describe a process for resource teacher and regular classroom teacher collaboration. They do not necessarily prescribe the specific instructional strategies, materials, or formats for intervention. These strategies will vary according to the needs of the students and the background and orientation of the teachers. However, principles of effective instruction and behavior management should be an integral component of the specific intervention designed for each student.

To be effective, resource teachers must recognize that regular classroom teachers are more likely to go along with a plan if they feel they have been meaningfully involved in developing it. Special education teacher consultants should work with regular teachers to define and assess the problem, set goals and objectives for the student, and discuss and select alternative intervention plans for meeting the program's objectives. Exhibit 8.2 outlines a generic model of the process of consultation with regular classroom teachers. Consultants should make a concerted attempt to have regular teachers generate alternative solutions by continually prompting them to consider potential outcomes of proposed solutions. This kind of problem-solving approach to consultation with regular classroom teachers may take more time than the "I'm the expert, here's the answer" approach, referred to as the doctor–patient model of con-

EXHIBIT 8.2   The process of consultation with regular classroom teachers

---

CONSULTING STEPS

Step 1:   Referral procedure

Step 2:   Consulting/regular teacher meeting(s) for baseline diagnosis procedures

Step 3:   Consulting/regular teacher meeting(s) to establish eligibility

Step 4:   Parent meeting for written permission

Step 5:   Consulting teacher classroom observations

Step 6:   Decision-making process for intervention procedures

Step 7:   Parent information meeting for intervention procedures

Step 8:   Implementation of intervention procedures

Step 9:   Evaluation of intervention procedures

Step 10:   Follow-through or confirmation

Source: From "Preparing Consulting Teachers Through a Collaborative Approach Between University Faculty and Field-Based Consulting Teachers" by P. Paolucci-Whitcomb and A. Nevin, 1985, *Teacher Education and Special Education, 8*, p. 135. Reprinted with permission from the Teacher Education Division of the Council for Exceptional Children and Special Press.

sultation (Neel, 1981), but it is more likely to produce the desired effect— improved school performance and adjustment by behaviorally disordered students.

The competencies consulting teachers require relate to the classroom learning problems for which their assistance is most often requested — academic and behavioral assessment, individual and group behavior management systems, academic learning problems, materials selection and adaptation, social skills problems, generalization and transfer strategies, and monitoring student performance. In addition, consulting teachers must also be skilled in collaborative consultation and problem solving with regular classroom teachers, other professionals, and parents.

Successful consultation requires adequate time and other resources. While some districts include consultation in the resource teacher's role description, others encourage special educators to serve as a resource to regular teachers but do not provide backup support or time to consult because the teacher's direct service caseload is too heavy. Obviously, if special educators are to be a resource to regular educators, they need to have time during the school day to observe in the regular classroom, to meet with regular teachers, and perhaps to actually demonstrate teaching procedures. It is unrealistic to expect special education teachers to serve as a resource only before or after school or on personal time.

Successful consultation also requires collaborative working relationships. Often, the success of the resource teacher's efforts will depend on interpersonal communication skills that facilitate collaborative problem solving (see Exhibit 8.3 and Pointer 8.2). The resource teacher will also need to develop public relations strategies. The attitudes of regular teachers and administrators and their expectations about the consultative role of the resource teacher can be significant impediments to effective and productive consulting. Idol-Maestas (1983) has offered the following suggestions for overcoming potential public relations problems:

- Ensure that the building principal offers strong support to the consultation model and positively communicates this to the teaching staff. Consultation should be communicated to teachers as a service that is available and one that the administration encourages them to use.
- Teacher consultants should not become involved in any type of teacher evaluation.
- Teacher consultants and/or other district personnel can offer inservice workshops that address such topics as the role of the consulting teacher, mainstreaming in the regular classroom, behavior management, construction of curriculum-based assessments.
- At the beginning of the year, teacher consultants should send memos to all staff members describing the available services.
- Teacher consultants can offer a brief presentation of consultation services at a faculty meeting at the beginning of the school year.
- Initially teacher consultants should emphasize the quality of consultation projects done rather than the quantity of contacts. The word will spread quickly if the consultant is doing a good job. It will spread quickly if the consultant's service is of poor quality.
- Results of successful consultation should be shared with the teaching staff. Teachers will be particularly interested in strategies that produce results. (p. 17)

In summary, we strongly recommend that the resource program be designed and implemented to maximize the consulting role of the resource teacher. The National Task Force on School Consultation identified a number of benefits of consultation as a special education service delivery option (Idol, 1986):

1. Provides for the efficient use of time and expertise of both regular and special education teachers because more students can be served
2. Intervention strategies learned by regular teachers can be applied to other nonhandicapped students as preventive measures
3. May reduce total number of referrals for special education services
4. Fosters greater understanding and closer working relationships among regular education and special education staff

EXHIBIT 8.3 Consultation communication skills

Do	Don't
. . . Remember that people are capable of solving their own problems.	. . . Tell a teacher you will help with a child without spelling out exactly what you think your responsibilities are.
. . . Try to accept others' values.	
. . . Be fully aware of your own values.	. . . Schedule yourself so tightly that you don't have time to meet with teachers for immediate consultation.
. . . Have a specific way that teachers can get your help.	
. . . Save time and help more teachers learn how to use your services; meet with a teacher team or department at meeting times.	. . . Act as if you have all the answers to solve a teacher's problem.
	. . . Become the "middle person" to take teacher's gripes to the principal.
. . . Have a wide variety of materials to help teachers.	. . . Push when the consultee is not ready to move.
. . . Let teachers know you value their knowledge.	
. . . Try to be involved in school activities.	. . . Let your need to help get in the way of the needs of the consultee.
	. . . Expect to see immediate results; you'll get discouraged.

Source: From *Data-Based Program Modification* by S. L. Deno and P. K. Mirkin, 1977, Reston, VA: Council for Exceptional Children, p. 215. Used with permission.

5. May serve as an effective means of inservice education
6. Increases the probability that behaviorally disordered students can be served in the least restrictive environment

PROMOTING GENERALIZATION FROM THE RESOURCE ROOM TO THE REGULAR CLASSROOM

The overall effectivenss of resource room programs can be measured by the extent to which academic and social/behavioral improvements generalize, or transfer, to the regular classroom and maintain over time. However, as was discussed in chapter 4, there is little evidence that gains in special education settings consistently transfer to regular classrooms. Procedures for promoting generalization are not usually used; they are often conspicuous by their absence (Wahler, Berland, & Coe, 1979; Wildman & Wildman, 1975).

Pointer 8.2

CONSULTATION IN THE REGULAR CLASSROOM

Target Behavior: Incomplete Assignments

A sixth grade teacher requested assistance with J., who did not complete his daily assignments. Sometimes J. completed partial assignments; thus the teacher believed that J. had the skills to complete assignments. Often J. would draw instead of completing work. He did not disturb others. The teacher had tried reminding him to get to work and withholding free time and library privileges.

Baseline

The percentages of daily assignments completed for spelling, reading, English, math, science, and social studies were recorded for 5 days. Only 3 subject assignments were completed, one each in spelling, reading, and social studies. The social studies lesson was an art project of drawing a map.

Design

A multiple-baseline design was used to monitor effects of contingencies upon targeted and nontargeted areas.

Condition A

The student and both teachers designed a contract stating that earned free time was contingent upon completion of spelling and reading assignments. Spelling and reading were subjects given priority by the teacher. The 30-minute reading period was divided into 5-minute segments. Using a kitchen timer, the classroom teacher checked on J. at five variable intervals. If he was working when the timer rang, the teacher would initial one box on a chart on J.'s desk. If he was not doing the assigned work, the teacher put a slash through the box and made no comment. Six points could be earned during spelling period.

Assignment completion was defined as (a) J. is working (eyes on paper, sitting at desk, proper book opened to correct page, and doing correct assignment) or (b) J. is talking to teacher regarding the assignment with appropriate questions. The teacher ignored him and put a slash in the box if any of these behaviors did not occur or if he was talking to other students.

The same procedure was used during a 40-minute reading period during which eight points could be earned. For both periods, when J. finished his work before the period ended, he could draw at his desk. After both periods had ended, J. brought a friend to the Resource/Consulting Teacher's (R/CT) room. They could play a chosen game for as many minutes as J. had earned points that day. Before starting the game, he reported to the R/CT the number of points earned and filled in the data on a chart. The R/CT spent a few minutes with J. discussing and congratulating him on his progress. Verifications were made between the chart in the regular classroom and the one in the R/CT's room. The R/CT made two reliability checks in the classroom. The two teachers had 100% agreement that J. was on task.

Criterion

J. was expected to complete 100% of the spelling and reading assignments.

Results

For spelling and reading, J. completed all of the assignments for every day of this phase. Assignment completion did not generalize to the remaining subject areas.

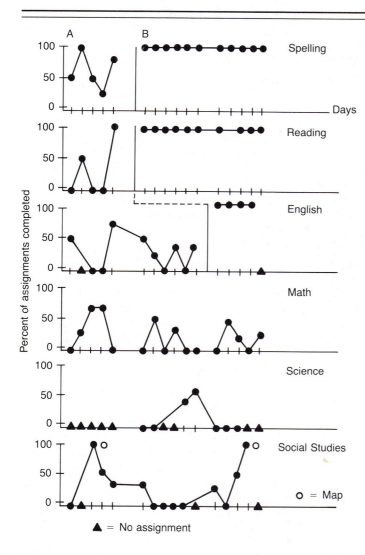

Completion of the regular classroom assignments with a multiple baseline measurement

○ = Map

▲ = No assignment

Condition B

Contingent teacher attention and free time were extended to English as well as spelling and reading.

Results

J. completed 100% of the English assignments, and spelling and reading assignments remained at 100%. Assignments were not completed in the other subject areas, with the exception of one day in social studies when the assignment was to draw a map.

Discussion

Contingent teacher attention and free time had a positive effect upon completion of daily assignments. The data indicate that the teachers could not expect J. to do as well in nontargeted subject areas.

Source: Drawn from "A Teacher Training Model: The Resource/Consulting Teacher" by L. Idol-Maestas, 1981, *Behavioral Disorders, 6,* 108–121. Used with permission.

Pointer 8.3

PROMOTING GENERALIZATION OF NEAT PAPER SKILLS

This study illustrates how direct instruction can be used to teach an academic skill (neat papers) in the resource room and how students can use self-monitoring strategies to promote transfer of the newly acquired academic skill to regular classroom settings.

This study involved 15 fourth, fifth, and sixth graders placed part-time in a resource room. The students, 13 boys and 2 girls, were identified as either mildly retarded, learning disabled, emotionally disturbed, or Chapter I (i.e., disadvantaged low-performers).

The "neat paper" skills that served as the targets were identified following a careful assessment of the expectations and standards in the students' regular classrooms. Nine features characteristic of neat papers were identified: use of margins, starting on the front side of the paper, proper placement of the student's name, identification of the assignment's content with a title, leaving the paper whole, no unnecessary marks or scribbling, writing on the lines, use of consistent spacing within and between sections, and neat and appropriate use of eraser.

The instructional program initially consisted of directly teaching these skills in the resource room. Instructional methods included demonstration, examples and nonexamples, guided practice, positive reinforcement, and corrective feedback. No attempt was made during the direct teaching phase to extend the program to a nontraining setting; i.e., no reinforcement or prompts were given to the students for using these skills outside the resource program.

A self-monitoring checklist was developed and students were taught to use it to evaluate their written assignments in both the resource room and other settings. After evaluating their written assignments on the criteria established for the nine fea-

When students are in the resource program itself, their behavior and performance may be significantly better than their performance and behavior in the regular classroom. This situation is a major source of frustration for resource teachers, who may respond to the concerns of equally frustrated regular classroom teachers by saying, "but he does it in my room" (Vaughn, Bos, & Lund, 1986). The technology of generalization has been evolving, and newly developed general principles for achieving generalization are now being applied with increasing frequency and success. The most important principle is: Do not assume that generalization will occur automatically; if you want generalization, you must actively program for it. Other intervention strategies based on the principles for promoting generalization discussed in chapter 4 include:

- Do not abruptly terminate a behavioral intervention prior to returning a student to the regular classroom. Instead, gradually fade selected components of the intervention.

tures of neat papers, the students would place a smiley-face sticker next to each of the nine target features they had performed correctly.

The results indicated that the direct instruction-only condition produced little effect on the neatness of writing in non-training settings. It did, however, improve neatness in the resource room. However, a significant improvement was evident when the self-monitoring checklist was used in the generalization setting.

This study illustrates the effectiveness of an intervention for promoting generalization of an academic skill taught in the resource room setting to nontraining settings using self-monitoring procedures. The authors offered several additional recommendations for increasing the effectiveness of self-monitoring checklists on the generalization of academic skills:

1. Self-monitoring checklists should be relatively easy for students to use; that is, unambiguous with yes–no criteria and decisions.

2. Identify a specific time for students to complete a self-monitoring checklist, usually immediately after completing the task.

3. Do not introduce the self-monitoring checklist in several settings simultaneously; use one to two settings or situations first and then extend it to more.

4. Monitor how the self-monitoring checklist is being used by students; accuracy should be occasionally checked by the teacher, but actual use should be carefully monitored at first.

Source: Drawn from "Neatness Counts: Effects of Direct Instruction and Self-Monitoring on the Transfer of Neat-Paper Skills to Non-Training Settings" by L. Anderson-Inman, S. C. Paine, and L. Deutchman, 1984, *Analysis and Intervention in Developmental Disabilities, 4,* 137–155.

- Increase the similarities between the resource program and regular classroom (see Pointer 8.3).
- A less intense form of the resource program's intervention may be required over a long period in the regular classroom.
- Prepare the regular classroom to support a returning student's academic and behavioral improvements.
- Teach self-monitoring and, perhaps, self-reinforcement procedures, enabling the student to assume more responsibility for managing his or her own behavior (see Pointer 8.3).
- Teach students to actively recruit reinforcement from their teachers.
- Implement an intervention used in the resource program (e.g., a daily report card) in the regular classroom while the student is still in the resource setting or after the student returns to the regular classroom setting (see Exhibit 8.4).

Exhibit 8.4   Daily report cards

Date_____

Classroom Work

☐ Good ☺

☐ Bad ☹

_____
Teacher's Signature

A

Date_____

Classroom Behavior

☐ Good ☺

☐ Bad ☹

_____
Teacher's Signature

B

Date_____

Social Behavior
    Acceptable
    Unacceptable

Academic Work
    Completed on time
    Not completed
    Accuracy acceptable
    Accuracy unacceptable

_____
Teacher's Signature

C

Date_____

Reading   _____
Math   _____
Spelling   _____
Science   _____
P.E.   _____
Lunchroom   _____
Playground   _____
Social Behavior _____
Bonus Points   _____
Fines   _____
Total Points   _____
Total Possible _____

_____
Teacher's Signature

D

Subject_____   Date_____

____ Is doing acceptable work and is keeping up with assignments
____ Work is not acceptable
____ Is behind on assignments
____ Social behavior is acceptable
____ Social behavior is unacceptable

Comments:

_____
Teacher's Signature

E

Source: From *Strategies for Managing Behavior Problems in the Classroom* by M. M. Kerr and C. M. Nelson, 1983, Columbus, OH: Charles E. Merrill, p. 284. Used with permission.

Producing generalized treatment effects should be the ultimate goal of all pull-out programs.

- Use several strategies to promote generalization.
- Follow up on student progress and provide "booster shots" if improved behavior has decayed in the regular classroom.

A prevalent theme in this book is the importance of active programming for generalization. Producing generalized treatment effects should be the ultimate goal of all pull-out programs for behaviorally disordered students. Planning, implementing, and coordinating all the elements is a major challenge for resource teachers. There are no short-cuts. As a now-famous line suggests, "In general, generalization should be programmed, rather than expected or lamented" (Baer, Wolf, & Risley, 1968).

SUMMARY

The basic purpose of a resource room program for behaviorally disordered students is to provide supportive instructional services that enable students to benefit from the regular classroom program. Assessment, intervention, progress monitoring, and follow-up are direct services provided by the resource program. Indirect services include consulting and advising with regular classroom teachers, inservice training, and coordinating all aspects of the special education program with regular classroom teachers, school administrators, and parents.

The primary purpose of the curriculum and instructional program provided in the resource program is to facilitate the student's successful adaptation in the regular classroom. The resource teacher serves as a support system to the regular classroom teacher by assisting in the development and implementation of interventions designed to increase academic skills and improve classroom behavior and social skills.

Central to the successful implementation of a resource program is the consultation of the resource teacher with the regular teacher. Close coordination and open communication between the regular classroom teacher and the resource teacher are vital if behaviorally disordered students are to receive quality educational programming.

REVIEW QUESTIONS

1. Outline a presentation you will make to a school faculty where you will explain why and how you will be providing indirect consultation services on a half-time basis and direct services the other half. What questions and concerns do you think will be expressed by the regular classroom teachers about your proposed role? How will you respond to these concerns?
2. How is the resource room program approach to service delivery used in your state? What special rules and regulations govern it?
3. Visit a school and ask the resource teacher if you can observe in the classroom for an entire day. Pay special attention to how behaviorally disordered students are served and how frequently the resource teacher consults with regular classroom teachers in the building.
4. Design a behavior management program that can be used in a resource program and can also be used as a generalization strategy in regular classrooms.

REFERENCES

Aloia, G. (1983). Special educators' perceptions of their roles as consultants. *Teacher Education and Special Education, 6,* 83–87.

Anderson-Inman, L., Paine, S. C., & Deutchman, L. (1984). Neatness counts: Effects of direct instruction and self-monitoring on the transfer of neat-paper skills to non-training settings. *Analysis and Intervention in Developmental Disabilities, 4,* 137–155.

Baer, D. M., Wolf, M. M., & Risley, T. R. (1968). Some current dimensions of applied behavior analysis. *Journal of Applied Behavior Analysis, 1,* 91–97.

Cartledge, G., & Milburn, J. F. (1978). The case for teaching social skills in the classroom. *Review of Educational Research, 48,* 133–156.

Cohen, J. H. (1982). *Handbook of resource room teaching.* Rockville, MD: Aspen Systems Corp.

Coleman, M. C. (1986). *Behavior disorders: Theory and practice.* Englewood Cliffs, NJ: Prentice-Hall.

D'Alonzo, B. J., & Wiseman, D. E. (1978). Actual and desired roles of the high school learning disability resource teacher. *Journal of Learning Disabilities, 11,* 390–397.

Demers, L. A. (1981). Effective mainstreaming for the learning disabled student with behavior problems. *Journal of Learning Disabilities, 14,* 179–188, 203.

Deno, S., & Mirkin, P. K. (1977). *Data-based program modification: A manual.* Reston, VA: Council for Exceptional Children.

Deshler, D. D., Alley, G. R., Warner, M. M., & Schumaker, J. B. (1981). Instructional practices for promoting skill acquisition and generalization in severely learning disabled adolescents. *Learning Disabilities Quarterly, 4,* 415–421.

Evans, S. (1980). The consultant role of the resource teacher. *Exceptional Children, 46,* 402–403.

Friend, M., & McNutt, G. (1984). Resource room programs: Where are we now? *Exceptional Children, 51,* 150–155.

Gickling, E., Murphy, L., & Mallory, D. (1979). Teachers' preferences for resource services. *Exceptional Children, 45,* 442–449.

Glavin, J. P. (1973). Follow-up behavioral research in resource rooms. *Exceptional Children, 40,* 211–213.

Glavin, J. P. (1974). Behaviorally oriented resource rooms: A follow-up. *Journal of Special Education, 8,* 337–347.

Glavin, J. P., Quay, H. C., Annesley, F. R., & Werry, J. S. (1971). An experimental resource room for behavioral problem children. *Exceptional Children, 38,* 131–137.

Greenwood, C. R., Hops, H., & Walker, H. M. (1977). The program for academic survival skills: Effects on behavior and achievement. *Journal of School Psychology, 15,* 25–35.

Hallahan, D. P., & Kauffman, J. M. (1986). *Exceptional children: Introduction to special education* (3rd ed.). Englewood Cliffs, NJ: Prentice-Hall.

Harris, W. J., & Schutz, P. N. B. (1986). *The special education resource program: Rationale and implementation.* Columbus, OH: Merrill.

Hawisher, M. F. (1975). *The resource room: An access to excellence.* Lancaster: South Carolina Region V Educational Services Center.

Hewett, F. M., & Forness, S. R. (1977). *Education of exceptional learners* (2nd ed.). Boston: Allyn & Bacon.

Hewett, F. M., & Taylor, F. D. (1980). *The emotionally disturbed child in the classroom: The orchestration of success* (2nd ed.). Boston: Allyn & Bacon.

Idol, L. (1986). *Collaborative school consultation: Recommendations for state departments of education.* Reston, VA: National Task Force on School Consultation, Teacher Education Division/Council for Exceptional Children.

Idol, L., Paolucci-Whitcomb, P., & Nevin, A. (1986). *Collaborative consultation.* Rockville, MD: Aspen Systems Corp.

Idol-Maestas, L. (1981). A teacher training model: The resource/consulting teacher. *Behavioral Disorders, 6,* 108–121.

Idol-Maestas, L. (1983). *Special educator's consultation handbook.* Rockville, MD: Aspen Systems Corp.

Idol-Maestas, L., & Ritter, S. (1985). A follow-up study of resource/consulting teachers. *Teacher Education and Special Education, 8,* 121–131.

Jenkins, J. R., & Mayhall, W. F. (1976). Development and evaluation of a resource teacher program. *Exceptional Children, 43,* 21–29.

Kerr, M. M., & Nelson, C. M. (1983). *Strategies for managing behavior problems in the classroom.* Columbus, OH: Merrill.

Knight, M. F., Meyers, H. W., Paolucci-Whitcomb, P., Hasazi, S. E., & Nevin, A. (1981). A four year evaluation of consulting teacher service. *Behavioral Disorders, 6,* 92–100.

McLoughlin, J. A., & Kelly, D. (1982). Issues facing the resource teacher. *Learning Disability Quarterly, 5,* 58–64.

Montgomery, M. D. (1978). The special educator as consultant: Some strategies. *Teaching Exceptional Children, 10,* 110–112.

Morse, W. C. (1976). The helping teacher/crisis teacher concept. *Focus on Exceptional Children, 8,* 1–11.

Neel, R. S. (1981). How to put the consultant to work in consulting teaching. *Behavioral Disorders, 6,* 73–77.

Nelson, C. M., & Stevens, K. B. (1981). An accountable consultation model for mainstreaming behaviorally disordered children. *Behavioral Disorders, 6,* 82–91.

Paolucci-Whitcomb, P., & Nevin, A. (1985). Preparing consulting teachers through a collaborative approach between university faculty and field-based consulting teachers. *Teacher Education and Special Education, 8,* 132–143.

Quay, H. C., Glavin, J. P., Annesley, F. R., & Werry, J. S. (1972). The modification of problem behavior and academic achievement in a resource room. *Journal of School Psychology, 10,* 187–198.

Robinson, S. M., Braxdale, C. T., & Colson, S. E. (1985). Preparing dysfunctional learners to enter junior high school: A transitional curriculum. *Focus on Exceptional Children, 18.*

Sargent, L. R. (1981). Resource teacher time utilization: An observational study. *Exceptional Children, 47,* 420–425.

Sindelar, P., & Deno, S. (1978). The effectiveness of resource programming. *Journal of Special Education, 12,* 17–28.

Speece, D. L., & Mandell, C. J. (1980). Resource room support services for regular teachers. *Learning Disability Quarterly, 3,* 49–53.

Thurlow, M. L., Ysseldyke, J. E., Graden, J., & Algozzine, B. (1983). Opportunity to learn for LD students receiving levels of special education services. *Learning Disability Quarterly, 7,* 55–57.

Vallecorsa, A. L., Zigmond, N., & Henderson, L. M. (1985). Spelling instruction in special education classrooms: A survey of practices. *Exceptional Children, 52,* 19–24.

Vaughn, S., Bos, C. S., & Lund, K. A. (1986). . . . But they can do it in my room: Strategies for promoting generalization. *Teaching Exceptional Children, 18,* 176–180.

Wahler, R. G., Berland, R. M., & Coe, T. D. (1979). Generalization processes in child behavior change. In B. B. Lahey & A. E. Kazdin (Eds.), *Advances in clinical child psychology.* New York: Plenum Press.

Weiderholt, J. L., Hammill, D. D., & Brown, V. L. (1986). *The resource teacher: A guide to effective practices* (3rd ed.). Boston: Allyn & Bacon.

Wildman, R. W., & Wildman, R. W. (1975). The generalization of behavior modification procedures: A review—with special emphasis on classroom applications. *Psychology in the Schools, 12,* 432–448.

9 Self-contained Classrooms for Behaviorally Disordered Students

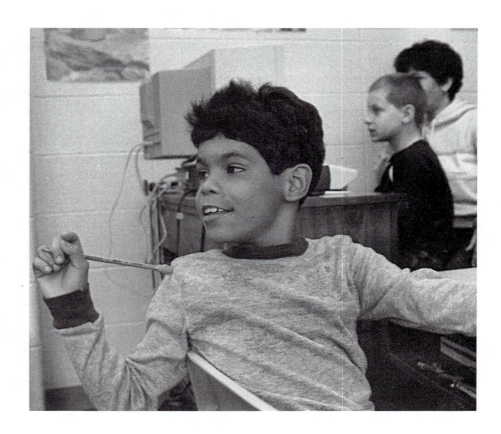

After completing this chapter, you should be able to

- *Identify types of problems displayed by students most often placed in self-contained classrooms.*
- *Explain the primary purpose of self-contained classrooms for behaviorally disordered students.*
- *Describe the purpose and operation of the classroom level system.*
- *Describe the purpose and operation of the classroom token economy.*
- *Discuss the basic process associated with coercion.*
- *Describe the precision request program.*

S ome behaviorally disordered students have very serious problems in school that interfere with their learning and the learning of other children in the class. These problems may be so severe that the child is placed in a self-contained classroom. Unfortunately, many self-contained classrooms focus only on controlling and containing the children instead of systematically teaching them the appropriate behaviors they need for school success (Walker, Severson, & Haring, 1985). Consequently, many of these students remain in self-contained classrooms for long periods.

We think that the primary purpose of a self-contained classroom should be proactive treatment and remediation to enable children to be returned to the regular classroom as quickly as possible. This chapter will emphasize the necessary skills teachers in self-contained classrooms need to design an effective treatment and remediation program for behaviorally disordered students. The model described here was developed and evaluated over a 10-year period at the Children's Behavior Therapy Unit in Salt Lake City.

This chapter begins with a review of the types of behavior problems most frequently found in self-contained classrooms. The design of a self-contained classroom is discussed next, with special attention to physical layout and daily schedule. Behavior management programs appropriate for use in self-contained settings comprise the core of the chapter. Procedures for implementing a level system and a token reinforcement program are specifically described. How to deal with noncompliance and aggression—two behavior problems frequently encountered in self-contained settings—is discussed in the next section. The chapter concludes with a review of the social skills training, academic instruction, and generalization programs recommended for use in self-contained settings.

WHO IS PLACED IN SELF-CONTAINED CLASSROOMS?

Almost all children referred to self-contained classrooms for the behaviorally disordered are referred because of misbehaviors or skill deficiencies so severe that the children cannot be effectively taught in a regular classroom or other part-time special education setting. The disruptive behaviors are frequently externalizing (Jenson, Reavis, & Rhode, 1987; Kazdin, 1985; Patterson, 1986; Walker et al., 1986; Walker, Reavis, Rhode, & Jenson, 1985); that is, they are directed toward the external environment (adults, peers, or property). This category includes such behaviors as noncompliance, tantrums, vandalism, fighting, arguing, inattentiveness, and theft. Externalizing behaviors are excesses in the sense that they occur too often and too intensely.

Behavioral excesses are only half of the referral picture, however. It is sometimes too easy to forget the children's behavioral deficits, particularly in self-control, academic, and social skills (Jenson et al., 1987; Patterson, 1986). In a sense, academic skills, self-control, and social skills are survival skills; without them a behaviorally disordered student is not likely to survive when reintegrated into a regular education setting.

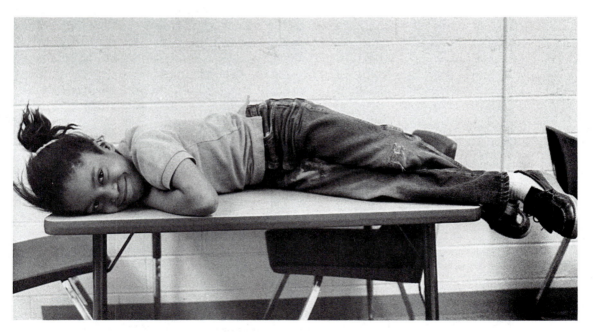

Most students placed in self-contained classrooms have significant externalizing behavior problems.

Some children are also referred for internalizing problems. These problems are called *internalizing* because they do not affect the external environment as much as they reflect "problems within the self" (Achenbach, 1982). For example, problems such as shyness, anxiety, fears, worrying, bodily complaints, and social withdrawal are internalizing behavior problems. In the past, these problems were given labels such as *severe emotional disturbance* and *personality disorders*. Many educators have considered these conditions to be more serious than externalizing behaviors (Jenson, 1978, 1985). However, longitudinal research has shown that an externalizing behavioral disorder is generally much more serious than an internalizing emotional disorder (Robins, 1979; Walker et al., 1986). Although some students with internalizing emotional disorders may be referred to self-contained classrooms, most can be educated in less restrictive settings. Thus, the majority of children referred to self-contained classrooms will demonstrate externalizing behavioral disorders.

DESIGN AND ORGANIZATION OF A SELF-CONTAINED CLASSROOM

As the name "self-contained" implies, a student who is placed in a self-contained classroom remains there for much of the school day. The actual amount of time varies, but most such students spend at least 50% of the school day in the self-contained classroom. Most self-contained classrooms serve fewer students than other classrooms; 10 to 15 students is the class size range in most states. The staffing ratio is higher in these classes because of more serious behavior problems require more attention.

Classroom Layout

A well-designed self-contained classroom begins with the physical design of the classroom and daily scheduling of activities within the classroom. Teachers may have little control over the physical structure of the classroom because administrators are reluctant to knock out walls or commit funds for new furniture and fixtures. Similarly, the daily schedule may need to conform to school-wide requirements for facilities such as the lunchroom, gym, and library. Even the curriculum may be determined by a district-wide adoption of a specific program or by instructional materials requisitioned by another teacher. In time, however, teachers can gradually shape the physical layout of their classrooms and gain some control over the daily classroom schedule, especially if they know what they want. Knowing the limitations of classroom design and how these limitations may affect the management of severe behavioral disorders is essential to the smooth organization of a self-contained classroom.

Exhibit 9.1 shows the physical design of the Oregon Experimental Classroom, a model self-contained classroom for behaviorally disordered children (Walker & Buckley, 1974). This classroom, designed for only six students at a time, has many of the basic requirements for a self-contained classroom. The classroom is centered around the six students' desks, with the teacher's desk behind them for easy monitoring. A display board at the front of the room indicates the number of token economy points earned by each student, and a store contains the reinforcers to be exchanged for points. A time-out room is also attached. If a student becomes severely disruptive, the teacher can use time-out without leaving the room. As noted earlier, the time-out room must be of a reasonable size, well-lighted, clean, ventilated, and sound-proofed to prevent disturbing the other children in the classroom. Observation rooms with one-way mirrors face into both the classroom and the time-out room to allow data collection. Observation of a student in time-out may be particularly important if the student is destructive or self-abusive. The bathroom is also attached to the room so that students do not have to leave the supervised area to go to the bathroom. Unattended bathrooms shared with regular classrooms can lead to all sorts of problems — plugged toilets, graffiti, disruption in the hallways. The teacher's desk is located near the exit so that the teacher can easily monitor children as they leave.

The Oregon Experimental Classroom may be considered ideal or even luxurious because of all the built-in fixtures, the observation windows and time-out room. Few school districts can provide this kind of facilities. Yet some basic components—a store with reinforcers, a supervised bathroom, quick access to a time-out room—are necessary before certain behavior management procedures can be implemented.

Scheduling for Self-contained Classrooms

Planning the classroom events for the day is an important aspect of a well-run classroom. The hallmark of a poor self-contained classroom is an unorganized or inefficient schedule. Poor organization is reflected in schedules that are unclear to the students and staff or schedules that continuously change. Students who are behind academically cannot afford wasted time, which is too often evident in schedules containing extended free times, play times, or arts or crafts at the expense of basic academic training (Paine, Radicchi, Rosellini, Deutchman, & Darch, 1983). These activities may have a place in a classroom schedule, but they should not dominate it. They do little to help a behaviorally disordered student prepare for re-entry into a regular classroom.

EXHIBIT 9.1   The physical layout of the Oregon Experimental Classroom

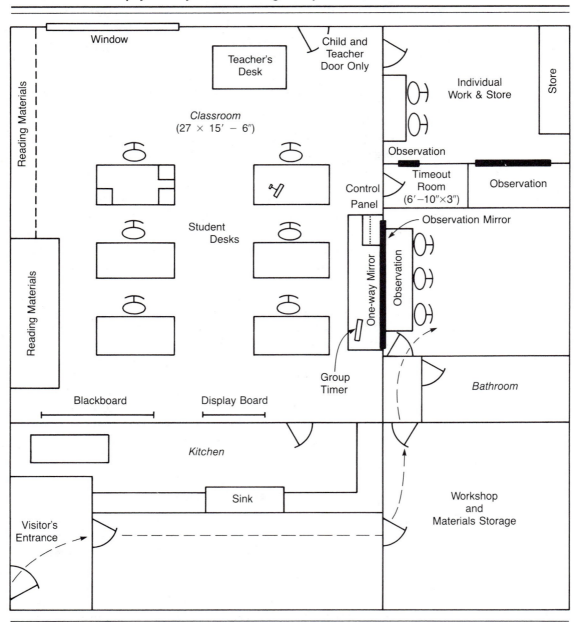

Source: From *Token Reinforcement Techniques: Classroom Applications for the Hard-to-Teach Child* by H. M. Walker and N. K. Buckley, 1974, Eugene, OR: E-B Press, p. 157.

EXHIBIT 9.2 Daily Schedule

8:30 Grooming or free time, 15 minutes

8:45 Self-report (report on transition times) and Calendar (explaining any schedule changes), 15 minutes

9:00 Direct Instruction Reading, 45 minutes

9:45 Direct Instruction Mathematics, 45 minutes

10:30 Earned Recess, 30 minutes

11:00 Writing Instruction, 30 minutes

11:30 Academic Checkout, Record Keeping, and Banking Points, 15 minutes

11:45 Lunch, 30 minutes

12:15 Social Skills Training, 45 minutes

1:00 Spelling or Writing, 45 minutes

1:45 Additional Afternoon Academics, 30 minutes

2:15 Academic Checkout, Record Keeping, and Banking Points, 15 minutes

2:30 Self-report on Daily Progress, Review of Social Skills and Academic Homework, and Checkout, 30 minutes

3:00 Earned Free Time or Additional Academic Make-up

3:30 End of Day

Exhibit 9.2 displays a sample schedule for a self-contained classroom. The initial morning events include grooming time, self-report, and calendar time. Grooming is needed with only those students who lack basic hygiene skills. It can be part of a social skills program to ensure that the students are not shunned by their peers (Walker, 1983).

Self-report and calendar time, which occupy a brief portion of the morning, allow students to report on their behavior on the way to school. Frequently, transition times such as the bus ride, the walk to school, and time in the halls are difficult for behaviorally disordered students. They are most likely to get into trouble when interacting with other students without supervision. The self-reports from the students should detail how they have behaved that day. If problems occurred, other students who were present can report as well. Checking with other personnel such as bus drivers or hall monitors can help settle disputes. Self-reports help reward the students' accurate reporting, and programs such as a "star bus rider list" can help reduce problems during transition times. Calendar time can be used to review daily events and expectations for the students each day. This time can also be used to talk about changes in the schedule or any special event planned that week.

As Exhibit 9.2 indicates, the bulk of the morning and early afternoon is used for academic instruction. Early mornings are particularly well-suited for basic instruction in arithmetic and reading because students are fresh and alert. Late morning or early afternoon can be excellent times for social skills training. Children can learn new skills and practice them in groups. Teachers can also give social skills and academic homework assignments. Students can practice specific social skills during recess, breaks, and lunchtime.

Additional academic sessions and arts and craft sessions are appropriate for the afternoon, which concludes with a daily wrap-up session. The wrap-up session is similar to the morning self-report for transition times. Here children rate themselves and report about how well they did during the day. Self-reports should include information about academics, social skills, and classroom behaviors. The self-reports are confirmed or disconfirmed by the teacher or other students. Teachers can reward accuracy with class points and movement upwards on the level system (to be discussed later). Self-report sessions can also help behaviorally disordered children develop accurate perceptions of their own behavior; they minimize opportunities for making excuses or blaming others.

BEHAVIOR MANAGEMENT PROGRAMS FOR SELF-CONTAINED CLASSROOMS

The review of basic behavior management techniques in chapter 3 emphasized interventions to increase or decrease behaviors, based primarily on a system of reinforcement and mild aversive consequences. The behaviors to be decreased were behavioral excesses that interfere with learning. Those to be increased were academic skills, social skills, and self-control behaviors. These goals are not too different from the goals of regular classrooms, and many of the behavior management techniques used in self-contained classrooms are similar to those used in regular classes. Yet there is one large difference. To be used successfully in a self-contained classroom, the techniques must be applied very systematically.

Systematically applying behavior management strategies may be the initial key to teaching behaviorally disordered children. However, children in self-contained classrooms can come to depend too heavily on the structured and behaviorally engineered environment. Therefore, an effective behavior management program for a self-contained classroom:

1. Decreases inappropriate behaviors (behavioral excesses)
2. Increases survival skills such as social and academic skills (behavioral deficits)
3. Transfers behavioral control from external sources to the student
4. Facilitates generalization to regular education settings as soon as possible

This section of the chapter will describe two specific procedures for achieving these goals: the classroom level system and the classroom token economy.

The Classroom Level System

The level system is the backbone of the behavior management program in a self-contained classroom. A level system shapes behaviors, fades behavior management techniques, and generalizes new skills. Level systems are commonly used in schools, institutions, and hospitals to shape behaviors and convey rules and privileges. They have been used as motivational systems in group homes for delinquents (Phillips, Phillips, Fixsen, & Wolf, 1971), in classrooms (Walker & Buckley, 1974), and in institutions for children with severe behavior disorders (Bauer, Shea, & Keppler, 1986).

In essense, a level system is a hierarchy of skills and behaviors a child is expected to master. It has four basic advantages:

1. Classroom rules are explicit.
2. Visual feedback about performance is available.
3. Classroom privileges are contingent on explicit and well-defined performance.
4. The system serves as a program for shaping, fading, and generalizing.

The initial levels start with simple fundamental skills that progress in complexity and shape the students' behavior as they move through the system (see Exhibit 9.3). Each level has certain privileges associated with it; these privileges are not available to children on lower levels.

A level system is also a *fading* and *generalization* tool. The beginning level behavioral requirements are designed to control behavioral excesses. At this level, the behavior management techniques feature external control devices such as a point system. The middle levels are used for learning and practicing replacement behaviors in academic and social skills. The upper levels are designed for generalization and self-control skills. As children reach the upper tiers of the system, they learn to monitor their own behavior, with occasional verification from the teacher. As they become more accurate in monitoring and controlling their own behavior, they are gradually faded from all external behavior management systems. The control systems at the highest level are essentially the same as in a regular classroom. All of the target behaviors in a level system, from the most rudimentary beginning behaviors to more sophisticated, upper-level behaviors, are designed to systematically shape, fade, and generalize a child back to the regular classroom.

The time a child takes to progress through the various levels is a type of continuous assessment data on the effectiveness of the level sys-

EXHIBIT 9.3   Color-coded level system for a self-contained classroom

				White
			Pink	Problem indentification Alternative solution problem solving
		Yellow	Self-reinforcement Accurate self-report Task completion Plus green, blue, and yellow behaviors	

	Blue	Polite language
		Cooperating with
		  friends
		Peer reinforcement
		Initiating play
		Plus green and
		  blue behaviors		

Green	Following directions Paying attention Raising hands Contributions Plus green level behaviors		SELF-TRACKING INITIATED	
Out of seat Hands Theft/cheating Physical aggressions				
Green Card	Blue Card	Yellow Card	Pink Card	No Card

↑ Starting   ↑ Half way through   ↑ Getting ready to go
back to regular class

→ Time

tem. Children who get stuck on one level or who frequently drop down a level because of inappropriate behaviors will need changes in their programs. A public display of the system, with the levels, rules and privileges, and names of the children on the various levels, gives the children continuous feedback about the teacher's expectation and their own progress. The system can only work, however, if the behaviors on the levels and the rules for movement up through the levels are objective, easily understood, and measurable. Teachers should avoid using their impressions or hunches about a child's progress to make decisions; they should use objective measures to move children from level to level.

Exhibit 9.3 shows an example of a five-step level system from a self-contained program for behaviorally disordered children (Jenson et al., 1987). Each level in this system is associated with a color that is displayed on a classroom bulletin board along with the names of the children on that level. On the first level, Green, children must remain in their seats, keep their hands and feet to themselves, engage in no aggressive behavior, and not cheat or steal. In addition, the children on Green start a social skills training program that emphasizes grooming. The privileges for the Green level include recess and lunch times and limited use of classroom equipment.

As students progress through the level system, they must handle each new set of social, academic, and behavioral requirements, plus continue to demonstrate their mastery of the requirements of the lower levels. Privileges continue to increase with each level and include making contracts for field trips, having a bank and token economy card, and earning a dot-to-dot chart and grab bag (to be discussed). The next two levels, Blue and Yellow, emphasize increasingly complex classroom behaviors and social skills.

When students reach the Pink level, they monitor their own behaviors and mark them on a point card. Teachers also select students at random and evaluate their progress on the same behaviors. If the teacher's and the student's ratings are the same, the child is reinforced. If they are significantly different, the child loses reinforcement (more of this will be discussed in the section on token economy). Children are taught to monitor themselves and match their teacher's perception because this self-control technique will be used when they return to the regular classroom.

While still on the Pink level, children gradually start working independently on academic subjects. At first independent work lasts 30 to 45 minutes at a time for at least one period of the day. The children obtain the necessary materials or read an assignment from the blackboard and start to work. The academic materials should be the same or similar to materials used in the regular classroom. Working independently with regular classroom academic materials is a critical step in generalization, because most regular classroom teachers require students to work from a blackboard. It is a major classroom survival skill and, frequently, one in which behaviorally disordered students are deficient.

When children reach the White level, they are no longer on the level system in the sense that all classroom privileges are available as long as they maintain their classroom behavior and academic progress. In addition, they spend more time in the regular classroom and carry a report note. The report note system enables the regular teacher to keep the self-contained teacher and parents informed about the child's progress. The child rates himself or herself on academic and social behaviors during the time spent in the regular classroom, and the regular teacher independently rates the same behaviors. As before, if the student's rating matches the regular teacher's rating, the student is rewarded — during self-report time in the self-contained classroom and at home by the parents. The child gradually spends more time in the regular classroom and the parents continue to receive the report note from the regular teachers. More detailed information about the report note system and working with parents is given in chapter 10.

The Classroom Token Economy

A token economy has been described as a "contingency package" in which target behaviors are reinforced by tokens that can later be exchanged for reinforcing objects or events (Sulzer-Azaroff & Mayer, 1977). The tokens can take several forms: actual plastic or metal tokens, marks on a blackboard, points marked on a paper card, beans in a mason jar, play money, or anything else suitable. The actual medium of exchange is not critical, except that it should not be easily counterfeited, stolen, or swallowed (for younger children). The effectiveness of a token economy depends on backup reinforcers, ease of use of the system, rules governing the exchange, and target behaviors to be reinforced by the tokens.

For maximum efficiency, a token economy should directly interact with a classroom level system. Exhibit 9.4 shows a series of daily token economy point cards that can be integrated with the five-step level system described in Exhibit 9.3. Each card color corresponds with a level of the same color. Students on the Green level have a green point card. The target behaviors from each level are listed on the corresponding point card. The teacher and classroom aides mark the points for class time, recess, and lunch in the boxes along the edges of the cards. They also record special contracts, social skills such as "warm fuzzies" (positive remarks to other children) and "zaps" (negative verbal remarks), depending on the level requirements. The center of the cards contains academic subjects with the notation "chartmoves," a motivation system for academic skills (to be discussed later in this chapter).

When students reach the Pink level and have a pink point card, they are self-monitoring and recording points for their own behavior. The Pink card contains a double row of boxes around the edge, one for the student to mark and the other for the teacher to mark. Students on the White level no longer have point cards; they receive all the basic privileges in the classroom. However, when these children are in the regular classroom for short try-out periods, they have a special report note on which they and the regular teacher rate their behaviors. Matches between the student and the regular classroom teacher are reinforced in the self-contained classroom.

This point system has several advantages. First, because the children carry their colored cards, the teachers can easily determine the child's level and what is expected of the child. The teacher has no trouble choosing the target behaviors for the token economy because they are standardized according to level. Second, to award points, the teacher simply marks the card, with none of the problems associated with managing bunches of plastic or metal tokens. At the end of the day, the teacher transfers the points to the child's bank and issues a new card. The classroom bank is simply a poster board containing student names, covered with plastic. The number of points earned each day is recorded with a grease pen that can be erased. Third, the daily point cards are the main source of continuous data used in assessing how well a child is doing in the program and deciding on level changes. At the end of each week, the teacher reviews the points earned, contracts fulfilled (see Pointer 9.1), and warnings and points missed.

It is easy to determine which students are having difficulty because they will have earned a minimum number of points and will have missed

EXHIBIT 9.4   Color-coded token economy cards for a self-contained classroom

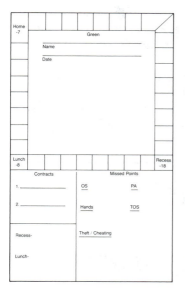

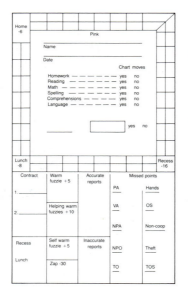

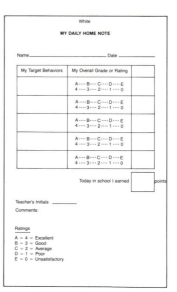

Pointer 9.1

BASIC COMPONENTS OF A BEHAVIORAL CONTRACT

1. Date agreement begins, ends, or is renegotiated (at least 1 week; no more than 3 weeks for behaviorally disordered students).
2. Behavior(s) targeted for change (measurable)
3. Amount and kind of reward or reinforcer to be used
4. Schedule of reinforcer's delivery

5. Signatures of all those involved: client, parents, mediator, and teacher
6. Schedule for review of progress (best daily)
7. Bonus clause for sustained or exceptional performance
8. Statement of the penalties that will be imposed if the specified behavior is not performed

Source: Text reprinted from *Writing Behavioral Contracts: A Case Simulation Practice Manual* by W. J. DeRisi & G. Butz, 1975, Champaign, IL: Research Press, p. 43. Used with permission.

earning points for some problematic behaviors. The number of points earned can be an objective criterion for deciding if a child should move to the next highest level. For example, a student earning the maximum points for 2 weeks for the target behaviors on one level moves to the next level.

Backup Reinforcers

Providing the backup reinforcers used in a token economy can present a problem; teachers may be on a very limited budget. Expensive reinforcers are not, however, necessary. In fact, some of the best reinforcers are free. Earning free time, playing video games, sitting at the teacher's desk for reading, running errands, being first in line, getting to wear a hat in the classroom, and choosing which desk to use are examples of inexpensive reinforcers. Other reinforcers were described in chapter 3. Some children may also want items such as small toys and treats if a teacher can afford them. This practice will require a classroom store (a cabinet or file drawer) that can be locked.

The cost to the students of backup reinforcers is an important consideration in a token economy. If items are too expensive, the children's motivation will likely decrease. If items are too inexpensive, then children will quickly earn all the reinforcers and satiate. For reinforcers that actually cost money, such as small toys, a number of points can be set for each cent the item costs. For example, using a factor of 5, a small toy that costs 35 cents might cost 175 points (i.e., 35 cents $\times 5 = 175$ points). For activities or privileges, time is used in computing the cost. For example, the exchange rate might be 15 points for each 5 minutes of an activity. Exhibit 9.5 shows a sample reinforcement "menu."

It is also important to remember that children should not be reinforced with points or material reinforcers alone. Teachers should also pair social praise and attention with the points and reinforcers. Pairing enhances the value of both the points and the teacher's attention. A workable formula for delivering social reinforcement and pairing it with points is given in the IFEED rules (see Exhibit 9.6).

Response Cost and Token Economies

To review, response cost is the loss of a positive reinforcer following an inappropriate behavior (Weiner, 1962). It is a mild punishment that is particularly useful with token economies and level systems because a child can lose points or be dropped a level for misbehavior. For example, behaviors such as not starting assignments, talking inappropriately in class, or constantly drifting off task can be consequated by taking away or cancelling a certain number of points on the token card. A teacher might use a warning with response cost: "You need to pay attention and work on your assignments for the next 30 minutes or you'll lose 10 points."

EXHIBIT 9.5   Example of a reinforcement menu from a classroom

Item	Cost
15 minutes free time	50 points
Getting to wear a hat to class	100 points
Extra snack from the classroom store	30 points
Not having to line-up for the day	100 points
Game with a friend for 30 minutes	300 points
Use of classroom video game for 10 minutes	50 points
Extra trip to the water fountain	50 points
Extra free reading time for 10 minutes	30 points
Getting to sit in any desk in the classroom	100 points
Classroom checker (check to see when lunch is ready or any messages)	30 points
Grab from the classroom treasure bag	100 points
Extra free time of 30 minutes in the arts and crafts area	200 points
Popcorn party for the whole class	500 points

Another example might be stating to the child that "If you cannot stop wandering around the classroom without permission for the rest of the day, you are in danger of losing points and being dropped a level." Actual warnings can be marked on the token economy card of children on beginning levels. For more advanced levels, no warnings would be given.

The basic drawback of response cost is the danger of overuse, especially if it is effective in reducing inappropriate behaviors. If the technique is overused and children lose too many points, they may actually go into the "hole" or in debt. It is hard to motivate children to earn points to get out of debt. If not closely monitored, this situation can lead to frustration and more inappropriate behaviors (Doty, McInnis, & Paul, 1974).

The advantages of response cost include its ease of use, particularly for milder forms of inappropriate behavior. Points or tokens can easily be subtracted from a classroom bank with few disruptive effects or physical harm. Response cost neither takes the child out of the classroom nor involves significant staff time. When the procedures, rules, and amounts are well-defined or used in combination with other management techniques, response cost is effective and fair.

Maximizing the Effectiveness of a Token Economy

Using a level system and pairing social praise and attention both increase the effectiveness of a token economy. There are also other methods, as suggested by Kazdin (1982):

EXHIBIT 9.6 The IFEED rules of positive reinforcement

Rule	Meaning
Reinforce **I**mmediately	Reinforce right after the behavior you like occurs. Delays weaken the effectiveness of the reward.
Reinforce **F**requently	Whenever you see your student performing a behavior you like, deliver a reinforcer. Let your student know you like what he or she is doing. Reinforce new behaviors each time they occur. Later on, you can reinforce less frequently.
Reinforce **E**nthusiastically	Listen to the tone of your voice. It can make your words positive reinforcers or a bland meaningless statement. Give a reinforcer some enthusiasm!
Reinforce **E**ye Contact	Look a student in the eyes when you reinforce, and let him or her know you really mean it. Don't look at the ground or another student when you are reinforcing a student who is doing a good job.
Reinforce **D**escriptively	Describe the behavior you like. Let the child know precisely what you like about the behavior. Detail a description at first, because a student may not know exactly what you like.

1. *Vary the magnitude of reinforcers.* Provide a range of reinforcers with different costs. Some should be relatively expensive and some, not so expensive. A classroom auction can also vary the available reinforcers. In an auction, the classroom staff members bring in their personal white elephants from garages and attics and the children bid competitively for them.
2. *Allow reinforcer sampling.* With this method, children are allowed to sample some of the reinforcers without having to buy. Children often become excited about backup reinforcers and are more willing to earn points.
3. *Use classroom peers.* Peers can be used in two ways to enhance the effectiveness of a token system. First, peers can be used to share the backup reinforcers a child earns. For example, all of the peers on the Blue Level can share the reinforcers earned by the children on Green Level. This is a form of a group contingency. Second, peers on the higher levels can help manage the token system by dispensing tokens or giving out reinforcers. Both methods foster positive peer attention and can improve the effectiveness of the token system.

Pointer 9.2

COERCIVE DANNY AND THE REQUESTING TEACHER

To understand how aggression, arguing, excuse making, delays, and noncompliance are associated, you must first understand the interactive–coercive process. First of all, coercion is a dynamic process that always involves two people: a *request maker,* usually a teacher or parent, and the *coercive responder,* usually a behaviorally disordered child. Second, coercion involves a *request* or a *command* given by an adult that is generally responded to with very aversive (coercive) behaviors. A child will seldom give excuses, argue, become aggressive, or delay in a behavioral vacuum unless a request is made.

Third, the coercive behaviors are *reinforced,* by the teacher. The sequence of negative reinforcement occurs when the adult (a) withdraws a request, (b) is inconsistent, or (c) is afraid to make a request. The reinforcement (the teacher withdrawing the request) is rationalized with such statements as, "It's too much trouble to make him do it" or "If I ask her, she'll throw an ugly fit." These statements reflect the fact that the teacher will withdraw the request if the child becomes sufficiently coercive. By withdrawing the request, a teacher is, in effect, rewarding the inappropriate behavior.

Each inappropriate behavior is a link in a *behavioral chain* that sets the occasion for the next and more inappropriate behavior. For example, delaying leads to excuse giving, which leads to whining, which leads to tantruming, which leads finally to aggression. If you wait to the end of the aversive behavior chain and then withdraw a request, the most intense coercive behaviors have been rewarded. The coercive process is a trap for both the teacher and the child in which yelling, ultimate threats (threats that are difficult or impossible to implement), name calling, and aggression

MANAGEMENT OF NONCOMPLIANCE AND AGGRESSION

Teachers in self-contained classrooms often must reduce high-rate inappropriate behaviors such as noncompliance and aggression before they can teach new behaviors. Physical and verbal aggression and persistent noncompliance can greatly disrupt the classroom and destroy the morale of both regular and special education teachers. Teachers should realize that these behaviors will occur in self-contained classrooms. More importantly, they must learn to manage them effectively.

Noncompliance and aggression are linked (Patterson, 1982, 1986) in the sense that they are likely to occur in combination. A teacher who requires a behaviorally disordered student to work on a difficult academic task may be the target of verbal and physical aggression. In addition, aggressive exchanges can lead to arguing, blaming, tantruming,

build with each escalating threat and counter threat.

An example between Danny, a behaviorally disordered student, and his teacher,
Mr. Setup, illustrates the coercive trap.

Mr. Setup's Responses	**Danny's Responses**
Danny, is it time to get started? (Question format)	Ignore the teacher and maybe he will go away.
Come on now Danny, let's get started.	Wait until I finish thinking. (Delay)
Now get started, so you can finish and go to recess.	How come the other kids don't have to do my type of work? It's too hard for me. (Excuse)
They have tough work too; now let's get going. (Yelling)	You always pick on me, for no reason. (Whining)
Now get started or else! (Even more yelling)	No, you can't make me—I'll never work for you. (Start of a tantrum)
You will work, or I'll have you expelled as a trouble maker! (Ultimate threat that can't be backed up easily)	Tough! And if you lay a hand on me, I'll kick your teeth in! (Beginning of an aggressive response)
Just sit then and be stupid, and see if you pass. (Request withdrawn, which reinforces child's worst behavior)	Danny just sits and stares out the window. (Reduction of his misbehavior, which reinforces the teacher)

whining, and other inappropriate responses. This process has been
termed *coercion* (Patterson, 1982) and is central to an understanding of
noncompliance and aggression. Pointer 9.2 explains the components of
coercion and provides an example of a coercive interaction between a
teacher and a behaviorally disordered child who does not want to do his
assignments. In this example, the behaviors in the process move from
noncompliance to increasing intensity and violence. Each behavior is
part of a chain that leads to and sets the occasion for the next one. As
yelling, delays, and excuses continue, the situation becomes more emotionally charged. To stop coercion, the teacher must implement a procedure with the initial behaviors in the chain instead of waiting until later.

The basic process involved here is noncompliance, not doing what
has been requested by another person. In addition, many annoying behavioral excesses such as arguing, making excuses, throwing tantrums,
and ignoring, are all directly linked to noncompliance. Some studies

(Russo, Cataldo, & Cushing, 1981) and reviews (Forehand, 1977; Jenson et al., 1987) have shown that changing noncompliance through a direct intervention may decrease some of these linked negative behaviors without an intervention.

Noncompliance includes three elements: (1) a child does not do what is requested, (2) within a reasonable amount of time, (3) up to a reasonable standard. Research has identified a number of factors that can increase or decrease compliance. First, compliance decreases with the number of commands given to a child in a short period (Forehand & Scarboro, 1975). That is, more commands will result in less overall compliance. Second, repeating instructions will not significantly increase compliance (Budd, Baer, & Green, 1974). For example, giving a command or request and then repeating it several times will not improve compliance. Using a request format when the child does not really have a choice also reduces compliance. For instance, asking a child "Would you like to start work?" instead of "Please start your work" reduces compliance. Giving a child enough time to comply with a request will increase compliance (Forehand, 1977). However, children are frequently not given enough time to comply before adults interrupt them with another command (Forehand & King, 1977; Forehand & McMahon, 1981). Being close to a child and making eye contact when making a request can increase compliance (Hamlet, Axelrod, & Kuerschner, 1984; Van Houten & Doleys, 1983). Increasing the specificity and clarity of a command by using nonambiguous terms has also been related to increases in compliance (Peed, Roberts, & Forehand, 1977). General statements that are unclear and broad may leave a child wondering exactly what the teacher wanted. For example, a statement such as "Do your arithmetic assignment, problems 1 through 10, before the recess break" is much better than "Go do your work." Exhibit 9.7 summarizes the variables found to either increase or decrease compliance in children.

Most noncompliance problems with behaviorally disordered children require direct intervention. Ignoring noncompliance is not likely to work because most coercive children would prefer to have a request forgotten (ignored). Using positive reinforcement for compliance is important; however, by itself, positive reinforcement is usually not effective in changing noncompliance (Drabman & Javie, 1977; Forehand, 1977; Roberts, 1985; Roberts, Hatzenbuehler, & Bean, 1981). A teacher cannot modify severe noncompliance by using only positive reinforcement and ignoring noncompliance. Instead, the teacher should give the child (a) specific requests and (b) time enough to respond, and (c) reduce multiple commands that interfere with compliance. The intervention should use built-in positive reinforcement for compliance and mild punishers for noncompliance.

EXHIBIT 9.7 Ten variables that affect compliance

1. *Using a Question Format* — The use of questions instead of direct requests reduces compliance. For example, "Would you please stop teasing?" is less effective than "I need you to stop teasing."

2. *Distance* — It is better to make a request from up close (i.e., 1 meter, one desk distance) than from longer distances (i.e., 7 meters, across the class-room).

3. *Eye Contact* — It is better to look into the child's eyes or ask the child to look into your eyes than to not make eye contact.

4. *Two Requests* — It is better to give the same request only twice than to give it several times (i.e., nag). Do not give many different requests rapidly (i.e., "Please give me your homework, please behave today, and do not tease the girl in front of you").

5. *Loudness of Request* — It is better to make a request in a soft but firm voice than a loud voice (i.e., yelling when making a request to get attention).

6. *Time* — Give the student time to comply after giving a request (3 to 5 seconds). During this short interval, do not converse with the child (arguing, excuse making), restate the request, or make a different request. Simply look the child in the eyes and wait for compliance.

7. *More Start Requests instead of Stop Requests* — It is better to make more positive requests for a child to start an appropriate behavior (e.g., "Please start your arithmetic assignment"). It is better to make fewer negative requests for a child to stop a misbehavior (i.e., "Please stop arguing with me.").

8. *Nonemotional instead of Emotional Requests* — It is better to control negative emotions when making a request (e.g., yelling, name calling, guilt-inducing statements, and roughly handling a child). Emotional responses decrease compliance and make the situation worse.

9. *Descriptive Requests* — Requests that are positive and descriptive are better than ambiguous or global requests (i.e., "Please sit in your chair, with your feet on the floor, hands on your desk, and look at me" is better than "Pay attention").

10. *Reinforce Compliance* — It is too easy to request a behavior from a child and then ignore the positive result. If you want more compliance, genuinely reinforce it.

Precision Requests

Several researchers (Forehand, 1977; Forehand & King, 1977; Forehand & McMahon, 1981; Hanf & Kling, 1973; Jenson et al., 1987; Neville & Jenson, 1984) have suggested procedures for making requests that maximize compliance. Suggestions for making a precision request include:

1. Do not to use a question format. Instead, use a direct request.
2. Phrase your request in positive, descriptive terms so the child knows exactly what is expected.
3. Give the child enough time to respond. It takes approximately 5 seconds to initiate a requested behavior.
4. During the 5-second interval, do not reissue the request, start the behavior for the child, or give a different request.
5. Make eye contact when making a request and, if possible, be within 3 feet of the child.
6. Keep arguing, prompting, and cajoling to a minimum; if possible, entirely eliminate them.
7. If the child complies, socially reinforce him or her genuinely and enthusiastically.
8. If the child does not comply, give a second request using the pivot word "need"; for example, "Now I need you to stop getting out of your seat." The word "need" signals a mild aversive consequence if the child does not comply within 5 seconds.
9. If the child complies on the second request, socially reinforce him or her.
10. If the child goes beyond 5 seconds on the second request, use the mild aversive consequence. After the mild consequence, reissue the request: "Now I need you to . . . ."

The precision request format is given in Exhibit 9.8. By following this format, a teacher gives the child enough time to respond and reduces yelling and repeated requests to a minimum. The child has two chances to respond, and consequences are in place for compliance and noncompliance. Consequences are critical to the effectiveness of precision requests.

Specific programs can be designed to reinforce social behaviors that are incompatible with noncompliance (see Pointer 9.3). However, if the child has not responded after the second request, a mild aversive consequence is needed. Teachers should plan consequences well in advance of making requests of noncompliant students. For example, mild noncompliance (e.g., not beginning an academic assignment right away) might be followed by a response cost of token points. For very disruptive or severe noncompliance, time-out procedures may be needed to increase compliance and reduce coercion.

EXHIBIT 9.8 Standard precision requires sequence; precision request sequence with the added "Sure I Will" program

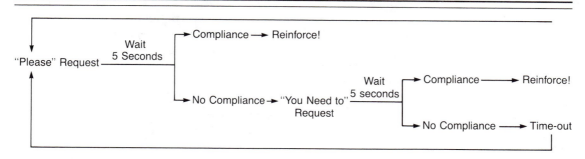

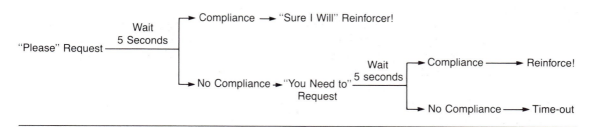

Source: From *Precision Commands and the 'Sure I Will' Program: A Quick and Efficient Compliance Training Sequence,"* by M. Neville and W. R. Jenson, 1983, *Journal of Child and Family Behavior Therapy, 6,* p. 64. Published by The Haworth Press, New York. Used with permission.

Time-out is a very effective mild consequence that can be used with precision requests. After the second precision request with the word "need," the time-out procedure is used. When time-out is over, the teacher then reissues the "I need you to . . ." request. If the child still refuses to comply, the time-out procedure is used again; however, this rarely happens. Generally, children are much more compliant after being in time-out. Time-out should be used only for severe noncompliance or aggression. Other mild aversive consequences, such as point loss, loss of a privilege, or a reprimand, can be used for less severe noncompliance. Two of the most common mistakes that teachers make when using precision requests with time-out are forgetting to reinforce children socially when they do comply and forgetting to re-issue the "I need you to . . ." request after the time-out is finished.

Group Contingencies

Sometimes, even with an effectively designed and implemented system, a teacher can not achieve optimal control of a self-contained classroom.

Pointer 9.3

"SURE I WILL"

Precision requests can help a behaviorally disordered child to begin complying. However, compliance may be difficult to maintain. The "Sure I Will" program involves selectively reinforcing an appropriate social skill that is incompatible with noncompliance.

To Make the "Sure I Will" program work, a teacher must first have implemented the precision request program outlined in this chapter, a simple "Please [plus the request]" followed shortly by "Now you need to [plus the request]." Once this program is working, the "Sure I will" component can be added. The child is told that after he hears "Please" and before the second request of "Now you need to," he should respond verbally with "Sure I will." If he says, "Sure I will," he will be rewarded (see Exhibit 9.8). The child is always rewarded by the teacher with social praise for saying "Sure I will" followed with compliance. However, on a random schedule (perhaps average of every three "Sure I wills"), the child may be given a bigger reinforcer such as bonus token points or free time. The points can be slowly faded out, and using them at random helps maintain the compliant behavior.

The advantages of "Sure I will" are that it is incompatible with noncompliance. It is difficult to say "Sure I will" and then immediately say "No, I am not going to do it." In a sense, it is the first positive step in the compliance chain. It also helps because the "Sure I will" response must precede the second precision request of "Now you need to" to be rewarded. This helps avoid a conflict and use of a mild aversive. Most important for the child, a cheery "Sure I will" followed by compliance is likely to be reinforced by other adults, which helps generalization.

Other verbal responses that signal compliance can also be used — "You bet!" "Okey-dokey," "As good as done," or "You can count on it." A group contingency compliance game can also be used for younger children (kindergarten to fourth grade). For example, a classroom can have three teams of children, the "Sure I will" team, the "You bet" team, and the "Okey-Dokey" team. The names of the teams are written on the blackboard. The teacher also writes a secret number on paper and puts it in an envelope at the beginning of the day. The children do not know the number. Throughout the day, if a member of a team responds to a teacher request with the correct team phrase (e.g., "Sure I will") and complies, the teacher puts a mark by the team name on the board. At the end of the day, the teacher reveals the written number from the envelope. If the team exceeds the number with their compliance requests, they receive a group reward (free time, group spinner, popcorn party). If they are at the number or below, then the whole team continues to work without a reward.

It is important to *not* count every compliance phrase from the children. Only some of the best and most genuine phrases are counted. In addition, if the child asks the teacher to count a request or points it out, it is never counted. The idea is to elicit genuine compliance phrases that can be used in a generalization program with regular teachers who will not recognize each phrase.

Group contingencies are very effective as a behavior management procedure.

Level systems, token economies, and precision requests may simply not be enough. Occasionally, using mild punishment procedures such as time-out can even make the situation worse. For example, students may be reinforced by their peers for the inappropriate behaviors that lead to time-out. The reinforcing effects of peer attention for inappropriate behaviors can be overwhelming. To counter this situation, a teacher can use a *group contingency.*

With group contingencies, the consequence for the whole group depends on the behaviors of a few children in the group. The "Good Behavior Game" (chapter 7) is an excellent example of a group contingency in a classroom out of control (Barrish, Saunders, & Wolf, 1969). The advantage of a group consequence is it turns peer attention and support from inappropriate behavior to appropriate behavior. Another use of a group contingency is an attending program based on variable beeps from a cassette recorder (Henderson, Jenson, & Erken, 1986). Children can be separated into teams or groups by rows. If all the children are working and attending when the beep goes off, then they all get their points. If one child is off-task, then the group or row loses points. With this group procedure Hendersen et al. improved on-task attending from 60% to 80% for

EXHIBIT 9.9   Steps for setting up a group contingency

Step 1: Is a group contingency necessary? Answer these questions:
1. Is there overt peer attention and support for misbehavior?
2. Have other behavior management methods failed?
3. Do you need to improve student cooperation?

Step 2: Defind the target behaviors observably and measurably (i.e., each student will be attending to work when the timer bell goes off). Ask this question:
1. Are all of the students capable of doing the target behavior? If not, redesign the target behavior so that each student is capable of mastering it.

Step 3: Decide on a criterion for the group contingency. Ask these questions:
1. Will the criterion be a group average (e.g., the whole class will do 80% of their homework for the reinforcement)?
2. Will the criterion be based on each individual's performance (e.g., if one student does not do 80% of the homework, then the whole class misses the reinforcer)?
3. Will the criterion be based on a high and low average (e.g., the average of the best homework performance and the worst performance will be above 80%)?
4. Will the criterion be based on an average of randomly selected students (e.g., three students will be picked randomly from class and their homework will be averaged to see if it is above 80%)?

Step 4: Decide on a positive reinforcement for the group if they make the criterion and a mild punisher if they do not make the criterion (e.g., free time if the criterion is met; no free time and the group will make-up the missed homework if the criterion is not met).

Step 5: Publicly post:
1. The target behavior—defined
2. The criterion
3. The consequences
4. A feedback system to inform the students how well they are doing

Step 6: Plan a backup procedure for a child who refuses to participate or sabotages the group contingency for the other children (make that child a group or team alone).

Step 7: Discuss the group contingency with the students, school principal, and parents to answer questions about the procedure and fairness.

groups of learning disabled, behaviorally disordered, and mentally retarded children.

With a group consequence, everyone on a classroom team has something to lose or gain depending on the behavior of classmates. The teacher must make sure that an individual does not find the punishment of the whole group reinforcing (Barrish et al., 1969). If this happens, that child can be treated as a team of one member. The basic procedures for properly implementing a group contingency are outlined in Exhibit 9.9 (Jenson, Sloane, & Young, in press).

SOCIAL SKILLS TRAINING IN A SELF-CONTAINED CLASSROOM

Social skills are important as replacement behaviors for students in a self-contained classroom. That is, after many of their behavioral excesses have been reduced through behavior management programs, they must replace them with appropriate social skills. If they are not replaced, the misbehavior will return. Behaviors such as arguing, throwing tantrums, showing off, interrupting adults, bossing peers, and being uncooperative are rewarded by others through attention, direct reinforcement, or escaping unwanted tasks. Therefore, replacement social skills must also be rewarded, with positive attention, negotiation, and reinforcement, if they are to replace the previous inappropriate behaviors.

Several social skills programs, reviewed in chapter 6, can be used in self-contained classrooms. A self-contained classroom should have access to several programs and combine them to maximize their different strengths.

In self-contained classrooms, social skills are best taught in a group every day or at least three times a week. The teacher should include at least one respected peer in the group to serve as a model, because some children may be reluctant to try a new skill unless they see a valued peer doing it first.

Social skills programs should be directly integrated into a classroom level system, with specific skills assigned to each step. For example, basic skills such as grooming, following directions, and not interrupting should be on the initial levels. Skills such as reinforcing peers, accepting negative feedback, making appropriate conversation, and cooperating should make up the intermediate levels. The more advanced skills of problem solving, resisting teasing, giving negative feedback, and being properly assertive should make up the more advanced levels. With this approach, the most basic skills are taught first in the beginning levels. The more advanced skills are taught later, when they can be used as generalization skills for re-entry into regular classrooms.

ACADEMIC INSTRUCTION IN SELF-CONTAINED CLASSROOMS

As we have seen, academic skills are critical to a behaviorally disordered child's overall school adjustment. The basic academic skills of reading,

CHARTMOVES FOR HOMEWORK

In this study, a chartmove system and a reward spinner were used to reinforce behaviorally disordered children for turning in correct homework. A chartmove system is a series of stars arranged in a square to make a border to a picture such as a comic face. An example is given below. The children can draw the pictures for the charts as an art project, with approximately 100 to 200 squares making up the border. The teacher places reinforcement stars in some squares with invisible ink. This study used

a "Secret Agent" pen, purchased at a novelty store for $1.50. On one end of this pen is invisible ink. On the other end is an ink that makes the invisible stars visible when touched. About 30 to 40 invisible reinforcement dots are placed on the picture at random.

A child who turns in homework 80% correct or better makes a chartmove on his chart. Using the Secret Agent pen, the child touches the next square on the chart. If it has an invisible-ink star, the star will appear and the child gets a reinforcer (a spinner or a grab bag). This happens randomly, about one out of every three chartmoves. A chart with 100 squares will last about 6 months. The teacher is the only person in the class allowed to have the Secret Agent pen.

In the study, homework production and accuracy doubled for the behaviorally disordered children. The system also has the advantage of using two random or variable reinforcement systems (the random invisible stars and a spinner reinforcement system), which helps maintain behavior without requiring too many expensive reinforcers (30 stars in a 100 squares is a variable ratio schedule 3). The chartmove system has been used to increase and then maintain classroom academic assignments, punctuality, and bus riding behavior, and also to reduce truancy, temper tantrums, and classroom talk-outs.

Source: Drawn from "Using Chartmoves and Spinners to Improve Homework Compliance in Behaviorally Disordered Children," by D. Malyn and W. R. Jenson, 1986, May, paper presented at the annual meeting of the Association for Applied Behavior Analysis, Milwaukee. Used with permission.

---

mathematics, spelling, and writing are literally survival skills for regular classrooms. However, most of these children have a long history of academic failure. Frequently they are embarrassed by their poor abilities and they use coercion to escape academic tasks.

Teachers must select academic materials and motivation systems that maximize success and ensure that the student performs at high levels. Pointer 9.4 gives an example of a motivation system used successfully with behaviorally disordered children to maintain high rates of correct assignment and homework completion.

No curriculum will meet the needs of all BD children. There are, however, preferred curriculums that will meet the needs of most children in a self-contained classroom. These systems are based on *direct instruction* teaching approaches (introduced in chapter 5) and emphasize specific and observable instructional objectives, sequenced skills, problem-solving skills, and extensive practice.

The generalization of academic skills from the self-contained to the regular classroom must be engineered. Like social skills, academic skills should be integrated in the level system. The lower levels should emphasize performing basic academic tasks correctly, under structured guidance, with immediate feedback. The middle levels stress accelerating academic performance. In the upper levels, the student should take more responsibility. For example, the student should pick up materials and start work without being prompted, do independent seatwork for long periods (30 to 45 minutes), and turn in completed homework. These are the minimal expectations of a regular classroom teacher.

The self-contained classroom teacher should also introduce academic materials from regular classroom at the upper levels. Although these materials may not be as effective as some direct instruction materials, they are the actual materials the student will be using. Introducing academic materials from the regular classroom is a major generalization step. The returning behaviorally disordered student should be able to work successfully with these academic materials in the regular classroom.

GENERALIZATION TO THE REGULAR CLASSROOM

This chapter has focused on the generalization of skills learned in the self-contained classroom to new settings and new people. Skills learned in a self-contained classroom should be viewed as an investment of resources, time, and money. Without generalization, the investment is lost. With generalization, it is a good investment and the child is more likely to adjust and benefit educationally.

Self-contained classrooms that do not have a formalized generalization program are generally based on a containment model. With the containment model, a child is expected to stay in the special classroom indefinitely. No real plans are made to return the child to regular education.

In this chapter we have presented a different approach, based on remediation and treatment. This approach promotes generalization through the classroom level system. The level system functions as a fading system that gradually shifts control from external behavior management systems to self-managed systems. In addition, the social skills and academic skills taught in the classroom are incorporated into the level system to ease the child's adjustment to the regular class. The child overlearns these skills while the teacher reinforcement and external behavior management procedures decrease. At the upper levels, the contingencies are much looser than at the lower levels. The students are also given numerous opportunities to try out their new skills in regular settings, rate their own behaviors, and receive feedback from regular teachers.

These generalization approaches, however, are not enough. Preferred practices for generalization from a self-contained classroom to a regular classroom require even more. Special education teachers design generalization programs that are based on the individual characteristics of the particular school district. The teacher must program for the "common stimuli" (discussed in chapter 4) found in regular classrooms (Epps, Thompson, & Lane, 1985). Because they are so critical to self-contained classrooms, they will be briefly reviewed here. The questions the special educator must ask include:

1. What natural student behaviors does the teacher reinforce?
2. What natural student behaviors does the teacher punish?
3. What is the physical arrangement of the classroom (i.e., desks, furniture, bulletin boards)?
4. How much feedback and reinforcement does the teacher give students? (What is the density of positive reinforcement per hour? Is the feedback primarily for mistakes and negative behavior, or does the teacher point out good progress and appropriate behavior?)
5. What are the work requirements in the class? (How much work? How long is a student expected to work independently? What accuracy level does the teacher expect?)
6. What type of instructional approach does the teacher use (i.e., group, in front of class, working individually with students)?
7. What verbal expressions does the teacher use in class to convey approval and disapproval?
8. What instructional materials are used in class?
9. What social skills are reinforced by the teacher?
10. What is the teacher's personal interaction style in the classroom?
11. What type of peers make up the class?

These are some of the regular classroom common stimuli to be assessed, so that the student can be trained to cope with them while in the self-contained classroom. Then the skills can be tested by try-out in the regular classroom. However, even with this training, a teacher in a self-contained classroom will need to assess the progress of a child who has been returned to a regular setting. A child who is failing may need to be re-placed into the self-contained classroom for a limited period to help him or her adjust. When this happens, a common stimuli assessment becomes critically important to pinpoint what unaccounted-for characteristic caused the failure.

SUMMARY

In this chapter, we have presented a treatment and remediation model for self-contained classrooms. This model is fundamentally different from the containment model, which does not emphasize training replacement skills or the return to regular education settings. Most behaviorally disordered children in self-contained placements will have major difficulties with externalizing behavior problems, including coercive behaviors such as noncompliance, arguing, aggression, and tantrums. However, most of these children will also have serious deficits in social, basic academic, and self-control skills. A successful self-contained classroom will first reduce the externalizing problem behaviors and then remediate the skill deficiencies before a child successfully returns to a regular classroom.

The self-contained classroom model uses a level system as a shaping, fading, and generalization tool within the classroom. At the beginning levels, the externalizing behaviors are decreased; in the middle levels basic academic and social skills are taught; in the upper levels self-control procedures and generalization skills are taught. A major function of the level system is to transfer control from external behavior management procedures to more internal self-control procedures of the student. Other useful procedures include a precision request compliance program, a point system that interacts with the level system, group contingencies, and direct instruction techniques to teach students social and academic skills.

Clearly, there is still much to be learned about self-contained classrooms. The model presented here is not appropriate for every student. However, it is designed to address the commonly referred behavioral problems in self-contained classrooms. This model is not a panacea for all severely behaviorally disordered children, but it is a systematic approach that emphasizes timely placement back in the regular classroom with improved survival skills.

REVIEW QUESTIONS

1. Throughout this book and in chapter 7 especially, we have stressed that behaviorally disordered students should be taught in regular classroom settings as much as possible. Why, then, are self-contained settings necessary? What are the advantages and disadvantages of self-contained placements for behaviorally disordered students? How can the disadvantages be overcome?
2. How does a classroom level system facilitate generalization?
3. Here is a self-observation project for you. When making requests of students, how do you issue the requests? Refer to Exhibit 9.7, the factors that affect compliance. How do you rate? What changes, if any, will you make in your request-giving behavior?

REFERENCES

Achenbach, T. M. (1982). *Developmental psychopathology* (2nd ed.). New York: John Wiley.

Barrish, H. H., Saunders, M., & Wolf, M. M. (1969). Good behavior game: Effects of individual contingencies for group consequences on disruptive behavior in a classroom. *Journal of Applied Behavior Analysis, 2,* 119–124.

Bauer, A. M., Shea, T. M., & Keppler, R. (1986). Level systems: A framework for the individualization of behavior management. *Behavior Disorders, 12,* 28–37.

Budd, K. S., Bear, D. M., & Green, D. R. (1974, August). *An analysis of multiple misplaced social contingencies in the mother of a preschool child.* Paper presented at the annual meeting of the American Psychological Association, New Orleans.

Doty, D., McInnis, T., & Paul, G. (1974). Remediation of negative side-effects of an on-going response cost system with chronic mental patients. *Journal of Applied Behavior Analysis, 11,* 191–198.

Drabman, R., & Jarvie, G. (1977). Counseling parents of children with behavior problems: The use of extinction and time out techniques. *Pediatrics, 59,* 78–85.

Epps, S., Thompson, B. J., & Lane, M. (1985). *Procedures for incorporating generalization and maintenance programming into interventions for special-education students.* Ames, Iowa State University, Project Iowa.

Forehand, R. (1977). Child noncompliance to parental requests: Behavior analysis and treatment. In M. Hersen, R. M. Eisler, & P. M. Miller (Eds.), *Progress in behavior modification* (Vol. 5). New York: Academic Press.

Forehand, R., & King, H. E. (1977). Noncompliant children: Effects of parent training on behavior and attitude change. *Behavior Modification, 1,* 93–108.

Forehand, R., & McMahon, R. J. (1981). *Helping the noncomplaint child.* New York: Guilford Press.

Forehand, R., & Scarboro, M. E. (1975). An analysis of children's oppositional behavior. *Journal of Abnormal Child Psychology, 3,* 27–31.

Hamlet, C. C., Axelrod, S., & Kuerschner, S. (1984). Eye contact as an antecedent to compliant behavior. *Journal of Applied Behavior Analysis, 17,* 553–557.

Hanf, C., & Kling, J. (1973). *Facilitating parent-child interaction: A two stage training model.* Unpublished manuscript, University of Oregon Medical School.

Henderson, H. S., Jenson, W. R., & Erken, N. (1986). Focus article: Variable interval reinforcement for increasing on task behavior in classrooms. *Education and Treatment of Children, 9,* 250–263.

Jenson, W. R. (1978). Behavior modification in secondary schools: A review. *Journal of Research and Development in Education, 11,* 53–63.

Jenson, W. R. (1985). *Severely emotionally disturbed vs. behavior disorders: Consideration of a label change.* (Field Rep. #2; University of Utah, Graduate School of Education Report Series). Salt Lake City: University of Utah.

Jenson, W. R., Reavis, K., & Rhode, G. (1987). A conceptual analysis of childhood behavior disorders: A practical educational approach. In B. K. Scott & J. E. Gilliam (Eds.), *Topics in behavior disorders.* Austin, TX: Behavioral Learning Center.

Jenson, W. R., Sloane, H. N., & Young, R. (In press). *Applied behavior analysis for teachers: A structured learning approach.* Engelwood Cliffs, NJ: Prentice-Hall.

Kazdin, A. E. (1982). The token economy: A decade later. *Journal of Applied Behavior Analysis, 15,* 431–445.

Kazdin, A. E. (1985). *Treatment of antisocial behavior in children and adolescents.* Homewood, IL: Dorsey Press.

Malyn, D., & Jenson, W. R. (1986, May). *Using chartmoves and spinners to improve homework compliance in behaviorally disordered children.* Paper presented at the annual meeting of the Association for Applied Behavior Analysis, Milwaukee.

Neville, M. H., & Jenson, W. R. (1984). Precision commands and the "Sure I Will" program: A quick and efficient compliance training sequence. *Child and Family Behavior Therapy, 6,* 61–65.

Paine, S. C., Radicchi, J., Rosellini, L. C., Deutchman, L., & Darch, C. B. (1983). *Structuring your classroom for academic success.* Champaign, IL: Research Press.

Patterson, G. R. (1982). *Coercive family process.* Eugene, OR: Castalia.

Patterson, G. R. (1986). Performance models for antisocial boys. *American Psychologist, 41,* 432–444.

Peed, S., Roberts, M., & Forehand, R. (1977). Evaluation of the effectiveness of a standardized parent training program in altering the interaction of mothers and their noncompliant children, *Behavior Modification, 1,* 323–350.

Phillips, E. L., Phillips, E. A., Fixsen, D. L., & Wolfe, M. M. (1971). Achievement Place: Modification of the behaviors of pre-delinquent boys within a token economy. *Journal of Applied Behavior Analysis, 4,* 45–49.

Roberts, M. W. (1985). Praising child compliance: Reinforcement or ritual. *Journal of Abnormal Child Psychology, 13,* 611–629.

Roberts, M. W., & Hatzenbuehler, L. C. (1981). Parent treatment of command-elicited negative verbalization: A question of persistence. *Journal of Clinical Child Psychology, 10,* 107–113.

Roberts, M. W., Hatzenbuehler, L. C., & Bean, A. W. (1981). The effects of differential attention and time out on child noncompliance. *Behavior Therapy, 12,* 93–99.

Robins, L. N. (1979). Follow-up studies. In H. C. Quay & J. S. Werry (Eds.), *Psychopathological disorders of childhood* (3rd ed.). New York: John Wiley.

Russo, D. C., Cataldo, M. F., & Cushing, P. J. (1981). Compliance training and behavioral covariation in the treatment of multiple behavior problems. *Journal of Applied Behavior Analysis, 14,* 209–222.

Sulzer-Azaroff, B., & Mayer, G. R. (1977). *Applying behavior analysis procedures with children.* New York: Holt, Rinehart and Winston.

Van Houten, R., & Doleys, D. M. (1983). Are social reprimands effective? In S. Axelrod & J. Apsche (Eds.), *The effects of punishment on human behavior.* New York: Academic Press.

Walker, H. M. (1983). *Walker Problem Behavior Checklist–Revised.* Los Angeles: Western Psychological Services.

Walker, H. M., & Buckley, N. K. (1974). *Token reinforcement techniques.* Eugene, OR: E-B Press.

Walker, H. M., O'Neill, R., Shinn, M., Ramsey, B., Patterson, G. R., Reid, J., & Capaldi, D. (1986). *Longitudinal assessment and long term follow-up of antisocial behavior in fourth grade boys: Rationale, methodology, measures, and results.* Unpublished paper, University of Oregon.

Walker, H. M., Reavis, H. K., Rhode, G., & Jenson, W. R. (1985). A conceptual model for delivery of behavioral services to behavior disordered children in educational settings. In P. H. Bornstein & A. E. Kazdin (Eds.), *Clinical behavior therapy with children.* Homewood, IL: Dorsey Press.

Walker, H. M., Severson, H., & Haring, N. (1985). *Standardized screening and identification of behavior disordered pupils in the elementary age range: Rationale, procedures, and guidelines.* Eugene, OR: University of Oregon, Center on Human Development.

Weiner, H. (1962). Some effects of response cost upon human operant behavior. *Journal of Experimental Analysis of Behavior, 5,* 201–208.

10 Working with Parents of Behaviorally Disordered Children

After completing this chapter, you should be able to

- *Discuss several myths about parents of behaviorally disordered students.*
- *Differentiate between family therapy and parent training.*
- *Describe the essential characteristics of several parent training programs.*
- *Describe how home note systems can be used with parents.*
- *Identify several characteristic types of difficult parents.*
- *Describe characteristics associated with abusive parents.*
- *Identify signs of child abuse and neglect.*

Parents are critically important to the development of their children. However, few parents realize the demands of parenthood, nor are many trained to meet those demands. Financial demands, time demands, marital stress, and just plain fatigue take their toll. This "want ad" from a recent book (Polster & Dangel, 1984) captures some of the often unrecognized challenges:

> One couple to procreate and raise a child. NO experience necessary. Applicants must be available 24 hours per day, 7 days per week, and must provide food, shelter, clothing, and supervision. No training provided. No salary; applicants pay $140,000 over the next 18 years. Accidental applications accepted. Single people may apply but should be prepared for twice the work. (p. 1)

If many couples had read an ad like this, they might have thought twice about having children.

The commitment necessary to raise a handicapped child is even greater, particularly if the child is behaviorally disordered. Many parents of these children feel guilty; they have trouble explaining their child's out-of-control behaviors. Parents may deeply love their behaviorally disordered child but, at the same time, intensely dislike or feel embarrassed by some of the child's behaviors (see Pointer 10.1). The conflict of love, dislike, and embarrassment can be confusing, resulting in mixed feelings for parents. They may feel powerless in their attempts to control a highly aggressive, noncompliant child. Many of these parents describe the home situation as being out of control. Families of handicapped children are additionally burdened with needs for special programs, higher rates of divorce, isolation from social support, and a number of emotional problems (Gallagher, Beckman, & Cross, 1983; Holroyd, 1974; McAndrew, 1976). Parents' emotional reactions may involve depression, anger, guilt, or anxiety (Holroyd, 1974; Marcus, 1977; Richman, 1977).

Pointer 10.1

TALES FROM THE FUNNY FARM

No matter how calmly you try to referee, parenting will eventually produce bizarre behavior, and I'm not talking about the kids. *Their* behavior is always normal, a norm of acting incomprehensibly with sweetly blank looks. But *you* will find yourself strolling down the road to the funny farm—like my mother, who used to get so angry that she would forget my name:

"All right, come *over* here, Bar—uh, Bernie . . . uh, uh — Biff . . . uh — what *is* your name, boy? And don't lie to me 'cause you live here and I'll find out who you are and take a stick and knock your brains out!"

All during my stormy boyhood years, I wanted to get some calves' brains and keep them in my pocket. Then, when my mother hit me in the head, I would throw them on the floor. Knowing her, however, she merely would have said, "Put your brains back in your head! Don't *ever* let your brains fall out of your head! Have you lost your *mind*?"

And thus, in spite of the joys that children do bring, does parenting take its toll on both father and mother. Mothers who have experience in the trenches of family warfare are sometimes even driven to what I call anticipatory parenting. They ask a child a question, he tries to answer, and they say, "You shut up! When I ask you a question, you keep your mouth shut! You think I'm talking to hear myself talk? *Answer* me!"

Source: From *Fatherhood,* by W. Cosby, 1986, Garden City, NY: Delphine Press, pp. 52-53. Used with permission.

School can help this situation or make it much worse. Imagine going through years of meetings with school personnel who describe in detail the serious misbehaviors and failings of your child. While few of us would blame the parents of a child born with a serious physical handicap, many would blame the parents of a behaviorally disordered child.

This chapter is designed to help teachers become a resource for parents and families of behaviorally disordered children. It will focus on accepting parents as partners in planning and implementing educational programs. It includes suggestions for conducting parent training programs and designing home behavior management programs. Special attention is devoted to the problems of working with difficult parents and identifying abused children.

MYTHS ABOUT PARENTS OF BEHAVIORALLY DISORDERED CHILDREN

Several myths about parents of behaviorally disordered children seem to persist in the minds of school personnel. These myths may lead to legal problems, damage relationships with parents, and interfere with children's educational programs.

Myth #1: "I can just do my job and teach without dealing with parents."

This myth reflects a pattern of educational isolationism in which the teacher excludes parents from the educational process. The logic might be that the teacher can do a better job without distractions from interfering parents. However, parents *must* be equal partners in deciding which assessment information to gather, which special placements to make, and which related services to provide. Federal law and regulations (PL 94-142) guarantee equal status to parents. Parents

> must be allowed to see any record the school relies upon in programming for the child, to be notified of each step before it is taken, to participate in annual planning and review of progress, and to be able to go to a hearing to challenge anything they dispute. (Martin, 1979, p. 9)

Working with parents of behaviorally handicapped children is now an essential part of the educational process. Including parents takes extra time and planning but, if it is effective, it can facilitate the teaching process and may actually reduce the demands on the teacher.

Myth #2: "Parents should accept the district's program or they might miss out by being choosy."

Parents should not be coerced into accepting the only special education program that the school district has to offer. Parents are coerced when they are told that if they do not accept the school's program their child may not receive any program or may need to wait until the next available space. A "take it or leave it" attitude does not recognize parents as equal partners. Waiting lists for special programs are inappropriate; not having sufficient funding to provide adequate special programs is not a legal excuse.

Myth #3: "Parents' values and attitudes should be similar to mine."

Well-meaning teachers can easily be victims of this third myth. Many teachers believe this myth and quite honestly make this mistake. They assume that they are acting in the child's and parents' best interests in making unilateral decisions about a student's education program. Clearly, similar values and attitudes toward appropriate behavior are strengths in developing a working relationship and different values can be the breeding ground of conflict, particularly if special techniques are used to

Parents are often wrongly blamed for the problems of their behaviorally disordered child.

teach a behavior the parents do not feel is important. For example, a teacher who expects a child to sit quietly and work hard all day may have a rude awakening when discussing these goals with the child's parents. The parents may think their child needs flexibility and freedom during the day. A teacher of behaviorally disordered children needs to meet parents to discover similarities and differences in values and attitudes.

Myth #4: "Parents are the primary cause of the disturbance."

This fourth myth may be the most destructive. It assumes that behavior problems are the sole result of an emotional disturbance. It is true that home environments may play a part in misbehavior. For example, poverty, divorce, abuse, and neglect may contribute to a child's behavior problems. However, behavioral disorders are generally too complex to be solely attributed to one or two individuals or to a single event. Genetics (Cadoret, 1978), biologically based temperament (Thomas, Chess, & Birch, 1969), and even environmental factors such as subtoxic levels of lead (David, Hoffman, Sverd, Clark, & Voeller, 1976) can contribute to behavior disorders. Nothing makes parents feel more guilty and defensive than an accusation from school personnel that they are bad parents, responsible for the behavior problems of their child.

Myth #5: "Parents do not have an important role to play in instructional programs designed to improve their child's school adustment."

This last myth may have the most damaging effect on the success of a special education program. Some teachers may believe that, while they should treat parents as equal partners in the general design of a program, implementing the program need not involve parents.

Cooperative parents of behaviorally disordered children can play a key role in generalizing the special education programming. They can extend a school behavior management program to the home, conduct social skills training, and supplement an academic program. All of these home-based activities ensure consistency across environments and generalization of the school program. Parents are often able and willing to carry on this work.

WHO SHOULD WORK WITH PARENTS?

Being responsible for all the daily tasks of teaching and then still being expected to work with parents can seem overwhelming. The entire responsibility should not be placed just on teachers. Other related service personnel, such as school psychologists, counselors, and social workers, should provide some of the services as well. However, because the teacher must request these services, it helps to know about what is available. An informed teacher who knows about quality parent training programs and makes specific requests is much more likely to obtain quality services than the teacher who simply requests "some kind" of help.

Frequently, teachers may want to be involved in parent training or a home assistance program. This interest generally develops after a teacher has successfully established the classroom and it is running smoothly. It may then become obvious that more intervention is needed, beyond the classroom, to help behaviorally disordered children. Teachers can conduct a parent training program or set up a home note program for a child with cooperative parents. However, teachers should not feel obligated to provide these extended services until their classroom is operating efficiently. Teachers can try to do too many things, especially early in their careers, and end up doing nothing well.

WORKING WITH PARENTS

In the past 20 years, researchers (Bijou, 1972; Gelfand & Hartmann, 1977; Hall, Copeland, & Clark, 1976; Herbert & Baer, 1972; O'Dell, 1974; Patterson, 1974; Polster & Dangel, 1984; Sloane, 1976; Wahler, Winkler, Peterson, & Morrison, 1965) have generated a great deal of interest in applying behavior management practices in the home and school. Especially noteworthy are programs that feature strong communication and intervention programs that overlap the home and school. These programs frequently take the form of parent training and home note systems. The advantage is the development of a working relationship between teachers and parents, who can then share information and resources to help manage problem behavior.

Parent Training

Parent training involves directly teaching specific skills or techniques to change a child's problem behavior. It is very different from parent or family therapy approaches, which are generally nondirective and assume that an underlying emotional problem causes a behavior problem. The goals of family therapy include gaining insight into the cause (often assumed to be a traumatic incident) of the emotional problem, unconditionally accepting the child (filial therapy), having the child relieve pent-up frustration in a socially acceptable manner such as punching a bozo doll (catharsis), and improving communication within a family. Although these goals may be laudable, their effectiveness with behaviorally disordered children has not been adequately demonstrated (as reviewed by Bandura, 1973; Gelfand, Jenson, & Drew, 1982; Herbert, 1978; Levitt, 1971). Furthermore, adults in daily contact with behaviorally disordered children can have trouble using these traditional therapies. For example, teachers *and* parents may have difficulty accepting a child's severely aggressive and noncompliant behaviors. Caretakers (teachers and parents) want techniques that result in fast and effective behavior change for a child.

Behavioral parent training programs share several characteristics (as reviewed by Polster & Dangel, 1984; O'Dell, 1974; Reisinger, Ora, & Frangia, 1976) well suited to school applications. First, behavioral parent training assumes that most of a child's behavior is maintained by its effect on the environment and that the behavior can be modified by people who interact with the child (Hall, 1984). Second, behavioral parent training is educationally oriented; parents learn specific techniques. Third, behavioral parent training emphasizes accurate measurement and charting of observable and measurable behaviors, especially positive behaviors. Fourth, intervention techniques generally involve positive reinforcement and limit the use of punishment. Fifth, most behavioral parent training approaches use step-by-step problem-solving skills, negotiation, contracting, and home-to-school notes to generalize the learned skills to new behaviors and new situations. Sixth, most published parent training approaches have written material for parents that forms a systematic curriculum of explanatory text, guide sheets, and prescribed homework assignments. Better programs have parents model and role-play new techniques before actually trying them with the child.

There are literally hundreds of parent training materials available. Some of the preferred behaviorally based programs and books are listed in Exhibit 10.1. To be a preferred practice for parent training with behaviorally disordered children, a program should be scientifically tested, stress direct teaching of techniques, emphasize positive techniques, and de-emphasize punishment. We will review five programs that meet these criteria and can be used in schools.

Responsive Parenting

This program was developed at the University of Kansas (Hall, 1981), and was offered to approximately 3,000 parents over an 8-year period in the Shawnee Mission School District suburban Kansas City. The basic intent of the Responsive Parenting model is to teach parents to accurately observe and measure behaviors and then use applied behavior analysis techniques to teach new behaviors in a home setting. The program is highly structured and is presented to a group of parents in eight, 2-hour weekly meetings.

Each weekly unit has a specific set of goals, objectives, and activities, outlined in the *Responsive Parenting Manual* (Hall, 1981). This manual has three sections that explain the responsibilities and instructions for the program director, the group leader, and the parent.

The parent manual is divided into eight training units revolving around a general model (Hall, 1984) of:

1. *Define* the behavior of concern.
2. *Measure* the rate, duration, and occurrence of the defined behavior.
3. *Intervene* using natural consequences readily available.
4. *Evaluate* the effectiveness of the treatment procedure.

Parents are encouraged to practice each new technique through behavioral rehearsals in small groups and then to apply the skill at home. In the first two sessions, parents learn to pinpoint and define target behaviors. The next three sessions emphasize systematic reinforcement, token systems, contracts, schedules of reinforcement, shaping, modeling, extinction, discrimination, and generalization. The sixth session

EXHIBIT 10.1   Additional parent training materials

Parents Are Teachers, by W. C. Becker, Research Press

Solving Child Behavior Problems at Home and at School, by E. A. Blechman, Research Press

SOS: Help for Parents: A Practical Guide for Handling Common Everyday Behavior Problems, by Lynn Clark, Parents Press

Troubled Families: A Treatment Approach, by M. J. Fleischman, A. M. Horne, and J. L. Arthur, Research Press

Helping the Noncompliant Child: A Clinician's Guide to Parent Training, by R. L. Forehand and R. J. McMahon, Guilford Press

Changing Children's Behavior, by J. D. Krumboltz and H. B. Krumboltz, Prentice-Hall

Systematic Parent Training, by W. H. Miller, Research Press

Families: Applications of Social Learning to Family Life, by G. R. Patterson, Research Press

Living with Children—New Methods for Parents and Teachers, by G. R. Patterson, Research Press

Positive Parenting, by R. C. Rinn and A. Markle, Research Media

The Good Kid Book: A Manual for Parents, by H. N. Sloane, New American Library

The Art of Parenting, by B. R. Wagonseller, M. Burnett, B. Salzberg, and J. Burnett, Research Press

covers the use of punishment techniques such as time-out and overcorrection, with a special emphasis on the dangers of misused punishment. The seventh session deals with specific problems of children such as fighting, noncompliance, tantrums, bed time, chores, and running away. The wrap-up session stresses the generalization and maintenance of the learned skills. At this last session, parents present the projects they have been working on with their children.

The effectiveness of this program has been demonstrated in several studies (Hall, 1984). These studies have consistently demonstrated the effectiveness of the program in teaching parents new skills, significant differences between children's pre- and post-scores on behavior checklists, and basic parent satisfaction with the program. The program is well suited to school applications, but requires well-trained and certified group leaders.

WINNING!

This parent-training program was developed to serve parents of children in the 3- to 12-year-old range. The model is unusual in that it emphasizes

EXHIBIT 10.2   Basic lesson mastery criteria

Basic lesson	Criteria
1. Praise and attention	10 descriptive praises.
2. Reward and privileges	Same as Lesson 1, plus two rewards and privileges
3. Suggestive praise	Same as Lesson 2, plus five suggestive praises
4. Ignoring	Same as Lesson 3, plus no attention to inappropriate child behavior
5. Time-out	Same as Lesson 4, plus one time-out
6. Removing rewards and privileges	Same as Lesson 5, plus two instances of removing rewards and privileges
7. Physical punishment	Same as Lesson 6, plus one physical punishment
8. Compliance	Deliver two instructions: follow one with positive consequences, one with negative consequences

Source: From "WINNING!: A Systematic, Empirical Approach to Parent Training" by R. F. Dangel and R. A. Polster, 1984. In R. F. Dangel & R. A. Polster (Eds.), *Parent training: Foundations of research and practice,* New York: Guilford Press, p. 168. Used with permission.

a *deductive* approach rather than the *inductive* approach of most other parenting programs (Dangel & Polster, 1984). According to Dangel and Polster, the deductive approach first teaches general behavior change skills without focusing on the child's specific problems. For example, a parent might learn about using praise and attention in a variety of settings with a number of different children. The basic idea is to facilitate generalization of a skill by teaching that a specific technique will work in a variety of settings. Watching 40 different scenes in which a specific technique is used reduces objections such as "This technique will not work with my child" or "My problems are different than other parents' problems." The basic lessons (see Exhibit 10.2) are taught in the first 8 weeks and use written material and videotapes.

If a parent does not generalize the basic techniques, then the WINNING! model shifts to an inductive approach, using videotaped scenes of specific applications of the techniques to common problems. These advanced lessons (listed in Exhibit 10.3) constitute a more detailed application of the basic techniques. If parents could not use the basic techniques to stop tantrumming, they would watch 40 to 50 scenes in which the intervention techniques were used to stop tantrumming, plus additional specific information on how to stop tantrums.

EXHIBIT 10.3 WINNING! advanced lessons

Temper tantrums	Homework
Fighting	School problems
Arguing and backtalk	Mealtime
Chores	Bedtime
Annoying habits	Good behavior in public places
Bedwetting and soiling	Allowances (Tokens)
Hygiene and appearance	Home school report cards

Source: From "WINNING!: A Systematic, Empirical Approach to Parent Training" by R. F. Dangel and R. A. Polster, 1984. In R. F. Dangel & R. A. Polster (Eds.), *Parent training: Foundations of research and practice*, New York: Guilford Press, p. 169. Used with permission.

The major advantage of this program is that the training model is used with parents. Each training module is relatively short and accompanied by a written manual and set of demonstration videotapes. Parents learn to define behaviors; each basic skill builds from the mastery of previous skills; modeling is emphasized; and parent homework assignments are closely monitored.

A validation research on the effectiveness of the program with 62 families in four studies has been impressive (Dangel & Polster, 1984). For example, positive consequences increased by an average of 95% and family interaction increased by 96% for all families after the program. In addition, the WINNING! program has had drop-out rates of only 20%, even though it has been used with parents of varying socioeconomic levels and minority backgrounds. The low drop-out rate for the WINNING! program is especially impressive when compared to drop-out rates reaching 50% for other parenting programs. A disadvantage of the WINNING! program is that its cost is relatively high.

Assertive Discipline for Parents

The Assertive Discipline Parent Training approach developed by Lee and Marlene Canter (1982) is an outgrowth of their school-based assertive discipline program for teachers. The main idea is teaching parents to take active charge of their child's behavior and to firmly communicate their wants and needs to the child. "Taking charge" implies that parents are willing and able to back-up their words with action. The assertive discipline program conveys two basic ideas to parents (Canter & Canter, 1982):

>First, you, the parent must assert your parental authority and be the boss
>when your children misbehave. Second, in order for you to do so, you
>will need to develop a systematic plan of action for how you will take
>charge with your children. (p. 16)

The assertive discipline program also draws a clear distinction between
an assertive response and a hostile response.

Hostile responses include physical punishment, threats, severe punishment, or responses that disregard the child's needs or feelings. For
example, hostile responses might be statements such as "You make me
sick," "Now you're going to get it," and "You can't leave your room for a
week." Assertive responses communicate clearly and firmly and recognize improvements in the child's behavior. For example, statements that
recognize children's accomplishments are; "I really like the way you followed my directions," or "Hey, we really like the way you did your chores
on your own."

The key to the program is the development of a plan including the
specific behaviors parents want the child to change and how parents will
back up their requests if the child complies and if the child does not comply. The general components of an assertive discipline plan are given in
Exhibit 10.4. In determining which behaviors are to be changed, parents
define the behaviors specifically, list them, concentrate on only a few
behaviors at one time, and communicate the goals to the child.

In backing-up requests with disciplinary actions, spouses should
agree on types of discipline used. The basic types include separating,
which is a form of time-out (e.g., sending a child to his or her room),
taking away a privilege, grounding, requiring a child to complete a requested action before being allowed to do something else, and taking
physical action (i.e., holding the child). The parents develop a disciplinary
hierarchy with increasingly severe consequences for children who frequently engage in the same misbehavior. For example, the first time the
child fails to cooperate, he or she is sent to the bedroom for 15 minutes,
the second time for 30 minutes, and the third time for an hour. Parents

EXHIBIT 10.4   Assertive Discipline training steps for parents: The Assertive
Discipline plan

Step 1:   Determining what you want your child to do and communicating the
          goals
Step 2:   Backing up your words with disciplinary actions
Step 3:   How to reinforce your child when they do behave
Step 4:   Laying down the law
Step 5:   Implementation

Source: From *Assertive Discipline for Parents* by L. Canter and M. Canter, 1982, Santa Monica, CA: Canter
Associates. Used with permission.

Pointer 10.2

MARBLE MANIA

Marble Mania is a group contingency that uses positive peer pressure with all of the children in a family. Whenever a child behaves appropriately, the parent positively comments on the behavior and puts a marble in a jar. When the jar is filled to a predetermined level (such as 50, 100, or 200 marbles), each child in the family earns an individualized reward. For example, one child might want a small toy, another child might want to stay up later at night, and another child might want to sleep over at a friend's house. Each child has a chance to earn marbles and add to the number. Positive peer pressure occurs when children prompt each other to behave so they can all earn a reward.

The essential rules for Marble Mania are as follows:

1. Make sure the children earn a large number of marbles each day (approximately one marble every hour to hour and a half).
2. If you need a reminder to give a marble for good behaviors, set a timer to ring every hour. When it rings each child who has been behaving appropriately should earn a marble for the jar.
3. Describe the appropriate behavior that earned the marble. For example, "Thanks for taking out the garbage the first time I asked. Now, you get a marble."
4. Never take marbles from the jar for any misbehavior. It will defeat the purpose of the system, and some children will go into "marble debt" for misbehavior and thus lose motivation.
5. At the end of the day, count the marbles in the jars with the children so they know how close they are to earning their rewards.
6. You must be able to control the marbles and the jar so that children will not secretly add their own marbles.

are also encouraged to describe explicit consequences for children's inappropriate behavior. Thus, the parents tell the child that he or she has *chosen* to receive a negative consequence by engaging in a particular misbehavior.

The next step in the plan is designing and practicing positive reinforcement when a child behaves well. Parental praise, the best reinforcer, is supplemented with special privileges, material rewards, and positive contracts. (See "Marble Mania," a positive group approach to reinforcing an entire family, in Pointer 10.2.)

The fourth and fifth steps of the plan include laying down the law and implementing the program. These steps show how a plan should be presented to children to avoid tears, belligerence, or indifference. Implementing a plan requires consistency, monitoring a child's progress, and immediate reinforcement.

The assertive discipline program is becoming increasingly popular with parents and teachers. The authors claim to have trained more than 300,000 educators (10% of all the educators in every state in the nation). However, despite its popularity and acceptance, little actual validation research has yet to appear in the scientific literature. One other caution should be mentioned as well. Users of this program should be especially careful to emphasize positive techniques. When this program is implemented inappropriately, there may be a tendency to overuse punishment.

The CBTU Parent Training Program

This program was developed at the Children's Behavior Therapy Unit (CBTU) and the University of Utah and has been used with hundreds of parents (Jenson, 1985). It parallels the behavior management techniques presented in chapter 9 on self-contained classrooms. This program is designed specifically for improving compliance in behaviorally disordered children.

The program is presented in six to eight weekly meetings that last approximately 2 hours each. Each parent receives written material that explains the basic intervention techniques with examples and illustra-

EXHIBIT 10.5   Parent training sequence from Children's Behavior Therapy Unit

Week 1:	Determining goals (pinpointing behaviors), Selection of reinforcers
Week 2:	How to use differential attention (ignoring inappropriate behaviors and reinforcing appropriate behaviors with attention), "Come Here Program" (getting a baseline on compliance)
Week 3:	Precision requests (how to make requests appropriately and consequate with time-out), Explanation of the coercive process (how coercion is tied to noncompliance, tantrums, aggression, delays, arguing, and excuse making)
Week 4:	Home reinforcement systems (star charts, spinners, grab bags, dot-to-dot posters), Reinforcing child for not going to time-out, "Sure I Will" program (teaching a social skill that is incompatible with noncompliance)
Week 5:	Using precision requests in public settings, Behavioral contracting, Home note systems, Overcorrection, and Response costs
Week 6:	Problem solving new behavior difficulties, Special problems (enuresis, encopresis, stealing, going to bed, not coming home, etc.), Planning for the future, Warnings about the overuse of punishment techniques
Follow-up:	Phone calls; Booster group session in two months

EXHIBIT 10.6 A star chart for recording, a spinner for reinforcement, and a dot-to-dot poster for reinforcement delivery

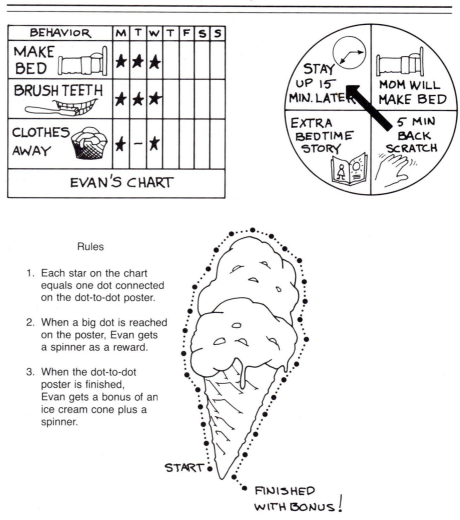

Rules

1. Each star on the chart equals one dot connected on the dot-to-dot poster.

2. When a big dot is reached on the poster, Evan gets a spinner as a reward.

3. When the dot-to-dot poster is finished, Evan gets a bonus of an ice cream cone plus a spinner.

tions (Jenson, 1980). The weekly sequence of topics is listed in Exhibit 10.5. During the initial training stages, the CBTU program is very similar to the other programs presented here. Parents learn to define, pinpoint, and measure appropriate behaviors they would like to increase. Along with their children, they also select a reinforcement menu. During the second week, parents begin to use differential attention as a positive behavior change technique. Differential attention involves ignoring inappropriate behavior, while giving positive attention to appropriate

---

Pointer 10.3

USING DOT-TO-DOT CHARTS AND GRAB BAGS
TO REDUCE SEVERE TANTRUMMING BEHAVIOR

This case study (Dachman, Halasz, & Bickett, 1984) used a simple dot chart and grab bag system for the CBTU program (Jenson & Sloane, 1979) to reduce severe tantrums in a 7-year-old boy. The boy, Josh, lived with his mother, who was single, in a trailer in a rural setting. The mother was referred to Project 12-Ways as a potential abuser. John had an average if only four tantrums each day; however, each tantrum lasted approximately 35 minutes. This meant that Josh was throwing tantrums for approximately 2 hours each day in a small, confined trailer. The tantrum was defined as "a minimum of 30 seconds occurrence of whining, crying, name calling, or foot stamping, in response to a denied request or command."

The materials for the intervention were a grab bag and dot-to-dot poster. The grab gab was a lunch sack containing slips of paper representing such rewards as small amounts of money, edible reinforcers, or preferred activities. The dot-to-dot posters consisted of unfinished drawings of

bonus rewards that Josh and his mother could do away from the trailer. For example, a poster might consist of a picture of an ice cream cone or eating at a restaurant. Each unfinished poster was composed of 50 to 150 small and large dots. (See Exhibit 10.6 for an example.)

The distance between each pair of dots on the poster represented a time contingency of 15 minutes of appropriate behavior. For example, if Josh did not throw a tantrum for 15 minutes, he could connect two dots on the chart. The larger dots on the chart represented reinforcement, and they were spaced so that Josh would connect them on an average of one every 75 minutes. When the larger dots were connected, John could reach into the grab bag for a slip of paper and receive the reward written on the paper. When all of the dots were connected on the poster (a matter of days), Josh received the bonus reward (the reward represented by the poster). Each time that the smaller (nonreinforcement) dots or the larger (reinforcement) dots

Source: Drawn from "The Use of Dot-to-Dot Posters and a Grab-Bag to Reduce Inappropriate Child Behavior," by R. S. Dachman, M. M. Halasz, and A. D. Bickett, 1984, *The Behavior Therapist, 7,* 14. Copyright 1984 by the Association for Advancement of Behavior Therapy. Reprinted by permission of the publisher and the author.

---

behavior. It is used with misbehavior that appears to be reinforced by a parent's attention (either positive or negative attention). The third week, parents learn about the coercive interaction that causes and maintains noncompliance, tantrumming, arguing, delays, and aggression in children. At this time, parents learn about the precision request and learn to use time-out as a consequence for noncompliance (for a more detailed explanation see chapter 9).

Parents receive information on reinforcement systems and behavior charts (Exhibit 10.6) on the fourth week. The reinforcement systems in-were connected, the mother would praise Josh for his appropriate, nontantrumming behaviors.

The results from this simple approach were impressive. The number of tantrums was cut in half during the first treatment phase (Phase B in the graph). In the second phase of training (Phase BI), the number of dots in the chart was reduced (cut in half) because it took too long for Josh to earn the bonus reward. This change reduced tantrumming even further, to barely 0.3 tantrums per day lasting only 3.4 minutes. A withdrawal of reinforcements to baseline showed a rapid return to higher rates and longer tantrums. Reinstatement of the treatment (Phase B2) showed, again, a rapid reduction in tantrums. Follow-up probes at 2 and 6 months showed a reduction of tantrums to near zero.

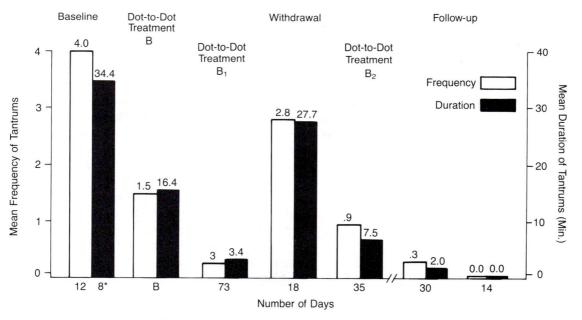

*Duration measure began four days after onset of baseline.

clude spinners, grab bags, and charts designed to use variable schedules of reinforcement. Parents are taught to positively reward their children for not going to time-out as part of the reinforcement system. The fifth week is devoted to home note systems and behavioral contracting. Home notes are important because they link the school and home. Behavioral contracting is used to generalize the program to new behavior, with the child as a primary negotiator for the behavior changes and consequences. The last week of the program is spent on special problem behaviors (e.g., enuresis, encopresis, stealing, fire setting, swearing) and problem solving. Parents present their home projects to the group. Throughout the CBTU parenting program, parents are encouraged to role play and model the various skills before they try them with the child at home (see Pointer 10.3).

Evaluation of the CBTU program (Jenson, 1986) indicates that parents are satisfied with the training received and the techniques learned. They seem particularly pleased with precision requests as a method to reduce noncompliance. Parents report increases in compliance from approximately 35% during baseline to 70 and 80% after they implement precision requests and reinforcement systems for compliance. More then 90% of the parents surveyed would recommend the group to other parents. However, follow-up data indicate that parents tend to drift into using punishment techniques such as time-out unless they receive problem-solving booster sessions.

Home Notes

Although parent training can greatly improve the quality of child–parent interactions in the home, some problems remain. Drop-out rates for structured parenting groups can be high. It can be difficult to train some parents to apply behavior management techniques. In addition, some parents may overuse punishment techniques such as time-out and may not use more positive techniques (Jenson, 1986). Teachers should be aware of the tendency of some parents to overuse punishment and should guard against its overuse. However, most parent training techniques are beneficial, particularly those that rely on close parent and teacher cooperation. One such technique is the use of home notes.

The home note system has also been called a *home-based* system and a *home contingency* system. These names suggest that something is happening in the home to change a child's behavior. Most of these systems (Atkeson & Forehand, 1979; Broughton, Barton, & Owen, 1981; Imber, Imber, & Rothstein, 1979; Schumaker, Hovell, & Sherman, 1977) include trained parents, a contingency management system at home and school, and an informative note that travels from the home, to the school, and back home (see Pointer 10.4). Home note systems work well with structured parent training because there must be some type of home reinforcement system for home notes to be effective. When a child brings the note home, the parent provides consequences for classroom performance and behavior.

For a home note system to be effective, parents and teachers must cooperate. The parent must be willing to review the note and reward appropriate behavior. The teacher must be willing to assess the student's daily performance and complete a note. Once the system is in place, the behavioral and academic improvements are substantial and well worth the effort (Atkeson & Forehand, 1979; Schumaker et al., 1977).

Problems can occur with a home note system. For example, the child may report that the note was lost or that the substitute teacher did not know how to complete the note. Children generally use these excuses when they are reluctant for their parents to see a note or when a punishment is part of the system (see Pointer 10.4). Children must understand that the note is their responsibility—no excuses! If a note is lost or not completely filled out, the child is responsible and should lose a privilege in the home and in the classroom. If the note does not come home, then the parent should call the teacher; if it is not returned to school, the teacher should call.

In most cases, notes are sent home daily. When a student has improved enough, the notes may be sent home only on Fridays, summarizing the child's progress for the week. If a child's performance declines, then the teacher can resume daily resports.

Unannounced, varible reports may be more effective than fixed time reports (Saudargas, Madsen, & Scott, 1977). For example, in one study, parents of 26 third-grade students first received a report on the quantity and quality of their child's academic work every Friday. In the variable time condition, the teacher selected seven to nine students at random each day to take notes home. When the students were not sure who would be selected to take home the note, the class as a whole performed better and completed more academic assignments. In addition, the teacher preferred the variable system to the fixed time system.

While some families may be willing to use a home note system, they may be unwilling or unable to deliver reinforcers at home. To overcome this problem, Larsson and Larsson (1982) designed a reinforcement kit for use with a minority population in a rural setting. Assembled by the classroom teacher, the kit contained 5 to 10 toys, food, and coupons. The parents awarded the coupons in the home, but children could exchange the coupons in the classroom for privileges. The parents received the kits and instructions to reinforce their children daily for good home notes. The teacher replenished the kits weekly. Eventually, the parents were told that the school was running out of money for reinforcers and encouraged to add some reinforcers themselves. Slowly, the school faded out delivering the reinforcement kits after the program had been successful and encouraged the parents to use home-generated reinforcers.

Home note systems have been very effective in increasing academic performance and reducing behavior problems in the classroom (Atkeson & Forehand, 1979) while at the same time being very time- and cost-efficient (Imber et al., 1979; Schumaker et al., 1977). Parents like a home note system because it keeps them informed and builds a needed communication link between school and home. They immediately know if

Pointer 10.4

AN EXAMPLE OF A HOME NOTE SYSTEM

The success of a home note system depends on (a) the teacher completing and initializing a note, (b) the child bringing the note home, and (c) parents applying consequences in the home dependent on the note. Most good home note systems have a reinforcement component for good behavior and a response cost or punishment component for inappropriate behavior. Using the examples of Tom's note in the figure, the following rules would outline a simple system for his parents:

Example of a Daily Home Note

Name: _____
Date: _____
Teacher: _____

Did the student...

	Yes	No	
Come on time?	☺		
Bring supplies?	☺		
Stay in seat?		☹	
Not talk inappropriately?		☹	
Follow directions?		☹	Rules Section
Raise his hand?	☺		
Not physically disturb others?	☺		
Clean up?	☺		
Pay attention?	☺		
Speak courteously?	☺		
Were you pleased with his performance today?	☺		Teacher Satisfaction Section
Points on today's classwork	20		Classwork Section
Grade on test assignment	C		Grades Section
Teacher's initials	A.B.		

1. For each + (or happy face) in the Rules Section, Tom gets an extra five minutes of TV time (or to stay up 5 minutes past his bedtime of 8:00PM). Because there are 10 squares for +'s in the Rule Section of the note, Tom could get a maximum of 50 minutes of extra TV time or stay-up time.

2. For each 0 (or sad face) [never use a −, because the child can change it to a +] in the Rules Section, Tom loses 5 minutes of TV time or stay-up time. Maximum loss would be 50 minutes.

3. If Tom receives more than 50 Class Work Points and gets a Grade on the Test Assignments of above a C each day, then Tom would get a bonus of 30 minutes extra play time outside. If these two scores are below the criteria, then Tom has to devote 30 minutes to extra homework or reading instead of play.

4. If the teacher is satisfied (Teacher's Satisfaction Section) 5 days (five notes), then Tom would get a bonus of his choice on Friday (movie, trip to a fast food restaurant, etc.)

5. If the note is lost, stolen, not filled out, or not initialed by the teacher, Tom loses 60 minutes of TV or stay-up time. The 60 minutes exceeds the maximum loss of a totally bad note (see Rule 2) by an extra 10 minutes penalty. This contingency will help ensure that he brings even bad notes home.

Source: Adapted from "An Analysis of Daily Report Cards and Parent-Management Privileges in the Improvement of Adolescent Classroom Performance," by J. B. Schumaker, M. F. Hovell, and J. A. Sherman, 1977, *Journal of Applied Behavior Analysis, 10,* 452. Copyright 1977 by the Society for the Experimental Analysis of Behavior, Inc. Used with permission.

their child is making progress or having problems. Teachers also like the system because it fosters parent participation and cooperation with school programs.

DIFFICULT PARENTS

The parents of most behaviorally disordered children are cooperative and actively solicit or accept assistance. However, some parents may be secretive, thinking the school has no right getting involved in family matters. Other families are so isolated and problem-ridden that other social service agencies must intervene. Some parents even abuse or neglect their children. Teachers must be aware of their legal and ethical obligations in these situations.

Patterson's Family Types

Gerald Patterson (1982) has conceptualized a family typology for difficult families. These families are difficult in the sense that the *"child and the parents* may be extremely resistive to doing what they agreed to do." In some of these families, up to 30 to 40% of the observed family behavior is resistive (Patterson, Reid, & Chamberline, in preparation). Although these family types are broad categories, they are useful to teachers in assessing and dealing with difficult parents.

The Parent-Sibling

This family type frequently shows up with antisocial children referred for treatment (Patterson, 1982; Patterson, Cobb, & Ray, 1973). In effect, this family has no responsible parent. The family is typically a single-parent family, "where the mother has given up the unpleasant features accompanying the role of caretaker" (Patterson, 1982). The mother tries to function as a peer, equal, or friend, buying her children's love by not setting limits or rules. She is isolated and cut off from other adults. There are virtually no rules or discipline in the family, with each family member defending his or her own territory (also see Pointer 10.5). The mother may have assumed some of the children's delinquent values such as believing that stealing and aggression are permissible.

Treatment for such families generally involves helping the parent form satisfactory contacts and relationships outside the family. It is important for the mother in this type of family to realize that needing to be unconditionally loved by her children has left her vulnerable to manipulation.

The Unattached Parent

This type of parent also does not set limits or rules in the family. Unlike the Parent-Sibling, this type of parent has no basic need to be loved by children. These parents are not attached to their children and not committed to the role of caretaker. Patterson (1982) has found that this type of parent-family situation is often associated with behaviorally disordered children who steal.

Unattached Parents are very difficult to involve in any type of intervention or school program. They would simply rather not be bothered. It is almost impossible to get them to attend a meeting. If they do attend, they are generally not motivated to change their child's behavior. Unattached Parents will miss or arrive late for appointments, fail to carry out agreed-upon assignments, and control the topics of discussion at all costs. The outlook for working with those parents is poor and the probability of abuse and neglect is high.

This Child Is Special

These parents represent a paradox in that they know what should be done to manage their child, but they choose not to do it. These families may

Pointer 10.5

INSULAR MOTHERS

Single mothers who have low incomes, are poorly educated (did not complete high school), and have very limited contact with the community may present particularly difficult problems for teachers. These mothers have been called *insular* (Wahler, 1980) because they are isolated from supportive and positive social contacts with the community. When studied (Wahler, Leske, & Rogers, 1979), these mothers had three or less contacts each day, most of which were with extended family or helping agencies. In addition, most of these contacts could be viewed as aversive. For example, a welfare worker might be checking on the mother to make sure the house was in order.

When the children of insular mothers are referred for treatment, their behaviors included a number common to behavior disordered children (Wahler, 1980; Wahler & Afton, 1980). In one study (Wahler, 1980), the behaviors included noncompliance, whining, verbal abuse, hitting, teasing, fighting, stealing, and property destruction. Insular mothers can be trained to change these problem behaviors effectively; however, the changes are generally only temporary. On follow-up after training, the positive training results vanish for most insular mothers. This outcome is very different from noninsular mothers, who generally maintain parent training effects and generalize the skills to new behaviors. Being isolated from social contacts *and* being left alone with difficult children without support dramatically reduces the effects of structured parent training. Insular mothers need both parent training and a positive social system to support their efforts. Special attention from teachers can help form this support.

include other siblings who behave appropriately. However, where the special child is concerned, all the family rules are suspended and firm limits are seldom imposed.

Parents of special children are often puzzled, confused, and frustrated by their child's onslaught of misbehavior. Patterson indicates that many of these parents resort to a "refrigerator" stance to minimize their contact with the child and reduce their frustration and hurt. A teacher or therapist may misinterpret this cold exterior as disinterest that causes the child's inappropriate behavior.

The challenge with this family problem is to convince the parents that normal limits and rules apply to this child. This task is not easy because some parents have great investments in their child's special problem and cannot lose face. However, Patterson (1982) reports that when this type of parent learns child management techniques, they often report increased affection and positive feelings between them and their child.

Overwhelmed

Overwhelmed parents are simply inundated by the day-to-day circumstances of living. Many of them know how to use child management techniques; however, they cannot seem to use them effectively. These families are frequently crushed by poverty. Both parents must work to survive economically and the families are large. There may be a prolonged parental illness. The children are unsupervised for long periods of time. They may steal or vandalize and associate with other unsupervised peers.

One asset in working with Overwhelmed parents is that they truly care for their children and are willing to cooperate if circumstances allow. It may be necessary for teachers to work with other social service agencies in obtaining basic resources for the family. In some instances, after-school day care or even a surrogate caretaker can be arranged.

Sadomasochistic Arabesque

This is a difficult family type because the parents undercut each other. One parent is harsh, strict, and punitive; the other parent is noncontingently warm, permissive, and inconsistent. Patterson (1982) has called this family configuration an Arabesque (a delicately balanced geometric design) because the family power is delicately balanced between two opposing parents—the permissive parent who attempts to balance the severity of the punitive parent, and the punitive parent who attempts to restore some type of order in the home. This type of family, with variations, has been identified by other researchers (Bandura & Walters, 1959; Glueck & Glueck, 1950; Hetherington & Martin, 1979; McCord, McCord, & Howard, 1961) as often correlated with aggressive, antisocial, and delinquent behavior.

Treatment is difficult. The family situation is often unstable because of marital difficulties, which are frequently made worse when the child gains the support of one parent. The behaviorally disordered child is generally managed, sometimes brutally, when the punishing parent is present. However, the permissive parent tries to balance the severe discipline by undercutting, behind the scenes and in secret, the rules laid out by the punishing parent. Any intervention will at least temporarily alienate one parent. Obviously consensus between parents on disciplinary techniques is critical because the child will exploit any rift between the parents. With this family, even if parents agree on child management strategies, there will be difficulties. The punitive parent may revert to harsh measures; the permissive parent may sabotage an agreed-upon approach by making secret deals with the child.

The Sadomasochistic Arabesque family has particular problems that show up in the classroom. Excessively harsh discipline from the punitive parent may result in child abuse. If there is a separation or divorce and the child is left with the permissive parent, the child's anti-social behavior may escalate. Frequently, outside professional will be required for this type of family.

Perfect Parents

These parents may have read a number of books on parenting and behavior management and seem well versed on child-rearing practices. They present a picture of a perfect middle-class family. The parents speak of love and responsibility, and they try to control their children through reasoning and lectures. They rarely set firm limits, but instead, try to talk their children into appropriate behaviors. These families can be obsessed with democracy and fairness and are extremely vulnerable to guilt induction or fairness arguments from their children. Patterson (1982) calls these arguments *Gotcha* arguments because the parents feel ashamed when the child accuses them of being unfair or illogically harsh.

As Patterson has noted, perfect parents are surprisingly difficult to treat. Many have had difficult childhoods themselves. Although perfect parents may appear to be logical and well read, they have tremendous difficulty applying a systematic child behavior management program. Rather, these parents revert to sweet reason and lectures to change their children's behavior. If a child looks sad, appears to listen, or claims repentance (learned manipulation strategies), the parent interprets these behaviors as evidence that the child has changed. Teachers should be particularly careful here because the child can portray the teacher as being an unreasonable disciplinarian. It is not uncommon for the parents to complain to a principal that the teacher is unreasonable and request a change in class assignment.

Misattribution

This type of family is associated with child abuse. The parents have expectations that are too high for the child's age or abilities. The discrepancy between what the child can do and the parents' high expectations is considered by these parents to be proof of the child's malevolent intentions. "The parent can become so preoccupied with negative attributes about the child that even his most innocent behavior is viewed as hostile" (Patterson, 1982). In assessing these families, a teacher should ask the parent to list 5 or 10 positive behaviors or qualities of the child. Often, these parents cannot do this.

Well-supervised child management practices that emphasize reinforcement and information on age-appropriate behaviors can be helpful with these families. Complications can occur when the child is difficult and behaviorally disordered. A social sevice agency may be needed to help a teacher if child abuse is evident.

CHILD ABUSE AND NEGLECT

The true incidence of child abuse and neglect in the United States is unknown because it is underreported. The U.S. National Center on Child Abuse and Neglect estimates that a million children each year suffer significant abuse and neglect (Broadhurst, Edmunds, & MacDicken, 1979). Within this total, 60,000 to 100,000 are sexually abused, 100,000 to 200,000 are physically abused, and the remainder are seriously neglected. Of the total, more than 2,000 children die each year from abuse and neglect. Teachers of behaviorally disordered children are likely to see more cases of abuse and neglect because difficult-to-handle handicapped children are more likely to be abused than nonhandicapped children (Burgess, 1979; Friedrich & Boriskin, 1976). Children who are particularly at risk for abuse have many of the same characteristics as behaviorally disordered children—being stubborn, demanding, resistive, negative, or overly active (Burgess, 1979; Wolfe, 1985).

Parents of abused children also have some common characteristics and behaviors. First, only a small proportion of abusing parents are psychotic or even psychiatrically impaired (Parke & Collmer, 1975; Spinnetta & Riglar, 1972). They are generally under intense stress that can involve marital discord, financial problems, unemployment, drug or alcohol abuse, poor health, parental dependency on the child, and unrealistically high expectations for the child (Burgess, 1979; Wolfe, 1985). Many abusing parents were also abused or neglected themselves as children (Goldstein, Keller, & Erne, 1985). The parents may be repeating a cycle where they are imitating the abusive behaviors of their own parents (Garberino, 1977). Another characteristic of abusive families is isolation of the family from the community at large (Garberino, 1977). The isolated, abusive family may not respond to the normal social controls of the community or may not have access to friends, relatives, or neighbors to help out during times of intense pressure and stress (Burgess, 1979). The size of a family is also related to abuse; families of four or more children have twice the incidence of abuse as families with few children (Gil, 1970; Young, 1964). Abuse is also found more frequently in poorer, lower-class homes (Garberino, 1977; Gil, 1970), though it can also occur (but less frequently) in affluent homes.

A special education teacher must be able to assess signs of physical abuse, sexual abuse, and significant neglect of children. More than 90% of physical abuse involves bruises or burns (Schmitt, 1979). Teachers should be particularly concerned if they find bruises on the lower back, buttocks, genitals, cheeks, ear lobes, or upper lip; these sites reflect possible abuse. Areas that are less indicative of abuse are bruises over bony areas such as an elbow, knee, or forehead. A general rule for identifying bruises caused by abuse is that if the bruises occur in a fleshy, soft part of the body and are numerous, then physical abuse should be suspected. Imprints such as small crescent shapes (pinch bruise), large crescent shapes (bite mark), hand prints with finger marks, two black eyes, long running designs with or without holes (strap or belt), or loops (bent lamp cords) are all commonly associated with physical abuse. Bruises around the neck, wrists, or ankles with or without abrasions suggest choking or being bound for long periods.

Burns make up the next most frequent category of physical abuse. The most common burn is a small circular burn made by cigarettes, matches, or incense. Parents may explain the burns by saying that they were "teaching the child not to play with matches or cigarettes." Scald burns confined to an area such as buttocks, total foot only (stocking burn), or hand only (glove burn) indicate that the child was immersed in hot water. Burns with no splash marks or a burned buttocks with an un-burned center (doughnut burn) suggest a child was held in hot water. The doughnut burn means that the child was forcibly held in hot water with the buttocks held tight against the bottom of a tub, thus escaping contact with hot water. This type of burn is common when children are being toilet trained.

Abdominal injuries caused by hitting or kicking can be lethal in children. Many of these injuries will not show bruises because the abdomen is fleshy and the force of the blow is absorbed by the inner organs. Symptoms associated with abdominal injuries include irritability, vomiting, breathing difficulty, and convulsions (Schmitt, 1979). Physically shaking a child can also be extremely dangerous because of the trauma to and possible hemorrhaging of the brain. Frequently, shaking will involve finger bruise marks on a child's shoulders or arms. In addition, any genital bruises, burns, or abrasions should be carefully monitored as possible child abuse. Children may be abused this way because they have toilet accidents or they masturbate.

Sexual abuse is also fairly common, particularly with girls (Brassard, Tyler, & Kehle, 1983). Females are reported as victims in 10 times as many cases as males, with 97% of the adult offenders being males (DeFrancis, 1969; Devine, 1980). One myth is that child sexual abuse is perpetrated by strangers who are child molesters. In fact, 75% of childhood sexual abuse involves people the child knows; 30 to 50% of the time relatives and parents are the abusers (DeFrancis, 1969). General signs of sexual abuse are bizarre or sophisticated sexual knowledge, seductive behavior towards adults, and unexplained fear of the opposite sex.

Possibly the form of abuse most difficult to identify and most damaging is severe neglect. It may be difficult to identify because many children who live in loving homes with severely limited resources for food and clothing are not neglected. Severe neglect involves the neglect of both physical needs and emotional needs.

EXHIBIT 10.7   Signs of possible abuse

I. Physical abuse
1. *Bruises* (most common sign of abuse)
   a. Bruises on fleshy (buttocks, cheeks, ear lobes, upper lip, throat, inner thighs) parts of the body, not over boney areas (knees, elbows, or foreheads)
   b. Bruises with the outline of a hand or finger outlines
   c. Bruises that are long or rectangular that could be made by belts, buckles, lamp cords, or fan belts (loop)
   d. Bruises or abrasions that are large crescents (bite marks) or small crescents (pinch marks)
   e. Tie marks (bruises or abrasions) around the ankles, wrists, or neck
   f. Any bruise or abrasion in the genital area
   g. Bruises that are bizarre in shape (made by a blunt object such as a toy or brush)
   h. Severe bruises on shoulder (possible shaking abuse)
   i. Numerous bruises

2. *Burns*
   a. Circular burns (could have been made by a cigarette or match)
   b. Severe design burns (made by a heating grate — children generally move before accidental burns become severe)
   c. Circular dunking burns around buttocks, doughnut burn, stocking burn of feet (clear burn line), or glove burn on hand (clear burn line)

3. *Other Injuries*
   a. Bald spots that are tender, torn hair, and no loose hair around edges (possible hair pulled out)
   b. Vomiting, breathing difficulty, swelling, irritability, convulsions, with or without bruises on abdomen (possible abdominal or shaking abuse with internal injuries)
   c. Tattoes, fork puncture marks, gag marks, black eyes

Neglect cases are difficult to prosecute because there are few overt physical signs. However, the effects of severe neglect can be more damaging than even physical abuse (Egeland & Sroufe, 1981). Severe neglect is a slow and insidious process where a child is deprived of nutrition for growth, safe supervision in the home, and most important, a caring and supportive adult. A neglected child may fail to grow (failure-to-thrive syndrome), be less intellectually capable, and have difficulty forming social relationships. The child may appear depressed (with a vacant, expressionless face), look unkempt, and dress inappropriately (particularly for the weather). These children may have characteristics

EXHIBIT 10.7 *continued*

II. Neglect—Failure to Thrive
1. *Basic Signs*
   a. Ravenous appetite at school; asks for more food
   b. Significantly underweight
   c. Inappropriately dressed, particularly for weather (no shoes in winter, no underwear, soiled clothing, always wears the same clothes)
   d. Poor hygiene, smells (urine or body odor)
   e. Difficulty attending or staying awake in class
   f. Depressed look (no eye contact, expressionless face, doesn't interact socially)

III. Sexual Abuse
1. *Basic Signs*
   a. Complaints of itching or pain in genital area
   b. Torn, stained, or bloody underclothing
   c. Difficulty walking or sitting
   d. Bruises or bleeding in external genital, vaginal, or anal area
   e. Venereal disease
   f. Fear or anxiety regarding opposite sex
   g. Bizarre, sophisticated, or unusual sexual knowledge or behavior
   h. Indiscriminate hugging, kissing, or seductive behavior with children or adults

IV. Parent Excuses
1. *Basic Signs*
   a. Parent denies obvious injury
   b. Parents delay in getting medical attention for child
   c. Parents have simple explanation for severe injury (i.e., child broke leg putting on his shoes)
   d. Parents consistently blame sibling for recurring injuries
   e. Parent who was present during the injury will not come in and talk about the circumstances surrounding the injury
   f. Child accuses parent of above, and parent denies the abuse, pointing out how difficult the child is to manage

Sources: Drawn from *Child Abuse/Neglect* by B. D. Schmitt, 1979, Washington, DC: American Academy of Pediatrics; and reprinted with permission from *School Psychology Review, 12,* M. R. Brassard, A. Tyler, and T. J. Kehle, "Sexually Abused Children: Identification and Suggestions for Intervention," copyright 1983, Pergamon Press, Ltd.

that are common to behaviorally disordered children in that they may appear irritable, sleepy, or inattentive. These characteristics can be paritally a function of poor nutrition, especially not eating a regular, nutritious breakfast.

Physical abuse, sexual abuse, and severe neglect are greatly disturbing to teachers. Unfortunately, teachers of the behaviorally disordered will see several abused children in their careers and they must recognize the signs of abuse (see Exhibit 10.7). If a child reports that he or she has been abused, the report must be taken seriously. A teacher's ethical and legal duties are clear in this situation. These cases *must* be reported either to the police or the appropriate social service agency for investigation. If the school principal does not want to get involved and asks the teacher not to report a case, it still must be reported. If a child begs not to have an incident reported (which is not uncommon in sexual abuse and physical abuse cases), it still must be reported. Most states have laws that require reporting abuse upon its discovery. The reporting laws protect the informant with immunity from an angry parent who may want to sue. If a case is not reported, the person discovering the abuse may be prosecuted by the state. Worse, not reporting abuse can condemn a child to physical injury, death, sexual exploitation (with pregnancy or disease), a life of squalor and filth, and the devastating psychological effects of abuse and neglect.

Most successful treatment programs for abusive parents involve relieving stress, retraining, and supportive monitoring. The services needed for the successful treatment of abuse go beyond what most schools can offer and require outside community resources. Programs such as Project 12-Ways (Lutzker, 1984) at the University of Southern Illinois involve intensive training that includes marital counseling, child management training, stress reduction, and a number of other skills. A cost-effective, direct training approach, Project 12-Ways has reduced child abuse dramatically, with only 10% recurrence (Lutzker, 1984). Most communities have child abuse treatment services, and teachers of behaviorally disordered children should be aware of these services and how to use them.

SUMMARY

In this chapter, we have discussed the importance of working with parents as equals in the education of behaviorally disordered children. We have also identified a number of myths concerning parents and shown how these myths can be destructive and interfere with effective education. We have presented the rationale for working with parents to establish home systems that aid both the child, parent, and teacher. Finally, the more problematic area of working with difficult and abusive parents was reviewed. Difficult parents and abusing parents present a challenge and frustration to special education teachers. However, even in the worst of family circumstances, a teacher can offer an abused or neglected child 5 hours of a stable and caring environment.

There is still a great deal more to be learned about working with parents. The field is relatively untapped. Only with the enactment of such laws as P.L. 94-142 has the need for working with parents been empha-sized. A great deal can be gained from working with parents apart from the legal mandates. Parents can contribute to improved classroom management of a child's behavior and to enhanced generalization of treatment gains. Some of the most rewarding experiences for special education teachers may be derived from successfully working with parents.

REVIEW QUESTIONS

1. What does it mean to view parents as "equal partners"?
2. Can teachers of behaviorally disordered students effectively do their job *without* dealing with the parents for their students? Explain your answer.
3. Why do you think behavioral approaches to parent training are effective?
4. One of your students comes to school with noticeable bruises and marks on his face, neck, and back. What is your responsibility as the teacher? To whom should this incident be reported? How should you behave toward the student?
5. Are behaviorally disordered children more or less likely to be abused or neglected than their normal peers? Why?

REFERENCES

Atkeson, B. M., & Forehand, R. (1979). Home-based reinforcement programs designed to modify classroom behavior: A review and methodological eval-uation. *Psychological Bulletin, 86,* 1298–1308.

Bandura, A. (1973). *Aggression: A social learning analysis.* Englewood Cliffs, NJ: Prentice-Hall.

Bandura, A., & Walters, R. H. (1959). *Adolescent aggression.* New York: Ronald Press Co.

Becker, W. C. (1971). *Parents are teachers.* Champaign, IL: Research Press.

Bijou, S. W. (1972). These kids have problems and our job is to do something about them. In J. B. Jordan & L. S. Robbins (Eds.), *Let's try doing something else kind of thing.* Arlington, VA: Council for Exceptional Children.

Blechman, E. A. (1985). *Solving child behavior problems at home and at school.* Champaign, IL: Research Press.

Brassard, M. R., Tyler, A., & Kehle, T. J. (1983). Sexually abused children: Identification and suggestion for intervention. *School Psychology Review, 12,* 93–96.

Broadhurst, D. D., Edmunds, M., & MacDicken, R. A. (1979). *Early childhood programs the prevention and treatment of child abuse and neglect.* National Center on Child Abuse and Neglect Children's Bureau. (DHEW Publication No. (OHDS) 79–30198). Washington, DC: U.S. Government Printing Office.

Broughton, S. F., Barton, E. S., & Owen, P. R. (1981). Home-based contingency systems for school problems. *School Psychology Review, 10,* 26–36.

Burgess, R. L. (1979). Child abuse: A social interactional analysis. In B. B. Lahey & A. E. Kazdin (Eds.), *Advances in clinical child psychology* (Vol. 2). New York: Plenum Press.

Cadoret, R. (1978). Psychopathology in adopted away offspring of biological parents with antisocial behavior. *Archives of General Psychiatry, 35,* 176–184.

Canter, L., & Canter, M. (1982). *Assertive discipline for parents.* Santa Monica, CA: Canter and Associates.

Clark, L. (1985). *SOS: Help for parents: A practical guide for handling common everyday behavior problems.* Bowling Green, KY: Parents Press.

Cosby, B. (1986). *Fatherhood.* Garden City, NY: Dolphine Press.

Dachman, R. S., Halasz, M. M., & Bickett, A. D. (1984). The use of dot-to-dot patterns and a grab bag to reduce inappropriate child behavior. *The Behavior Therapist, 7,* 4, 14.

Dangel, R. F., & Polster, R. A. (1984). WINNING! A systematic, empirical approach to parent training. In R. F. Dangel & R. A. Polster (Eds.), *Parent training: Foundations of research and practice.* New York: Guilford Press.

David, O. J., Hoffman, S. P., Sverd, J., Clark, J., & Voeller, K. (1976). Lead and hyperactivity. Behavioral response to chelation: A pilot study. *American Journal of Psychiatry, 133,* 1155–1158.

DeFrancis, V. (1969). *Protecting the child victims of sex crimes committed by adults.* Denver: American Humane Association.

Devine, R. A. (1980). Incest: A review of the literature. In *Sexual abuse of children: Selected readings.* Washington, DC: U.S. Department of Health and Human Services, DHHS Publication No. (OHDS) 78–30161, November.

Egeland, B., & Sroufe, A. (1981). *Developmental sequelae of maltreatment in infancy.* In R. Rizely & D. Cicchetti (Eds.), *Developmental perspectives on child maltreatment, 11,* 77–92.

Fleischman, M., Horne, A., & Arthur, J. L. (1983). *Trouble families: A treatment program.* Champaign, IL: Research Press.

Forehand, R., & McMahon, R. J. (1981). *Helping the noncompliant child: A clinician's guide to parent training.* New York: Guilford Press.

Friedrich, W. N., & Boriskin, J. A. (1976). The role of the child in abuse: A review of the literature. *American Journal of Orthopsychiatry, 46,* 580–590.

Gallagher, J. J., Beckman, P., & Cross, A. H. (1983). Families of handicapped children: Sources of stress and its amelioration. *Exceptional Children, 50,* 10–19.

Garberino, J. (1977). The human ecology of child maltreatment: A conceptual model for research. *Journal of Marriage and the Family, 39,* 721–735.

Gelfand, D. M., & Hartmann, D. P. (1977). The prevention of childhood behavior disorders. In B. B. Lahey & A. E. Kazdin (Eds.), *Advances in child clinical psychology* (Vol. 1). New York: Plenum Press.

Gelfand, D. M., Jenson W. R., & Drew, C. (1982). *Understanding child behavior disorders.* New York: Holt, Rinehart and Winston.

Gil, D. G. (1970). *Violence against children: Physical child abuse in the United States.* Cambridge: Harvard University Press.

Glueck, S., & Glueck, E. T. (1950). *Unravelling juvenile delinquency.* Cambridge: Harvard University Press.

Goldstein, A. P., Keller, H., & Erne, D. (1985). *Changing the abusive parent.* Champaign, IL: Research Press.

Hall, M. C. (1981). *Responsive parenting.* Shawnee Mission, KS: Responsive Management.

Hall, M. C. (1984). Responsive parenting: A large-scale training program for school districts, hospitals, and mental health centers. In R. F. Dangel & R. A. Polster (Eds.), *Parent training: Foundations of research and practice,* New York: Guilford Press.

Hall, R. V., Copeland, R. E., & Clark, M. (1976). Management strategies for teachers and parents: Responsive teaching. In N. Haring & R. Schiefelbusch (Eds.), *Teaching special children.* New York: McGraw-Hill.

Herbert, E. W., & Baer, D. M. (1972). Training parents as behavior modifiers: Self-recording contingent attention. *Journal of Applied Behavior Analysis, 5,* 139–149.

Herbert, M. (1978). *Conduct disorders of childhood and adolescence: A behavioural approach to assessment and treatment.* New York: John Wiley.

Hetherington, E. M., & Martin, B. (1979). Family interaction. In H. C. Quay & J. S. Werry (Eds.), *Psychopathological disorders of childhood* (2nd. ed.). New York: John Wiley.

Holroyd, J. (1974). The questionnaire on resources and stress: An instrument to measure family response to a handicapped member. *Journal of Community Psychology, 2,* 92–94.

Imber, S. C., Imber, R. B., & Rothstein, C. (1979). Modifying independent work habits: An effective teacher-parent communication program. *Exceptional Children, 45,* 218–221.

Jenson, W. R., & Staff (1980). *Children's Behavior Therapy Unit's parenting group.* Unpublished manuscript.

Jenson, W. R. (1985). Skills preference in two different types of parenting groups. *Small Group Behavior, 16,* 549–555.

Jenson, W. R., & Sloane, H. N. (1979). Chart moves and grab bags: A simple contingency management system. *Journal of Applied Behavior Analysis, 12,* 334.

Krumboltz, J. D., & Krumboltz, H. B. (1972). *Changing children's behavior.* Englewood Cliffs, NJ: Prentice-Hall.

Larsson, D. G., & Larsson, E. V. (1982). *Parent training and generalization of skills in economically depressed rural areas.* Paper presented at the Association for Behavior Analysis, Milwaukee.

Levitt, E. E. (1971). Research on psychotherapy with children. In A. E. Bergin & S. L. Garfield (Eds.), *Handbook of psychotherapy and behavior change: An empirical analysis.* New York: John Wiley.

Lutzker, J. R. (1984). Project 12-Ways: Treating child abuse and neglect from an ecobehavioral perspective. In R. F. Dangel & R. A. Polster (Eds.), *Parent training: Foundations of research and practice.* New York: Guilford Press.

Marcus, L. M. (1977). Patterns of coping in families of psychotic children. *American Journal of Orthopsychiatry, 47,* 388–398.

Martin, R. (1979). *Educating handicapped children: The legal mandate.* Champaign, IL: Research Press.

McAndrew, I. (1976). Children with a handicap and their families. *Child: Care, Health and Development, 2,* 213–237.

McCord, W., McCord, J., & Howard, A. (1961). Familial correlates of aggression in nondelinquent male children. *Journal of Abnormal and Social Psychology, 62,* 79–93.

Miller, W. H. (1975). *Systematic parent training.* Champaign, IL: Research Press.

O'Dell, S. (1974). Training parents in behavior modification: A review. *Psychological Bulletin, 81,* 418–433.

Parke, R., & Collmer, C. (1975). Child abuse: An interdisciplinary analysis: In M. Hetherington (Ed.), *Review of child development research* (Vol. 5). Chicago: University of Chicago Press.

Patterson, G. R. (1974). Interventions for boys with conduct problems: Multiple settings, treatments, and criteria. *Journal of Consulting and Clinical Psychology, 42,* 471–481.

Patterson, G. R. (1979a). *Families: Applications of social learning to family life.* Champaign, IL: Research Press.

Patterson, G. R. (1979b). *Living with children: New methods for parents and teachers.* Champaign, IL: Research Press.

Patterson, G. R. (1982). *Coercive family process.* Eugene, OR: Castalia.

Patterson, G. R., Cobb, J. A., & Ray, R. S. (1973). A social engineering technology for retraining the families of aggressive boys. In H. E. Adams & I. P. Unikel (Eds.), *Issues and trend in behavior therapy.* Springfield, IL: Charles C Thomas.

Patterson, G. R., Reid, J. B., & Chamberlin, P. (in preparation). *Family typology and clinical resistance.* Eugene: Oregon Social Learning Center.

Polster, R. A., & Dangel, R. F. (1984). Behavioral parent training: Where it came from and where it's at. In R. F. Dangel & R. A. Polster (Eds.), *Parent training: Foundations of research and practice.* New York: Guilford Press.

Reisinger, J J., Ora, J. P., & Frangia, G. W. (1976). Parents as change agents for their children: A review. *Journal of Consulting Psychology, 4,* 103–123.

Richman, N. (1977). Behavior problems in preschool children: Family and social factors. *Journal of Psychiatry, 131,* 525–527.

Rinn, R. C., & Markle, A. (1977). *Positive parenting.* Cambridge, MA: Research Media.

Saudargas, R. W., Madsen, C. H., & Scott, J. W. (1977). Differential effects of fixed and variable time feedback on production rates of elementary school children. *Journal of Applied Behavior Analysis, 10,* 673–678.

Schmitt, B. D. (1979). *Child abuse/neglect.* Washington, DC: American Academy of Pediatrics.

Schumaker, J. B., Hovell, M. F., & Sherman, J. A. (1977). An analysis of daily report cards and parent managed privileges in the improvement of adolescent classroom performance. *Journal of Applied Behavior Analysis, 10,* 449–464.

Sloane, H. N. (1976). *Classroom management: Remediation and prevention.* New York: John Wiley.

Sloane, H. N. (1979). *The good kid book: A manual for parents.* New York: New American Library.

Spinnetta, J. J., & Rigler, D. (1972). The child abusing parent: A psychological review. *Psychological Bulletin, 77,* 296–304.

Thomas, A., Chess, S., & Birch, H. G. (1969). *Temperament and behavior disorders in children.* New York: New York University Press.

Wagonseller, B. R., Burnett, M., Salzberg, B., & Burnett, J. (1977). *The art of parenting.* Champaign, IL: Research Press.

Wahler, R. G. (1980). The insular mother: Her problems in parent-child treatment. *Journal of Applied Behavior Analysis, 13,* 207–219.

Wahler, R. G., & Afton, A. D. (1980). Attentional process in insular and noninsular mothers: Some differences in their summary reports about child problem behaviors. *Child Behavior Therapy, 2,* 25–41.

Wahler, R. G., Leske, G., & Rogers, E. S. (1979). The insular family: A deviance support system. In L. A. Hamerlynck (Ed.), *Behavioral systems for developmentally disabled: I. School and family environments.* New York: Bruner/Mazel.

Wahler, R., Winkler, G. H., Peterson, R. F., & Morrison, D. C. (1965). *Behaviour Research and Therapy, 3,* 113-124.

Wolfe, D.A. (1985). Child-abusive parents. An empirical review and analysis. *Psychological Bulletin, 97,* 462-482.

Young, L. (1964). *Wednesday's children: A study of child neglect and abuse.* New York: McGraw-Hill.

11 Legal Issues in Educating Behaviorally Disordered Children

John E. B. Myers, J. D.
Associate Professor
McGeorge School of Law
University of the Pacific

After completing this chapter, you should be able to

- *Define special education, related services, and appropriate education.*
- *Describe basic elements of due process.*
- *Explain the distinction between legitimate behavior management techniques and interventions that are abusive.*
- *Describe the basic elements of informed consent for behavior management programs.*
- *Explain legal guidelines for the use of punishment and other aversive techniques.*
- *Identify the current legal status of the use of corporal punishment and suspension and expulsion of behaviorally disordered students from school.*

During the past two decades, the law has played an increasingly important role in the regulation and operation of special education programs. To plan and implement effective educational programs for behaviorally disordered children, educators, psychologists, and other professionals must acquire a working knowledge of the principal laws and regulations in this field. Familiarity with the law can lead to better educational services for children and reduced friction between professionals and parents.

This chapter discusses the major legal issues related to the education of behaviorally disordered students, beginning with an historical overview of major state and federal court decisions and legislation. The concepts of least restrictive environment and due process are included. Information concerning legal issues in behavior management, school discipline, and the use of medications is also provided. Finally, the chapter reviews issues associated with the liability of school personnel.

HISTORICAL BACKGROUND

Legislative bodies and courts have only recently become involved in issues relating to special education. Prior to 1970, there was little legal activity in this field, and educators were left on their own to operate special education programs at the state and local levels. During the 1960s, however, the nation awakened to many forms of discrimination, including discrimination against the handicapped (Gee & Sperry, 1978). Attention was focused on the plight of intellectually and physically handicapped children who were either receiving inadequate educational opportunities or were excluded from school (Martin, 1979a). As late as 1971, for example, some states excluded mentally retarded and behaviorally disordered children from the public schools. The total number of handicapped children denied the basic right to an appropriate education will never be known, but it was certainly in the hundreds of thousands.

Two landmark court cases from the early 1970s spelled the beginning of the end of systematic exclusion of the handicapped from public school (Pullin, 1982). In the first case, *Pennsylvania Association for Retarded Children* v. *Commonwealth of Pennsylvania* (P.A.R.C.) (1971), parents of retarded children sued the state over its policy of excluding the retarded from school. The parents charged that to treat handicapped children differently than their nonhandicapped peers violated the constitutional guarantee of equal protection of the laws. When the judge decided the case in favor of the parents and their children, education opportunities and services became available for the handicapped in Pennsylvania and across the nation (Martin, 1979a). Following in the footsteps of the P.A.R.C. case, parents in the Distict of Columbia sued their school board over its policy of excluding many mentally retarded and behaviorally disordered children from school. In this case, *Mills* v. *Board of Education* (1972), the judge ordered the school system to establish a plan for the education of all handicapped children.

Following the parents' victories in *P.A.R.C.* and *Mills,* many states took steps to provide improved special education programs to handicapped children. At the same time, public pressure caused Congress to increase funds for distribution to the states to help pay for special education programs. Through the combined efforts of parents, educators, and legislators, work began on what eventually became the most important legislation in history relating to education of handicapped children—the Education for All Handicapped Children Act and Section 504 of the Rehabilitation Act of 1973. With passage of these two statutes came a veritable revolution in American special education. The statutes provide incalculable educational benefits to millions of handicapped children and their families.

The Education for All Handicapped Children Act

Congress passed the Education for All Handicapped Children Act in 1975. This federal statute, which is commonly known as Public Law (PL) 94-142, marks a major step forward in the education of handicapped children. The law serves two principal functions. First, it is a funding statute under which federal monies are distributed to the states to supplement state and school district special education budgets. In 1986, for example, more than a billion dollars was distributed under a complicated formula that considers the number of handicapped children living in each state.

The second principal function of the statute is to establish the requirement that all school-aged handicapped children in states receiving PL 94-142 funds be provided a "free appropriate public education." This is a lofty goal; to ensure its fulfillment, the statute sets forth detailed procedures the states must follow. As is normally the case with complex federal legislation, the federal agency charged with responsibility for the statute's administration—in this case the U. S. Department of Education—wrote specific regulations to clarify the broad statutory language. The regulations promulgated uner PL 94-142 are complex and detailed. Special educators should become familiar with them so they can develop programs that meet all the requirements. While this chapter focuses on the federal regulations, keep in mind that in each state where PL 94-142 applies, there are state statutes and regulations as well as rules and policies within each school district. At times the shear volume of rules and regulations seems overwhelming; however, their importance makes them deserving of careful study.

Definitions

Before discussing the requirements of the PL 94–142 regulations, it is important to study the way the regulations define certain key terms.

Special Education

This term is defined as "specially designed instruction, at no cost to the parent, to meet the unique needs of a handicapped child, including classroom instruction, instruction in physical education, home instruction, and instruction in hospitals and institutions" (34 C.F.R. 300.14(a)(1)). The key to understanding this regulation is to remember its emphasis on individualized instruction designed to meet the unique needs of the child (Larson, 1985). The definition makes clear that educational services for behaviorally disordered children must be available in an array of settings, ranging from the regular education classroom to residential programming.

The word "education" has a special meaning in the context of programming for handicapped children. It is given an expansive definition, going well beyond the traditional academic subjects. Certainly, for many handicapped children, educational programming places primary emphasis on traditional subjects, but it is easy to see that, for the more seriously handicapped, the term embraces nontraditional interventions. Several examples will illustrate the point. For a severely mentally retarded child who is also physically handicapped, educational programming might consist of learning basic self-care skills such as eating and toileting; for an autistic child, it might consist primarily of learning alternative means of communication such as signing. For a behaviorally disordered child, a behavior management program aimed at decreasing noncompliance is education. "Education" is a flexible term, and educational programming for handicapped children takes many forms, depending on the needs of the child. It is this very flexibility that makes special education so exciting because professionals working with handicapped children can creatively shape programs to meet individual needs.

Related Services

Recall that PL 94-142 guarantees every handicapped child a free appropriate education. As defined in the law, "education" includes both special education and such "related services" as needed to enable a child to benefit from special education. Related services are defined as "developmental, corrective, and other supportive services (which) are required to assist a handicapped child to benefit from special education" (34 C.F.R. 300.13(a)). The term includes such services as speech therapy, language development, physical and occupational therapy, recreation, social work services, counseling services, psychological services, and school health services.

A good deal of debate surrounds the concept of related services. One of the most controversial issues is whether schools are required to provide psychological counseling and psychotherapy (Akin, Black, Guarino, Klebanoff, & Rosenfeld, 1981–82; *McKenzie* v. *Jefferson,* 1983). School administrators frequently argue that those services are outside the traditional role of the schools and should be provided by other agencies such as community mental health centers. Parents, on the other hand, take the position that their children cannot benefit from educational programming without those services.

While there is still confusion over this issue, it appears that psychological services, including psychotherapy, can sometimes be related services. To determine whether the services are required by PL 94-142 as related services, the question to ask is whether they are necessary for the child to derive educational benefit from an individualized education program. If the answer is yes, and the services "are coordinated with the intent to directly reinforce a student's special education program," then they may be related services *(In re Carlisle Area School District,* 1981–82). If the services are not directly related to the child's edcuational needs, however, or if they can be administered "other than during the school day" they may not be related services *(Irving Independent School Dist.* v. *Tatro,* 1984; *In re P.,* 1982).

It is not possible to determine in advance whether psychological services are related services. Each case must be evaluated on its own merits. In the final analysis, the unique needs of each child should dictate the ser-

Every handicapped child is guaranteed an appropriate education.

vices provided. Fortunately, some progressive school districts around the country have instituted excellent programs for behaviorally disordered children that include psychological services, psychotherapy, group therapy, and social case work (Knitzer, 1982).

Appropriate Education

Under PL 94-142, every handicapped child is guaranteed an "appropriate" education. Because a program that is appropriate for one handicapped child may be inappropriate for another, the appropriateness of a particular child's program depends largely on whether it is specially designed to meet the child's unique educational needs. Because every child's education needs are unique, it is difficult to formulate a generic definition of the word "appropriate." It is possible, however, to establish parameters for appropriateness of education services under the law. In general, a child's educational program meets the requirement of appropriateness if it satisfies all of the following criteria:

1. The child's program meets the legal requirements of PL 94-142 and the rules and regulations of the state educational agency where the child lives.
2. The program is tailored to meet the unique educational needs of the child.
3. The program ensures that the child has meaningful access to educational services.
4. The program is sufficient in content and scope to afford meaningful educational benefit to the child (*Board of Education* v. *Rowley,* 1982).

PL 94-142 in Operation

The Education for All Handicapped Children Act established a four-step sequence that every handicapped child follows on the path toward an appropriate education. Each step follows logically from the one before it, and each contains numerous technical nuances. The steps are as follows.

1. First, every school district receiving PL 94-142 funds must locate all handicapped children living within its boundaries.
2. Once a child is located, he or she must be evaluated by a multidisciplinary team of professionals.
3. When the necessary evaluation and diagnostic data are available, educators and parents meet to formulate an individualized education plan (IEP) for the child.
4. Finally, the child's IEP is implemented by the teachers and other professionals working with the child.

EXHIBIT 11.1   Education of handicapped children

Step 1

Child Find
School districts try to find and identify every handicapped child within their boundaries. Children gain access to special education through their school district's child find effort.

Step 2

Evaluation
When a child is first identified as possibly handicapped, he or she must be evaluated by a multidisciplinary team of professionals knowledgeable about the particular handicap. Every handicapped child must be reevaluated every three years. More frequent reevaluations may be appropriate for some children. Parents must give their consent to the evaluation. If parents believe the school's evaluation of their child is not appropriate, they can request an independent educational evaluation by professionals who are not employed by the district. In some cases, parents can require the district to pay for the independent educational evaluation.

Step 3

IEP
Every handicapped child must have a written IEP. The IEP must be rewritten once a year. It can be rewritten more often if the child's needs change. The IEP is formulated and written by an IEP team at a meeting usually called an IEP meeting. The IEP team consists of the parents, teacher, an administrator, and the child, if appropriate. For an initial IEP, a member of the evaluation team must be present. The IEP contains:
- long term goals
- short term instructional objectives
- the child's placement
- related services

Step 4

Implementation
When the child's IEP has been written, the last step in the P.L. 94-142 process takes place: The IEP is implemented by the teachers and other professionals who will work with the child throughout the year.
If major program changes need to be made during the year then it is necessary to go back to Step 3, call a new IEP meeting, and change the child's IEP. The new IEP is then implemented.

This four-step process, illustrated in Exhibit 11.1, is the heart of PL 94-142.

Least Restrictive Environment

As the IEP team formulates the child's program of specialized instruction and related services, it must consider the educational placement where these services can be most appropriately provided. For example, should the child be mainstreamed full-time, or is a resource room or self-contained classroom necessary? Is the child's condition so serious that the only appropriate placement is in a setting where intensive intervention is possible 24 hours a day?

When deliberating the crucial question of placement, the IEP team is guided by PL 94-142's overriding mandate that, to the maximum extent appropriate, handicapped children should be educated with nonhandicapped children. This principle is known as education in the *least restrictive environment,* or mainstreaming (Martin, 1979a). It is a touchstone for placement decisions under the law.

According to PL 94-142, the regular education classroom is normally considered the least restrictive environment because it is the normal educational environment for school-aged children. Children can be placed outside the regular, mainstream classroom only "when the nature or severity of the handicap is such that education in regular classes with the use of supplementary aides and services cannot be achieved satisfactorily" (34 C.F.R. 300.550(b)(2)). Placement outside the regular classroom is considered more restrictive than placement within the regular classroom, and it is inappropriate unless it is required to enable the child to benefit from education. For example, placement in a resource room two periods a day is more restrictive than full-time placement in the regular classroom. Placement in a self-contained classroom all day is more restrictive than the resource placement. Institutional care is, of course, still more restrictive.

This sequence of placements, which begins with the least restrictive and moves to progressively more restrictive placements, is easy to understand. Where behaviorally disordered children are concerned, however, there is one placement that at first glance appears to be less restrictive than the regular classroom, but is actually more restrictive. This group of deceptively restrictive placements is sometimes called *home-study.* It is unfortunately true that many behaviorally disordered children are inappropriately placed on "home study." A home study placement is restrictive because the goal of PL 94-142 is to educate handicapped children *with* their nonhandicapped peers. Any removal of a child from the mainstream, including home study, is more restrictive than the regular classroom, and unless the child needs the increased restrictiveness, is inappropriate. For example, if educators decide to educate a child at home and to permit no attendance at school or participation with nonhandicapped students, this seemingly unrestrictive placement is actually *very* restrictive (*Department of Education* v. *Katherine D.,* 1982).

It is especially important for professionals working with behaviorally disordered children to realize the inappropriate restrictiveness of home study, because some schools have failed in their duty to mainstream these children. Rather than provide needed programming, they have simply gotten rid of behaviorally disordered youngsters by telling them they cannot return to school and euphemistically calling their "non-placement" home study. This abandonment of troubled youth must be avoided because it violates PL 94-142 and does a tremendous disservice to children, their families, and the community. Exhibit 11.2 illustrates the principles of the least restrictive placement.

Schools are responsible for all of the educational and related services contained in the IEP. These services must be provided at no cost to the parents of the handicapped child. The services required by a child's IEP cannot be significantly altered unless a new IEP meeting is held to reassess the child's needs. This is not to say that professionals are powerless to make minor changes during the academic year. As long as changes in programming are not major, they can be made. If parents or educators want to alter the IEP, however, it is necessary to go through the IEP process, including an IEP meeting.

The law requires educators to provide the services contained in a child's IEP and to make reasonable efforts to assist the child to achieve his or her goals and objectives. However, PL 94-142 does not make professionals working with children legally accountable if a child falls short of those goals and objectives. There are simply too many variables at work to guarantee that even the best program will bring about all of the goals established in an IEP. On the other hand, when an educationally sound IEP is implemented by dedicated and caring professionals working closely with parents, there is every likelihood of substantial progress.

RESOLVING DISAGREEMENTS OVER IDENTIFICATION, EVALUATION, OR EDUCATIONAL PLACEMENT

The four-step process described above forms the basic structure for delivery of special education services under the Education for All Handicapped Children Act. Children enter the system and receive individualized programming as long as they need it. The procedure works smoothly and efficiently for most handicapped children and ensures that they derive substantial benefit from their schooling. As is true with any system affecting large numbers of people, however, there are bound to be occasional disagreements. Parents and educators sometimes part ways

EXHIBIT 11.2 Least restrictive placement

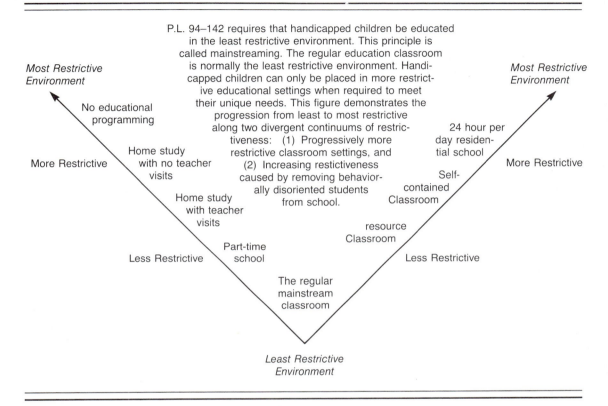

Most Restrictive Environment

No educational programming

More Restrictive

Home study with no teacher visits

Home study with teacher visits

Less Restrictive

Part-time school

The regular mainstream classroom

Least Restrictive Environment

P.L. 94–142 requires that handicapped children be educated in the least restrictive environment. This principle is called mainstreaming. The regular education classroom is normally the least restrictive environment. Handicapped children can only be placed in more restrictive educational settings when required to meet their unique needs. This figure demonstrates the progression from least to most restrictive along two divergent continuums of restrictiveness: (1) Progressively more restrictive classroom settings, and (2) Increasing restictiveness caused by removing behaviorally disoriented students from school.

Most Restrictive Environment

24 hour per day residential school

More Restrictive

Self-contained Classroom

resource Classroom

Less Restrictive

over issues relating to the special education of particular children. PL 94-142 contains a detailed mechanism for resolving disagreements.

The law encourages parents to work closely with teachers, administrators, and other professionals to ensure appropriate programming for the handicapped child. Under the law, parents are equal partners with educators in the decision-making process. Most agreements can be resolved in a friendly manner through cooperative and flexible negotiation. In some cases, however, when parents and educators simply cannot come to terms about some aspect of a child's evaluation, IEP, or placement, PL 94-142 provides a process for their resolution. Because teachers may have occasion to be involved in the resolution of disputes, it is important that they understand how the mechanism works.

Under our legal system disputes are resolved in a number of ways, ranging from informal negotiation through administrative hearings, which are more formal, to adversarial court litigation. Whatever the mechanism chosen or required to resolve a dispute, the legal system seeks to reach the correct outcome while providing fairness and impartiality to both sides. The fundamental requirement of fairness in legal proceedings derives from the *due process* clause of the U. S. constitution.

Due process of law is a flexible concept. It does not require a single set of procedures and rules for all types of legal proceedings. On the contrary, it mandates different procedures in different contexts. For example, in court proceedings before a judge, formal rules of evidence and procedure apply. Either the judge or a jury decides who wins. In an administrative hearing, on the other hand, due process requires less formalistic procedures. The formal rules of evidence and procedure are relaxed or not used. The decision maker in administrative proceedings is often called an *administrative hearing officer* or *administrative law judge*. Sometimes, as in the case of PL 94-142 administrative hearings, the hearing officer need not be a judge or an attorney. The hearing officer in a PL 94-142 case might be a special educator who has been trained in how to conduct a hearing.

While due process requires different procedures to ensure fairness in different contexts, it is possible to list several basic requirements that apply in most proceedings, including PL 94-142 hearings. Due proess requires that notice be given to the parties so they can prepare their case. Each side has the right to an attorney. Both sides may subpoena and cross-examine witnesses. A record must be kept of the proceedings. Usually, the losing party has the right to appeal. Finally, an impartial judge or hearing officer presides over the proceedings to ensure fairness and to make a decision.

In special education, most disagreements are resolved through informal negotiation between parents and educators. When negotiation is unsuccessful, however, the PL 94-142 regulations state that an administrative hearing can be requested to resolve the dispute. The hearing is called a *due process hearing*. Either parents or school districts can initiate due process proceedings. In most cases, however, it is the parents who request a hearing. A hearing can be requested if a parent disagrees with a school district proposal to change a child's identification as handicapped or to alter a child's individualized program. A hearing can also be requested if a district refuses a parent's request to change a child's identification or program. Additionally, parents can request a hearing if they disagree with the way in which a child's IEP is implemented.

When a parent requests a due process hearing, the school district appoints an impartial hearing officer, who cannot be an employee of the district. After being appointed, a hearing officer conducts the hearing and makes a decision on the case. If either party is dissatisfied with the decision, an appeal may be filed. The appeal is to a higher administrative body or directly to court. When a final decision is reached, either at the due process hearing or after appeal, it is binding on both parents and educators.

Due process proceedings can take considerable time, especially if there is an appeal. While the proceedings are pending, the child usually must remain in the educational placement he or she was in when the process began. For example, suppose a child is enrolled in a self-contained classroom for behaviorally disordered children. After 6 months, the

EXHIBIT 11.3 Due process procedures for resolving educational disputes over programming

Step 4. COURT ACTION: After Steps 2 and 3 are completed, the losing party may commence a court action in federal or state court. The judge considers all the evidence produced at Steps 2 and 3. He or she may also consider further evidence. The judge then renders a decision which is final unless the losing party appeals to a higher court.

Step 3. APPEAL TO STATE BOARD OF EDUCATION: In many states the party who looses the due process hearing may appeal the decision to the State Board of Education. The State Board appoints an official to conduct an impartial review of the due process hearing. After reviewing all the evidence, the offical makes an independent decision on the case.

Step 2. DUE PROCESS HEARING: A hearing officier is appointed. A due process hearing is scheduled promptly. The hearing officer hears the evidence presented by the parents and the school district. The hearing officer's decision is final unless the losing party appeals.

Step 1. INITIAL DISAGREEMENT: Parents and educators disagree about some aspect of a child's identification, evaluation, placement, or educational program. If the disagreement cannot be worked out through negotiation or mediation, then the parent or the school district requests a due process hearing.

teachers feel the child is ready to be mainstreamed into the regular class-room. The parents, however, feel strongly that the move would be inappropriate. A due process hearing is requested by the parents after negotiations with the educators fail to resolve the dispute. During the due process proceedings, the child remains in the self-contained classroom.

There are three limited exceptions to the rule that a student's placement cannot be changed during due process proceedings. First, if parents and the school district agree, the change can be made while the proceedings are pending. Second, if the disagreement involves an initial application for admission to public school, the child must be admitted until the proceedings are completed. Third, if remaining in a program would cause a child serious harm, parents or educators may request a court to order a change in placement.

The due process hearing procedures established by PL 94-142 have been used by parents around the nation to resolve disagreements over special education programming. Hundreds of hearings have been held, some of which have been appealed to the courts. A few have gone all the way to the United States Supreme Court. Teachers, psychologists, social workers, administrators, and others have been called to testify regarding the programming needs of particular children. Fortunately, the decisions in some cases have set valuable precedents that are of great assistance in the effort to ensure appropriate special education programming for all handicapped children. While use of due process hearings to resolve disagreements has positive aspects and is sometimes the only solution, in most cases the expense, delay, and frequent ill-will generated by the procedure can be avoided. When parents and educators join together in an honest and even-handed effort to keep the focus squarely on the best interest of the child, most disagreements can be amicably resolved. Exhibit 11.3 illustrates the appeal process under PL 94-142.

LEGAL ISSUES IN THE USE OF BEHAVIOR MANAGEMENT

Behavior management strategies are frequently used in the education and treatment of behaviorally disordered children. Professionals using behavior management techniques should be familiar with their legal implications so they can use the technology effectively and avoid running afoul of the law.

The courts become embroiled in controversies over behavior management when the practices of certain institutions were questioned (Martin, 1979b). In the early 1970s several law suits were filed against institutions for the mentally ill and the mentally retarded, prisoners, and juvenile delinquents (*Knecht* v. *Gillman*, 1973; *Pena* v. *New York State Division of Youth*, 1976; *Wyatt* v. *Stickney*, 1972). The challenged practices included undue physical restraint, isolation, and overuse of tran-quilizing drugs. These practices were abuses of both human rights and the legitimate uses of behavior management. An "experiment" carried out in a California prison is a good example of the misuse of behavioral technology. Inmates who demonstrated "inappropriate" behavior were given a drug called *anectine* (*Mackey* v. *Procunier,* 1973). The drug caused temporary paralysis of the of the respiratory system resulting in a terrify-ing feeling of suffocation and impending death. It was theorized that as-sociating the aversive state with the unwanted behavior would suppress the behavior. The court ruled that such treatment could not be employed. The 1976 case of *Gary W.* v. *Louisiana* also involved an institution. The court challenge was made on behalf of behaviorally disordered children in a juvenile detention facility. Among other things, the children's attor-neys attacked the use of seclusion. The lawyers argued that long periods of seclusion violated the children's right to adequate and humane treat-ment. In his thoughtful decision, the judge prohibited excessive use of seclusion as a behavior management technique. At the same time, how-ever, the judge was careful to distinguish this nontherapeutic practice from the legitimate use of time-out. The judge ruled that, when properly planned and supervised, time-out can be used.

The *Gary W.* case illustrates a crucial legal distinction between legitimate behavior management techniques and excessive, abusive interventions. With the former, competent professionals create individ-ualized treatment plans based on behavioral techniques recognized in the literature as effective. Treatment plans are written down, and data are col-lected regularly to measure program effectiveness. Abuses of behavior management are found when poorly trained or overworked staff mem-bers use behavioral techniques for such unjustifiable purposes as sup-pressing unwanted behavior for their own convenience or merely punish-ing for the sake of punishment (Brogan, 1981). Abuses frequently involve use of aversive stimuli, punishment, restraint, seclusion, or tranquilizing drugs. As long as professionals using behavior management do not stray close to the line separating sound treatment from potentially damaging misuse, they need not fear the law. Perhaps the best way to make sure the line is never approached is to ensure that those involved are well-trained professionals who keep abreast of developments in the literature and use only these methods directly related to legitimate and documented pro-gram goals (Harris & Kapche, 1978; Matson & Kazdin, 1981).

Informed Consent to Behavior Management

Use of behavior management techniques with behaviorally disordered children is both justified and productive. However, behavior management often goes beyond the traditional techniques of classroom instruction used with nonhandicapped children. Use of behavior management takes the professional into the realm of treatment, where the legal doctrine of informed consent to treatment becomes applicable (Ludlam, 1978; Miller, 1980; Myers, Jenson, & McMahon, 1986; Tryon, 1976). For this reason, it is important to obtain informed consent from parents, and in some instances children, before initiating a behavior management program (Shapiro, 1982).

Under the law, minors are usually considered legally incompetent to give informed consent to treatment (Myers, 1982), so their parents have authority to consent on their behalf. It is generally necessary, therefore, to obtain the written informed consent of parents before using therapeutic techniques with children (Bersoff, 1982: Wilson, 1978). As students enter adolescence, it is good practice to involve them in the informed consent process so that they feel a part of their treatment program.

To give proper informed consent to a child's behavior management program, parents must be given a full explanation of the proposed program (Gutheil & Appelbaum, 1982). They must be informed about any risks or side effects inherent in the technique and about the potential benefit from its use. They should be informed about alternative techniques and why they were not chosen. Finally, they should be encouraged to ask questions. It should be impressed on parents that their consent must be voluntary, and educators must be careful to avoid pressuring parents into consenting to a particular program (Martin, 1979b). The person obtaining informed consent from parents should be a professional who is competent to answer questions about the technique to be used. The consent process should take place in a quiet and unhurried setting so that parents have time to consider their decision.

It is good practice to ask parents to sign a consent form that indicates their informed and voluntary consent to the proposed program. The consent form should become part of the child's school record. It is especially important to obtain voluntary written informed consent from parents whenever a behavior management program includes use of aversive stimuli, medication, restraint, or time-out. Furthermore, if experimental or unproven techniques are to be used, parents must be informed about them. Consent to those procedures is essential. Even if a technique has been well researched and reported in the literature, it should be considered experimental if it is employed in an unproven or novel way. Finally, parents should be told that they can withdraw their consent to a procedure at any time.

By obtaining informed consent to behavior management techniques before they are instituted, educators working with behaviorally disordered children can be confident they have satisfied the legal requirement that parents be consulted about interventions on behalf of their child. What is more, the informed consent process can be used as an additional opportunity to involve parents in their child's program.

Use of Punishment or Aversive Stimuli

The repertoire of behavioral techniques at the disposal of educators working with behaviorally disordered children includes punishment and aversive stimuli. While these techniques are legitimate in certain severe cases, care must be taken to ensure that they are not misused (Myers et al., 1986; Schwitzgebel & Schwitzgebel, 1980). Before using these techniques, all less drastic and less restrictive methods of behavior management should be considered (Feldman & Peay, 1982). Less drastic techniques should be tried before punishment or aversive stimuli are used unless the teacher can document that those techniques would not be effective (Martin, 1979b). For example, if positive reinforcement of socially appropriate behavior can be used to replace inappropriate behavior, then it should be used instead of punishment. Care must be taken to ensure that punishment and aversive stimuli are employed only as long as necessary to modify undesirable behavior. Once problem behaviors are reduced or eliminated, the treatment plan should be altered to discontinue their use. Punishment and aversive stimuli should be used only under the direct control and supervision of highly qualified professionals. The need for the intervention should be included in the child's IEP along with a statement about why less drastic techniques are not appropriate. The child's record should contain data to substantiate the use of punishment or aversive stimuli.

Use of Restraint

There are times when behaviorally disordered children must be restrained to prevent them from harming themselves or others. In the past, physical restraint was occasionally abused and overused, especially in large institutions. As a result, the law looks askance on this form of behavior control (Brogan, 1981). Restraint should only be used if it is necessary to protect the safety of children and staff. Great care must be taken to assure that it is used only when absolutely necessary (*Romeo* v. *Youngberg,* 1982). Restraint should never be used as a substitute for meaningful programming, nor should it be employed simply for the convenience of the staff as a device to control unwanted behavior (*Wyatt* v. *Stickney,* 1972). In other words, physical restraint, either in a locked room or with body restraint devices, must be a technique of last resort. When it is necessary, it should be used for very limited periods, and the child should be observed every few minutes. Restraint can be approved only by qualified professionals and should be carried out under their close supervision. Furthermore, if restraint is part of a child's program, it should be included in his or her IEP.

Sometimes behaviorally disordered children have unexpected and potentially dangerous outbursts of aggression. In such rare emergencies, educators may take prompt action to restrain a child to prevent injury. The child may be removed from the classroom so that the education of other students can continue. Emergency restraint should continue only long enough for the educator to help the child regain control.

On rare occasions, tranquilizing drugs are misused as a form of chemical restraint to reduce undesirable behavior (Brogan, 1981). While there are legitimate uses for medication with behaviorally disordered children, it is improper to use these drugs—which can have serious side effects—for the convenience of staff or as a substitute for meaningful programming. Use of drugs must be carefully monitored by professionals trained to detect side effects, and there must be prior parental consent. Finally, as is true with physical restraint, use of medication should be part of the IEP.

Time-Out

The definition and uses of time-out were presented in detail in chapter 3. Time-out is indispensible with certain children; when employed in conformity with an appropriate individualized treatment plan, it is sanctioned by the law (*Gary W.* v. *Louisiana,* 1976; Martin, 1979b; Myers et al., 1986). It should be kept in mind, however, that time-out can be abused. For example, placement in a time-out room for a period longer than 55 minutes may be considered seclusion rather than time-out, and seclusion is a very restrictive procedure of questionable therapeutic value (Martin, 1979b). The generally accepted rule is that seclusion in a locked room should occur only in emergency situations "to prevent serious harm to the child or to others" (Brogan, 1981, p. 382). Time-out used in schools generally calls for short periods that do not resemble seclusion.

To make sure time-out is properly used, a few simple principles should be followed. Time-out should be used only when it is determined by qualified professionals to be a necessary component of a behavior management plan. It should last only long enough to be effective. The child should be carefully monitored while in time-out to ensure safety. The procedure should be included in the child's IEP, and careful data should be kept. Finally, parents should be made aware of its use with their child and should give their informed consent (Gast & Nelson, 1977).

Token Economies

The use of a token economy with behaviorally disordered children is an accepted practice. From a legal perspective, the technique poses few problems. In the small number of court cases that have considered token economy systems, the aspects of the programs that were challenged were the degree to which individuals were required to participate involuntarily and the extent to which they were stripped of basic necessities when they entered the program (Martin, 1979b; Wexler, 1981: *Wyatt* v. *Stickney,* 1972). In one, for example, institutionalized adult subjects were required to participate. At the first level of the program, they were deprived of such basic necessities as privacy and minimally adequate living facilities (*Clonce* v. *Richardson,* 1974). The courts reviewing these token economy systems decided that individuals could not be coerced into participation, and that they could not be deprived of such basic necessities as privacy, decent food, and minimally adequate living conditions.

Educators working with behaviorally disordered children can avoid potential legal roadblocks to use of a token economy by structuring the economy so that children are not deprived of basic necessities such as good food, reasonably pleasant surroundings, and access to other people (Schwitzgebel & Schwitzgebel, 1980; Wexler, 1974). Again, parental informed consent should be obtained. Teachers should be concerned about depriving a child of lunch, clothes, bathroom use, reasonable recreation, and so on. One common, but questionable, aspect of classroom token economies is a program in which a child can lose so many tokens that he or she goes into the hole and misses opportunities.

STUDENT RECORDS

School systems generate and retain many types of records on students, from report cards to results of standardized achievement tests. Most of the material is private and should not be released to anyone who does not have a legitimate educational need for the information. The school records maintained on behaviorally disordered children frequently contain extraordinarily confidential and sensitive material such as reports by psychologists, psychiatrists, and social workers; results of psychological testing; and sensitive teacher records. Access to these confidential records must be carefully limited to parents and professionals who need the records to provide appropriate programming.

There are two important federal laws that govern student records. The first is the Family Education Rights and Privacy Act, commonly known as the *Buckley Amendment;* the second is the Education for All Handicapped Children Act. Under these laws, *student records* are defined as all records directly related to a student maintained by the child's school district (Bersoff, 1982; Martin, 1979a.) This definition is intended to be very broad, so that almost everything written about a handicapped child is considered a school record.

Parents have the right to review all educational records relating to their child that are collected, maintained, or used by a school system. In other words, parents must be permitted access to their child's entire education record. If a parent needs copies of portions of the record to review them thoroughly, the school must provide copies. In particular, parents are entitled to a copy of their child's IEP.

There are two exceptions to the general rule that parents can review everything relating to their child. First of all, teachers and other professionals working with students are not required to disclose their personal notes on a student if they retain them in their sole possession and do not share them with anyone except substitute teachers. If, however, personal notes are made a part of the child's educational record, or if they are shared with other professionals, they must be revealed to parents. The second exception to the rule of full disclosure pertains to treatment records written by psychiatrists, psychologists, social workers, and similar professionals, which pertain exclusively to treatment such as psychotherapy, and which are not disclosed to other individuals providing services to the child. An example of the records within this exception are a therapist's progress notes, retained in the therapist's possession. The exception does not apply to records describing activities and interventions that are part of the child's program of instruction. For example, data maintained by a teacher to document progress toward IEP goals would not be covered by the exception.

The rule of thumb for all student records is that parents have the right to inspect them. The exceptions to the rule are narrow. Rather than keep parents from their child's record, teachers and other professionals should offer to assist them in understanding the sensitive and technical information the records contain. By taking such an approach, professionals are given another opportunity to involve parents.

With certain exceptions, schools must obtain the parents' written consent before they disclose student records to anyone other than parents. This rule is designed to protect the privacy of children and their families. Prior written consent is not required for school officials, teachers, and other professionals employed by the school district so long as they have a legitimate educational interest in obtaining information on the child. Furthermore, if a medical emergency arises, necessary information may be revealed without advance consent to individuals such as police officials or physicians.

If parents believe information contained in their child's education record is inaccurate or misleading, they may ask the school to amend the record. If the school declines to make a requested amendment, parents have the right to a hearing to challenge the content of the record. If records become outdated and are "no longer needed to provide educational services to the child" (34 C.F.R. 300.573(a)), the school must notify parents of this fact, and the parents may ask the school to destroy the outdated material.

Under PL 94-142, handicapped students in many states are entitled to special education services until they are 22. When students turn 18, the law states that the right of access to student records shifts from parents to the student. After that time, the student has the right to inspect his or her records. Furthermore, records cannot be released to nonschool personnel without the advance consent of the student.

SCHOOL DISCIPLINE

During school hours, students are subject to reasonable discipline by teachers, principals, and other school employees. Educators have the authority and the responsibility to ensure the orderly functioning of the schools so that the process of learning can go forward. While children are in school, the legal doctrine of *in loco parentis* gives educators disciplinary authority somewhat similar to that parents have over their children. Educators are said to stand in the place of parents when they are acting *in loco parentis*. Their authority ends when children are away from school. The legal authorities are in general agreement that school officials may not dictate parents' disciplinary practices. While the law defers substantially to educators on matters of student discipline, two forms of discipline have drawn close scrutiny from judges. These are corporal punishment and suspension and expulsion.

Corporal Punishment

Corporal punishment has been part of American education since colonial times. While there have always been some educators who abused the practice, it was only recently that there were legal challenges to its use. The most important court case on corporal punishment is the U..S Supreme Court case of *Ingraham* v. *Wright* (1976) (Mahoney, 1985; Weckstein, 1982). The parents of a child who had been paddled sued the school district, taking the position that the U.S. constitution prohibits corporal punishment in the schools. The Supreme Court rejected the parents' argument and ruled that the constitution does not prohibit corporal punishment in the schools (Overcart & Sales, 1982). The Supreme Court Justices pointed out, however, that children have a right to freedom from excessive or malicious corporal punishment. In cases of excessive physical punishment, parents can sue the teachers and administrators involved.

Some states and school districts prohibit corporal punishment entirely. Others place strict limits on its use. If a teacher decides to use corporal punishment, he or she should consult with district authorities to determine the applicable policies and procedures. It should be employed, if at all, as part of a child's individualized educational program, reflected in the child's IEP with parental consent. All punishment should be recorded and its effectiveness assessed. The child's record should contain an explanation of the behavior that necessitated corporal punishment. As a final note, the use of corporal punishment with behaviorally disordered children is uncalled for in *nearly all* cases. Using the techniques discussed in chapter 3 should eliminate the need to fall to the level of physical punishment.

Suspension and Expulsion

The term *suspension* is normally used to describe the disciplinary technique by which educators require children to remain away from school for a relatively short time. *Expulsion,* on the other hand, refers to enforced absence for a substantial period such as a semester or even an entire year (Simon, 1984). No group of students are as often unfairly or adversely affected by suspension and expulsion as the behaviorally disordered. It is an unfortunate fact that some school administrators use suspension and expulsion as a means to rid the schools of "difficult" children. Rather than serve these students as the law requires, many of them are effectively excluded from public education. While most educators do not knowingly abuse suspension and expulsion, they sometimes lose patience with behaviorally disordered children and resort to these counterproductive methods. Fortunately, the law regulates the use of suspension and expulsion, and the legal rules reduce inappropriate use of these disciplinary techniques.

In 1974 the U.S. Supreme Court decided the case of *Goss* v. *Lopez,* ruling that for short-term suspensions, such as 10 days or less, the due process clause of the constitution requires the disciplinarian to give the offending student written or oral notice of the charges against him or her (Weckstein, 1982). A student who disputes the charges must have an opportunity to explain his or her side of the story. The required notice and opportunity to explain should usually take place before the suspension; however, in cases where a student poses an immediate threat to other students or school property, suspension may precede notice of the charges and the opportunity to explain (*S-1* v. *Turlington,* 1981).

In cases where a disciplinarian intends to suspend a student for an extended period, such as a month, or to expel a student altogether, the constitution requires more formal procedures. For example, it might be necessary to give written advance notice of the charges. A formal administrative hearing might be required so that the student could present a case. The student would be permitted to present witnesses and have the assistance of an attorney. As a general rule, the more serious the intended punishment, the more likely the law will require educators to follow formalized, legalistic procedures before imposing discipline. In some states, for example, there are statutes and regulations that set up complex suspension and expulsion procedures. The purpose behind those laws is to ensure that children are disciplined fairly. Behaviorally disordered children are the beneficiaries of those rules because they are too often the victims of unwarranted suspension or expulsion.

Suspension and Expulsion Under PL 94-142

The procedures required by *Goss* v. *Lopez* apply to all children, handicapped and nonhandicapped alike. In the past several years, a special procedure for suspension and expulsion of handicapped students has emerged in court decisions (Rossow, 1984). This special procedure supplements the *Goss* procedure. The rule is of particular relevance to professionals working with behaviorally disordered children.

Recall that every handicapped child must have an IEP that, among other things, describes the child's educational placement. The placement cannot be changed without changing the IEP, which requires an official IEP meeting. At the meeting, the IEP team, which includes the parents, considers whether a change in educational placement will serve the student's educational needs.

With these requirements of PL 94-142 in mind, the parents of a behaviorally disordered child who is threatened with suspension or expulsion from school can argue that that discipline would amount to a change in their child's education placement (*Stewart* v. *Nappi,* 1978). In other words, the child's placement would be changed from school-based special education programming to no programming at all! The parents could argue that the change in placement has to be made in compliance with the IEP procedures.

Several court decisions support this position. Judges intepreting PL 94-142 have ruled that before educators may suspend or expel a handicapped child, they must convene an official IEP meeting. At the meeting the IEP team decides whether the conduct that prompted disciplinary action is related to or caused by the student's handicapping condition. If the misbehavior is *not* related to the child's handicap, the IEP may be altered to include suspension or expulsion. If, however, the behavior that caused the problem *is* related to the child's handicap, the child should normally not be suspended or expelled. For example, if a child with attention deficit disorder is frequently aggressive due to some aspect of his or her disability, school officials should not suspend or expel the child for misbehavior related to the condition. Rather, the child's IEP should be amended to incorporate programming to control the aggression. Alternately, the child's placement might be changed to a more restrictive setting with more intensive programming.

A final point should be made regarding suspension and expulsion. In most cases, these procedures should be satisfied before discipline is administered. In some cases, however, educators must act immediately to remove a child from the classroom. This is so, for example, when a student poses an immediate threat to him or herself, other students, staff, or property. Teachers and other professionals have the authority to act immediately in these cases to remove children from explosive situations. After the emergency abates, however, the child should be returned to the classroom.

MEDICATION IN THE SCHOOLS

A substantial number of behaviorally disordered students receive medication, which has legal as well as educational and medical implications (Courtnage, 1982). The first question to ask is whether the law allows teachers to administer medication. In many cases, state law requires administration by medical personnel such as nurses. Certainly, school nurses could administer drugs to students. As a practical matter, however, in many schools the teacher has to do the job. Fortunately, several states have passed laws that specifically allow teachers to administer prescribed drugs to their students. As long as teachers do not act negligently, these laws protect them from personal liability.

Teachers who administer medication should have a working familiarity with the effects and purposes of the drugs to be used, the range of acceptable dosages, the possible adverse reactions, the emergency treatment for reactions, and the probable effect of the medication on the child's ability to perform in school. It is good practice to have a letter in the child's record from the physician who prescribed the medication that addresses these important factors (Gadow, 1982). When medication is given, it should be recorded in the child's school record. Medications should be kept in a safe, locked place, and should be protected from wide temperature changes on holidays if the heat or air conditioning is turned off. Finally, if the teacher believes a particular drug is doing more harm than good, he or she should inform the parents. The teacher might also seek the parents' permission to consult directly with the physician.

If medication is to be administered at school, it should be mentioned in the IEP. In some cases, the physician may be invited to attend the IEP meeting to help other professionals and parents understand the effect the drug treatment may have on the student's educational performance.

LIABILITY OF EDUCATORS

Few things are more distressing than being sued. With the law's increased involvement in the daily operation of the schools, teachers and administrators are understandably distressed about the possibility of liability. In recent years several suits have been brought against schools and their employees for what is commonly called *educational malpractice.* For example, in the case of *Peter W. v. San Francisco Unified School District* (1976), the parents of a nonhandicapped child found that when their son was graduated from high school he was functionally illiterate. His reading and writing skills were at a fifth grade level. The parents sued the school district, taking the position that the school had a legal duty to provide an appropriate education and that it failed to do so. They argued that this failure amounted to professional malpractice, similar to malpractice by doctors or lawyers. The judges ruled against the parents. They held that, for reasons of public policy, lawsuits based on educational malpractice should not be allowed. The trend established by this and other cases appears to be against recognizing educational malpractice (Coultas, 1979; *Tubell v. Dade County Public Schools,* 1982).

While teachers do not need to be overly concerned about malpractice liability, an increasing number of suits are being filed against educators and their employers on other grounds. One of the common grounds for liability is violation of students' constitutional rights (Cambron-McCabe, 1982). While the constitutional rights of children are not precisely the same as those of adults, there is no doubt that minors have such rights (*In re Gault,* 1967; *Tinker v. Des Moines,* 1969). For example, students have a constitutional right to be free from unreasonable physical restraint. In the context of suspension and expulsion, students have a right to be notified of the charges against them and to give their side of the story. If educators violate these or other constitutional rights, they may find themselves in court (*Wood v. Strictland,* 1975).

The law of tort presents a potential area of legal liability. A tort is an act by one person that causes injury to another person, for which the law permits the recovery of monetary damages. For example, an individual who negligently causes an auto accident can be sued for the tort of negligence. If a person writes material about another that is false and damaging to the person's reputation, a suit based on the tort of libel may be filed. If an individual causes intentional physical injury to another by striking him or her, a suit based on the tort of battery is appropriate. To make the law of torts relevant to education, we can use the torts just described in the context of a school. If a teacher fails to properly supervise students on a field trip and one of them wanders off and is injured, the parents might sue the teacher and the school for negligence. If the teacher of a behaviorally disordered child writes untrue and harmful statements about the child or the parents, they might sue for libel. Finally, if a teacher uses uncalled for and punitive physical punishment that exceeds the limits of permissible corporal punishment, a suit for battery might follow.

While the types of situations leading to liability are large in number, responsible educators exercising sound judgment will probably never have to face the unpleasant reality of litigation. Awareness of legal issues in education helps avoid potential legal problems (Reddick & Peach, 1982). In well-organized and professional education programs there is very little likelihood that the rights of students will be infringed. As long as those who declare their careers to educating troubled children exercise responsible professional judgment in the best interest of their students, they will probably never become involved in legal action.

SUMMARY

Since its passage in 1975, the Education for All Handicapped Children Act has been a major force in improving educational opportunities for millions of handicapped children, including behaviorally disordered children. Understanding this important law enables professional educators to deal more effectively with the complex issues surrounding education of children with special needs.

Every handicapped child is entitled to an individualized program that will afford him or her an opportunity to make measurable progress toward the long-and short-term goals contained in the IEP. Setting realistic goals and providing the programming and related services needed to achieve them is the basic requirement of PL 94-142.

To ensure appropriate placements, all school districts must provide a continuum of alternative placements, including regular classrooms, special classes, special schools, home instruction, and education in institutions. If a school district does not have a particular placement option available, it may contract for the needed services. The IEP team places the child in the least restrictive setting that is likely to provide educationally beneficial programming. Educators and parents should be creative and flexible to assure that each child's placement satisfies the mainstreaming requirement and is also beneficial.

Properly conceptualized and implemented behavior management programs are of great value to many children. The law will not stand in the way of such beneficial programming. It is only in those rare cases where children are harmed or even abused that the law intervenes. Professionals who care about children and use established methods of intervention can be confident that the law will protect appropriate behavioral programming.

REVIEW QUESTIONS

1. You are planning to implement a time-out procedure with a particular student in your classroom. You realize that you will need to obtain informed consent from the student's parents. Develop a written statement to explain how you will implement the procedure.
2. What is your school's policy concerning corporal punishment? Does it conform to the guidelines discussed in the chapter?
3. You are the teacher in charge of a self-contained classroom for children with severe behavior disorders. Describe the steps you will take to create an IEP for a new student, 10-year-old John. John has been diagnosed as psychotic. When frustrated, he sometimes becomes violent. He finds it very difficult to make and keep friends. John is 2 years behind in all academic subjects and needs speech therapy as well as psychotherapy. He takes medication to control his psychotic symptoms.

REFERENCES

Akin, R. A., Black, J. C., Guarino, R., Klebanoff, H. M., & Rosenfeld, S. J. (1981–82). Psychology as a "related service." *Education of Handicapped Law Reporter,* Decisions, AC 15–45.

Bersoff, D. N. (1981). Testing and the law. *American Psychologist, 35,* 1047–1056.

Bersoff, D. N. (1982). The legal regulation of school psychology. In C. R. Reynolds & T. B. Gutkin, *The handbook of school psychology.* New York: John Wiley.

Board of Education v. *Rowley,* 458 U.S. 176 (1982).

Brogan, M. T. (1981). Recent developments in behavior modification. *Nebraska Law Review, 60,* 363–399.

Cambron-McCabe, N. H. (1982). School district liability under section 1983 for violations of federal rights. *NOLPE School Law Journal, 10,* 99–108.

In re Carlisle Area School District. 1981–82. *Education of Handicapped Law Reporter,* Decisions, 504: 198.

Clonce v. *Richardson,* 379 F. Supp. 338 (W.D. Mo. 1974).

Coultas, F. M. (1979). Educational malpractice and special education law. *Chicago-Kent Law Review, 55,* 685–712.

Courtnage, L. (1982). A survey of state policies on the use of medication in schools. *Exceptional Children, 49,* 75–77.

Davison, G. L., & Stuart, R. B. (1975). Behavior therapy and civil liberties. *American Psychologist, 1975, 30,* 755–763.

Department of Education, State of Hawaii v. *Katherine D.,* 531 F. Supp. 517 (D. Hawaii 1982).

Feldman, M. P., & Peay, J. (1982). Ethical and legal issues. In A. S. Bellack, M. Hersen, & A. E. Kazdin (Eds.), *International handbook of behavior modification and therapy,* 250.

Gadow, K. D. (1982). Problems with students on medication. *Exceptional Children, 49,* 20–7.

Gary W. v. *Louisiana,* 437 F. Supp. 1209 (E. D. La. 1976).

Gast, D. L., & Nelson, C. M. (1977). Legal and ethical considerations for the use of timeout in special education settings. *Journal of Special Education, 11,* 457–467.

In re Gault, 387 U.S. 1 (1967).

Gee, E. G., & Sperry, D. J. (1978). *Education law and the public schools.* Newton, MA: Allyn & Bacon.

Goss v. *Lopez,* 419 U.S. 565 (1974).

Gutheil, T. G., & Appelbaum, D. S. (1982). *Clinical handbook of psychiatry and the law.* New York: McGraw-Hill.

Harris, A., & Kapche, R. (1978). Behavior modifications in schools: Ethical issues and suggested guidelines. *Journal of School Psychology, 16,* 25–33.

Ingraham v. *Wright,* 430 U. S. 651 (1976).

Irving Independent School District v. *Tatro,* 52 U. S. L. W. 5151 (1984).

Knecht v. *Gillman,* 488 F.2d 1136 (8th Cir. 1973).

Knitzer, J. (1982). *Unclaimed children: The failure of public responsibility to children and adolescents in need of mental health services.* Washington, DC: Children's Defense Fund.

Larson, L. (1985). Beyond conventional education: A definition of education under the Education for All Handicapped Children Act of 1975. *Law and Contemporary Problems, 48,* 63–91.

Ludlam, J. (1978). *Informed consent.* Chicago: American Hospital Association.

Mackey v. *Procunier,* 477 F.2d 877 (9th Cir. 1973).

Mahoney, D. J. (1985). Corporal cunishment and school discipline. *Journal of Juvenile Law, 1,* 178–179.

Martin R. (1979a). *Educating handicapped children: The legal mandate.* Champaign, IL: Research Press.

Martin, R. (1979b). *Legal challenges to behavior modification.* Champaign, IL: Research Press.

Matson, J. L., & Kazdin, A. E. (1981). Punishment in behavior modification: Pragmatic, ethical and legal issues. *Clinical Psychology Review, 1,* 197–210.

McKenzie v. *Jefferson,* 566 F. Supp. 404 (D. D. C. 1983).

Miller, L. (1980). Informed Consent I, II, III, IV. *Journal of the AMA,* 2100–2103, 2347–2350, 2556–2558, 2661–2662.

Mills v. *Board of Education,* 348 F. Supp. 866 (D. D. C. 1972).

Myers, J. E. B. (1982). Legal issues surrounding psychotherapy with minor clients. *Clinical Social Work Journal, 10,* 303–314.

Myers, J. E. B., Jenson, W. R., & McMahon, W. (1986). *Legal and educational issues affecting autistic children.* Springfield, IL: Charles C Thomas.

Overcart, T. D., & Sales, B. D. (1982). The legal rights of students in the elementary and secondary public schools. *The handbook of school psychology.* New York: John Wiley.

In Re P. (1981–82). *Education of Handicapped Law Reporter,* Decisions, 504:148.

Pena v. New York State Division of Youth, 419 F. Supp. 203 (S. D. N. Y. 1976).

Pennsylvania Association for Retarded Children v. Commonwealth of Pennsylvania, 334 F. Supp. 1257 (E. D. Pa. 1971).

Peter W. v. San Francisco Unified School District, 131 Cal. Rptr. 854 (Cal. Ct. App. 1976).

Pullin, D. (1982). *Special education: A manual for advocates.* Cambridge, MA: Center for Law and Education.

Reddick, T. L., & Peach, L. E. (1982). What secondary school teachers should know about tort liability. *Clearinghouse Review, 55,* 529–530.

Romeo v. Youngberg, 451 U.S. 982 (1982).

Rossow, L. F. (1984). Administrative discretion and student suspension: A lion in waiting. *Journal of Law and Education, 13,* 417–440.

S–1 v. Turlington, 635 F. 2d 342 (5th Cir. 1981).

Schwitzgebel, R. L., & Schwitzgebel, R. K. (1980). *Law and psychological practice.* New York: Praeger.

Shapiro, M. H. (1982). Legislating the control of behavior control: Autonomy and the coercive use of organic therapies. *Biological and Behavioral Technologies and the Law.* New York: Praeger.

Simon, S. G. (1984). Discipline in public schools: A dual standard for handicapped and non-handicapped students? *Journal of Law and Education, 13,* 209–237.

Stewart v. Nappi, 443 F. Supp. 1235 (D. Conn. 1978).

Tinker v. Des Moines School District, 393 U.S. 503 (1969).

Tryon, W. W. (1976). Behavior modification treatment and the law. *Professional Psychology, 7,* 468–474.

Tubell v. Dade County Public Schools, 419 So.2d 388 (Fla. Dist. Ct. App. 1982).

Weckstein, P. (1982). *School discipline and student rights.* Cambridge, MA: Center for Law and Education.

Wexler, D. B. (1974). Of rights and reinforcers. *San Diego Law Review, 11,* 957–971.

Wexler, D. B. (1981). *Mental health law: Major issues:* New York: Plenum Press.

Wilson, J. (1978). *The rights of adolescents in the mental health system.* Lexington, MA: D. C. Heath.

Wood v. Strictland, 420 U.S. 308 (1975).

Wyatt v. Stickney, 344 F. Supp. 373 (M. D. Ala. 1972).

Index